Red October

Historical Materialism Book Series

More than ten years after the collapse of the Berlin Wall and the disappearance of Marxism as a (supposed) state ideology, a need for a serious and long-term Marxist book publishing program has arisen. Subjected to the whims of fashion, most contemporary publishers have abandoned any of the systematic production of Marxist theoretical work that they may have indulged in during the 1970s and early 1980s. The Historical Materialism book series addresses this great gap with original monographs, translated texts, and reprints of "classics."

Editorial board: Paul Blackledge, Leeds; Sebastian Budgen, London; Jim Kincaid, Leeds; Stathis Kouvelakis, Paris; Marcel van der Linden, Amsterdam; China Miéville, London; Paul Reynolds, Lancashire.

Haymarket Books is proud to be working with Brill Academic Publishers (http://www.brill.nl) and the journal *Historical Materialism* to republish the Historical Materialism book series in paperback editions. Current series titles include:

Alasdair MacIntyre's Engagement with Marxism: Selected Writings 1953–1974, edited by Paul Blackledge and Neil Davidson

Althusser: The Detour of Theory, Gregory Elliott

Between Equal Rights: A Marxist Theory of International Law, China Miéville

The Capitalist Cycle, Pavel V. Maksakovsky, translated with introduction and commentary by Richard B. Day

The Clash of Globalisations: Neo-Liberalism, the Third Way, and Anti-Globalisation, Ray Kiely

Critical Companion to Contemporary Marxism, edited by Jacques Bidet and Stathis Kouvelakis

Criticism of Heaven: On Marxism and Theology, Roland Boer

Criticism of Religion: On Marxism and Theology II, Roland Boer

Exploring Marx's Capital: Philosophical, Economic, and Political Dimensions, Jacques Bidet, translated by David Fernbach

Following Marx: Method, Critique, and Crisis, Michael Lebowitz

The German Revolution: 1917–1923, Pierre Broué

Globalisation: A Systematic Marxian Account, Tony Smith

The Gramscian Moment: Philosophy, Hegemony and Marxism, Peter D. Thomas

Impersonal Power: History and Theory of the Bourgeois State, Heide Gerstenberger, translated by David Fernbach

Lenin Rediscovered: What Is to Be Done? in Context, Lars T. Lih

Making History: Agency, Structure, and Change in Social Theory, Alex Callinicos

Marxism and Ecological Economics: Toward a Red and Green Political Economy, Paul Burkett

A Marxist Philosophy of Language, Jean-Jacques Lecercle, translated by Gregory Elliott

Politics and Philosophy: Niccolò Machiavelli and Louis Althusser's Aleatory Materialism, Mikko Lahtinen, translated by Gareth Griffiths and Kristina Köhli

The Theory of Revolution in the Young Marx, Michael Löwy

Utopia Ltd.: Ideologies of Social Dreaming in England 1870–1900, Matthew Beaumont

Western Marxism and the Soviet Union: A Survey of Critical Theories and Debates Since 1917, Marcel van der Linden

Witnesses to Permanent Revolution: The Documentary Record, edited and translated by Richard B. Day and Daniel Gaido

Red October

Left-Indigenous Struggles in Modern Bolivia

Jeffery Webber

Haymarket Books
Chicago, IL

First published in 2011 by Brill Academic Publishers, The Netherlands
© 2011 Koninklijke Brill NV, Leiden, The Netherlands

Published in paperback in 2012 by
Haymarket Books
P.O. Box 180165
Chicago, IL 60618
773-583-7884
info@haymarketbooks.org
www.haymarketbooks.org

ISBN: 978-1-60846-258-2

Trade distribution:
In the US, Consortium Book Sales and Distribution, www.cbsd.com
In Canada, Publishers Group Canada, www.pgcbooks.ca
In the UK, Turnaround Publisher Services, www.turnaround-uk.com
In Australia, Palgrave Macmillan, www.palgravemacmillan.com.au
In all other countries, Publishers Group Worldwide, www.pgw.com

Cover design by Ragina Johnson.

This book was published with the generous support of
Lannan Foundation and the Wallace Global Fund.

Printed in Canada with union labor.

10 9 8 7 6 5 4 3 2 1

Library of Congress Cataloging-in-Publication data is available.

For Tieneke,
and my parents,
Roger and Elaine

Contents

Acknowledgements

A doctoral award from the International Development Research Center of Canada (IDRC) made the fieldwork necessary for this book materially possible.

The book grew out of my doctoral dissertation in political science at the University of Toronto. I am grateful to have had a supportive committee that carefully read various drafts of my dissertation and provided me with instructive suggestions and critique throughout the process. Thanks to Dickson Eyoh, Paul Kingston, and Antoinette Handley. A special thanks to Judith Teichman, my supervisor, for reading multiple drafts of an enormously long initial manuscript, commenting incisively and extensively, and providing me space to draw my own conclusions. Lesley Gill's engaged scholarship on Bolivia, Colombia, and US-imperialism in Latin America has long been an inspiration, and she was an exemplary external examiner who read my dissertation closely and provided insightful comments on the final product.

In Toronto, I have a large network of friends who have been invaluable throughout the last several years. Todd Gordon and Jackie Esmonde are genuinely good people. During various return visits to Toronto, they put up with me staying in their house for extended periods at different intervals, during which time sections of this book were written up. Ongoing research and writing collaboration with Todd has made me smarter, and his presence in various stints of fieldwork has kept me relatively sane. Weekly pitchers and political discussions with Shiraz Vally at our local bar are some of the best memories of my time in Toronto, as are the take-out dinners we gorged on with the whole gang at his and Naomi Dachner's place. Keith O'Regan and Juliane Edler are another pair of wonderful people who I am privileged to know. Fernando Soto, Seth Clarke, Susan Bender, Clarice Khuling, Alan Sears, Greg Sharzer, Katherine Grzejszczak and Sandra Sarner are great friends, some of whom took money from me regularly at the poker table. From Toronto, to London, to New York, Clarice has been a consistent comrade – in politics, friendship, and after-hour excess – on the circuit of *Historical Materialism* conferences. David McNally is a model of the scholar-activist, and his friendship and interest in my work on Bolivia has been rewarding. Jasmin Hristov's work on Colombia is reflective of her deeply felt commitment to social justice. Our discussions over coffee have been an education in the politics of that country, and she's a fountain of kind advice and support. I didn't actually spend much time in the halls of the University of Toronto political-science department, but when I was around I was heartened by the friendship of Asya El-Meehy, Elena Cirkovic, Anil Varughese, and Glen Coulthard, among others. I learned a lot from each of them. Thanks also to all the comrades of the Toronto branch of the New Socialist Group for their commitment to transforming this world, and for sharpening my political education.

From Winnipeg, David Camfield has taught me more about politics than he probably knows. He has also been a good friend, and I am glad he was already out there on the prairies as I made my way as I made my way to teach in Regina for 2009 and 2010.

In the United States, I was fortunate to attend the summer-school of Solidarity in 2006, where we had a round of important discussions about developments in Bolivia. I have benefited particularly from conversations in subsequent years with Charlie Post, and David Finkel and Dianne Feeley (both editors of the great magazine *Against the Current*). The folks at Haymarket Books and *International Socialist Review* have provided important outlets for my writing on Bolivia. Thanks to Anthony Arnove, Ahmed Shawki, Julie Fain, John Macdonald, and Tom Lewis. Sinclair Thomson of New York University has shown a sustained interest in my work since we met briefly in Montreal. It is always refreshing to encounter a great scholar who is also a down-to-earth human being. Greg Grandin, likewise, took time to read my manuscript, in what must have been the few available insomniac moments between writing a tide of books and articles condemning the US empire and exploring the contours of the Latin-American Left today. His enthusiastic encouragement meant a lot, as did the advice, commentary, and constructive critique of Henry Veltmeyer and Marc Becker. Vanessa Bohm, in between Latin-American newscasts for the excellent San Francisco-based KPFA radio show, La Raza Chronicles/Crónicas de La Raza, read the manuscript and provided valuable feedback. Sasha Lilley, co-host of another amazing KPFA radio-programme, *Against the Grain*, helped sharpen my ideas on Bolivia by inviting me on the show, and cutting through trivialities with a series of incisive questions. Ronald Chilcote, managing editor of *Latin American Perspectives*, has supported my work in various ways over the years and I was happy to join the collective of participating editors of that journal recently.

In the Netherlands, a number of individuals made my year there a rewarding one. Peter Thomas and Sara Farris showed Tieneke and I around Amsterdam, gave us a place to stay for a couple of nights, talked politics, and gave us an excuse to go to Sardinia for their wedding. Peter Drucker and Christopher Beck were gracious hosts in Rotterdam. Great meals, great conversation, and great friendship. Antonio Carmona Báez was an important friend in Amsterdam, and I only wish I could have stayed longer to discuss Latin-American politics with him over several pints.

While in Regina, I was lucky to be a part of the Critical Political Economy working group. Discussions with George Buri, Emily Eaton, Phil Hansen, André Magnan, and David Webster taught me a lot. Jenn Wallner and Steve White are good friends. Conversations with Annette Desmarais about her important work with Vía Campesina provided me with a better grasp of their international peasant-struggle. Mainly because of Miguel Sánchez I gained a better grasp of Chilean-community politics in Regina and the history of migration of Chilean revolutionary refugees to that part of the world. My former colleague Joyce Green is an example for all committed anti-racist, feminist activists. She was also constant source of new students for the Marxist-theory class I taught at the University of Regina. Dave Mitchell, the former editor of the important magazine *Briarpatch*, has also been a good friend in the short time I have known him. Val Zink, one of the new editors of *Briarpatch*, is an inspiration. She exemplifies how a revolutionary life is to be led in non-revolutionary times. The anticapitalist discussion group in town evolved into a dynamic space over the course of the year, with lots of young inspiring radicals involved. I am happy to learn it has since been transformed into the Regina Solidarity Group, responsible, among other things, for the city's first Israeli Apartheid Week in 2010.

In London, where I moved in 2010, the editors of *Historical Materialism* have been a wellspring of intellectual exchange. Special thanks to Demet Dinler for letting me stay at her place during my visits to London in 2008 and 2009, and for always interesting discussions on politics, and to Peter Thomas and Sebastian Budgen for encouraging me to publish this text as part of the *Historical*

Materialism Book Series. I have had many rich political discussions over pints with editorial comrades, particularly Adam Hanieh, Rob Knox, Giorgos Galanis, and Lucia Pradella. Also in London, the kindness of Feyzi Ismail, Saskia Fischer, Paul Rekret, and Honor Brabazon quickly made the city liveable. Colleagues in the School of Politics and International Relations at Queen Mary, University of London have been a supportive and collegial group of scholars. I have particularly benefitted from getting to know Claes Belfrage, Rick Saull, Lee Jones, Bryan Mabee, Clive Gabay, and James Dunkerley. James, Sara Motta, and Ben Selwyn were kind enough to read the manuscript and provide critical commentary for a panel at the *Historical Materialism* conference in London in 2010. Their sophisticated interventions, from distinct angles, have spurred me to think through a number of the implications of the arguments advanced in *Red October*, some of which I hope to address in future research projects. Presenting my work on Bolivia at the University of Nottingham, at the invitation of Sara, and at the University of Sussex, at the invitation of Ben, was equally rewarding.

In Bolivia, I have accrued so many debts as to make a list impossible. I thank all of those who agreed to be interviewed and whose names appear in the Appendix to this volume. Forrest Hylton helped me with initial contacts, and our stays in Bolivia thankfully overlapped. On several occasions we got together for coffee, and for many hours discussed uninterruptedly developments that were unfolding. For me, these were intensive training sessions on getting serious about Bolivian history and committed scholarship. I learned a great deal and met a good friend and comrade. Forrest also read the manuscript for this book and provided invaluable commentary and advice. Ben Kohl and Linda Farthing were also in La Paz when I was there, and it has been nice to have stayed in touch with them ever since. Luis A. Gómez helped me out in more ways than I can describe. I benefited from our conversations, and continue to value the work he does with Jean Friedman-Rudovsky on their website, *Ukhampacha Bolivia* <www.ubnoticias.org>. My roommate, friend, and comrade in Bolivia, Susan Spronk, was a veritable fountain of ideas and conversation during my time in La Paz, and has read and commented on most of what I have written in the last number of years. If it was not for her extroverted personality, and the constant stream of new faces in her milieu, I would not have met half the people I ended up meeting in Bolivia.

My indebtedness to the writings of Bolivian scholars and activists will be clear to anyone who takes a cursory glance at the bibliography. I have also relied on the courageous and gifted journalism, commentary, and analysis of the Bolivian scene by the likes of Marxa Chávez, Claudia Espinoza, Jorge Viaña, and Gonzalo Gosalvez, among many others. Much of the economic analysis in this book draws from the rich work of economists based at the Centro de Estudios para el Desarrollo Laboral y Agrario (CEDLA) in La Paz. During my fieldwork I was a research associate at the Centro Boliviano de Estudios Multidisciplinario (CEBEM), also in La Paz. Thanks to José Blanes for his support at that institution.

It is difficult to record what I owe my family. My sisters Elizabeth, Ruth, and Theresa have been alongside me unstintingly for the last three decades. I treasure them. Ruth's husband Roy, and their kids, Tasman and Sage, are always fun to visit when I make it back to Vancouver.

Gerry Dykstra and Olga Shustyk have shown me an extraordinary kindness over the last 13 years, not least when I stayed at their place in Copetown for a month and a half writing up parts of this book. Rebecca Dykstra has also been great to me, even as Tieneke and I camped in the living room of her Hamilton apartment and I turned her kitchen into my temporary office.

This book is dedicated to Tieneke Dykstra, because she is everything to me. It is also dedicated to my parents, Roger and Elaine Webber, for their love.

Acronyms

ADN	Acción Democrática Nacionalista, Nationalist Democratic Action
ANPOS	Asamblea Nacional Permanente de Organización Sindical, Permanent National Assembly of Union-Organisation (ANPOS)
AP	Asamblea Popular, Popular Assembly
AP	Acuerdo Patriótico, Patriotic Accord
APDHB	Asamblea Permanente de Derechos Humanos de Bolivia, Permanent Assembly of Human Rights of Bolivia
APG	Asamblea del Pueblo Guaraní, Assembly of Guaraní People
ASP	Asamblea por la Soberanía de los Pueblos, Assembly for the Sovereignty of the Peoples
CAINCO	Cámara de Industria y Comercio, Chamber of Industry and Commerce
CAO	Cámara Agropecuaria del Oriente, Eastern Agricultural Chamber
CDHCD	Comisión de Derechos Humanos de la Cámara de Diputados, Human-Rights Commission of the Chamber of Deputies
CEBEM	Centro Boliviano de Estudios Multidisciplinarios, Bolivian Centre for Multidisciplinary Studies
CEPB	Confederación de Empresarios Privados de Bolivia, Confederation of Private Entrepreneurs of Bolivia
CIB	Comité Indigenal Boliviano, Bolivian Indigenous Committee
CIDOB	Confederación Indígena del Oriente, Chaco y Amazonia de Bolivia, Indigenous Confederation of the Bolivian East, Chaco, and Amazon
CMUB	Confederación de Maestros Urbanos de Bolivia, Confederation of Urban Teachers of Bolivia
CNIO	Confederación de Naciones Indígenas y Originarios, Confederation of Aboriginal and Indigenous Nations
CNTC	Confederación Nacional de Trabajadores Campesinos, National Trade-Union Confederation of Peasant-Workers

COB	Central Obrera Boliviana, Bolivian Workers' Central
COD	Central Obrera Departamental, Departmental Workers' Central
COES	Centro Obrero de Estudios Sociales, Workers' Centre for Social Studies
COMIBOL	Corporación Minera de Bolivia, Bolivian State-Mining Company
CONDEPA	Conciencia de Patria, Consciousness of the Fatherland
COPAP	Consejo Político del Acuerdo Patriótico, Political Council of the Patriotic Accord
COR-El Alto	Central Obrera Regional de El Alto, Regional Workers' Central of El Alto
CPB	Confederación de la Prensa de Bolivia, Bolivian Press-Confederation
CPESC	Coordinadora de Pueblos Étnicos de Santa Cruz, Co-ordinator of Ethnic Peoples of Santa Cruz
CPSC	Comité Pro Santa Cruz, Pro Santa Cruz Committee
CSFTC	Coordinadora de las seis federaciones del trópico de Cochabamba, Co-ordinator of the Six Coca-Growers' Federations of Tropical Cochabamba
CSTB	Confederación Sindical de Trabajadores de Bolivia, Trade-Union Confederation of Bolivian Workers
CSUTCB	Confederación Sindical Única de Trabajadores Campesinos de Bolivia, Trade-Union Confederation of Bolivian Peasant-Workers
CUTAL	Confederación Única de Trabajadores de El Alto, Workers' Confederation of El Alto
EAP	Economically Active Population
EGTK	Ejército Guerrillero de Tupaj Katari, Tupaj Katari Guerrilla-Army
EMP	Estado Mayor del Pueblo, Peoples' High Command
ENDE	Empresa Nacional de Energía, National Energy-Company
ENTEL	National Telephone-Company
Fabriles	Federación de Fabriles de Cochabamba, Federation of Factory-Workers of Cochabamba
FDI	Foreign Direct Investment
FEDECOR	Federación Departamental de Regantes de Cochabamba, Departmental Federation of Peasant-Irrigators of Cochabamba

FEJUVE-El Alto	Federación de Juntas Vecinales de El Alto, Federation of Neighbourhood-Councils of El Alto
FEPB-SC	Federación de Empresarios Privados de Bolivia – Santa Cruz, Federation of Private Entrepreneurs of Bolivia Santa Cruz
FETCTC	Federación Especial de Trabajadores Campesinos de Trópico de Cochabamba, Special Federation of Peasant-Workers of the Tropics of Cochabamba
FMUC	Federación de Maestros Urbanos de Cochabamba, Urban Teachers' Federation of Cochabamba
FOF	Federación Obrera Femenina, Womens' Labour-Federation
FOL-La Paz	Federación Obrera Local de La Paz, Local Workers' Federation of La Paz
FOT	Federación Obrera del Trabajo, Workers' Labour-Federation
FRT	Federación Regional de Transporte 1 de Mayo, May 1st Regional Federation of Truckers
FSB	Falange Socialista Boliviana, Bolivian Socialist Phalange
FSTMB	Federación Sindical de Trabajadores Mineros de Bolivia, Trade-Union Federation of Bolivian Mine-Workers
FTGACM	Federación de Trabajadores, Gremiales, Artesanos y Comerciantes Minoristas, Federation of Organised Workers, Artisans, Small Traders and Food-Sellers of the City of El Alto
FTI	Federación de Transportes Interprovincial, Federation of Inter-Provincial Truckers
FTS	Federación de Trabajadores en Salud, Federation of Health-Care Workers
FUDTCLP-TK	Federación Única Departamental de Trabajadores Campesinos de La Paz Tupaj Katari, Departmental Federation of Peasant-Workers of La Paz – Tupaj Katari

FUTECRA   Federación de Trabajadores en Carne de El Alto y La Paz, Federation of Meat-Workers of El Alto and La Paz

GES   Grupo Especial de Seguridad, Special Security-Forces

GNI   Gross National Income

GTA   Grupo Tupac Amaru, Tupac Amaru Group

IB   Izquierda Boliviana, Bolivian Left

IDB   Inter-American Development-Bank

IMF   International Monetary Fund

INRA   Instituto Nacional de Reforma Agraria, National Agrarian-Reform Institute

IPSP   Instrumento Político por la Soberanía de los Pueblos, Political Instrument for the Sovereignty of the Peoples

ISI   Import-Substitution Industrialisation

IU   Izquierda Unida, United Left

LPP   Ley de Participación Popular, Popular-Participation Law

MAS   Movimiento al Socialismo, Movement Towards Socialism

MBL   Movimiento Bolivia Libre, Free Bolivia Movement

MCB   Movimiento Campesino Base, Grassroots Peasant-Movement

MIP   Movimiento Indígena Pachakuti, Pachakuti Indigenous Movement

MIR   Movimiento de la Izquierda Revolucionaria, Movement of the Revolutionary Left

MITKA   Movimiento Indio Tupaj Katari, Tupaj Katari Indian Movement

MNR   Movimiento Nacionalista Revolucionario, Revolutionary-Nationalist Party

MRTK   Movimiento Revolucionario Tupaj Katari, Tupaj Katari Revolutionary Movement

MRTK(L)   Movimiento Revolucionario Tupaj Katari (de liberación), Tupaj Katari Revolutionary-Liberation Movement

MST   Movimiento Sin Tierra, Landless Peasant-Movement

MUPS   Movimiento de Unión Popular Socialista, Movement of Popular-Socialist Unity

NEP   Nueva Política Económica, New Economic Policy

NFR   Nueva Fuerza Republicana, New Republican Force

NGO   Non-Governmental Organisation

NIC   National Indigenous Congress

PCB   Partido Comunista de Bolivia, Bolivian Communist Party

PCML   Partido Comunista Marxista Leninista, Marxist-Leninist Communist Party

PIR   Partido de la Izquierda Revolucionaria, Party of the Revolutionary Left

PMC   Pacto Militar-Campesino, Military-Peasant Pact

POR   Partido Obrero Revolucionario, Revolutionary Workers' Party

PS   Partido Socialista, Socialist Party

PS – 1   Partido Socialista – 1, Socialist Party – 1

RADEPA   Razón de Patria, Patriotic-Reason Party

SAP   Structural-Adjustment Programme

SEMAPA   Servicio Municipal de Agua Potable y Alcantarillado (Cochabamba), Municipal Service of Drinking Water and Sewerage

SIB   Sociedad de Ingenieros Bolivianos, Society of Bolivian Engineers

UCS   Unión Civica Solidaridad, Solidarity Civic Union

UDP   Unidad Democrática Popular, Popular-Democratic Unity

UMSA   Universidad Mayor de San Andrés, University of San Andrés (Public University of La Paz)

UMSS   Universidad Mayor de San Simón, University of San Simón (Public University of Cochabamba)

UPEA   Universidad Pública de El Alto, Public University of El Alto

US   United States

YPFB   Yacimientos Petrolíferos Fiscales de Bolivia, Bolivian State Petroleum-Company

Chapter One

Politics of Indigenous Resistance and Class-Struggle

Evo Morales, leader of the Movimiento al Socialismo (Movement Towards Socialism, MAS), was elected President of Bolivia on 18 December 2005, with an historic 54 per cent of the popular vote. Not even the 'most optimistic [MAS] militants had imagined such a result'.[1] The percentage of votes obtained by the MAS exceeded by almost 15 points the top showing of any party since the return of electoral democracy in 1982.[2] Moreover, the electoral turnout was an impressive 85 per cent of eligible voters, up 13 per cent from the 2002 elections. Morales is the first indigenous president in the republic's history, a particularly salient fact in a country where 62 per cent of the population self-identified as indigenous in the last census in 2001.[3] As part of a wider shift to the left in Latin-American electoral politics since the late 1990s, the government of Evo Morales has drawn both vilification and idolisation in the existing literature. To focus exclusively, or even primarily, on the electoral politics of Bolivia's new Left, however, is to miss some of the fundamental social and

---

1. Stefanoni and Do Alto 2006, p. 17.
2. Romero Ballivián 2006, pp. 49–50.
3. INE 2001.

political dynamics of the current epoch that are rooted in extra-parliamentary social movements with complex histories.

Following fifteen years of neoliberal economic restructuring (1985–2000), élitist 'pacted democracy' between ideologically indistinguishable political parties, and the concomitant decomposition of popular movements, left-indigenous struggle in Bolivia was reborn with a vengeance in the 2000 Cochabamba Water-War against the World-Bank-driven privatisation of water in that city. This monumental uprising initiated a five-year cycle of rural and urban re-awakening of the exploited classes and oppressed indigenous majority that gradually spread throughout most of the country. The rebellions reached their apogee in the removal of two neoliberal presidents: Gonzalo Sánchez de Lozada, in October 2003, and Carlos Mesa Gisbert, in June 2005. These two moments were dubbed the 'Gas-Wars' because of the centrality of the demand to re-nationalise the oil-and gas-industry in Bolivia – the country has South America's second largest natural-gas deposits after Venezuela.

This book provides an analytical framework for understanding the left-indigenous cycle of extra-parliamentary insurrection between 2000 and 2005, and the long historical backdrop that preceded it. The central argument is that a specific combination of elaborate infrastructures of class-struggle and social-movement unionism, historical traditions of indigenous and working-class radicalism, combined-oppositional consciousness, and fierce but insufficient state-repression, explain the depth, breadth, and radical character of recent left-indigenous mobilisations in Bolivia. The coalition of insurrectionary social forces in the Gas-Wars of 2003 and 2005 was led by indigenous informal workers, acting in concert with formal workers, peasants, and to a smaller degree, middle-class actors. The indigenous informal working classes of the city of El Alto, in particular, utilised an elaborate infrastructure of class-struggle in order to overcome structural barriers to collective action and to take up their leading role. The supportive part played by the formal working class was made possible by the political orientation toward social-movement unionism adopted by leading trade-union federations. Radicalised peasants mobilised within the broader alliance through their own rural infrastructure of class-struggle. The whole array of worker- and peasant-social forces drew on longstanding popular cultures of indigenous liberation and revolutionary Marxism which they adapted to the novel context of the twenty-first century. These popular political cultures ultimately congealed in a new combined oppositional consciousness, rooted simultaneously in the politics of indigenous resistance and class-struggle. This collective consciousness, in turn, strengthened the mobilising capacities of the popular classes and reinforced the radical character of protest. At key junctures, social-movement leaders were able to synthesise oppositional consciousness into a focused collective-action frame of nationalising the natural-gas industry. Finally, throughout the left-indigenous cycle, ruthless state-repression was nonetheless insufficiently powerful to wipe out opposition altogether and therefore acted only to intensify the scale of protests and radicalise demands still further. The legitimacy of the neoliberal social order and the coercive power required to reproduce it were increasingly called into question as violence against civilians increased.

This chapter begins with a brief survey of the migration of European and American social-movement theory to the Latin-American context and the insights and limitations of these extant frameworks. Next, it highlights some of the weaknesses of the dominant liberal-institutionalist approach to understanding indigenous politics in contemporary Latin America. Finally, it defines in detail the core theoretical concepts that inform the alternative Marxist and indigenous-liberationist analytical framework offered in the book.

1.1 Social-movement theory

In a seminal work on social-movement studies in the mid-1980s, Jean Cohen (1985) describes a fundamental divide between the European 'identity-oriented'[4] approach to the study of contemporary (1970s–80s) movements, and the 'resource-mobilisation' or 'strategy'-oriented theories emerging out of American academia. Together, the two bodies of literature challenged classical theories of social-movements and shared the following assumptions: social movements involve contestation between well-organised groups with developed forms of communication; contentious collective action is normal and the individual participants typically rational; and, finally, there are two levels of collective action consisting, on the one hand, of large-scale mobilisations

---

4. Often referred to in the contemporary literature as the 'New Social Movement' (NSM) approach or theory.

and, on the other, underlying forms of organisation and communication that sustain participation and allow for wide-scale mobilisation.[5]

Both schools formed in response to earlier frameworks. 'New Social Movement' (NSM) theorists were reacting against what they deemed to be the inapplicability of Marxism to the heterogeneous movements in Europe in the 1970s and 1980s. Movements rooted in ecology, peace, gender, ethnicity, age, neighbourhood, environment, and sexual diversity were seen as the new loci of contention in 'postindustrial' society. According to these theorists, the new movements could not be explained or understood in terms of Marxist notions of class and the primacy of the economy and the state. Instead, the movements were said to engage in self-limiting, reformist struggles, primarily in the domain of civil society.[6]

While not a uniform set of thinkers, these theorists generally agreed on where Marxists had gone wrong. First, Marxists were allegedly guilty of a set of two reductionisms: (i) economic reductionism, in the sense that an economic logic determines social formations and political and ideological processes, such that politics and ideology are epiphenomena of the economic realm; and (ii) class-reductionism, in the sense that the identity of social actors is derived primarily from their class-position.[7] In contradistinction to this, NSM-theorists suggested that the heterogeneity of the 'new' movements were concerned more with the 'process of symbolic production and the redefinition of social roles' than the economy.[8] These were expressive rather than instrumental movements. The following emphases, then, characterised the NSM-perspective: culture; the struggle over meaning and the social construction of new collective identities; the pre-eminent role of civil society as the domain of contention, as opposed to the state; and the stress on discontinuity, the 'newness' of these movements when compared to the 'traditional' collective actors of old.[9]

Across the Atlantic, resource-mobilisation (RM), or strategy-theorists took as their starting point a rejection of the psychological categories, and empha-

---

5. Cohen 1985, p. 673.
6. See Cohen 1985; Habermas 1981; Laclau 1981, 1983; Laclau and Mouffe 1985; Melucci 1980, 1984, 1985, 1989; Mouffe 1979, 1984, 1988; Offe 1985; Touraine 1981, 1985, 1988.
7. Canel 1997, p. 190.
8. Ibid.
9. Canel 1997, p. 189.

sis on breakdown, characteristic of the functionalist collective-behaviour approach.[10] The strategy-school dominated the study of social movements in North America.[11] This school concerned itself with organisations, interests, resources, opportunities, and strategies.[12] In particular, the strategy-perspective emphasised the following: the political orientation of social movements; the conception of movements as conflicts over goods in the political market; the strategic and instrumental components of collective action and the simultaneity of struggle at the levels of civil society and the state; and the continuity between 'new' and 'old' collective actors.[13]

Overwhelmingly, Latin-American social-movement studies in 1980s and 1990s favoured the 'identity'-approach, often uncritically applying the European lens to the Latin-American setting.[14] Despite some incorporation of strategy, economy, formal politics, and the state, the emphasis remained on NSM-themes of analysis in Latin-American social-movement studies.[15] Culture, civil society, and the heterogeneity of movement-identities were front and centre in the contributions of this school. These theoretical foci have been applied to topics as wide-ranging as the methodology of social science, citizenship, democracy and the state, cyber-politics, ethnicity, race and gender, globalisation, and transnationalism. The NSM-paradigm had critical cross-disciplinary influence throughout the 1980s and 1990s, and retains its hegemony in anthropology as well as considerable weight in social-movement studies in political science, sociology and history.

Diane E. Davis points out that, in addition to the positive appeal of the civil-society focus of the NSM-perspective, the 'strategy-oriented' paradigm was often seen as state-centred by Latin-American scholars.[16] She argues this was essentially a 'kiss of death' for the paradigm in a region where the state was generally conceived of as the enemy given the proliferation of authoritarian régimes in the 1960s and 1970s.[17] Moreover, she suggests, the role of

---

10. Cohen 1985, p. 674.
11. See Jenkins 1981, 1982, 1983; McAdam 1996; McAdam, McCarthy, and Zald 1996a; McAdam, McCarthy, and Zald 1988; McAdam 1982; McCarthy and Zald 1973, 1977a, 1977b; Tilly 1978, 1981, 1985; Tilly and Tilly 1981; Zald and Ash 1966; Zald and McCarthy 1987.
12. Cohen 1985, p. 674.
13. Canel 1997, pp. 189–190.
14. Foweraker 1995, p. 3.
15. Álvarez, Dagnino, and Escobar 1998; Escobar and Álvarez 1992; Slater 1985.
16. Davis 1999, pp. 586–8.
17. Davis 1999, p. 589.

'anti-Americanism' among Latin-American social-movement scholars/ activists, and (at that time) a pervasive intellectual Eurocentrism, may also have played some role in determining the hegemonic status of the 'identity'-school.[18] There were also important empirical realities of the changing Latin-American political, demographic, and economic contexts that help to explain the character of social-movement studies in Latin America during the period in question. From the 1930s to the 1960s, much of Latin America was characterised by populist politics and highly interventionist states. The pre-eminent collective-action domains during this period were generally considered to consist of urban-labour and agrarian-peasant activity rooted in social class. In short, there was a circumscribed range of collective actors. Two subsequent developments were important in shaping the social-movement context of the 1980s and 1990s. First, by the 1970s, rapid rural-to-urban migration in Latin America had contributed to a serious transformation of urban life. Second, the crisis of the populist and developmentalist state in the region led to the proliferation of military and authoritarian régimes. The combination of urban expansion and state-repression fuelled the rise of new social actors, especially women's movements.[19]

Latin-American literature during this period emphasised the discontinuity between the explosive heterogeneity of contemporary movements and the relatively limited range of social actors that were said to characterise Latin America twenty-five years earlier.[20] The NSM-perspective shared these thematic emphases and provided a useful optic for many Latin-American thinkers. However, influenced as they were by the wider intellectual concerns of postmodernism, NSM-studies tended to bend the analytical stick too far, toward a seemingly autonomous cultural sphere. They had the effect of shifting the focus of social-movement studies almost entirely 'from political-economy and history' toward 'literature and 'culture, an approach which entailed both the conceptual deprivileging of economic development ('post-development'), and the political rejection of Marxism, meta-narratives, and European Enlightenment-discourse ('post-Marxism')'.[21] Recent Marxist litera-

---

18. Davis 1999, p. 588.
19. Foweraker 1995, p. 5. See also Bouvard 1994; Isbester 2001; Jaquette 1989; Kampwirth 2002, 2004; Nash and Safa 1986.
20. Foweraker 1995, p. 38.
21. Brass 2002a, pp. 2–3.

ture on social movements in Latin America, particularly in peasant-studies, challenges this exaggerated cultural turn, calling for the continued applicability of political-economy methods to the study of peasants, and the role of a reconstituted class-analysis that can take into account issues of gender and ethnicity.[22] They point out that the NSM-framework is deeply ahistorical and is also unable to identify crises of capitalism, such as stagnation and financial panics, or the social contradictions of increasing inequality at national, regional, and international scales, which impose structural constraints on the local-level problems with which NSM-studies tend to be preoccupied.[23]

These Marxist theoretical and sociological critiques correspond closely to historian Greg Grandin's important interpretation of twentieth-century Latin-American history. Grandin points out that many scholars, in celebrating the focus of 'new social movements' on 'culture, community, sexual, and gender identities and interests and for moving away from class analysis', sometimes lose perspective both on the continuing relevance of class and the continuities between 'old' movements of the Left and 'new' identity-based movements. 'Despite their inability to incorporate culture and race into their analyses and visions of progress', Grandin contends, 'left political parties and labor organizations in Bolivia, El Salvador, Guatemala, Chile, and Peru, for some examples, drew significant support from rural, often indigenous communities'.[24] And, in the current context, in many of these same countries, 'movements led by native Americans are the most forceful agents of the kind of democratic socialism that was advanced by the old left'.[25] In short, NSM-studies neglect class, political economy, and history.

As regards the strategy-literature, it is important to point out that, given the authoritarian setting of much of Latin America during this period, it was difficult for many to think of 'political opportunities', so central to this school, as important variables.[26] Following the transition to electoral democracies

---

22. Brass 2002b; Hertzler 2005; Hristov 2005; Petras 1997, 1999; Petras and Veltmeyer 2000.

23. Petras 1999.

24. Grandin 2005, pp. 192–3.

25. Grandin 2005, p. 193. Grandin points out, for example, that in Guatemala the contemporary Maya movement is populated with leaders who began their politicisation in the guerrilla-organisations of the 1960s and 1970s. He argues that, 'more than just a direct connection, many of the identities that drive today's social-movements were shaped in the crucible of old left politics' (Grandin 2005, p. 193).

26. Edelman 2001, p. 292.

throughout the 1980s, however, mainstream-studies of social movements have increasingly drawn from the strategy-oriented theoretical frameworks;[27] although, even where strategy-oriented approaches have been used in the Latin-American context, the theoretical component of these works has typically been understated. The strategy-framework – and, more recently, the related political-process approach which focuses specifically on political-opportunity structure (POS)[28] – has also come under considerable fire. Critics emphasise that little attention is paid to the roles of identity and gender in social movements, and the social construction of the structure of political opportunities.[29] Another common line of criticism aims at the imprecision of the notion of political-opportunity structure. Gamson and Meyer put it this way: '...[POS is] a sponge that soaks up virtually every aspect of the social-movement environment...an all-encompassing fudge factor...[which] may explain nothing at all'.[30] Most seriously, the political-process approach tends to focus on institutional régime-change and political democratisation without addressing adequately the accompanying economic transformations issued forth by changes in the structure of capitalism – most importantly for this book, the changes wrought by neoliberalism since the mid-1970s. Class-analysis is largely expunged from this school's examination of institutions and amorphous social movements. In sum, then, the strategy-school suffers from a relative neglect of class, identity and gender, the socially constructed and contested nature of political-opportunity structures themselves, and a pre-eminent focus on political and institutional change at the expense of political economy.

Some neo-Marxist theorising in the Latin-American context has addressed the centrality of the structure of the political economy in framing the institutional and cultural environs of social movements. For example, Susan Eckstein develops an elaborate framework for a 'historical-structural' approach to understanding social movements in the region.[31] On this view, social structure is important to any understanding of popular movements: 'Those

---

27. See Brockett 1991, 2005; Haber 1996; Hipsher 1998; Schneider 1995.
28. See Tarrow 1998; Wong 2004.
29. Edelman 2001, p. 290.
30. Ibid.
31. Eckstein 1989.

who control the means of physical coercion and the means of producing wealth have power over those who do not.... When the poor and working classes rebel, it is not because they are intrinsically troublemakers. They rebel because they have limited alternative means to voice their views and press for change.'[32] Changes in economic relationships are seen as the principal cause of protest and collective action in hopes of change.[33] However, protest is mediated by 'contextual factors', such as 'cross-class, institutional, and cultural ties; state structures; and real, or at least perceived, options to exit rather than rebel'.[34] Similarly, Kenneth M. Roberts argues, 'In general, the literature on social movements has paid more attention to issues of régime change and democratisation than to the challenges posed by economic restructuring'.[35] His measure of the staying power of the Latin-American Left at the end of the 1990s focuses on the mobilising capacities of the poor and working classes. He identifies 'social structure', 'the organizational density and forms of collective action in civil society', and 'agents of political representation' (i.e. the relationship between social movements and political parties), as the central variables determining left strength.[36] Neo-Marxist social-movement theorising improves on NSM- and political-process frameworks, emphasising as it does the importance of structural economic change in understanding social-movement dynamics. However, neo-Marxists tend to emphasise the reformist characteristics of actually-existing social movements and are ill-equipped to understand sociologically the recent explosion of radical, anticapitalist struggles in Latin America, just as they are frequently opposed to them ideologically. Furthermore, neo-Marxism usually employs a limited Weberian structural class-analysis, seeing class merely as a position in a stratified social hierarchy, rather than as a social relationship and historical process rooted in the antagonistic struggles of different social classes.[37]

Against this backdrop, the theoretical approach advanced in this book attempts to bring back to the fore themes of political economy and history

32. Eckstein 1989, p. 3.
33. Eckstein 1989, p. 5.
34. Eckstein 1989, p. 4.
35. Roberts 1997.
36. Roberts 1998, pp. 53–78.
37. I discuss the benefits of treating class as a social relationship and historical process in the section below on working classes as historical formations.

which have been neglected in both the NSM- and strategy-oriented social-movement literatures, and theorised from a reformist ideological perspective and Weberian-influenced sociological framework in the case of many neo-Marxists. It also argues that social class and class-struggle must be taken much more seriously than they have been in the reigning paradigms of social-movement studies in the Latin-American context over the last two and a half decades. At the same time, by consciously incorporating other social relations – such as gender and race – into our class-analysis, we need not succumb to the sort of economic reductionism against which NSM-theorists initially reacted.

In order to avoid the all-encompassing sponge-effect of some POS-research mentioned above, I deliberately avoid this tradition's tendency to accumulate new concepts and variables at an alarming rate, concepts and variables which are then incorporated into an ever-more complicated environmental network constituting the political-opportunity structure. I draw selectively from this literature when appropriate – particularly regarding state-repression and collective-action frames –, but have attempted to simplify and clarify the analytical edifice necessary to understand social movements in Bolivia, with an emphasis on bringing out the centrality of class-struggle and indigenous resistance. Before elaborating the core-concepts that distinguish my approach – working classes as historical formations, infrastructures of class-struggle, social-movement unionism, popular cultures of resistance and opposition, and combined-oppositional consciousness – it is important first to trace the contours of the theoretical framework through which specifically indigenous movements and parties in Bolivia, and Latin America more widely, are most commonly understood today.

The 1994 Zapatista rebellion in Chiapas, Mexico fuelled scholarly interest in indigenous movements in Latin America. Apparently, more books were published on the Latin-American 'Indian question' between 1994 and 1999 than during the rest of the twentieth century.[38] Despite the attention the Zapatistas received, the proliferation of studies of indigenous movements across the region showed that the Mexican rebels were, in fact, latecomers in the most recent cycle of indigenous political activity. Elsewhere in the continent, many of the indigenous movements of this wave had engaged in direct action, mass-mobilisations, and roadblocks as far back as the 1960s. By one estimate,

---

38. Otero 2003, p. 249.

there are approximately 34 million to 40 million indigenous people in Latin America.[39] Indigenous movements have emerged as key political actors in the current conjuncture, whether in countries with relatively large indigenous populations, such as Bolivia, Guatemala, and Ecuador, or in countries where those populations are minorities, such as Chile, Colombia, and Brazil.

1.2 Liberal institutionalism and neoliberal multiculturalism

During the 1990s, mainstream political science in North America was mostly devoted to the study of the 'third wave' of democratisation.[40] Consequently, one of the first areas of interest with respect to the politicisation of indigenous identity in Latin America was how it would have an impact upon liberal democracy, and specifically, its 'consolidation' in the region.[41] A key normative concern driving this work was the idea that the exclusion of indigenous communities from participation in the political system intensifies ethnic conflict and slows the process of liberal-democratic consolidation. This turn in the literature was part of a general shift toward liberal institutionalism in the study of identity-politics in Latin America. Liberal institutionalism in this field focuses on state-institutions and how they shape indigenous movements.[42] Liberal democracy, and the system of capitalism that undergirds it, is seen to be at least potentially favourable to Latin-American indigenous peoples. Liberal-institutionalist analysis focuses on the transition from corporatist to neoliberal citizenship-régimes in Latin America in the 1980s and 1990s and the ways in which this shift in the institutional arrangements of the state challenged enclaves of indigenous local autonomy in several different countries.[43] It also pays close attention to processes of constitutional reform.[44] Beginning in the 1980s, a number of Latin-American states drew up new constitutions. Many of these constitutions officially recognised the pluricultural and multiethnic nature of Latin-American states for the first time since independence from colonial rule in the early nineteenth century.[45]

---

39. Assies 1998, p. 4.
40. Huntington 1991.
41. Van Cott 1994.
42. See Van Cott 2005; Yashar 2005.
43. Yashar 2005, p. 8.
44. Van Cott 2003a.
45. Stavenhagen 2003, pp. 32–3.

Linking constitutional reform in Latin America in the late 1990s to the democratisation-literature, some scholars contend that, 'constitutional transformation', represents a 'new type of democratisation'.[46] The recognition by the state of society's multiethnic and pluricultural natures is presented as a major step forward.[47] A final central concern of liberal institutionalism has been the formation of ethnic parties and the changes in state-institutions, party-systems, and social movements that account for their formation.[48] From this perspective, shifts to more permissive institutional environments – 'constitutional provisions, laws, and rules that structure electoral competition' and/or shifts to more open party-systems are necessary conditions for the formation and better performance of ethnic parties.[49]

The liberal-institutionalist framework suffers from a number of important weaknesses. It tends, first, to emphasise the 'newness' of indigenous movements, situating them in a wave of allegedly non-class identity-movements that emerged in the region in the 1970s, 1980s, and 1990s. A number of historians working in different Latin-American countries have called this emphasis on the novelty of contemporary indigenous movements into question, and it is now clear that discussion of indigenous movements as separate phenomena from class-struggle is misleading at best.[50] In the Bolivian case, I found it striking that the most important social movements in recent years have been rooted in the largely indigenous and informal proletarian urban centres, such as El Alto, and have been a response in large part to the social costs resulting from neoliberal economic restructuring. They have, therefore, been about race and class together, and are best seen as part of an emergent and dynamic indigenous Left, rather than a phenomenon that has replaced the death of the Left. Rather than being totally new movements, the contemporary left-indigenous struggles in Bolivia are deeply linked to longstanding insurrec-

---

46. Van Cott 2000, p. 6.
47. See Albó 2002a; Assies, van der Haar, and Hoekemaet 1998; Cojtí Cuxil 2002; Davis 2002; de la Peña 2002; Laurie, Andolina, and Radcliffe 2002; Plant 2002; Sieder 2002; Van Cott 2000, p. 265.
48. Birner and Van Cott 2007; Van Cott 2003c, 2005.
49. Van Cott 2005, p. 8.
50. See Larson 1998; Larson, Harris, and Tandeter 1995; Mallon 1992; Quijano 2005; Thomson 2002, 2003.

tionary traditions of indigenous and working-class resistance stretching back centuries.[51]

Liberal institutionalism also naturalises the existence of capitalism and therefore assumes its essential uncontestability. How the contradictions of capitalist social relations impinge on the varied aspects of indigenous reality in Latin America is left largely unexamined. Such an approach has important ideological and sociological implications. While liberal institutionalists include extensive theoretical exploration of theories of citizenship, for example, they tend to obscure the way in which capitalism, in uniquely separating the political sphere from the economic, circumscribes dramatically what citizenship can possibly mean within that system.[52] The separation of indigenous political struggles from the wider sphere of capitalist social relations leads liberal institutionalists to political conclusions that seem remote from the far-reaching, often anticapitalist, demands of many actual indigenous movements in Latin America.

Because liberal institutionalism treats ethnicity and culture as separate spheres from the economy and the historical and material foundations of social life, it exaggerates the significance of indigenous cultural gains in the 1990s, such as the constitutional reforms mentioned above. In this regard, we ought to be especially cognisant of the historical-material reality underpinning the emerging ideology of 'neoliberal multiculturalism' in that decade. The 1990s, in the Latin-American context, were characterised both by massive indigenous mobilisations and neoliberal capitalist expansion. Neoliberal political and economic reforms accompanied the shift in state-policies toward multicultural recognition of indigenous communities, and these reforms are well known to exacerbate or sustain existing material inequalities between

---

51. Historians Forrest Hylton and Sinclair Thomson remind us that the protagonists of the explosive wave of left-indigenous insurgency in early twenty-first century Bolivia borrowed from past struggles 'a set of signs and scripts' that helped them to understand 'their world, their actions and their aims' (Hylton and Thomson 2007, p. 6). This book seeks in part to complement their foundational 'excavation of Andean revolution, whose successive layers of historical sedimentation comprise the subsoil, loam, landscape, and vistas for current political struggle in Bolivia' (Hylton and Thomson 2007, p. 31).

52. For a liberal-institutionalist treatment of citizenship see Yashar 2005, pp. 31–53. On the separation of the political from the economic sphere under capitalism and a devastating Marxist critique of liberal notions of citizenship, see Wood 1995, pp. 19–48.

social classes. 'Since the culturally oppressed, at least in the case of Latin America's indigenous people, occupy the bottom rung of the class hierarchy in disproportionate numbers', Charles Hale observes, 'they confront the paradox of simultaneous cultural affirmation and economic marginalisation'.[53] Hale's notion of the *indio permitido*, or 'authorised Indian', refers to the way in which neoliberal states in Latin America in the 1990s adopted a language of cultural recognition of indigenous people and even enacted modest reforms in the area of indigenous rights. At the same time, these states set strict limits on the extent of reform. Neoliberal multiculturalism, in this way, played the role of dividing and domesticating indigenous movements through selective co-optation. The 'unauthorised' indigenous movements that refused to accept the parameters of neoliberal multiculturalism were frequently targeted and repressed by these 'multicultural' states. In particular, the era of the *indio permitido* has meant that cultural rights are to be enjoyed on the implicit condition that indigenous movements will not challenge foundational neoliberal economic policies and their accompanying forms of capitalist class-power and exploitation. Indigenous movements that have submitted more or less to the framework of neoliberal multiculturalism fall into Hale's socio-political category *indio permitido*, or 'authorised Indian'.[54]

Insights from historical materialism, I argue, push this critical approach still further. They help us to understand key dynamics and obstacles within indigenous struggles, and their relationship to class-struggle and potential emancipation from class-exploitation. They transcend the limitations of liberal institutionalism and easy celebration of neoliberal multiculturalism. Marxist theory has come a long way in enveloping the multidimensionality of social reality through an appreciation of anti-oppression politics, and the incorporation of race, gender, sexuality, and other social relations, into its analysis without forgetting about social class and the totalising power of capitalism.[55] My own work builds more specifically on a growing Latin-American literature that treats indigenous struggles from the perspective of Marxism and/or critical-race theory, taking into account the relationship between indigenous

---

53. Hale 2002, p. 493.
54. See Hale 2002, 2004, 2006.
55. Bannerji 2000; Becker 1993, 2006; Brenner 2000; Dore 2006; Gordon 2006a, 2007; Roediger 1999; Stephen 2005.

resistance and class-struggle in particular.[56] The point here is to highlight the necessity of considering indigenous struggles in contemporary Latin America within a greater system of domestic capitalist social relations – class-struggle from above and below.[57] Analyses of the contemporary indigenous question must also take into account the longer history of the relevant countries, their traditions of indigenous struggle or lack thereof, their long trajectories of capitalist development, state-formation, and insertion into the global capitalist economy, and what all of this has meant for shifting class-formations and class-struggle.

Despite the general neglect of social class in the dominant liberal-institutionalist literature, then, a number of recent studies attempt to deal with the ways in which class-struggle and indigenous political contention interact. What stands out, however, is that, thus far, these contributions are focused by and large on rural settings.[58] For example, Henry Veltmeyer, through an examination of the Chiapas uprising in Mexico in 1994 and 'new peasant-movements' proliferating throughout Latin America in the 1990s, argues for a 'reconstituted form of class-analysis that takes into account gender, ethnic, and development issues'.[59] In doing so, Veltmeyer positions himself amidst other sociological studies of peasants and social movements in Latin America, such as Thomas Benjamin's *A Rich Land, A Poor People: Politics and Society in Modern Chiapas*, and Gavin Smith's *Livelihood and Resistance: Peasants and the Politics of Land in Peru*.[60] Such studies have not 'been trapped in the rather sterile debate between an economistic form of class-analysis that ignores the subjective aspects of class-formation on the one hand, and an overly subjectivist and idealist postmodernist interpretation on the other'.[61] Jasmin Hristov's analysis of struggles of the smallholding peasant-indigenous peoples of Cauca, Colombia, and especially their resistance-efforts through the Consejo Regional Indígena de Cauca, or CRIC) since the early 1970s, is exemplary

---

56. Escárzaga and Gutiérrez 2005; García Linera 2005b; Gould 1990, 1998; Grandin 2005; Gutiérrez and Escárzaga 2006; Hale 1996, 2006; Harvey 1998; Hristov 2005; Hylton 2006; Hylton and Thomson 2007; Rivera Cusicanqui 2003 [1984]; Sawyer 2004; Stephen 1996, 2002; Veltmeyer 1997.
57. The impact of imperialism on these domestic class-struggles is also extremely important, but mostly beyond the scope of this study.
58. Otero 2004; Otero and Jugenitz 2003.
59. Veltmeyer 1997, p. 141.
60. Benjamin 1989; Smith 1989.
61. Veltmeyer 1997, p. 149.

in the sense of placing indigenous movements within the broader context of class-struggle and the expansion of neoliberal capitalism within the Colombia.[62] The analyses of issues of culture and class in Veltmeyer and Hristov's contributions are noteworthy for their erudition and sophistication and my analysis in this book grows explicitly out of this tradition of historical materialism. At the same time, however, the urban dimension of class-formation and indigenous struggle, as well as the rural-urban dynamics of these issues, have not been adequately theorised. This is one of the gaps I hope to fill with this study.

1.3 Working classes as historical formations

According to Ellen Meiksins Wood, 'There are really only two ways of thinking theoretically about class: either as a structural *location* or as a social *relation*'.[63] Static structural pictures may be useful as a starting point for the determining logic of class-relations, but there is a very long way to travel in order to identify how a class 'in itself' becomes a class 'for itself', to use Marx's terminology for the movement between an objective class-situation and class-consciousness, or from social being to social consciousness.[64] In order to get there, we need to think of class as a social-historical process and relationship. 'The working class did not rise like the sun at an appointed time', E.P. Thompson famously argues in *The Making of the English Working Class*, for '[i]t was present at its own making'.[65] Here he is firmly asserting the importance of human agency in the class-struggle, agency that is, however, bounded by the logic of a set of class-situations that each person enters into involuntarily. Understanding class as a relationship in which the common experiences of real people living in real contexts matter, and which takes place in historical time, means that it 'evades analysis if we attempt to stop it dead at any given moment and anatomise its structure'.[66]

Thompson has been criticised for neglecting the objective structure of productive relations in favour of a conception of class which centres on

---

62. Hristov 2005.
63. Wood 1995, p. 76.
64. Camfield 2004, p. 436.
65. Thompson 1963, p. 9.
66. Ibid.

consciousness and subjectivity.[67] However, as David Camfield points out, in Thompson's framework, common experience, human agency, culture, and subjectivity 'are not free-floating. They have a material foundation'.[68] For Thompson, '[t]he class experience is largely determined by the productive relations into which men are born – or enter into involuntarily'.[69] Yet, as Camfield suggests, in Thompson's schema, '[t]he relations of production are only the point of departure'.[70] 'Class consciousness', writes Thompson, 'is the way in which these experiences', the experiences of being thrust through birth or an alternative form of involuntary entry into a class-situation, 'are handled in cultural terms: embodied in traditions, value-systems, ideas, and institutional forms'.[71] Ultimately, class-analysis requires looking at real people in real contexts: 'Class is defined by men as they live their own history, and, in the end, this is the only definition'.[72]

David Camfield's theoretical formulation of *working classes as historical formations* flows out of the Thompsonian tradition and travels nicely to Bolivian context.[73] Camfield conceptualises class 'as a structured social process and relationship that takes place in historical time and specific cultural contexts'. Such a conceptualisation, for Camfield, 'must consciously incorporate social relations other than class, such as gender and race'.[74] Class-formations in this theory flow from the historical relations people experience with the relations of production and other antagonistic social classes.[75] Such an historical approach to understanding class-formations reveals that, while class 'is ultimately anchored and sustained' at the point of production, 'class-relations pervade all aspects of social life'.[76] Because, '[p]eople do not stop belonging to classes when they leave their workplaces', a useful theory of class-formation will have to examine class in households and communities, as well as in workplaces.[77]

---

67. Anderson 1980; Cohen 1978.
68. Camfield 2004, p. 434.
69. Thompson 1963, p. 9.
70. Camfield 2004, p. 437.
71. Thompson 1963, p. 10.
72. Thompson 1963, p. 11.
73. Camfield 2004.
74. Camfield 2004, p. 421.
75. Camfield 2004, p. 424.
76. Ibid.
77. Ibid.

Camfield's interpretation is also influenced by the Italian Marxist Antonio Gramsci, who was preoccupied with the social origins of new classes, a view that emphasised the importance of history in studying class-formations.[78] Working classes are not constructed abstractly out of theoretical structures, but, rather, are formed 'out of pre-existing social groups whose particular traditions, aspirations and cultural practices – modified by the devastating experience of proletarianisation – will be those of an emergent proletariat'.[79] If we take these insights seriously, it follows necessarily that any serious approach to class-formation will require a 'profound appreciation of the society in question', and a deep understanding that '[n]ational particularities have real significance'.[80] Taking this theoretical contribution seriously has led me to contextualise the period of left-indigenous insurrection in Bolivia between 2000 and 2005, through an extended, long-view discussion of working-class formation and traditions of indigenous resistance in the country's history since the eighteenth century.

I use urban 'working classes' throughout this book in an expansive sense to refer to those whose labour has been commodified in various ways and who do not live off the labour of others.[81] Such a definition avoids simplistic and formulaic notions of a worker of an ideal type. It recognises that 'the boundaries between "free" wage-labourers and other kinds of subaltern workers in capitalist society are in reality rather finely graded or vague', that 'there are extensive and complicated "grey areas" replete with transitional locations between the "free" wage laborers and slaves, the self-employed and the lumpenproletarians', that 'almost all subaltern workers belong to households that combine *several* modes of labor', and that 'the distinction between the different kinds of subaltern workers is not clear-cut'.[82] In combining the workplace, the household, and the community into our discussion of working-class formation, we also take into account the often gendered role of unpaid repro-

---

78. Camfield 2004, p. 431.
79. Ibid.
80. Camfield 2004, pp. 432–3.
81. Olivera 2004b, p. 157; Spronk 2007a, p. 186; 2007b, p. 13. Likewise, when discussing the countryside throughout this study I have chosen expansive expressions. By 'peasants', following Catherine LeGrand 1986, I mean 'small rural cultivators who rely on family labor to produce what they consume. Sharecroppers, service tenants, small proprietors, and frontier settlers would, by this definition, all be called peasants' (quoted in Hylton 2006, p. 140).
82. van der Linden 2008, p. 32.

ductive labour that occurs in the household and elsewhere. Working-class families, and even individual workers, in many Third-World countries may hold different jobs simultaneously, or may be both urban and rural, with back and forth movement between the two worlds. Smooth and permanent transitions from peasant to proletarian, for example, are outside the norm.[83] This is true in many cases of immigrant-labour in the advanced capitalist countries as well.[84] Classes, therefore, ought to be understood as 'complex and heterogeneous formations'.[85]

1.4 Infrastructure of class-struggle

As a way of capturing the concrete processes by which working-class formation and working-class struggle developed in Bolivia during the neoliberal era, I have adopted and altered components of Alan Sears's concept of *infrastructure of dissent*, by introducing what I call the *infrastructure of class-struggle*.[86] The development of an infrastructure of dissent, for Sears, facilitates the growth of individual and collective capacities of the oppressed and exploited to mobilise and challenge the hierarchical power-structures responsible for their exploitation and oppression; that infrastructure can include formal and informal networks in workplaces, unions, communities and political organisations, various informal gathering places for radical dissidents, and an array of alternative media. That infrastructure, furthermore, strengthens the collective memory of past struggles, fosters more sophisticated theoretical debate and analysis among radicals, and facilitates unofficial and non-commercial communicative ties between various dissident groups and individuals.[87]

Working-class formation does not spring up straightforwardly. Common experience is necessary both within and outside the workplace. The infrastructure of class-struggle might be thought of as the incubator of that common experience. My use of Sears's term is adapted to the particular context of

---

83. Striffler 2004, p. 12.
84. Thanks to Forrest Hylton for stressing this point.
85. Camfield 2007, p. 38.
86. See Sears 2007. Because I see class-struggle in the Bolivian context as highly racialised, I use 'racialised class-struggle' and 'class-struggle' interchangeably throughout the text.
87. Sears 2007, pp. 8–9.

Bolivia, and to my more specific thematic focus on Bolivia's left-indigenous insurrectionary cycle between 2000 and 2005. At the heart of this insurrectionary wave is racialised class-struggle. I use the term 'infrastructure of class-struggle' to embrace the multi-sited locales of class-struggle, particularly, but not only, after neoliberal restructuring radically reduced the capacities of traditional trade-unions to lead the battles of the Bolivian Left. Informal workers in this setting have often found organising primarily in the community as the only feasible way of building resistance and protest-movements for their class-interests. Yet, as I show in the discussion of the Gas-Wars, the links between community-based organisations of informal workers depended upon alliances with the older trade-union structures of sectors of the formal working class as well as those of the peasantry. I mean by the infrastructure of class-struggle *all those formal and informal networks – in the workplace, community, household, land, and territory – that orient, organise, politicise, and mobilise the class-struggles of the largely-indigenous proletarian and peasant-majority.*[88] A key facet of any infrastructure of class-struggle is the way it provides a means through which longstanding revolutionary memories and popular cultures of resistance and opposition can be sustained and adapted to changing contexts of struggle.

The historical parts of this book chart the multifaceted contours of the development of various infrastructures of rural and urban racialised class-struggle over the *longue durée*. My discussion of neoliberalism reveals the purposeful decomposition of this popular infrastructure by the ruling class between 1985 and 2000, particularly the state's attempt to demobilise and fragment the Federación Sindical de Trabajadores Mineros de Bolivia (Trade-Union Federation of Bolivian Miners, FSTMB) and the Central Obrera Boliviana (Bolivian Workers' Central, COB) through the privatisation of the tin-mines. The twenty-first century in Bolivia, I then argue, has witnessed the recomposition of that infrastructure in novel ways that borrow from the repertoires of struggle and popular cultures of resistance and opposition of the past.

---

88. I exclude political parties from this expansive definition for analytical clarity, even as I recognise the centrality of political parties to the unfolding of class-struggle.

1.5 Social-movement unionism

Social-movement unionism, for our purposes, is understood as militant unionism that is deeply democratic, fights for increased power and organisation of workers in the workplace, and at the same time seeks to multiply 'its political and social power by reaching out to other sectors of the class, be they other unions, neighbourhood-based organisations, or other social movements. It fights for all the oppressed and enhances its own power by doing so'.[89] Alliances between unions and community-based social movements are seen as an integral component of the move 'toward the "organisation of the proletarians into a class", as Marx put it a hundred and fifty years ago'.[90] In the Bolivian case, I show how an orientation toward social-movement unionism by important sectors of the labour-movement was essential in facilitating the links between community-based organisations of informal proletarians and the formal working class, all of which together formed a dense infrastructure of class-struggle.

1.6 Defining ethnicity and what it means to be indigenous in Bolivia

It is important to be clear about what is meant by ethnicity and indigenous identity. For our purposes here, we follow the definition offered by anthropologist Suzana Sawyer in her study of indigenous movements in modern Ecuador. For Sawyer, 'Ethnic identity is a process of constant negotiation over collective senses of being that naturalises certain attributes (anything from skin color to religion) as innate possessions stemming from a mythical history'.[91] Ethnicity, then, 'is a relation, not a thing, and consequently, a terrain of struggle', through which different groups engage in the 'political act' of defining 'who is and is not indigenous'.[92] Because it is relational, 'the content of ethnic identity is forged from ongoing historical conflicts'.[93] Sawyer's notion of ethnicity contains certain shared elements of our theory of working-class formation: process, relation, history, and contestation. Just

---

89. Moody 1997, p. 5.
90. Moody 1997, p. 207.
91. Sawyer 2004, pp. 220–1.
92. Sawyer 2004, p. 221.
93. Ibid.

as in the case of social class, such a conceptualisation of ethnicity avoids transhistorical, essentialist renderings that exist outside of historical time and concrete settings. Race and ethnicity are social constructions, terrains of social struggle and political contestation that are altered in accordance with shifts in the wider balance of social forces within a particular society.[94]

In terms of ethnicity's relationship to class, there are those who suggest that ethnicity is an analogue for social class.[95] This perspective strikes me as ahistorical. More attractive is the notion that ethnicity has a heterogeneous relationship to class that is contingent on the historical and social relations of a particular time and a particular place: 'As ethnic identities and relations are variously constituted historically and socially, their relationship to class is highly variable. Under some circumstances, Comaroff's thesis that ethnicity is an analogue for class holds, in others not'.[96] In the case of Bolivia, there has been an historical tendency – not unbroken or free of contradiction – for ethnicity to stand in as an analogue for class. In contemporary El Alto, to use the strongest example, roughly 93 per cent of the population is working class – in the sense that their labour is commodified in various ways and they do not live off the labour of others –, and 82 per cent self-identify as indigenous.[97] *Alteños* (residents of El Alto) often take pride in their indigenous and working-class identities simultaneously, and are, at the same time, stigmatised by the Bolivian élite along the same cultural and socio-economic axes.

Much of this book is devoted to the *how* of indigenous ethnicity in its relationship to class over the history of modern Bolivia. For an introductory comment on the specificity of Bolivian race-relations, however, it is useful to have a synchronic portrait of the contemporary period. Bolivia's indigenous population is comprised of at least 37 distinct groups. The Quechua and Aymara, concentrated in the western highlands, are the largest by far, followed by the Guaraní of the eastern lowlands. As Table 1.1 indicates, the so-called *media luna* (half-moon) departments of Beni, Pando, Santa Cruz and Tarija have the lowest proportion of self-identified indigenous people. This is an important part of the explanation for the racist component of a bourgeois-autonomist

---

94. Wade 1997, pp. 12–13.
95. Camaroff 1987.
96. Dore 2006, p. 32.
97. See Chapter Six for a fuller explanation of the claim that 93 per cent of El Alto is working-class.

Table 1.1   Indigenous self-identification, 2001

Department	Total Aged 15+	Total Indigenous 15+	% Indigenous
Beni	202,169	66,217	32.75
Chuquisaca	308,386	202,204	65.57
Cochabamba	900,020	669,261	74.36
La Paz	1,501,970	1,163,418	77.46
Oruro	250,983	185,474	73.90
Pando	30,418	4,939	16.24
Potosí	414,838	347,847	83.85
Santa Cruz	1,216,658	456,102	37.49
Tarija	239,550	47,175	19.69
Total/average	5,064,992	3,142,637	62.05

Source: Van Cott 2005, p. 51.

movement of the eastern lowlands that re-emerged in 2005 and which tends to pit the idea of a light-skinned *camba nation* (comprising the white-*mestizo* élite of the *media luna* departments) against a *colla nation* (predominantly Aymara and Quechua) of the western highlands.[98]

Racial categories of Quechua, Aymara, Guaraní, and so on, have been fluid and mutable over time. Some working-class and peasant-individuals of Aymara or Quechua descent, for example, have not self-identified as such given the stigma that has been attached to these identities for much of the colonial and republican periods.[99] This situation has begun to change since the 1990s, however, as rates of indigenous self-identification increased parallel to the recomposition of infrastructures of racialised class-struggle by the end of the 1990s, and the explosion of left-indigenous resistance in the early 2000s. In the interest of further semantic clarification, 'mestizo' in this book will refer to 'racial or cultural mixture of Indian and European ancestry', yet in the highlands it carries a marked sense of difference from 'Indians' or popular sectors of 'Aymara descent' (also referred to as 'cholos'). In valley-regions like Cochabamba, 'mestizo' is more frequently applied to the peasantry and

---

98. See Lowrey 2006; Webber 2005. Bolivia is divided into nine departments, or states. In local parlance, they have been separated traditionally into those of the *altiplano*, or high plateau (La Paz, Oruro and Potosí), the valleys (Cochabamba, Chuquisaca and Tarija), and the eastern lowlands (Pando, Beni and Santa Cruz). In the contemporary period, the term *media luna* (half moon) has gained political currency as a way of describing Pando, Beni, Santa Cruz and Tarija. The *media luna* departments are also frequently called the 'eastern lowlands' today despite Tarija's traditional positioning in the 'valley'-departments, and Pando's location in the northwest of the country.

99. Hylton and Thomson 2007, p. 155.

urban popular sectors'.[100] Finally, 'creole' denotes 'people thought to be of predominantly European ancestry who are raised (from the Spanish *criar*) in the Americas)'.[101]

1.7 Popular cultures of resistance and opposition

In addition to, and intricately rooted in, long-term historical and material factors that helped to shape the character of contemporary social movements in Bolivia – capitalist development, state-formation, and racialised class-struggle – are the ways in which organised groups of people come to understand and make sense of the political and economic change going on around them. In other words, how do subjective understandings of the changing times intersect with more structural economic and political-processes to inform the dynamics and outcomes of social and revolutionary movements? Eric Selbin argues that a 'crucial component of the revolutionary potential in any population is perception of the options available and plausible to them'.[102] Collectively, and to a lesser extent individually, people draw on a 'repository of knowledge' available in society to help them form the parameters of what they conceive as possible or imaginable. Revolutionary processes are more likely to develop, receive widespread support, and come to fruition in societies 'where revolution is considered a viable response to oppression – due to a long-standing history of rebellious activities being celebrated in folk culture, or to revolutionary leaders having fashioned, restored, or magnified such traditions in the local culture or some combination of these'.[103]

Repositories of knowledge about and celebrations of rebellious activities in folklore are important for revolutionary and non-revolutionary popular movements alike. One component of social-movement theory emphasises the role of symbols being drawn by social-movement leaders from the dynamic cultural reservoirs of the wider society in which a social movement is embedded. These historical symbols help form collective frames of the injustice the social movement is struggling to overcome.[104] Social movements, 'draw on

---

100. Ibid.
101. Ibid.
102. Selbin 2008, p. 135.
103. Ibid.
104. Tarrow 1998, p. 112.

the cultural stock for images of what is an injustice, for what is a violation of what ought to be'.[105] Necessarily, movements relate to, and selectively borrow from, 'the larger societal definitions of relationships, of rights, and of responsibilities to highlight what is wrong with the current social order, and to suggest directions for change'.[106]

Just as they source cultural reservoirs for understanding injustice, they learn from the past, 'of how to protest and how to organise.... Cultural stocks are not static, and over time repertoires of contention grow and change. Some items fall out of the repertoire', while new ones are added.[107] The same is true of rebellious symbols which movements interpret dynamically from the past in order to connect them to the challenges and specificities of the present: 'the symbols of revolt are not drawn like musty costumes from a cultural closet', rather they are, 'woven from a blend of inherited and invented fibers into collective action frames in confrontations with opponents and élites'.[108] A collective-action frame, such as the one that formed around the call to nationalise the natural-gas industry in 2003 and 2005, can be understood as an interpretive schema 'that simplifies and condenses the "world out there" by selectively punctuating and encoding objects, situations, events, experiences, and sequences of actions within one's present or past environment'.[109]

In order to capture this cultural component of social and revolutionary movements in the Bolivian case, and to ground it in the historical and material processes of capitalist development, state-formation, and racialised class-struggle, I borrow John Foran's concept of *political cultures of resistance and opposition*.[110] These are cultures that 'tap everything from historical memories of past conflicts to inchoate sentiments about injustice, to long-standing religious idioms and practices, to more formally elaborated political ideologies'.[111] Foran's argument is that in pre-revolutionary moments, 'different groups in society elaborate multiple political cultures of opposition to the régime, and that these may draw on diffuse folk beliefs and historical memories of struggle, shared "structures of feeling" fashioned out of common experiences, and

---

105. Zald 1996, p. 266.
106. Zald 1996, p. 267.
107. Ibid.
108. Tarrow 1998, p. 118.
109. Snow and Benford 1992, p. 137.
110. Foran 1997, p. 208.
111. Ibid.

eventually, perhaps, explicitly revolutionary manifestos and formally articulated ideologies'.[112] Foran's perspective does not pretend that these political cultures of resistance and opposition are merely discursive practices that float above and outside the material world. Instead, he insists that they be linked 'with actual social forces for the study of revolution'.[113]

An integral part of the historical analysis developed in this book is, therefore, a mapping of the contours of the main political cultures of resistance and opposition that were formed, transformed, and re-articulated at various stages in the development of Bolivian capitalism and state-formation, as popular classes and indigenous movements battled for their rights within and sometimes against the capitalist system. These battles took place in ever-changing material and temporal conditions; the political cultures of resistance and opposition were consequently reworked and re-invented regularly to speak to the novel community-, workplace-, and popular organisational settings that were formed as the dynamics of capitalist development and the balance of racialised class-forces in society shifted in historical time.

I focus on the resistance-cultures of indigenous liberation stretching back to the eighteenth century and the working-class oppositional cultures of revolutionary Marxism that were forged alongside the development of the tin-mining industry in the twentieth century. I show how resistance and oppositional cultures based on indigenous liberation from internally-colonial race-relations at times developed separately from and in tension with working-class cultures seeking freedom from class-exploitation, and at other times coalesced with working-class oppositions, making both traditions stronger as they engaged in real struggles on the ground. Nowhere is this clearer than in the interlacing of these two popular cultures of resistance and opposition during the left-indigenous insurrectionary cycle of 2000 to 2005; the synergistic intersection of the two helped to fuel a dual challenge to racial oppression and class-exploitation in the urban cityscapes and rural countryside alike. Throughout the book, the discussion of these popular cultures is always linked with the actual social forces driving them – an eclectic mix of changing class-forces, social movements, infrastructures of class-struggle, and political parties. Moreover, analysis of the interaction between these popular cultures

---

112. Foran 1997, p. 209.
113. Foran 1997, p. 208.

and competing ruling-class ideologies is interwoven into the larger narrative of racialised class-struggle.

1.8 Combined-oppositional consciousness

We have now reflected on some of the theoretical issues of class-formation and class-consciousness, ethnicity and its relationship to class, and popular cultures of resistance and opposition. In order to describe the specific coming together of the politics of indigenous resistance and class-struggle in the collective worldview of leading social-movement activists in 2003 and 2005, I introduce the more precise concept of *combined-oppositional consciousness*, building on Jane Mansbridge's notion of 'oppositional consciousness'. For Mansbridge, this sort of consciousness 'is an empowering mental state that prepares members of an oppressed group to act to undermine, reform, or overthrow a system of domination'.[114] Not merely a consequence of cold calculation, oppositional consciousness 'is usually fuelled by righteous anger over injustices done to the group and prompted by personal indignities and harms suffered through one's group membership'.[115]

As oppositional consciousness is raised, it transforms individuals and collectivities, by taking 'free-floating frustration and direct[ing] it into anger', by turning, 'strangers into brothers and sisters', and by building 'on ideas and facts to generate hope'.[116] By definition, consciousness is 'internal to an individual's mind', but it is also 'inextricably derived from the social world'.[117] The contours of oppositional consciousness take shape in 'particular historical moments when certain political opportunities, certain mobilising institutions, and certain repertoires of collective action and self-understanding become available'.[118] It would be simplistic to suggest that collective or individual oppositional consciousness is something that a group or individual has or does not have full stop; it is best to think in continua rather than binaries, and

---

114. Mansbridge 2001b, pp. 4–5.
115. Ibid.
116. Mansbridge 2001b, p. 5.
117. Ibid.
118. Ibid.

through the lens of historical processes of formation rather than static pictures of consciousness.[119]

Combined-oppositional consciousness in this study refers to a collective consciousness achieved at the height of the Gas-Wars of 2003 and 2005 in which the politics of class-struggle and indigenous liberation are tightly interwoven. My arguments here are rooted in the perceptions, beliefs, and values of the activists I interviewed, and, more specifically, the perceptions of members of the most important social-movement and trade-union organisations in El Alto and La Paz regarding their understandings of the Gas-Wars of 2003 and 2005. In El Alto, one of the most important ways in which the combination of class and indigenous consciousness manifested itself was through the multilayered notion of *vecino*. Literally translated, *vecino* means *neighbour*. Yet, in the context of Latin-American shantytowns, *vecino* often 'implies important bonds of community, characterised by common experiences, values, and reciprocal ties of solidarity'.[120] In El Alto, the *vecino* identity valorised the mixed character of racial and class-consciousness among indigenous workers. A comparable combined-oppositional consciousness prevailed outside of the *alteño* setting in city of La Paz and in the rural *altiplano* (high plateau), although without the use of *vecino*. Activist workers of the formal working class tended to emphasise their class-identities over their indigenous ones, but this certainly did not imply the negation of the latter. Similarly, radicalised Aymara peasants tended to stress their indigenous identities over class-consciousness, but, again, this did not preclude their conscious participation in peasant class-struggle, and worker-peasant alliances. Moreover, I discovered that when specific individuals stressed class- or indigenous consciousness in their narration of events, this almost invariably included an implicit reference to the interpenetration of class- and indigenous identities.

An interrogation of the combined-oppositional consciousness that emerged during the Gas-Wars also reveals the profound interpenetration of Bolivia's two most important popular cultures of resistance and opposition. In the street-battles of El Alto and La Paz, the traditions of revolutionary Marxism and indigenous liberation intertwined in everyday-practice and ideological expression to such an extent that identifying where one tradition ended and

---

119. Mansbridge 2001b, pp. 6–7.
120. Oxhorn 1995, p. 113.

the other began became impossible. Revolutionary memories of indigenous heroes in insurrectionary moments in Bolivian history were weaved together with the idols of revolutionary-left culture and the highlights of twenty-century tin-mining struggles. The ritualised remembrance of past heroes and popular battles helped fortify the twenty-first century combined-oppositional consciousness. One way that these memories were sustained, I discovered, was through 'family-traditions of resistance'.[121] Multifaceted anti-imperialist critique, connected in different ways to analyses of capitalism and racial domination as systems of oppression and exploitation, comprised an additional part of the emergent combined-oppositional consciousness. At the same time, a more focused opposition to the privatisation of natural resources – especially natural gas and water – allowed activists to concentrate in concrete terms the revolutionary Marxism, indigenous resistance, and anti-imperialism of their combined-oppositional consciousness.

One important facet of getting at oppositional consciousness through the concrete process of interviewing activists, particularly in situations where revolutionary change or important structural reform of a social system seems possible, is to ask them about their 'freedom-dreams': what they are fighting for, what society they envision for the future, and how it differs from the one they are currently living in.[122] 'Revolutionary dreams', historian Robin D.G. Kelley points out, 'erupt out of political engagement; collective social movements are incubators of new knowledge…new theories, new questions. The most radical ideas often grow out of a concrete intellectual engagement with the problems of aggrieved populations confronting systems of oppression'.[123] The best social movements do 'what great poetry always does: transport us to another place, compel us to relive horrors and, more importantly, enable us to imagine a new society. We must remember that the conditions and the very existence of social movements enable participants to imagine something different, to realize that things need not always be this way'.[124]

Most important in the Bolivian case are the ways in which the principal protagonists of the Gas-Wars envisioned a better society along four principal lines: (i) equality, the end of poverty, and the abolition of social classes; (ii) a

---

121. Kampwirth 2002, p. 10.
122. Kelley 2002.
123. Kelley 2002, p. 8.
124. Kelley 2002, p. 9.

future free of racism; (iii) dignity, social justice, and basic necessities; and (iv) socialist and indigenous-liberationist democracy.

1.9 Neoliberalism

Neoliberalism on a world-scale ought to be understood as a political project of the ruling classes in the advanced capitalist countries – especially in the US – to create or restore capitalist class-power in all corners of the globe in response to the crisis of embedded liberalism in the late 1960s, the decline in profitability and the growth of stagflation by the 1970s, and the rise of leftist political threats to capital in the shape of radical popular struggles, labour-movements, and peasant-insurgencies across large parts of the world during that period.[125] Rather than 'a core set of ahistorical neoclassical economic policies', often cited as 'the Washington Consensus', neoliberalism is better understood as 'a historical, class-based ideology that proposes all social, political, and ecological problems can be resolved through more direct free-market exposure, which has become an increasingly structural aspect of capitalism'.[126]

The purist theory of free-market economic fundamentals which provides the bedrock for neoliberal ideology should be understood as a flexible tool-kit for justifying the project for restoring capitalist class-power, rather than as a guide to the actual policy-practice of states during this period. The extent to which state-policy has conformed to the precepts of the purist theory of neoliberalism has varied tremendously across different cases. Globally, neoliberalism has failed miserably in terms of its declared objectives of increasing economic efficiency and improving human well-being. However, seen as a political project for the formation or restoration of capitalist class-power, neoliberalism has been successful. Nonetheless, its implementation has created massive social contradictions, and in Latin America in particular, organised popular rejection of the model is widespread and resistance is growing faster there than anywhere else in the world.[127]

---

125. See Albo 2007; Gowan 1999; Harvey 2003, 2005; Saad-Filho 2005.
126. Marois 2005, pp. 102–3.
127. Katz 2007; Robinson 2007, 2008; Sader 2008.

The expansion of neoliberal capitalism in the last quarter of the twentieth century and the opening years of the twenty-first had a number of defining characteristics. To start, given the fact that its economic dominance in the realm of production was threatened by the late 1960s, the US-state placed its bets in finance. Financial capital in the US increasingly played a central role in the renewed project of capitalist imperialism initiated through the neoliberalisation of the globe.[128] In order for this to be successful, the US required the liberalisation of markets, and, in particular, capital-markets. Taking advantage of the leverage over Third-World countries offered up by the debt-crisis of the 1980s, both the US-state, and, to a lesser but important degree, other core imperialist powers, utilised their control of the most important international financial institutions – commercial banks, the multilateral lending institutions such as the International Monetary Fund (IMF) and the World Bank, and various regional banks – to push through structural-adjustment programmes (SAPs) in a vast number of countries.[129] SAPs, which were often imposed by IMF and World-Bank conditionality, typically included demands for Third-World countries to commit to fiscal austerity with minimal to zero-deficits, cut-backs in spending for social services and subsidies for food and other basic necessities, reform of the tax-system, liberalisation of financial markets, unification of exchange-rates, liberalisation of trade, elimination of barriers to foreign direct investment (FDI), deregulation of industry, and strengthening of guarantees of private-property rights.[130]

Within the international context so described, between the mid-1970s and the mid-1990s, virtually all Latin-American countries more or less rapidly reconstructed their economies according to the dictates of the 'Washington Consensus'.[131] While, in the 1980s, the transition away from import-substitution industrialisation (ISI) toward models of export-led growth coincided with a transition from authoritarianism to electoral democracy, we should understand that, in the preceding decades, Latin-American state-terror backed by American imperial might was key to the necessary destruction of the political Left, labour-unions, and other popular class-organisations in civil society. The mass-movements, and revolutionary and populist projects, that

---

128. Harvey 2003, pp. 63–6; Panitch and Gindin 2003, 2004; Magdoff 2006.
129. Gordon 2006a, p. 54; Green 1999, 2003a; Soederberg 2004, 2005, 2006.
130. Williamson 1993, pp. 1332–3.
131. Green 2003a, b; Oxhorn and Ducatenzeiler 1998; Robinson 2008.

had proliferated throughout large sections of the region since the end of the Second World-War needed to be quite definitively expunged from the scene if neoliberalism was to take hold.[132] This was the process, seen most dramatically in the authoritarian régimes of the Southern Cone beginning in the 1970s and the counter-insurgency terror-operations throughout the 1980s in much of Central America, which made feasible the path toward neoliberal economics. Moreover, it should be stressed, that the régime-transitions in the 1980s and 1990s were generally from authoritarianism to 'low-intensity' democracy, or 'polyarchy', 'a system in which a small group actually rules, on behalf of capital, and participation in decision making by the majority is confined to choosing among competing élites in tightly controlled electoral processes'.[133]

The monumental shift from attempts at establishing state-capitalist development based on import-substitution with populist redistribution, to a model of export-driven, 'free-market' capitalism, based on the utilisation of the region's comparative advantage in mostly primary commodities, and the importation of manufactured goods and technology from advanced-capitalist economies, had tremendously negative social, political and economic repercussions in a region already widely recognised as the most unequal in the world.[134] A very small minority of economic and social élite in Latin America have benefited enormously from accelerated integration into the global economy through processes of structural adjustment.[135] The movement from developmentalist states to neoliberal states has meant the hollowing out or destruction of the state's social responsibilities to citizens; social-welfare services are now increasingly left to private-market forces with the predictable, in fact inevitable, unequal distribution of benefits.[136] As the portrait above suggests, neoliberal capitalism in Latin America has intensified capitalism's general pattern of increasing inequality, pauperisation, marginalisation and cultural atomisation and alienation. Ecological devastation and rising crime and insecurity are plaguing the region in the neoliberal era.

By the close of the twentieth century, the neoliberal model in Latin America was plainly in crisis. It was unable to sustain a development-model that 'lifted

---

132. Grandin 2005, p. 14.
133. Robinson 2004.
134. Bulmer-Thomas 1996.
135. Korzeniewicz and Smith 2000; Roberts 2002.
136. Robinson 2004, p. 144.

all boats', nor even prevent the escalation of preexsiting social and economic problems. Politically, the polyarchic régimes were 'increasingly unable to contain the social conflicts and political tensions generated by the polarising and pauperising effects of the neoliberal model'.[137] Even advocates of polyarchy, as the best of bad alternatives, began signalling the dangers to its survival in Latin America given the context of inequality and social crisis.[138] Discontent with polyarchic régimes and neoliberal capitalism found expression in extra-parliamentary social movements in rural and urban areas. Road-blockades, strikes, IMF food-riots, land-invasions, and mass peasant- and urban unemployed-movements chequered the landscapes of the region, as did an explosion of indigenous resistance. Such movements almost invariably met with state- or paramilitary repression, increasingly showing the polyarchic régime's propensity to use coercion when necessary in the interests of capital. In Chapter 4, we analyse in considerable detail how these general dynamics of neoliberalism at the international and regional levels played themselves out in the specific Bolivian context between 1985 and 2000, setting the stage for the left-indigenous cycle of insurrection thereafter.

1.10   The state, crisis, and repression

The nature of capitalism generates social contradictions and political crises through which the stability of social order is challenged. Historically, 'the nation state has provided that stability and predictability by supplying an elaborate legal and institutional framework, backed up by coercive force to sustain the property relations of capitalism, its complex contractual apparatus and its intricate financial transactions'.[139] In the era of neoliberalism, the radical economic restructuring (breakdown of internal barriers within financial markets, wide-scale privatisation and so on) relied on the 'legalisation' and 'juridification' capactites of the state to 'rule' the relations of 'free-markets'.[140] The state is understood, for our purposes, as the political expression of dynamic racialised class-struggle occurring in historical time. The state 'assumes a specific form that expresses politically the contradictory

---

137. Robinson 2004, p. 137.
138. Huber, Rueschemeyer, and Stephens 1997; Karl 2000, p. 150.
139. Wood 2003, pp. 16–17.
140. Panitch 2000, p. 15.

nature of capitalist social relations, just as the production process expresses the relations economically'.[141] The specific form of state-power under neoliberalism in Bolivia saw the further concentration of authority in the executive, the frequent use of coercion to control popular resistance, and even greater distancing of democratic control over policymaking, particularly in the economic sphere, as élite-technocrats were provided enormous powers in the most powerful ministries. Lesley Gill has described the Bolivian experience of ongoing deployment of coercive state-power to reproduce the interests of capital, and the thorough liberalisation of certain parts of the economy through state-policy, as the 'armed retreat' of the state.[142] Neoliberalism is characterised, in other words, by 'authoritarian hardening of the central state and the reorganisation of its administrative apparatus'.[143]

When I refer to a *crisis of the state*, I am referring to historical moments when the balance of racialised class-forces undergirding the specific social form the state has taken is altered to such an extent that the reproduction of that form of state-power is undermined. In order to flesh out the particular dynamics of state-repression and popular-movement response at the height of state-crisis, I draw from theories of social movements and revolutionary change. Sidney Tarrow argues that, 'governments that categorically reject all challengers' claims and back their rejection with force will either destroy the opposition – where repression is effective – or bring about a revolutionary polarization where it is not'.[144] My findings from the Bolivian Gas-War of September and October 2003 show that the government of Gonzalo Sánchez de Lozada was always reticent to negotiate seriously with the mobilised forces of the indigenous peasantry of the *altiplano* and the insurrectionary working classes of El Alto and La Paz. Instead, the state's response at this juncture was fierce repression in an attempt to stifle popular opposition through force and intimidation. While brutal, the extent of repression was evidently too weak to utterly destroy the key opposition-groups and to intimidate the rank and file. To the contrary, the state-repression in the countryside of the department of La Paz and the cities of El Alto and La Paz actually intensified the spiral of

---

141. Gordon 2006b, p. 31.
142. Gill 2000.
143. Albo 2007, p. 359.
144. Tarrow 1998, p. 149.

political, racial and class-based polarisation in the country and solidified new solidarities within those sectors at the receiving end of the state's coercion.

Widespread moral outrage at the repression quickly led to fractures within the political and economic ruling bloc. These ruptures fed the hopes of the insurgents who saw the overthrow of Sánchez de Lozada as increasingly plausible. Again, social-movement theorists have long suggested, 'conflicts within and among élites encourage outbreaks of contention'.[145]

What the findings on the Gas-War of September–October 2003 revolts illustrate is that the traditional social-movement literature on political opportunities is unhelpful as a tool to explain the rise in social protest that occurred in Bolivia subsequent to an increase in state-repression. State-repression, because it dampens opportunity, should have led to a diminishment of protest according to the traditional political-opportunity thesis.[146] As it turns out, the relationship between social protest and state-response – repression, concession, or some combination of the two – is often more dynamic and dialectical. State-élites react, adjust, and counter oppositional mobilisation in dynamic ways that affect the patterns in which oppositional groups react, adjust, and counter in their interactions with the state. Transhistorical models of political opportunities and threats are unable to take into account how both oppositional groups and state-élites function with highly imperfect knowledge of their own strength and popular support as well as of those enjoyed by the other side. Thus, formulae that claim collective action accelerates as opportunities open up, and falls as opportunities contract, are too simplistic. In reality, the dynamic interplay between state-action and reaction – concession/repression – and oppositional action and reaction – heightened mobilisation/retreat – can lead to variegated outcomes in specific concrete historical circumstances. The empirical record of aborted rebellions, successful revolutions, mass-protests, and modest contentious activity across the world and historical time testifies to these complexities.[147]

In the second Gas-War of May and June 2005, President Carlos Mesa, in contrast to Sánchez de Lozada, made opposition to state-repression a central facet of the legitimacy of his government. He was thus constrained in his

---

145. Tarrow 1998, p. 79.
146. McAdam, McCarthy and Zald 1996b.
147. Goldstone and Tilly 2001, pp. 180–92.

ability to deploy state-coercion in response to the left-indigenous insurrection that was launched in May. While using tear-gas, rubber-bullets, and water-cannons extensively, Mesa stopped short of lethal force. At the same time, he would not concede to the demands of social movements. This untenable state-response led to a rising tide of revolt in late May and early June that could not be restrained. The right-wing forces of the eastern lowlands, what I call the eastern-bourgeois bloc, ultimately abandoned their support for Mesa because they wanted the popular movements crushed. With support from neither the popular left-indigenous movements nor the most powerful fractions of the capitalist class, Mesa was forced to resign on 6 June 2005. He was the second neoliberal president to be overturned in less than two years.

1.11 Structure of the book

Chapter 2 examines the complex processes of capitalist development, state-formation, and racialised class-struggle in Bolivia between the late eighteenth century and the National Revolution (1952–64). It demonstrates how the popular cultures of liberation and revolutionary Marxism emerged out of these historical processes. Chapter 3 explores how the period between 1964 and 1985 was marked by the return of authoritarianism, the reversal of many gains of the National Revolution, cycles of state-repression and popular resistance, and, finally, the successful worker- and peasant-led struggle to restore electoral democracy by 1982. How the shifting balance of racialised class-forces in a context of extreme economic and institutional crisis led to the neoliberal counterrevolution between 1985 and 2000 is then the subject of Chapter 4.

Chapter 5 explains how a left-indigenous insurrectionary cycle emerged out of the social, economic, and political contradictions of neoliberalism after fifteen years of experimentation with that model of development. It focuses specifically on the Cochabamba Water-War of 2000, a series of Aymara peasant-insurrections in the western *altiplano* in 2000 and 2001, and a working-class anti-tax revolt in La Paz and El Alto in February 2003. These events were precursors to the September–October 2003 and May–June 2005 Gas-Wars that are taken up in Chapters 6 and 7. Chapter 8 then rounds out the book with a close examination of the contours of combined-oppositional consciousness.

Chapter Two

Indigenous Insurgency, Working-Class Struggle, and Popular Cultures of Resistance and Opposition, 1781–1964

This chapter examines the ways in which the history of capitalist development, state-formation, and racialised class-struggle in Bolivia fuelled rich popular cultures of opposition between the late eighteenth century and the National Revolution (1952–64). This history contains the origins of Bolivia's left-indigenous cultures of resistance and opposition that later shaped and fed the twenty-first century insurrectionary cycle between 2000 and 2005. The long period connecting the eighteenth and twenty-first centuries was characterised by racialised repression, exploitation, and dispossession, punctuated with repeated explosions of resistance and insurgency. The ongoing use of state-coercion to reinforce élite-control often paradoxically strengthened the resistance of the exploited and oppressed, because despite its frequent brutality it never reached the ferocious levels of neighbouring Argentina and Chile during the 1970s and early 1980s, or the genocidal state-terror of Guatemala in the early 1980s. In Bolivia repression was often strong enough to help bring popular classes together in opposition to élite-rule, and, at the same time, too weak to wipe out the social and political organisations that provided the popular classes with their mobilisational capacities.

Various cycles of repression and resistance gave rise eventually to the 1952 National Revolution, which although a movement of heterogeneous classes, led by the reformist Movimiento Nacionalista Revolucionario (Revolutionary-Nationalist Movement, MNR), contained within itself a powerful strain of worker-radicalism fed by a confluence of militant organisations and left ideologies. Ultimately, however, the revolution was betrayed by divisions that emerged between the peasantry and the workers, as peasant militancy temporarily subsided in the wake of land-redistribution in 1953. Following a rightist military coup in 1964, Bolivian politics returned to the familiar cycles of state-repression and militant popular resistance.[1]

Between the eighteenth century and the coup that reversed the National Revolution, the resilient features of popular Bolivian politics were independent indigenous resistance and militant working-class activity sustained by powerful worker-organisations and myriad left ideologies. These two traditions of struggle – indigenous resistance and worker-radicalism – came together at various junctures in powerful unison, despite other periods of mutual tension and hostility. Together the processes of capitalist development, state-coercion, and racialised class-struggle created the context for these radical traditions of struggle, which, in turn, came to constitute the origins of Bolivia's left-indigenous cultures of resistance and opposition in the early twenty-first century.

2.1 Late colonialism and early republicanism: silver-capital, the state, and indigenous rebellion

In their discussion of indigenous rebellions spanning from pre-republican to post-colonial Bolivia, Forrest Hylton and Sinclair Thomson argue that an overarching *Andean culture of insurrection* is discernible.[2] The insurrectional indigenous culture apparent in Bolivia's *altiplano* and the city of El Alto at the opening of the twenty-first century is inspired in part by the memory of anticolonial uprisings of the past. The most visible manifestation of this comes to light in the frequent portrayal of and allusion to indigenous heroes

---

1. The new authoritarian régimes after 1964 clearly had novel characteristics, however, in no small part a consequence of the regional Cold-War dynamics of the period. Thanks to Forrest Hylton for drawing my attention to this point.
2. Hylton and Thomson 2005b, p. 7.

from earlier struggles – Tomás Katari, Tupaj Katari, Bartolina Sisa, Zárate Willka – by indigenous rebels and organic intellectuals of contemporary movements.[3] The origins of indigenous-state relations are to be found, in the first instance, at the moment of initial Spanish colonisation. But the specific forms of the initial republican-oligarchic race-relations of the nineteenth century have their most immediate start in the crisis of the colonial system in the eighteenth century and the popular movements that grew out of this crisis. In Bolivia and Peru, the apotheosis of this moment took its shape in the Great Andean Civil War of 1780–2, when indigenous forces led respectively by Túpaj Amaru and Túpaj Katari laid siege to the colonial power.[4] State-repression in response to the Andean insurgency was fierce and 'ethnically based', helping to 'recreate and deepen cultural and spatial distances between whiteness and Indianness, lending a more hierarchical and exclusionary quality to the independence process [in the early nineteenth century], in which Indian communities scarcely participated'.[5]

The underlying historical and material dynamics of nineteenth-century Bolivian race-formations, indigenous-state relations, and processes of indigenous rebellion, are rooted in the contraction of silver- and large land-holding agricultural economies in the first few decades after independence in 1825, the rapid expansion of the silver-economy in the last decades of the nineteenth century, and, subsequently, the displacement of the silver-economy by tin around 1900. All of these turns in the country's political economy dialectically shaped, and were shaped by, highly racialised domestic class-struggle and fluctuations in the prices of the relevant commodities on the world-market.

---

3. The idea of 'insurgent memory' to which Hylton and Thomson refer, is not a simple formula which sees an unbroken continuity between the eighteenth and twenty-first centuries, but rather conveys a 'temporal consciousness' of today's movements which are cognisant of the ruptures and disjunctures in historical time. The process of drawing from the reservoirs of Andean insurgency strengthens the bases for contesting the legitimacy of the extant dominant order today and proposing a new set of social relations in its place (Hylton and Thomson 2005, pp. 8–9). As Hylton and Thomson argue, 'insurrectional political culture, then, does not imply a transcendental Andean logic that exists in a metaphysical and invariable manner above the vicissitudes of history. Rather, it means values and practices adapted by subjects in accordance with concrete historical conditions…' (Hylton and Thomson 2005, p. 12).
    4. Serulnikov 2003; Stern 1987; Thomson 2002.
    5. Mallon 1992, p. 44. Looking ahead a century, Mallon (1992, p. 46) draws the conclusion that Bolivia entered the twentieth century with an oligarchical state-formation that excluded popular indigenous classes from the national project, after having been 'constructed on the corpses produced by repression'.

Since as far back as the Spanish exploitation of the Potosí silver-mines in the sixteenth century, mining had been the central axis around which the Bolivian economy turned. However, the seventeenth century was marked by a generalised depression in mining, the eighteenth century saw the rise of competitive mining in Mexico, and the early nineteenth century introduced the disruptive wars of independence in Latin America.[6] Combined, these three factors meant that by the 1820s the Bolivian economy was in dire straits.[7] By 1846, the year of Bolivia's first national census, there were still roughly ten thousand abandoned silver-mines in the country, 'two-thirds of which retained silver but were now under water and could not be developed without pumping machinery'.[8] The 1846 national census determined that 89 per cent of the approximately 1.4 million inhabitants of Bolivia (excluding the indigenous communities of the eastern lowlands), lived in rural areas, and only 20 per cent of the national population was conversant – monolingually or bilingually – in Spanish.[9] Nonetheless, Spanish was the only official language of the republic, perhaps the clearest indication of the chasm between the white-*mestizo* ruling class and the indigenous majority.

The agrarian racial-class structure was divided into roughly equal parts: servile tenantry (*yanaconas* or *colonos*) living on *haciendas* (large landholdings), and *comunarios*, or members of *ayllus* (independent indigenous communities).[10]

---

6. Volk 1975b, p. 28.

7. This period is described by historian James Dunkerley as 'the first Bolivian revolution' (Dunkerley 2007, p. 154). The revolution began on '16 July 1809, when Pedro Domingo Murillo issued a proclamation denouncing three centuries of despotism and the fact that the creole elite suffered "a form of exile in the bosom of our own land"'. It was punctuated by 'the arrival of the Patriot army under Sucre' and 'Bolívar's fleeting visit later in 1825', but it did not come to a close until 'the Battle of Ingavi, in November 1841, when independence from Peru was finally guaranteed and a creole republic...was given precedence over both the old viceregal limits of Peru and the market links between La Paz, Arequipa and Tacna' (Dunkerley 2007, p. 154). The revolutionary epoch of independence – from 1809 to 1841 – bequeathed a complex historical sequence of events.

8. Klein 2003, p. 120.

9. Klein 2003, p. 121.

10. Grieshaber 1980; Larson 2004. The complexity of the situation of indigenous peasants in fact defies such a straightforward bifurcation of *comunarios* and *colonos*. Institutional and class-positions were different whether a peasant was a *comunario*, *colono*, or peasant free-holder. Complicating the picture further is the fact that these class-positions were not always clearly demarcated, but rather often bled into one another. However, Brooke Larson argues persuasively that, 'Despite these different, often overlapping, positions in relationship to land and the state, and the proliferation of cultural *mestizos* and *cholos* in Bolivia's eastern valleys and cities, the republic

With mining in a slump, the tribute paid collectively by indigenous *ayllus* contributed 54 per cent of total state-revenue.[11] Thus, on the one hand, accepting the relative autonomy of free indigenous communities in exchange for tribute to the state was functional for the ruling class during this extended period of economic crisis.[12] From the other side, indigenous *ayllus* valued their relative autonomy and agreed to the tribute-system.[13] This Andean 'pact' between the state and *ayllus*[14] was maintained relatively securely until the age of silver-expansion in the late nineteenth century shifted the balance of racialised class-forces, and fostered an orgy of state-sponsored enclosures of indigenous land and territory through processes of accumulation by dispossession.[15] All of this, in turn, stoked the flames of Andean indigenous insurgency once again.

---

cemented the system of socio-racial stratification' (Larson 2004, p. 206). Whatever the class- and geographical complexities to peasants' relationships to land and the state, racialisation from above had a certain degree of homogenisation attached to it: 'To be perceived as Indian, or as one of the amorphous mixed strata (*mestizos, cholos, castas*), was not simply a legal-administrative fiction but an every day reality, reconstituted through daily practice. Landed and regional elites often saw Indians as belonging to one seamless race, destined by birth, history, and biology to a life of field labour, servility, and humility' (Larson 2004, p. 207).

11. Larson 2004, p. 211.
12. Irurozqui 2000, p. 90.
13. Platt 1987, p. 280.
14. Mallon 1992, p. 45.
15. See Harvey 2003. Geographer David Harvey's concept of accumulation by dispossession is an elaboration of Karl Marx's 'primitive accumulation' (Marx 1977, pp. 873–940). Ellen Meiksins Wood explains how primitive accumulation in Marx's writings refers to 'the expropriation of direct producers, in particular peasants' that 'gave rise to specifically capitalist social property relations and the dynamic associated with them' (Wood 2002, p. 48). Marx writes of those epoch-making 'moments when great masses of men are suddenly and forcibly torn from their means of subsistence, and hurled onto the labour-market as free, unprotected and rightless proletarians. The expropriation of the agricultural producer, of the peasant, from the soil is the basis of the whole process. The history of this expropriation assumes different aspects in different countries, and runs through its various phases in different orders of succession, and at different historical epochs' (Marx 1977, p. 876). For Harvey, Marx rightly highlighted these processes of capital accumulation 'based upon predation, fraud, and violence', but incorrectly imagined them to be exclusively features of a 'primitive' or 'original' stage of capitalism. With the concept of accumulation by dispossession, Harvey wants to point rather to the continuity of predatory practices that have risen dramatically to the surface once again in the era of neoliberalism (Harvey 2003, p. 144). Since the mid-1970s, around the world, assets previously held under collective ownership, either by the state or in common, have been forced on an unprecedented scale into the realm of the market, often through fraud, coercion, and innumerable forms of predation both by the state and powerful private actors. In other words, many forms of public property have been commodified, have entered into the market as commodities

The period between 1873 and 1895 is widely considered 'the great age of nineteenth-century altiplano silver mining', characterised by phenomenal growth in Bolivia's silver-output.[16] The silver-expansion introduced new dynamics into the class-struggle and the race for land, positioning the 'Indian problem' in the centre of politics with renewed vigour. Migrants and settlers were amassing in the highland hamlets and cities, agricultural commodities were finding new and expanding markets, and thus, the '1860s also fortified the Creole landholding class, which began to covet neighbouring lands under the control of the *ayllus*'.[17] Arm in arm with the Creole landholding class, the new silver-mining capitalists, enamoured with ideas of modernisation drawn from nineteenth-century liberal ideology, 'touted the benefits of government deregulation of mining and minting, the end of protectionism, and the promotion of railroad building to give the mine owners cheaper access to the world market'.[18] With new revenues from mining, the state's relative dependence on the indigenous tribute was receding, providing it the space and initiative to tackle indigenous collective holdings with a new determination.[19] While an aborted attempt at land-reform was made as early as 1863 under President José María de Achá, the most sustained attack on indigenous communities for decades was fostered by an 1866 decree issued by President Mariano Melgarejo (1864–71).

With the mine-owners behind him, Melgarejo's administration marked the beginning of a long series of racialised class-battles waged from above and resisted from below in which indigenous communal lands were attacked and the liberalisation of the economy attempted. Melgarejo's confiscation-decree declared that indigenous communally held land was in fact state-property and established measures for putting the land up for public auction. Indigenous inhabitants of *ayllus* were now required to purchase individual plots of this 'state-owned' property.[20]

Embarking on this initiative, however, the ruling class had ill-considered the limited strength and reach of the Bolivian state in the 1860s and totally

---

for buying and selling. The intensification of commodification has included the commodification of labour, or the proletarianisation of peasantries, on a grand scale.

16. Klein 2003.
17. Larson 2004, p. 214.
18. Ibid.
19. Irurozqui 2000, p. 91.
20. Irurozqui 2000, p. 93; Klein 2003, p. 136; Larson 2004, pp. 216–17.

miscalculated the level of indigenous discontent the proposed measures would engender. Resistance to the commodification of land was especially potent in the departments of Potosí, Oruro, and La Paz, where, unlike Cochabamba's more entrenched traditions of peasant petty-commodity production and weak communal-land structures, *ayllu*-patterns of communal life were the norm.[21] Between 1869 and 1871, indigenous uprisings in the Aymara communities of the *altiplano* – particularly in Pacajes and Omasuyos – gathered to a scale 'unprecedented since Túpac Catari's siege of La Paz almost one hundred years earlier', culminating in January 1871 as 'thousands of Indians allied themselves with Melgarejo's political enemies to lay siege to La Paz and drive the *caudillo* into permanent exile'.[22]

As mining activities, railroad-building, and expanding markets for agricultural commodities continued to expand, the pressure on *ayllu*-land invariably increased.[23] In 1874, under President Tomás Frías Amattler, the Ley de Exvinculación was introduced. This law threatened the end of indigenous communities through the break up of communal lands into individual parts and reforms to the tributary system.[24] It thus 'unleashed a process of expropriations which led to an escalation of the wretched situation of the Indians and radicalised their reactions'.[25]

---

21. For the greater part of the nineteenth century, state-authority was barely exercisable outside the urban centres of La Paz, Cochabamba, Potosí, Santa Cruz, Sucre, and Oruro, 'and any form of state presence in remote highland areas or tropical lowlands was generally happenstance – a result of mining activities, the presence of trade routes, or the natural course of rivers' (Grindle 2000, p. 98). There were no 'Indian rural schools, a modern judicial system, or government agents to assimilate the Indian masses into civilised life' (Larson 2004, p. 215). The policing and military apparatuses of coercion were likewise underdeveloped. As late as the 1850s, for example, only 1,500 to 2,000 men were active in the military, a paltry number in the face of a population of roughly 1.8 million by that time (Klein 2003, p. 131).
22. Larson 2004, p. 218.
23. The wave of insurrection successfully fended off the incursions of Melgarejo and the class-interests his régime represented, but the élite-dream of uprooting the indigenous from their corporate landholdings was not so easily vanquished.
24. The law sought to transform the indigenous *comunario* into a small peasant-landowner, and to convert land into a commodity, free for buying and selling on the market.
25. Irurozqui 2000, p. 94. The vicious dispossession of indigenous land through force, fraud and purchase was resisted heroically, but the unequal concentration of power in the hands of mine owners, the *hacendados*, foreign capital, and the state eventually overwhelmed much of that resistance.

Historian Herbert S. Klein is correct to point out that, '1880 to 1930 saw Bolivia's second great epoch of hacienda construction. Still holding half the lands and about half the rural population in 1880, the [indigenous] communities were reduced to less than a third of both by 1930'. At the same time, he overstates the case when he claims that the, 'power of the free Indian communities was definitively broken'.[26] The impact on the indigenous peasantry was, in fact, variable by region. In northern Potosí, for example, the resistance of the *ayllus* was more effective than most places, such that their fiscal autonomy actually improved entering the twentieth century, and a new 'pact' with the state was similarly solidified.[27] As Tristan Platt suggests, 'the ayllus were rejecting the most visible of a series of 'modernising' tactics, developed by a creole oligarchy anxious to complete the process of 'primitive accumulation' that had preceded the success of its European models'.[28] In the Bolivian case, these processes were quickened and expanded as silver-capital and the state expanded its reach and viciously confronted rural indigenous populations in the late nineteenth century.[29]

2.2   The Federalist War of 1899 and early twentieth century

By the mid-1890s, the price of silver on the international market was falling and this quickly fed into the erosion of Conservative power.[30] At the same time, the tin-economy was growing and La Paz became the centre

---

26. Klein 2003, p. 147.

27. Platt 1987, p. 318.

28. Platt 1987, p. 294.

29. One of the unique aspects of accumulation by dispossession in Bolivia was that this process unfolded in a highly racialised pattern, from above, and from below. Peasants' defensive resistance of communal lands was class-struggle distinctly inflected with *indigenous* content, as the resisting agricultural producers came up against white and *mestizo*-capital with the backing of an increasingly powerful state. The ruling class, moreover, invented and reinvented a string of racist ideologies to justify and legitimate the mass-expropriation of indigenous land and territory in which they were engaged.

30. The period of silver-expansion and indigenous dispossession was also the period in which the Conservative Party (called the Constitutionalist Party by the late 1890s) dominated national politics. The Conservative party represented the class-interests of the silver-capitalists rooted geographically in the Sucre-Potosí area. The Liberal Party, by contrast, represented the class-interests of the emerging tin-capitalists and burgeoning commercial interests in the rapidly growing city of La Paz and its surrounding areas (Klein 2003, p. 154).

of economic activities servicing the regions of the tin-industry. The shift in mining from silver to tin happened rapidly, moving the centre of mining production only slightly, but decisively, to northern Potosí and southern Oruro, while catching the silver-oligarchs off guard with too much sunk capital in silver-investments to make the transition to tin. Instead, 'a plethora of foreign companies entered the market, and a new group of Bolivian entrepreneurs emerged for the first time on the national scene'.[31] Despite the withering away of their economic basis, the Conservatives continued to cling to political power with force, leading inexorably to the militarisation of politics and immanent conflict with the economically and politically ascendant Liberals. What became known as the Federalist War of 1899, in fact began in December 1898 as 'a combined Liberal and regionalist revolt...whereby the largely Liberal élite of La Paz called for local Federalist rule and the overthrow of the Conservatives'.[32] This was the material basis of the war at an élite-level, but indigenous insurgency from below also formed a major part in the development of the war and its outcome.[33]

The most contentious theme in the historical understanding of this period has to do with the nature of the formation and unravelling of the Liberal-indigenous alliances that emerged and broke down before, during, and after the Federal War.[34] The two most prominent leaders of the Liberals and indigenous forces were Colonel José Manuel Pando and Pablo Zárate Willka respectively.[35] The ideological binds that linked these men together were tenuous. As Larson notes, Pando's enemy 'was simply the opposition party that had kept the Liberals out of power since the beginning of civilian oligarchic rule in

---

31. Klein 2003, p. 156.
32. Ibid.
33. Condarco Morales 1965; Hylton 2004.
34. Irurozqui 1999, 2000; Langer 1989; Platt 1987. By the late 1880s, the macro-political setting provided nascent bases for tactical if tenuous alliances between the Liberals and indigenous communities rooted in their shared antipathy for the ruling Conservatives (Larson 2004, p. 229). In the late nineteenth century, the Liberal Party was distinctive for its surface heterogeneity and conflicting ideological appeals to diverse social classes and castes (Platt 1987, pp. 311–14). Its narrow ostensible aims in the 1880s and 1890s were 'to share power at the top and restructure the bureaucracy along federalist lines'. The Liberals 'wanted clean elections' more than anything else, 'and they were willing to forge unholy alliances and espouse pro-Indian causes (e.g., the restitution of communal lands and the repeal of land reforms) to mobilise Indians against their Conservative enemies' (Larson 2004, p. 230).
35. Other important indigenous leaders in the Federalist War were Lorenzo Ramírez, Mauricio Pedro, and Juan Lero.

1880'.[36] In stark contrast, the aims of indigenous-peasant communities, 'under siege for more than two decades', included the transformation of 'the whole social and moral order'.[37]

Within the war-pact coalition, the indigenous forces forged a Quechua-Aymara 'insurgent federalism', inflected with considerable ethnic content and their own political understanding of 'justice, law, honour and ownership of the land'.[38] The tenuous initial pillars of the Liberal-indigenous alliance wore even thinner as the war progressed. Villages subsumed in the violence of advancing Liberal-Federalist and Conservative-Constitutionalist armed forces were the horror settings for the rape and murder of indigenous peasants of varied political allegiances.[39] In this context, ethnic and class-struggle blurred the boundaries of Liberal-Constitutionalist battles.[40]

The enhanced obsession with race in the early 1900s was very much intertwined with the threat to the established order evoked by the indigenous insurgency of 1899, the Liberal victory in the Constitutionlist-Federalist battle, and the terrible Liberal repression of their erstwhile indigenous allies once they had treaded outside the circumscribed boundaries of Liberal politics. The new political class 'inherited the mantle of modernisation from their Conservative rivals', and 'paved the way for unbridled capitalism in tin mining, railroad building, and land grabbing after 1900', but 'their main mission necessarily had to be the domestication of the Indian race'.[41] The Liberals could ill afford another insurrectionary 1899.

2.2.1 *Tin-capital, working-class formation, and indigenous-socialist alliances, 1900–32*

In some respects, despite the drama of the Federal War, the new century looked like a continuation of the one it replaced. The Liberals turned out to

---

36. Larson 2004, p. 231.
37. Ibid.
38. Hylton 2004, p. 112. If the Quechua and Aymara insurgents were Liberals, Forrest Hylton contends, they were Liberals who challenged every basic tenet of liberalism. They called into question the supremacy of the individual, representative politics, and private property, and at the same time demanded self-government, communal management of their land and territories, and an end to taxes that fell disproportionately on *comunarios* (Hylton, 2004, p. 112).
39. Larson 2004, p. 234.
40. Larson 2004, p. 236.
41. Larson 2004, p. 242.

have much in common with their bitter Conservative rivals.[42] Indeed, if there was a difference between the old and new régimes with respect to the expansion of racialised capitalism it was that the Liberals brought to it an even greater enthusiasm – more rapacious, systematic, and vicious.[43] Nonetheless, the 1899 Federalist War was a key turning moment in Bolivian history. The nature of the War's resolution gave rise to a number of novel developments in the country's political and economic spheres.

2.2.2   Racial ideologies of the ruling class

The first decade of the twentieth century was pivotal in shaping the trajectory of racial ideologies in Bolivia. As studies of the literary, political, philosophical, and ethnographic works of leading white intellectuals and statesmen of the period have shown, the new paceño-élite[44] developed a 'culture of anti-mestizaje', a 'racial project' which formed 'the basis of Bolivia's emerging political culture of paternalism, authoritarianism, and exclusion'.[45] By the end of the first decade of the new century, it had become clear that the predicted inflows of white migrants and 'natural' indigenous decline had not transpired. Capitalist development in Bolivia would require access to indigenous land and would need to turn indigenous community-members into proletarians. Moreover, these labourers would have to be disciplined, something the vast indigenous rebellion of 1899 had already shown to be no simple task. A new rigidity to racial categories arose in which Indians were fit only to be labourers with no access to the public sphere, citizenship, or

---

42. The string of liberal régimes between 1899 and 1920 – José Manuel Pando (1899–1904), Ismael Montes (1904–9, 1913–17), Eliodoro Villazón (1909–13), and José Gutiérrez Guerra (1917–20) – mirrored their predecessors' subsidisation of railroad-construction, mining industry and urbanisation, as well as their assault on indigenous communal landholdings and support of hacienda-expansion, free trade, and minimal corporate taxes.

43. Meanwhile, presidential elections continued to be rigged and congressional elections were open only to white and mestizo-élites (Klein 2003, p. 157). The Liberals also dropped their commitment to federalism and simply shifted centralised rule from Sucre to La Paz once they had conquered the Conservatives.

44. Residents of La Paz are known as paceños.

45. Larson 2005, pp. 231–2. The opening decade of the twentieth century brought with it a shift from the social Darwinism of the nineteenth century, which had stressed that the indigenous population would atrophy with time due to the combined pressures of natural selection, survival of the fittest, and mass levels of white migration to Bolivia (Larson 2005, p. 231).

political and civil rights.[46] Meanwhile, urban *cholos* and provincial *mestizos* were singled out for distinct demonisation. These dangerous upstarts were also deemed unfit for equal participation in the public sphere.[47] The overarching turn in racial ideologies in early twentieth-century Bolivia was driven by the state's efforts to exclude the indigenous population from formal politics, appropriate their lands and transform them into propertyless and disciplined agrarian proletarians.[48]

2.2.3 The labour-movement

Alongside the changes in racial formation, the labour-movement was experiencing quite dramatic growth and dynamism. Following Volk's useful periodisation, 1914 to 1932 is best understood as the 'expansive' period of the Bolivian labour-movement.[49] In the major tin-mines of Caracoles, Llallagua, and Uncía the class-consciousness of miners was developing quickly. The complex combination of increasing consciousness and organisational strength among the miners, and, at the same time, their ongoing vulnerability to replacement by other workers and repression by the state is apparent in the events leading up to the infamous Massacre of Uncía on 4 June 1923. Beginning on May Day, there was a series of miners' demonstrations in support of trade-union organising rights.[50] On 4 June, large protests erupted as miners and their families peacefully denounced arrests and detentions of union leaders. In response, the army was ordered to fire on the crowds, killing 'several dozen'.[51] Despite elaborate attempts by the Bautista Saavedra government to cover up the killings – closure of opposition-newspapers, presidential

---

46. To be clear, the rigidity in racial categories was novel, not the exclusion of indigenous people from basic rights.

47. Larson 2005, pp. 249–50.

48. Larson 2004, p. 243. The racist ideologies of the ruling-class intelligentsia were designed to construct 'an informal system of apartheid: Indians would be civilised and molded into a labouring class yet simultaneously separated, protected, and their political aspirations contained' (Larson 2004, p. 243).

49. Volk 1975b, p. 33.

50. Earlier that year, local mine-unions had succeeded in creating a larger federation of unions in Uncía called the Federación Central de Mineros de Uncía (Central Federation of Miners of Uncía, FCMU).

51. Klein 1969, p. 81.

lies to congress – the Massacre of Uncía became a potent historical symbol of heroism in the working-class struggle.[52]

Outside the mining districts, urban centres such as La Paz, Oruro, Potosí, and Cochabamba were increasingly home to Marxist and anarchist study-groups, emergent socialist parties, student-organisations, and labour-federations. Railway and street-car worker-federations led organised labour in the cities. During the sharp depressive cycle of 1920–1, the Railway-Federation led a series of urban strikes.[53] In February 1922, the Federación Obrera del Trabajo de La Paz (Workers' Labour-Federation of La Paz, FOT-La Paz), called for Bolivia's first general strike with the support of street-car operators, railroad-workers and typographers.[54]

The two labour-federations founded in the expansive period of the Bolivian workers' movement, and their wider social and political milieus, reflected the general ideological division between anarcho-syndicalism and Marxism pervasive in contemporary circles of militant Bolivian theorists and activists. The Marxist FOT was established in 1918. The FOT disseminated its political perspective through the *Bandera Roja* (Red Flag) publication. Marxist study-circles and political theatre groups, such as the Centro Obrero de Estudios Sociales (Workers' Centre for Social Studies, COES) and the Rosa Luxemburg Drama-Group, added to the political and cultural ferment in the cities of this era.[55] Progressive students and intellectuals were debating Marxist ideas and organising along Marxist lines in the universities.[56] In 1926, the anarcho-syndicalist Federación Obrera Local de La Paz (Local Workers' Federation of La Paz, FOL-La Paz) was formed out of a split in the FOT. The anarcho-syndicalists attempted to spread their analyses through their short-lived newspaper, *Humanidad*.[57] The Federación Obrera Femenina (Womens' Labour-Federation,

---

52. Lora 1977, p. 120.
53. Volk 1975b, p. 35.
54. Klein 1969, p. 76. The same sectors of the working class, joined by miners, commercial employees, and the federation of artisans, met in Oruro in 1921 for the first congress of Bolivian workers. A second congress, held in La Paz in 1925, attracted a wide array of anarchists and Marxists, although Marxist positions and proposals were apparently more widely supported (Lora 1977, pp. 138–40).
55. Lora 1977, pp. 100–2.
56. Lora 1977, p. 147.
57. Volk 1975b, p. 38. In the case of La Paz, the FOL became a serious mass-organisation with a membership outnumbering that of the La Paz FOT. The FOL-La Paz boasted 38 affiliated unions including woodworkers, bricklayers, tailors, and factory-workers (Lora 1977, p. 151).

FOF), founded by women street- and market-vendors in La Paz in 1927, also played an historic role in the anarcho-syndicalist movement.[58] Both Marxist and anarchist political currents were developing powerful anti-imperialist critiques of foreign capital's increasing influence in Bolivian affairs, a perspective which left an indelible mark on all subsequent popular movements and parties.

One of the most important theoretical innovations in radical politics in this period was the experimental blending of *indigenismo* and Marxism.[59] The most well-known theorist of this vein of thinking in Latin America was the Peruvian Marxist José Carlos Mariátegui.[60] In the Bolivian case, however, much more influential was the local novelist, political writer, and contemporary of Mariátegui, Gustavo Navarro, better known by his pseudonym, Tristán Marof. In fact, Marof was a correspondent for Mariátegui's journal *Amauta*.[61] By 1926, Marof had published *La Justicia del Inca* in Belgium. *La Justicia*, perhaps his most famous book after *La tragedia del altiplano*, included the phrases 'Tierras al Indio [Land to the Indians]' and 'Minas al Estado [Mines to the state]', that would find their echo in a number of revolutionary currents over the following decades.[62]

58. Lehm A. and Rivera Cusicanqui 1988, pp. 164–81; Volk 1975b, p. 33.
59. García Linera 2005a.
60. See Becker 1993, 2006; Löwy 1998; Mariátegui 1971; Vanden 1986.
61. See Thomson 2003. Born in Sucre in 1898, Marof's political debut was certainly within the mainstream. As a member of the Republican Party, he supported the coming to power of Bautista Saavedra, and was sent to be consul in Genoa soon after Saavedra gained the presidency in 1920. However, in Europe he 'became a left-wing revolutionary and openly espoused Marxism', a change in perspective resulting from 'the influence of the powerful left-wing current which stirred Europe after the First World War and the Russian Revolution' (Lora 1977, p. 165).
62. Klein 2003, p. 185. As historian Sinclair Thomson suggests, 'Marof sought to root a socialist modernity in Andean soil, and he drew upon radical *indigenismo* in order to accomplish this' (Thomson 2003, p. 127). Marof was the most influential of a small group of radical theorists challenging the racism and oligarchic features of Bolivia in the early twentieth century from a revolutionary perspective. According to Thomson, 'The Andean socialist tradition of Marof…was the only radical tendency that could imagine a past and future at least partially in terms of Indian community struggle and political autonomy' (Thomson 2003, pp. 130–1). As will be described further when we address Bolivian Trotskyism, Marof was a political activist in addition to being a theorist. Between 1925 and 1935 he was the preeminent revolutionary figure on the Bolivian scene (Klein 1969, p. 195).

2.2.4 *Indigenous-peasant resistance: the Chayanta rebellion, 1927*

In amidst the development of the new tin-economy, the formation of new racial ideologies and categories, and the expansion of the labour-movement, the 1910s and 1920s also witnessed a cycle of indigenous-peasant resistance. Broadly, this resistance was a response to hacienda-expansion, racism, the persistence of the indigenous tribute under new names, and the abusive labour-conditions and sexual exploitation suffered by indigenous *colonos* and their families working on large estates under the reign of white *hacendados*. The rebellions of Pacajes in 1914, Caquiaviri in 1918, the 'endemic and intermittent' movements in Achacachi, and the 1921 insurrection in Jesús de Machaca (brutally repressed) stand out.[63] However, without doubt the largest and most politically significant indigenous revolt of the period was the Chayanta rebellion of 1927.[64] The rebellion began on 25 July 1927 in the Chayanta province of northern Potosí, but spread quickly to include the participation of roughly 10,000 peasants in four of Bolivia's nine departments in the sacking and burning of *haciendas*, attacks on landowners, and destruction of orchards and cattle-herds. The revolt was put down with machine-gun laden troops, leaving hundreds of indigenous dead alongside the small number of landowners they had killed. A rebellion of such scope had not occurred in Bolivia since 1899.[65]

Independent indigenous-peasant agency was absolutely pivotal to the Chayanta rebellion.[66] But, while the predictable élite-thesis of a communist-socialist plot wrongly dismissed the agency of the indigenous rebels in a distinctly racist fashion, their fears of socialist-indigenous alliance were not merely reactionary fabrication. Lawyers, tailors, artisans, and urban intellectuals aligned with the Partido Socialista had real ties with the indigenous movements who led the revolt.[67] Together, the urban radicals and indigenous insurgents shared the objectives of radically redistributing the wealth and property of Bolivia, building rural schools for the indigenous population, and re-establishing the sovereignty of *ayllu*-communal control over rural indigenous territory and land. The indigenous rebels drew from and reinvented the

---

63. Choque Canqui and Alejo Ticona 1996; Rivera Cusicanqui 2003 [1984], p. 78.
64. Harris and Albó 1986 [1974], pp. 59–71.
65. Hylton 2005b, pp. 135–6; Langer 1990, pp. 228–9.
66. See Langer 1990.
67. Hylton 2005b, pp. 187–8.

repertoires of contention from 1781 and 1899, but they also were persuaded by urban and revolutionary-socialist ideas of equality, building alliances between all the oppressed and exploited, and engaging in direct action on these bases.[68] In the end, the revolutionary aspirations of the indigenous-urban-radical coalition did not come to fruition as the insurrection never spread to the department of La Paz or to any of the cities, and was therefore vulnerable to state-repression.[69] However, for the first time since the accelerated processes of dispossession in the 1880s, an indigenous rebellion effectively slowed to a halt the expansion of haciendas in Potosí and Chuquisaca.[70]

2.3 The Chaco War, left-party formation, revolutionary workers, and indigenous rebels (1932–52)

2.3.1 The Great Depression and the Chaco War

The Great Depression hit Bolivia with blunt force. The Bolivian tin-industry entered a precipitous decline as other major tin-producing countries such as Nigeria, Malaya, and Indonesia were able to produce higher-grade ore at lower cost. There were massive layoffs in the mines, and some miners were forced to retreat to the countryside in search of alternative livelihoods.[71] The agricultural economy also suffered and hacienda expansion slowed. It was in this context that the increasingly authoritarian régime of Daniel Salamanca (1931–4) led Bolivia into the disastrous Chaco War (1932–5) with Paraguay. The causes and motivations of the Bolivian side in this conflict have been the subject of vast scholarly and political dispute, all of which is beyond the

---

68. Hylton 2005b, p. 141.
69. Hylton 2005b, p. 145.
70. Harris and Albó 1986 [1974], p. 71. From a historical perspective, this period in Bolivian history is unique for the ties that existed between Marxists and indigenous rebels, a relationship in which indigenous radicalism and political autonomy were not subordinated to a revolutionary nationalism premised on the dominance of cultural *mestizaje*. As the sociologist and political activist Álvaro García Linera suggests, this era saw a 'fruitful, very beautiful, relationship between Indians and Marxists' (personal interview, 10 April 2005), the likes of which did not arise again until the 2000–5 wave of indigenous-left struggle (Webber 2005).
71. Klein 2003, p. 170.

scope of this study.[72] Suffice for our purposes to highlight the consequences. Of the two million inhabitants of the republic in the early 1930s, 250,000 men fought in the Chaco War. 52,400 died, 21,000 were captured, and 10,000 deserted. Most of the dead succumbed to 'natural' causes rather than bullets, fighting most of the war as they did in isolated terrains, distant from Bolivian towns and villages.[73] Bolivia also ceded hundreds of kilometres of territory in a war it instigated.

Left dissidents who protested against the war were imprisoned, exiled or conscripted into the army. On the front, the battalions were organised in sync with the caste-system, meaning officers were white, the middle ranks were predominantly *cholo*, and indigenous were the cannon-fodder engaging the Paraguayans directly. As Klein notes, 'The only group to violate these divisions were the workers and radicals seized by Salamanca who were sent to the front lines'.[74] For these white radicals and workers, 'the experience was a bitter one and committed many of them to a radical stance toward the racial divisions of their society', while for the indigenous rank and file, 'it meant the continuation of the standard patterns of exploitation'.[75] The calamitous fallout from the Bolivian state's aggression in the Chaco War called into question the legitimacy of the old régime, the racist foundations of Bolivian society, and the exploitative bases of an economy organised around the interests of *la rosca* (the tin-barons) and the landed élite. The traditional Liberal and Republican Parties were entirely discredited in the process.

2.3.2 *Military socialism*

Changes at the national level came quickly. Before the war had even ended, the army forced Salamanca to resign and declared José Luis Tejada Sorzano, then Vice-President and leader of the Liberal Party, the new President in 1934.[76] Tejada Sorzano soon faced a massive general strike and lost control of the police and the army. Filling this power-vacuum, colonels David Toro and

---

72. Arze Aguierre 1987; Díaz Machicao 1955; Dunkerley 2003 [1987], pp. 203–62; Farcau 1996; Guachalla 1978; Querejazu Calvo 1975; Zavaleta Mercado 1998 [1963], pp. 18–40; Zook 1961.

73. Dunkerley 2003, pp. 144–5.

74. Klein 2003, pp. 182–3.

75. Klein 2003, p. 183.

76. Klein 2003, p. 181.

Germán Busch orchestrated a successful *coup d'état* on May 17, 1936, placing Toro in the presidency. Thus the self-styled era of 'military socialism' commenced.[77] Toro's régime was, in fact, reformist rather than socialist. It created Bolivia's first Ministry of Labour, and, most significantly, nationalised the New Jersey-based Standard Oil Company of Bolivia, establishing in its place the state oil-company, Yacimientos Petrolíferos Fiscales de Bolivia (YPFB).[78] The Toro régime was itself overthrown in July 1937 by Germán Busch, an erstwhile ally of Toro and a war-hero from the Chaco theatre. Rather than an abrupt change in course, however, the Busch régime perpetuated military socialism with the introduction of additional moderate labour-reforms that in no way threatened the basic sanctity of private property or other pillars of capitalism, but did modestly improve the political and working conditions of Bolivian labour.[79] The period of military socialism reached its ceremonious and premature ending in August 1937 when Busch committed suicide, garnering, with this act, a popularity and respectability he had never enjoyed during his lifetime.[80]

In the restricted elections of 1940, General Enrique Peñaranda, the joint candidate of the Liberal and Republican Parties, won the presidency. However, this penultimate gasp of the oligarchy was extinguished in December 1943 by a group of dissident, fascist-oriented junior officers in the armed forces known as Razón de Patria (RADEPA), in alliance with the increasingly important Movimiento Nacionalista Revolucionario (Revolutionary-Nationalist Movement, MNR), the party that would eventually lead the April Revolution of 1952. The 1943 coup brought to power the hitherto unknown Major Gualberto Villarroel, whose régime reflected the nascent, reformist nationalism of the MNR.[81] Villarroel, lasting about as long as his predecessor, was captured and hanged by protesters in the central plaza of La Paz, outside the presidential palace, on 14 July 1946. The protests were organised by the far-right traditional parties and the Stalinist Partido de la Izquierda Revolucionaria (Party of the Revolutionary Left, PIR).[82]

---

77. Klein 1969, pp. 228–33; Zavaleta Mercado 1998 [1963], pp. 40–3.
78. Klein 2003, p. 190.
79. Código Busch, the first modern labour-code in Bolivian history, was likely the most important legislation introduced under that régime.
80. Klein 2003, pp. 193–4.
81. Klein 2003, pp. 201–2.
82. Lora 1977, p. 244.

The period between 1946 and 1952 – under the régimes of Enrique Hertzog (1947–9), Mamerto Urriolagoitia (1949–51), and Hugo Ballivián (1951–2) – came to be known as the *sexenio*. The era was marked by authoritarianism and repression in the face of rural and urban unrest, constituting essentially the ultimate effort to restore the oligarchy before it was crushed in the National Revolution.

2.3.3 *The MNR and radical-left parties*

Without doubt, the MNR was the most influential political party in Bolivia during the twentieth century. The party's intellectual origins are to be found in *La Calle* newspaper, run by the prominent intellectuals Agusto Céspedes and Carlos Montenegro, both of whom produced books with a lasting legacy in Bolivian political culture. There were distinct ideological currents within the MNR from its beginnings, but important figures in the party's development, notably Céspedes and Montenegro, were enamoured with the fascist parties of Europe, published pro-Nazi articles in *La Calle* in the late 1930s, and were hostile to Jewish immigrants in Bolivia.[83] Despite their initial fascination with German and Italian fascism, however, on the domestic front the MNR appealed broadly to the small but growing middle class, emphasising social reform and economic nationalism. As noted, the MNR exercised heavy influence in the Villarroel régime after the coup of 1943, and had begun to solidify its prominence on a national level as an alternative both to the oligarchic parties and the revolutionary Left before Villarroel was overthrown. Somewhat paradoxically, the MNR's moments of greatest growth took place during the period in which it experienced its most brutal and sustained repression: the *sexenio* from 1946–52. During this time, the MNR abandoned its fascist inclinations[84] and focused much more resolutely on building its middle-class

83. Klein 1969, pp. 337–8. The MNR's formation was in part a response to the Peñaranda government's pro-Allied stance at the outset of World-War II. A group of congressional deputies, including Víctor Paz Estenssoro, joined with Céspedes and Montenegro 'to form a party nucleus from almost the first sessions of the regular 1940 congress', and, 'by the end of the year the name *Movimiento Nacionalista Revolucionaria* began to become a popular term for describing the group…' (Klein 1969, p. 337).
84. Klein 2003, p. 203.

base and extending its tentacles into the mines and the rest of the labour-movement, as well as into the indigenous countryside.[85]

In 1949 the MNR led opposition forces in a short-lived civil war that ended in bloodshed but uncovered the weakness of the régime.[86] In 1950, the MNR supported an armed labour-insurrection that was likewise repressed. The 1951 presidential elections witnessed the MNR's electoral victory and its last attempt to access the presidential palace through legal channels. In the immediate aftermath of the MNR's victory, however, the army intervened and imposed General Hugo Ballivián in the presidency before the MNR could assume power.[87] The next revolt led by the MNR ended with the National Revolution.

Outside the MNR's sphere of reformist nationalism, the epoch between the Chaco War and the National Revolution also saw the emergence of an array of radical-left political parties. The most influential, initially, was the aforementioned PIR, founded in 1940. The PIR was established at a labour-congress in Oruro at which 150 representatives of radical leftist parties and the labour-movement were present. The first programme of the Party came out of this congress and declared that class-struggle and a neocolonial position within the international imperialist system characterised Bolivia's reality. The *rosca*, the programme argued, served the interests of international capital and needed to be replaced.[88] José Antonio Arze was the PIR's most important theorist and leader, as well as one of Bolivia's best-known Marxist sociologists.[89] He briefly served as a legal advisor to the Ministry of Labour under the

---

85. Alexander 1973, p. 124.
86. de Mesa et al. 2003, p. 616.
87. Klein 2003, p. 206.
88. Klein 1969, p. 339. The PIR apparently encompassed an eclectic grouping of somewhat different ideological factions, at least in its early history. For example, there was a 'very strong indigenista group (which wholeheartedly echoed the agrarian reform plans of Mariátegui)', and, at the same time, 'a pro-communist wing...heavily oriented toward the international scene' (Klein 1969, p. 340). Historian Robert J. Alexander reports that the PIR described itself as adhering to independent Marxism, but 'had within its ranks those elements who were loyal to Stalinism...' (Alexander 1973, p. 118). For Guillermo Lora, the PIR, since its foundation, was straightforwardly a Stalinist political party (Lora 1977, p. 198).
89. Graduating with a law-degree from the Cochabamba university in 1925, he devoted much of his life to sociology. Inspired by the Russian Revolution and the university-reform movement of Córdoba, Argentina, he played a leading role in the 1928 student-congress at which the Bolivian University-Federation (FUB) was formed (Lora 1977, p. 200). He was also an important organiser in the movement against the

Toro régime before being exiled to Chile in 1936. Arze later ran as the presidential candidate for the PIR, surprisingly winning 10,000 of the 58,000 votes cast in the 1940 elections.[90]

Parallel to Stalinist developments on the far Left in Bolivia during the 1930s and 1940s, there emerged a vibrant Trotskyist movement which became the most important in all of Latin America. Indeed, outside of Ceylon (now Sri Lanka), no other country in the globe would match the importance Trotskyism came to have in national political life in Bolivia.[91] Tristán Marof, whom we have already considered briefly, was the first personality of national significance linked to the development of Trotskyism in the country. After returning to Bolivia from diplomatic duties in Europe in 1926, Marof was instrumental in the formation of the short-lived Socialist Party (PS). The Party was repressed and Marof was forced into exile in Argentina in 1928. There he became part of the Grupo Tupac Amaru (GTA), a loosely-knit revolutionary group with ties to both the Socialists and Communists in Argentina. The GTA, along with other exiled Bolivian radicals – the Izquierda Boliviana (Bolivian Left, IB) based in Chile, and Exiliados en el Peru (Exiles in Peru) – met for a congress in Córdoba, Argentina in 1934 where the POR, Bolivia's preeminent Trotskyist party, was formed.[92] The Party immediately affiliated with the International Left Opposition, which was under the leadership of Leon Trotsky. Despite Marof's elevated public status, José Aguirre Gainsborg was actually

---

Chaco War, for which he was exiled in Peru. Even Lora, a bitter rival of Arze's political line, suggested that, 'he showed great courage in denouncing the imperialist character of the war...and in going against the wave of chauvinism which gripped the country at that time' (Lora 1977, pp. 200–1). Ricardo Anaya was the other prominent founding figure of the Party.

90. Klein 2003, p. 196. Despite Peñaranda's victory that year, the PIR's performance was of monumental significance in its challenge to the oligarchic order. From this point until the mid-1940s the PIR was the most important party in the labour-movement and a national force to be reckoned with (Klein, 1969, p. 341). However, because of its allegiance to the Soviet Union, and concomitant position in favour of the Allies and anti-fascist fronts, the Party joined together with the far-right parties to bring down the Villarroel-MNR government which it had determined to be 'fascist'. Because of its role in bringing forth the nightmare of the *sexenio*, the Party lost all credibility in the popular classes by the late 1940s. The Partido Comunista Boliviano (Bolivian Communist Party, PCB) emerged out of the ashes of the PIR when the latter split into near-total disintegration in 1950, disappearing for all intents and purposes by the 1960s (de Mesa, 2003, pp. 600–1). The vacuum left by the PIR's exit from the stage was another factor explaining the subsequent surge of the MNR.

91. Alexander 1973, p. 111.

92. Alexander 1973, pp. 111–12.

the principal force in pushing for the POR's Trotskyist identification. It was Aguirre Gainsborg – an important activist in the radical university-movement in Cochabamba in the late 1920s, a major revolutionary in the 1930s, a prisoner in an *altiplano* jail, and an exile in Chile – who authored the POR's initial platform.[93]

By the late 1930s, the POR had adopted Trotsky's theory of permanent revolution as a fundamental basis of its programme. For the POR, revolution in Bolivia would be shaped by the country's particular semi-colonial position in the world-system. The revolution would be a combined one, meaning a bourgeois-democratic revolution with warfare and peasant-uprisings would run alongside a proletarian-socialist revolution, consisting of working-class insurrection.[94] In further accord with the theory of permanent revolution, the POR insisted that the socialist revolution must flow beyond the borders of Bolivia and become international if it was to survive. Moreover, the Party argued, within the Bolivian context, revolution could be successful only if the workers and peasants did not ally themselves with the national bourgeoisie.[95] The POR began entering the mines and by the late 1940s it enjoyed formidable power in the miners' unions, although still less than that of the MNR.[96] The depth of the Trotskyist pull in the mines was best illustrated with the approval of the Tesis de Pulacayo (Thesis of Pulacayo), which was approved as the new manifesto of the miners' movement and which essentially adapted Trotsky's Transitional Progamme to the Bolivian context.[97] After Villarroel was overthrown, the POR co-operated extensively with the MNR in resisting the attempts of the oligarchy to re-establish its reign over Bolivian society.[98]

---

93. Lora 1977, pp. 209–13.
94. Alexander 1973, p. 116.
95. Alexander 1973, pp. 116–17. In October 1938, Aguirre Gainsborg surreally 'fell to his death from the big wheel at a fun fair' in La Paz at the age of twenty-nine (Lora 1977, p. 213). It was not until the early 1940s that Guillermo Lora provided a similar style of protagonistic leadership to the POR, becoming in the process the most recognisable figure in Bolivian Trotskyism. Lora was a prolific author of political tracts, pamphlets, and a five-volume history of the Bolivian labour-movement. Far more decisively characterising his life, however, was political leadership and association with the radical tin-miners.
96. Alexander 1973, pp. 118–19.
97. See Trotsky 1977.
98. Alexander 1973, p. 123.

2.3.4   *Working-class formation*

Steven S. Volk characterises the period between 1936 and 1946 as the 'semi-cooptive' phase of the Bolivian labour-movement.[99] The Great Depression beginning in 1929, repression under the Salamanca government (1931–4), and the enhancement of the national crisis engendered by the Chaco War, together served to weaken Bolivian labour's capacities to resist capital.[100] The rise of military socialism under Toro and Busch raised for the first time the realistic possibility of state-strategies of co-optation. After the objective weakening of the labour-movement following depression and war, workers reignited their militancy in the 1936 general strike that helped bring down the Tejada Sorzano régime and allowed space for Toro's ascent to office. Of the many ideological currents visible in Bolivia's military-socialist period, state-corporatism was one important force. Volk points out, for example, that the creation under Toro of the Permanent National Assembly of Union-Organisation (ANPOS), and the efforts to make the unionisation of all workers obligatory under this umbrella-institution, 'represented thinly veiled attempts to place the organised labour movement at the disposal of the state'.[101] Despite the fact that 'some labour elements demonstrated a willingness to collaborate with Toro and Busch', the co-optive efforts of the 'military socialists' were ultimately unsuccessful. In opposition to the 'government-directed labor bureaucrats' the majority of unions in the country managed to construct their own national organisation, the Confederación Sindical de Trabajadores de Bolivia (Union-Confederation of Bolivian Workers, CSTB).[102]

With the rise of new political parties in the post-Chaco epoch, bourgeois-reformist and revolutionary-socialist approaches to the union-movement increasingly penetrated the working class, the former associated with the MNR and the latter linked to the (early) PIR and POR. While the MNR's approach to union-organising privileged working through the labour-bureaucracy, the POR and PIR, 'worked through the base of the unions and tried to guide the unions – albeit with some deviations – to revolutionary action'.[103] In the late 1930s and early 1940s, the objective strength of the working class once again

---

99. Volk 1975b, p. 38.
100. Volk 1975b, p. 40.
101. Volk 1975b, p. 43.
102. Ibid.
103. Volk 1975a, pp. 180–4.

increased as the tin-economy recovered parallel to the onset of World-War II. Bolivia became by far and away the principal producer of tin in the world, and in particular began producing for the US-market through a contract with the US Metal Reserve Company.[104]

In late September 1942, in the Catavi mine of the huge Llallagua-Uncía complex owned by Patiño, the miners' union demanded wage-increases between 20 and 70 per cent for different jobs in the mine, calling attention to the record-profits being generated as a result of the elevated international price of tin.[105] When negotiations with the government failed, the union declared that a strike would begin on 14 December 1942. Declaring the strike illegal, the government sent army-troops to the mining camps, preventing all miners and their families from leaving the area, while at the same time closing the company-stores [pulperías] and therefore access to food. On 21 December, over 8,000 workers and family members, led by women and children in the front-lines, marched in protest and were met with the machine-gun fire of the army. Hundreds were dead by the end of the day.[106] The Catavi massacre became one of the tragic anniversaries of the labour-movement, but it also had an impact on national politics. In a parliamentary inquiry that followed the massacre, the MNR ably denounced the Peñaranda government and began making further inroads into the workers' movement. Any pre-existing legitimacy of the Peñaranda régime was now unrecoverable and the stage was set for the successful takeover by MNR-RADEPA contingents and the installation of Villarroel as President.

The Villarroel-MNR régime introduced the Fuero Sindical, 'a basic labour bill of rights which granted unions and their members the essential legal rights of organisation', but in exchange, 'the MNR demanded the support of organised labor and control over its most important institution'.[107] A measure of the Villarroel-MNR's semi-cooptive success came during the founding congress of the Federación Sindical de Trabajadores Mineros de Bolivia (Trade-Union Federation of Bolivian Mine-Workers, FSTMB) in Huanuni in

---

104. Volk 1975a, pp. 184–5.
105. Lora 1977, pp. 218–19.
106. Lora 1977, pp. 221–2; Volk 1975a, pp. 185–6.
107. Volk 1975a, pp. 188–9.

June 1944.[108] The government's Ministry of Labour funded the congress and 'prevented the participation of delegates from the politically active mines of the Llallagua-Uncía complex'.[109] The Third Congress of the FSTMB in March 1946 was of quite a different nature, however. Held just months before the July 1946 right-wing overthrow of Villarroel, the FSTMB broke off its relations with the Villarroel-MNR régime and introduced a new platform influenced by the political perspective of the POR under the leadership of Guillermo Lora.[110] At this point, the exploitation of minerals accounted for roughly 95 per cent of Bolivia's exports. Tin-exports alone constituted some 60 per cent. The mining sector as a whole contributed 15 per cent of GDP.[111] The strategic character of the tin-sector, with the historical experience of its wild fluctuations subject to the vagaries of major international wars and commodity-price swings, combined with the domestic trajectory of state-repression, workers' resistance, layoffs, and booms and busts.[112] These factors contributed to the historical formation of a militant, revolutionary and anti-imperialist working class, with the miners at the head. In the First Extraordinary Congress of the FSTMB, held in the town of Pulacayo in November 1946, the miners adopted as their central guiding doctrine what would become the most famous document of Bolivian labour-history, the Thesis of Pulacayo.[113]

Between 1947 and 1952, labour and the popular sectors of the countryside were engaged in full-scale battle with the state, the *rosca*, and the landlords, and the miners were a favoured target of vicious state-repression and generalised political assault. In 1948, for example, 'more than 800 miners and members of their families were killed in a battle with police and army units' at Catavi-Siglo XX mines.[114]

108. The FSTMB from this founding conference until the privatisation of the tin-mines in the mid-1980s was unquestionably the most powerful union in the Bolivian labour-movement, and its actions typically gave direction to the working-class struggle as a whole.
109. Volk 1975a, p. 189. The platform of the first congress was therefore characterised by moderation and resolutions centred on the state's recognition of basic labour-rights.
110. Volk 1975a, p. 192.
111. Knight 2003, p. 61.
112. See Bergquist 1986 on Latin-American labour-movements in strategic sectors.
113. Dunkerley 1984, p. 17; Lora 1977, pp. 246–52.
114. Volk 1975a, p. 197.

2.3.5 *Indigenous resistance: the 1945 National Indigenous Congress and the 1947 uprisings*

Traditional scholarship on the Bolivian National Revolution has tended to privilege the role of workers in the mines and the cities, the MNR, and middle-class sectors in the defeat of the oligarchy in 1952. The preceding tumult of the 1940s, however, extended deeply into the indigenous countryside as well. Moreover, historical episodes such as the 1945 National Indigenous Congress (NIC), which brought together over 1,500 indigenous representatives, and the 1947 indigenous-peasant uprisings in its aftermath, reveal that networks between urban workers, miners, intellectuals, and revolutionary and reformist party-militants, on the one hand, and grassroots-indigenous leaders in the countryside, on the other, increased dramatically in scope and depth during this period. What is most critical about the NIC is that it emerged as a result of indigenous popular agency in the countryside in alliance with various progressive allies, even if it also epitomised the Villarroel-MNR strategy of co-opting and regulating popular movements to advance a reformist and nationalist state-building project quite different from that envisioned by the indigenous movements themselves.[115] If, in the Chayanta insurrection of 1927, networks linking urban radicals and indigenous rebels were tenuously entering their birth-pains, by the mid-1940s linkages between labour-radicals, reformist and revolutionary party-militants, and indigenous rebels in the countryside, were better established and expanding rapidly in a period of mass-mobilisation. Political relationships between different indigenous groups were also maturing.[116] The fact that the oligarchy was unwilling to consider even the limited agrarian reforms proposed by the Villarroel-MNR helps to explain the overthrow of that régime and the subsequent widespread repression in the countryside during the *sexenio*. The generalised hostility of the *hacendados* to any reform whatsoever in the wake of the 1945 NIC and the subsequent right-wing overthrow of Villarroel, then, provide much of the

---

115. Dandler and Torrico 1987, p. 344; Gotkowitz 2003, p. 165.

116. For Gotkowitz, worker-involvement enhanced rather than displaced indigenous-peasant agency in this period: 'The burgeoning labour-movements of the 1940s coalesced with and gave new impetus to longstanding struggles by indigenous leaders for land, education, and citizenship' (Gotkowitz 2005, p. 143).

background for the 1947 indigenous uprisings that spanned the departments of Cochabamba, Chuquisaca, La Paz, Oruro and Tarija.[117]

Immediately prior to Villarroel's ascension to the presidency, rural strikes had proliferated. This was one of the key impetuses for the government considering a National Indigenous Congress. However, before Villarroel had even issued the official green light, indigenous leaders had already established a Comité Indigenal Boliviano (Bolivian Indigenous Committee, CIB) to plan for the NIC.[118] The CIB facilitated the expansion of rural infrastructures of class-struggle and urban-rural alliances at a rapid pace. It acted as 'coordinator and promoter', historians have observed, 'pushing for the collective organisation of the peasantry', and 'relating peasant leaders from diverse regions not only with one another, but also with national authorities, union leaders, printers, miners, factory workers, and others'.[119] The CIB issued a 27-point agenda for the NIC without the approval of the government prior to the NIC's inauguration and had it published in the national press:

> Of the many demands in this richly detailed plan, the most notable include: 'That the Indian be free, secure in his life and work, and respected the same as everyone; that there be special laws and authorities for the Indian; and that there be committees of lawyers paid by the government to defend the Indian'. Not coincidentally, the list begins and ends with the longstanding claim that all the land 'belongs to the Indians' – that it be 'returned to the Community' and belong to 'those who work it...the Indian'.[120]

---

117. One other longer-term factor stands out in regions like the Ayopaya province of Cochabamba, site of the widest scale and most radical insurrection during the 1947 phase of rebellion. Ayopaya is located in the Cochabamba highlands, and in the 1940s was dominated by *haciendas*, with very few free indigenous communities, and extreme systems of servitude for the indigenous *colonos* tied to the large estates. As the markets in the mines and cities expanded in the late 1930s and early 1940s, the landlords in Ayopaya intensified the exploitation of their *colonos* and ratcheted up the free services they were forced to provide. Larger numbers of 'supervisory personnel' were also hired to ensure worker-discipline in these new environs (Dandler 1987, pp. 338, 370). The underlying causes of the 1947 revolts combined the escalating levels of labour-exploitation on the haciendas, opportunities posed by the Villarroel reformist interlude in government, and the subsequent repression and failure to implement the reforms of the NIC.

118. Gotkowitz 2003, p. 166.

119. Dandler and Torrico 1987, p. 344. Important oral histories of participants in the 1947 uprisings further reveal that the PIR, POR, and MNR were all active in forging ties with the indigenous peasantry in this period, although with distinct purposes and degrees of success (Dandler 1987, pp. 345–7).

120. Gotkowitz 2003, p. 167.

These radical objectives were accompanied by increasing levels of contentious peasant-action in the countryside in the lead-up to the NIC, including
a wave of sit-down strikes.[121] The signs of rural unrest were sufficient for
the MNR to declare prominent indigenous leaders 'agitators' and jail them
before they could attend the congress.[122] It should not be surprising, therefore,
that the official agenda of the congress and the presidential decrees passed
therein managed to domesticate or leave out altogether many of the objectives of the indigenous movements who had been staging actions against
landlords in various regions of the country.[123] Nonetheless, the NIC brought
together different indigenous activists from across the country, and indigenous movements on the ground began interpreting the decrees announced
by Villarroel at the congress in ways that matched their much more revolutionary aims. At the same time, Villarroel's reforms were duly ignored by
landlords.[124] Radicalised indigenous peasants sought to enforce them through
the mobilisation of their own social power, from below, with direct action
against landowners and local authorities. Repression began soon after the
NIC under the direction of the Villarroel-MNR government. It reached new
and sustained heights after the hanging of Villarroel. Hertzog, the next president, refused to recognise the decrees setting off the massive 1947 rural insur-
gencies.[125] Although the uprisings of that year failed to break the landlord's
grip on power, the collective memories and infrastructure of rural insurgency
were reawakened powerfully very soon after the mainly urban revolution of
April 1952 successfully installed the MNR at the helm.

---

121. Dandler and Torrico 1987, p. 351.

122. Gotkowitz 2003, p. 167.

123. The preeminent questions of land distribution and communal control, for
instance, were sidelined.

124. Resembling, in some respects, what Forrest Hylton has termed, in the case of
Colombia, the 'parcellization of sovereignty' (Hylton 2006, p. 80), landlords and local
authorities had tremendous sovereign authority in the Bolivian countryside of the
1940s due to the weakness of the central state (Dandler 1987, p. 338).

125. The insurgents were met with naked brutality: 'The repression unleashed
against the 1947 rebels was virulent and almost unprecedented. Planes were employed
against rural insurgency for the first time ever; in addition to the army, landlords called
out their own civil guards' (Gotkowitz 2005, p. 176).

2.4 National Revolution, 1952–64

Between 9 April and 11 April 1952 an MNR-led insurrection under the leadership of Hernán Siles Zuazo quickly escaped the boundaries of the basic coup envisioned by the MNR-leadership. Popular militias of factory-workers and miners, and MNR rank-and-file militants and urban dwellers, overran most of the armed forces of the *ancien régime*, compelled swathes of low-ranking troops to switch sides, and sent many of the remaining hostile forces fleeing into exile. Chaco veterans were armed with their twenty-year-old weapons, miners were equipped with the dynamite of their trade, and the mutinous troops who joined the revolutionary forces brought with them arms of the state. The coercive apparatuses of the old order caved in almost completely under the weight of revolutionary advance. The immediate consequence was a remarkably low level of revolutionary and counter-revolutionary violence, although many more would die over the following decades as those seeking to defend the nationalist-populist revolution, and others attempting to steer it toward socialism, were repeatedly subjected to the brutalities of military authoritarianism and state-terror.[126]

2.4.1 *The legacies of revolutionary nationalism*

The militancy of the working class, led by radical miners, drove forth the initial radicalisation of the revolution. While the peasantry played a limited role in the initial insurrectionary phase, by the end of 1952, as we will see, they were also mobilising *en masse* in the countryside and pushing forward agrarian reform. It also seems to be, as Leon Trotsky once pointed out, that 'a revolution needs from time to time the whip of the counter-revolution'.[127] In the Bolivian case, two right-wing coup-attempts against the new MNR régime further engendered a hardening of resolve within the popular forces and made clear the necessity that the MNR-leadership take quick measures to ensure the irreversibility of the National Revolution. In this context, between 1952 and early 1956, the major advances of the revolution – those associated to this day with the *estado de '52* ('state of 52') – were consolidated: (i) the

---

126. In the April fighting of 1952, 90 died in Oruro, and 400 in La Paz, the two focal points of insurrection, whereas in Cochabamba, the MNR simply assumed control without serious opposition resistance (Dunkerley 1984, p. 39).

127. Trotsky 2005 [1932], p. 774.

nationalisation of the three big mining companies and the establishment of the state-mining company, COMIBOL; (ii) agrarian reform; and (iii) universal suffrage.[128]

The MNR enjoyed tremendous legitimacy in 1952 because of its links to the martyred Villarroel, its leading role in opposition to authoritarian reaction during the *sexenio* (1946–52), its initiation of the 1949 civil war, its victory in the 1951 elections, and its leadership in the opening hours of the 1952 insurrection. When Paz Estenssoro returned from exile in Buenos Aires, he became president, and Hernán Siles Zuazo took over the vice-presidency. The ideological terrain in Bolivian politics was overwhelmingly dominated by the MNR's revolutionary nationalism.[129]

The party encompassed a broad array of social forces, ranging from militant miners and other sectors of the working class, the indigenous peasantry, and reformist and conservative nationalists from the middle class. The party frequently employed radical rhetoric, and opposed the *rosca* and the landed oligarchy in practice; but it was never committed to socialism and, in fact, harboured a deep anti-communism. In the first three years following the revolution, the MNR made its deepest reforms and absorbed many leftist militants into its ranks. At the highest levels of the state, for example, the working class was represented in the Ministry of Mines (Juan Lechín), Ministry of Labour (Germán Butrón), and Ministry of Peasant Affairs (Ñuflo Chávez).[130] The MNR also developed an elaborate system of state-patronage and clientelist networks connecting the highest echelons of the party to the smallest local levels of the cities, municipalities, and villages. Political support was ensured through petty favours and a steady distribution of jobs. Indeed, the size of the civil service apparently doubled in the first four years of the new government as loyalists reaped their rewards.[131] Thus, the net of co-optation was cast wide and functioned remarkably well in terms of consolidating the party's power.[132]

---

128. Dunkerley 1984, pp. 38–82; Malloy 1970, pp. 167–310; Mitchell 1977, pp. 38–59; Whitehead 2003, pp. 27–32.

129. Antezana 1983, pp. 60–84.

130. Dunkerley 1984, p. 40.

131. Dunkerley 1984, p. 80.

132. At the same time, those who could not be co-opted were selectively repressed, as the Trotskyists discovered as early as 1953. The Partido Obrero Revolucionario (Revolutionary Workers' Party, POR) was frequently targeted for seeking to foment 'communist subversion'. High-profile *porista* figures, such as the brothers Guillermo

The United States, for its part, recognised the anti-communist character of the MNR régime early on, and provided increasing levels of aid to tame the leftist elements of revolutionary nationalism and fortify the Right over the coming decades.[133]

Another facet of the revolutionary nationalism of the MNR in this period left an indelible print on Bolivia's cultural politics. The indubitable advances in citizenship for the indigenous peasantry, reflected in universal suffrage, agrarian reform, and access to rural education, were granted at a cost. In the process of becoming citizens, indigenous peasants were expected to assimilate into the newly dominant conceptualisation of race, cultural *mestizaje*. Citizenship was to include the westernisation of indigenous political practices and traditional economies. The political and economic system of the postrevolutionary era, in this way, 'created a precarious hegemonic model of a mestizo citizen: a consumer and producer of merchandise, a speaker of Spanish and an aspirant to a western ideal of civilisation'.[134] *Mestizaje* conceived of in this way, 'implied a distillation of Bolivia's distinct Spanish and Indian racial and civilisational essences into a blended national unity', where 'cross-class alliance and unitary citizenship' were seen by the MNR as 'the fulfillment of the earlier yet frustrated promise of independence in 1825'.[135] Rural and urban indigenous movements began to challenge these ideas by the 1970s, but, in the 1950s and 1960s, the mythology of cultural *mestizaje* was one of the most powerful inheritances bequeathed by the MNR's revolution.

2.4.2 *Developmental capitalism – a nationalist-populist régime of accumulation*

At the time of the 1952 Revolution, the Bolivian economy was characterised by the uneven development of capitalism, 'in which a relatively advanced, export-oriented capitalist sector – in this case tin mining – coexisted and inter-related with an archaic, stagnant and predominantly provincial organisation of agriculture'.[136] The country was wrought with profound economic, social, and regional inequalities rooted in unique patterns of intense, enclave

---

and César Lora, spent a year in prison early in the postrevolutionary period (Dunkerley 1984, p. 77).
133. Scott 1972; Whitehead 1969; Wilkie 1969; Zunes 2001.
134. Rivera Cusicanqui 2004, p. 21.
135. Hylton and Thomson 2007, p. 80.
136. Dunkerley 1984, p. 6.

capitalist development and the survival of precapitalist social formations.[137] The tin-barons generated 95 per cent of Bolivia's foreign exchange, accounted for 50 per cent of central-government revenues, and controlled the banks which partially financed the weak central state.[138] Prerevolutionary Bolivia had the highest inequality of land-concentration in all of Latin America, with 82 per cent of land in the possession of four per cent of landowners.[139]

After the MNR assumed power in 1952, however, the aim was to establish a 'developmentalist state', or the acceleration of state-led capitalism, in which unproductive, semi-feudal social relations in the countryside would be uprooted through land-reform, nationalisation of the mines would provide the state with control over the main source of foreign exchange, industry would be promoted, and diversification of the economy would flourish through state-direction and planning.[140] In the postrevolutionary period, the state controlled and led the productive process through the establishment of various state-enterprises. The development-model established was based on a centralised state-administration, state-ownership of natural resources, extensive state-employment, and a host of limited yet real social citizenship and welfare-rights guaranteed by the state.[141] Finance, agriculture, and mining were the major activities of capitalists in this period, with manufacturing industries still employing only 3 per cent of the economically active population by the 1970s.[142]

2.4.3 The Revolution moves rightwards

The Bolivian conjuncture of 1952 engendered, on the one hand, major reforms to land-tenure, mining, and the state's involvement in the productive process of the economy more generally, that were difficult to uproot for many years to come. On the other hand, within four years of the Revolution, the political Right within and outside the MNR went on the offensive in an effort to roll-

---

137. Grebe López 1983, pp. 87–8.
138. Eckstein and Hagopian 1983, p. 66.
139. Eckstein 1983, p. 108.
140. Eckstein and Hagopian 1983, p. 66.
141. Orellana Aillón 2006, p. 265. Sociologist Lorgio Orellana Aillón calls this development-model a nationalist-populist régime of accumulation, which he argues lasted from the 1952 Revolution until the neoliberal counter-revolution in 1985.
142. Conaghan, Malloy, and Abugattas 1990, p. 24.

back what it could from the popular advances of the opening saga of the revolutionary process. A distinct right-wing shift in the régime was concretised
by 1956, under the presidency of Siles Zuazo (1956–60), when it introduced
a Stabilisation-Plan for the economy, backed by the International Monetary
Fund (IMF) and the US-state.[143] The decree did succeed in curbing inflation,
but, at the same time, suffocated production, increased unemployment-levels,
and slashed the real incomes of all working-class sectors. The peasantry, on the
other hand, enjoyed increases in the prices of their produce.[144] The trajectory
to the right signalled by the Stabilisation-Plan was enriched and extended
under Paz Estenssoro's second administration (1960–4), as was the escalation
of foreign ties with the United States.[145]

After the construction of a highway linking the department of Santa Cruz
to the rest of the country in 1954, the eastern lowlands were gradually transformed over the next several decades into the new dynamic geographical
centre of Bolivian capitalism, rooted in agro-industry, forestry, commercial
ranching, oil and natural gas, and, eventually, the higher tiers of the cocaine-
trade. The social and political repercussions of these developments would
become enormous over time; not least of them was an increasing polarisation
between the regional-ethnic-political identity of white-*mestizo cambas* (low-
landers in Pando, Beni, Santa Cruz and Tarija) and the more indigenous *collas*
(populations of the valleys and highlands of the rest of the country).[146]

Parallel to the Stabilisation-Plan, the MNR rebuilt the nation's armed forces
with the assistance of the US in order to wrestle control from the popular
armed militias and reassert the authority of the state over the popular classes.
Between 1960 and 1964, it should be stressed, US aid to Bolivia catapulted
by over 600 per cent.[147] Recall that, as early as 11 April 1952, the masses in
the streets of La Paz were demanding 'the complete dismantling of the military apparatus, nationalisation and workers' control of the mines, an agrarian

---

143. The United States and the IMF made $25 million in funding for their 1956
Stabilisation-Plan contingent on Bolivia's adoption of a series of monetarist measures, including an end to dual exchange-rates, a wage-freeze, cuts to credit-lines, and
the abolition of tariffs protecting local industries. As a consequence, GNP per capita
declined and manufacturing industry fell to 14 per cent of GDP in 1960, after reaching
18 per cent in 1955 (Eckstein and Hagopian 1983, p. 76).
144. Dunkerley 1984, p. 87.
145. Dunkerley 1984, pp. 104–5.
146. Gill 1987a, b; Healy and Paulson 2000, pp. 7–8.
147. Dunkerley 1984, p. 108.

revolution, and the formation of popular militias'.[148] Between 1958 and 1964, the army's troop-base increased threefold from 5,000 to 15,000 men, its share of the budget increased from 6.8 per cent to 16.8 per cent of GDP, and its officers were sent to the School of the Americas in the Panama Canal Zone for specialised training in the enforcement of US-imperial security-doctrine for the Americas.[149] Hence, while the armed forces had been crushed in 1952, by 1964, under MNR-impetus, in alliance with US-imperial financing and direction, they had been fully reconstituted. Wide-scale repression of the popular classes was once again possible, indeed, inevitable.

2.4.4   The working class, 1952–64

One of the most salient features of the revolutionary period of the early 1950s was the consolidation of the miners as the vanguard of the labour-movement. This leadership was facilitated in part through the extraordinary wealth of the popular cultures of resistance and opposition in the mining camps. In Bolivia, in addition to the ideological traditions of revolutionary Marxism and anarcho-syndicalism, the miners' radicalism was amplified by their ongoing allegiances and attachments to pre-conquest, precapitalist Quechua-Aymara indigenous traditions and rituals, adapted to the new settings of capitalist exploitation.[150] These beliefs and rituals 'provide[d] deep roots' for the miners' sense of identity, helping to 'generate a sense of self that reject[ed] subordination and repression'.[151] The working class of the mining communities tended to 'encapsulate in a unitary worldview the widely disparate, apparently contradictory ideologies to which they ha[d] been exposed', including 'primordial figures of the Quechua- and Aymara-speaking population who work in the mines; the saints and diabolical agents that have been intro-

---

148. Dunkerley 1984, p. 4. The popular militias that did arise were of two sorts. On the one hand, there were the MNR's *grupos de honor* which were effectively subordinate to the party's leadership. On the other hand, there were popular militias rooted in workplaces, linked to local unions, and from that level extended up to the Central Obrera Boliviana (Bolivian Workers' Central, COB). Paz Estenssoro was always opposed to these developments and, by 1953, had already begun taming the capacity of the independent, workers' militias through the formation of the Control Político, an institution which incorporated all MNR-militias into a centralised command-structure (Dunkerley 1984, p. 81).
149. Dunkerley 1984, p. 114.
150. Nash 1993, pp. 310–34.
151. Nash 1989.

duced by Spanish conquerors and missionaries; and Marxist, Trotskyist, and developmentalist ideologies that inspire the political and labor movements in which they have been involved since the early part of the twentieth century'.[152] A further defining feature of the miners' popular cultures of resistance and opposition was the emphasis on participatory democracy in their unions and communities. This manifested itself in the primacy of independent syndicalism over party-politics, frequent mass-assemblies in the mining camps, a tradition of popular control of mining delegates sent to higher federations, autonomy of strike-committees from the national executives of union-organisations, and annual elections for the leadership of union-locals. Such an environment made the union much more than a union. Instead, it acted as a pivotal reference-point for all aspects of working-class life in the mining zones. The union fought for workers basic material interests. It stressed mass-participation and active engagement with national politics. It was through the union that popular militias were formed and cultural activities organised.[153] In other words, the tin-miners were engaged in precisely the sort of social-movement unionism described in Chapter One.

Paradoxically, the geographical isolation of the mining zones did not prevent the miners from assuming a vanguard-role in the wider social and political milieus of the labour-movement in the cities, the student-movement of the universities, and, in certain extraordinary historical moments, the countryside of the indigenous peasantry as well. This led Bolivia's most incisive sociologist René Zavaleta Mercado to write of a *locus minero* of the workers' movement, and to describe the phenomenal *irradiación*, or reach, of the miners' influence in the wider array of popular struggles throughout Bolivian society.[154] While the centrality of the miners was already well-established in the popular struggles of the 1930s and 1940s, the 1952 Revolution solidified this relationship between the miners, the state, and the rest of society with such strength that it really could not be extinguished until the neoliberal counter-revolution of the mid-1980s. As popular power aggregated in the streets, mining communities, and, soon after, in the countryside, the Central Obrera Boliviana (Bolivian Workers' Central, COB) was formed in the immediate aftermath of the

152. Nash 1989, p. 182.
153. Roddick and van Niekerk 1989, p. 139.
154. Zavaleta Mercado 1983a, pp. 222–5.

revolt in April 1952. More than merely a labour-confederation, the COB, at that time, acquired characteristics of a soviet, and the seeds of a dual-power situation were sown. Embracing under its fold miners, salaried workers, the peasantry, public-sector employees, university-students, and sections of the urban petty bourgeoisie, the COB represented the sovereign authority of the Bolivian masses at this juncture in the revolutionary upswing.[155]

In the three years following the Revolution, support for the MNR was a generalised phenomenon within the working class. However, the traditions of assembly-style popular democracy in the local mining camps facilitated a more nuanced unionism at the grassroots-level. Tactical support for the MNR, in other words, was combined with strategic loyalty to a radically democratic project of revolutionary-socialist *sindicalismo*. Throughout 1952, militants of the POR and the Partido Comunista Boliviano (Bolivian Communist Party, PCB) were active in local assemblies and the MNR's control at this level was much less pronounced; furthermore, 'whatever their sympathies, the majority of workers were organised independently through the unions and the COB, with no direct links between them and the party apparatus'.[156] Beginning in 1953, the MNR started persecuting the POR, often with the assistance of the PCB, but the traditions of popular democracy and independent syndicalism persisted. The MNR was able to sweep the COB-congress in 1954, but union-locals and local camp-activity continued to embrace a more eclectic and diverse politics of radicalism. There began to emerge a significant cleavage between the labour-movement and the MNR as early as 1956. Commencing with the Stabilisation-Plan, the MNR's grip on workers' sentiments began to deteriorate. At the 1957 congress of the FSTMB, for example, a resolution inspired by the POR was passed demanding an end to *co-gobierno* and the declaration of a general strike.[157] The same resolution was supported soon after in the national congress of the COB, but it was never successfully carried out.[158]

---

155. Lora 1983, pp. 178–9. The nationalisation of the mines, a compromised form of *control obrero* (workers' control) in COMIBOL, and *co-gobierno* (co-government), or the designation of several important ministries to trade-unionists, were all expressions of this power.

156. Roddick and van Niekerk 1989, p. 141.

157. Roddick and van Niekerk 1989, p. 146.

158. The Stalinists of the PCB organised against such an orientation, arguing that the working class should support the MNR-government – now led by President Hernán Siles Zuazo – to avoid any possibility of a right-wing coup (Roddick and van Neikerk 1989, p. 146).

A fundamental fissure between the MNR and the labour-movement was only secured, however, in the fallout from Paz Estenssoro's implementation of the Triangular Plan in 1961. The details of the plan – including mass-layoffs and stricter labour-discipline – drove the FSTMB and the COB to support a lengthy and bitter strike in the mines in 1963.[159] The strike lasted 100 days and was centred in Catavi-Siglo XX. At the pinnacle of the strike, miners, still armed from 1952, sealed access to Siglo XX and took US government-representatives and foreign technicians hostage in order to leverage their demands.[160] The strike failed to reverse the policies of the Triangular Plan, but it did rupture the relationship between the MNR and the workers, and, in so doing, spurred the fragmentation of the MNR itself.[161]

2.4.5 *The indigenous peasantry, 1952–64*

The MNR revolutionary government enacted a series of reforms that substantially altered social relations in the countryside, as well as the relationship between indigenous peasants and the state. Agrarian reform satiated landless-peasant and agrarian-labourer demands for land. It challenged the gross concentration of *latifundia*, or large landholdings. Universal suffrage enfranchised huge numbers of illiterate rural indigenous producers previously excluded from basic citizenship-rights. The expansion of free rural education responded to a key grievance expressed in the indigenous-peasant activism of the first half of the twentieth century.[162]

Despite the peasantry's minimal role in the initial April insurrection – the importance of which is easy to overstate in relation to the revolutionary developments that preceded and followed it – responsibility for the depth of agrarian reform lies with the direct-action tactics and independent land-occupations orchestrated by radicalised peasants in Cochabamba, La Paz, and Oruro, and, to a lesser extent, in northern Potosí and Chuquisaca, by the end of 1952.[163] Sociologist Silvia Rivera Cusicanqui has described

---

159. Dunkerley 1984, p. 111.
160. Nash 1993, p. 221.
161. Roddick and van Niekerk 1989, p. 147.
162. Albó 1987, p. 382; García Linera 2005b, p. 7; Ticona A., Rojas O., and Albó 1995, pp. 35–6.
163. Albó 1987, p. 383; Dunkerley 1984, p. 67. Thanks to Forrest Hylton for insisting that I not exaggerate even implicitly the significance of the relative absence of the peasantry in April.

indigenous peasants' relationship to the state between 1952 and 1958 as *active subordination*.[164] Peasants took the initiative in the countryside through mobilisation and self-organisation, but, even in this early period, their actions were steadily subordinated to the MNR's project of populist state-led capitalism.[165] In spite of the MNR's relatively slow initial instincts on agrarian reform, the party was able to build an infrastructure in the countryside in the wake of peasant-mobilisations and land-occupations. It soon controlled the political processes of much of rural Bolivia by effectively balancing an acceptance of many initial popular demands for reform with the channelling of the social power of the peasants into the party-machine through elaborate patron-client networks and state-controlled peasant-unions.[166] The networks were co-ordinated through the Ministry of Peasant-Affairs, established shortly after the Revolution.[167] The MNR-government, sensing the fragility of its clutch on the peasantry in the immediate postrevolutionary period, decisively changed course and implemented the Agrarian-Reform Law in August 1953. The law recognised the seized *haciendas* in Ucureña and the Cochabamba valley, and

---

164. Rivera Cusicanqui 2003 [1984], p. 139.

165. Rivera Cusicanqui 2003 [1984], pp. 122–3.

166. In large parts of the *altiplano*, state peasant-unions were superficially established as the intermediary institutions through which state-peasant relations were conducted; in reality, however, the unions were subordinated to the organisational and political traditions of the indigenous *ayllus* which had survived more robustly than in Cochabamba. In northern Potosí, where precapitalist social formations were most widespread, and where *ayllus* maintained a depth of sovereignty unparalleled in other regions, the state-unions were seen as overt instruments of internal colonialism and conduits of racial domination and oppression. Traditional indigenous authorities consequently resisted their imposition on the domain of the *ayllus* more fervently than anywhere else (Rivera Cusicanqui 2003 [1984], p. 137). It is also vital to point out that in regions where indigenous communal structures were maintained more fully, the limits of *hacienda*-expansion meant that indigenous-peasant demands for land were far less vociferous. As a consequence, the agrarian reform did not have the same deeply pacifying effect (Albó 1987, p. 385), even if loyalty to the MNR was still cultivated through other, weaker channels of clientelism.

167. Albó 1987, p. 383. While the depth of hegemony established by the party varied along regional lines, it nonetheless constructed a remarkable social base, loyal to its political project, in most parts of the country. This loyalty tended to extend to an acceptance of – even enthusiasm for – the MNR's vision of cultural homogenisation through the promotion of *mestizaje*. Indigenous peasants were increasingly 'de-ethnicised', referred to as *campesinos* rather than *indios* (García Linera 2005b, p. 7; Rivera Cusicanqui 2003). The early period of agrarian reform, therefore, was driven by social movements from below that were subsequently co-opted by the MNR at substantial cost to their independence.

redistributed large tracts of land in the *altiplano*.[168] In so doing, the MNR effectively seized control of the popular rural momentum and steered it to toward the government's own ends. The basic material impact of land-reform in quelling peasant-radicalism and binding peasant-communities to the MNR cannot be overstated.[169] By 1958, the peasant-relationship to the state had therefore shifted to *passive subordination*, a situation that would only thicken with time under the Barrientos régime.[170] Nonetheless, it is also true that these expansive peasant-networks created by the MNR, which were interlaced in heterogeneous patterns with pre-existing indigenous communal structures as we have seen, provided an infrastructural basis for independent peasant-politics and peasant-worker alliances decades in the future.[171]

Conclusion

The historical forces of capitalist development, state-formation, and racialised class-struggle between the eighteenth and twentieth centuries provided the material context for rich popular cultures of indigenous liberation and revolutionary-leftist politics. The cultures of resistance forged over this long period laid the bases for the left-indigenous insurrectionary politics of the early twenty-first century. The Bolivian political and social history navigated in this chapter was distinctive for its racialised state-repression, economic exploitation, and processes of primitive accumulation. But the interruption of these abusive ruling-class practices by periodic rebellions, and even revolutions, were just as important. State-repression fuelled the escalation of resistance from overwhelmingly indigenous popular classes more often than it silenced their efforts to defend their rights. The names of the indigenous leaders of 1781 and 1899 continue to ring out to this day.

The early twentieth century witnessed the rise of powerful tin-barons on the one hand, and a militant tin-miners' movement on the other. Developing alongside this advance in the formation of the working class was the flowering of new radical ideologies in the labour-movement, including Marxism, anarchism, socialism, and communism. At the same time, the example of Zárate

---

168. Rivera Cusicanqui 2003 [1984], p. 123; Eckstein 1983, p. 109.
169. Dunkerley 1984, pp. 73–5; Lora 1983, p. 185.
170. Rivera Cusicanqui 2003 [1984], pp. 139–40.
171. Rivera Cusicanqui 2003 [1984], p. 141.

Willka and the insurgent indigenous peasantry he represented, in conjunction with the further development of capitalism, spurred a pivotal shift in the trajectory of ruling-class racial ideologies that sought to shape and to justify the transformation of indigenous peasants into a disciplined labour-force while expropriating their communal lands. Willka's example and the expansion of capitalism also facilitated the rise of new cycles of indigenous-peasant struggles and the formation of novel popular cultures of resistance and opposition. In the midst of this complex and multifaceted social setting, Bolivia witnessed experimental ideological convergences and political alliances between urban radicals informed by Marxism and indigenous peasants informed by earlier uprisings. The Chayanta rebellion of 1927 is the most important early example of this phenomenon, one that was repeated and extended in the 1947 revolts. The Great Depression and the Chaco War helped to precipitate the breakdown of the traditional political-party system and oligarchic régime, and the birth of an unstable reformist epoch known as 'military socialism'. Far-left political parties were established. Perhaps the most consequential outcome of the historical sequence set in motion by the Chaco War was the formation of the nationalist-reformist political party, the MNR. Working-class radicalism and indigenous-peasant mobilising continued to expand in bold forms. Cumulative cycles of repression and resistance eventually led to the 1952 National Revolution, which contained an important component of worker-radicalism sustained by militant unionism and revolutionary ideologies. The multi-class revolutionary alliance eventually unravelled as a consequence of divisions between the peasantry and the workers. Peasant-radicalism waned in the wake of land-redistribution.

By the end of the 1950s, 'intraparty strife was as intense as that among parties, classes, and groups'.[172] The party fragmented, labour abandoned the MNR, and the armed forces were rebuilt into a relatively effective coercive force. The ground was set for Barrientos's coup in November, 1964, a coup that would usher in a period of authoritarian dictatorships lasting almost twenty years. The familiar cycles of state-repression punctuated by explosions of militant popular resistance returned to Bolivian politics.

---

172. Malloy and Gamarra 1988, p. 7.

Chapter Three

Authoritarianism, Democracy, and Popular Struggle, 1964–85

The new régime of General René Barrientos, whose slogan was *revolución restauradora* [restorative revolution], endured until April 1969. The social bases underpinning it included the military, nascent bourgeois interests in Cochabamba and Santa Cruz, and parts of the urban middle class. In terms of foreign relations, the government adopted an avidly pro-American stance, tying itself closely to the US-state and the International Monetary Fund (IMF).[1] Another fundamental facet of the new administration – indeed, second only in importance to the support of the military – was the alliance Barrientos forged with the peasantry. That alliance came to be known as the Pacto Militar-Campesino (Military-Peasant Pact, PMC). The new president fused his fluency in Quechua with a personalistic authoritarian style and able employment of the established channels of patronage to develop this decisive alliance.[2] It was an alliance predicated on the continuity of the cultural *mestizaje* introduced by the MNR, but inflected now with a much harder edge in its dealings with dissident-sectors of the indigenous popular classes that dared stray outside its perimetres.

---

1. Malloy and Gamarra 1988, p. 18.
2. Barrientos's mother spoke Quechua.

With an unstable coalition of domestic social forces and a more reliable network of imperialist support in place, the régime positioned itself to continue the economic trajectory introduced by the post-1956 MNR, yet with a dose of brutality and repression unavailable to its civilian predecessor.

Hugo Bánzer's régime (1971–8) signalled the hardened extension of the authoritarian historical sequence set into motion by the 1964 coup of Barrientos. After a short window in time in which this sequence was challenged by the labour-movement and the radical Left (1969–71), Bánzer reclaimed the ferocious authority of capital and imperial power through the exercise of naked military might. By the end of the 1970s, however, a confluence of factors came together to force Bánzer from power, kicking off a popular battle to restore democracy (1978–82). This battle witnessed a convergence of radical movements of the working class and the peasantry, as well as the rise to office of the centre-left Unidad Democrática Popular (Popular-Democratic Unity, UDP) in 1982.

This chapter demonstrates how the period between 1964 and 1985 was marked by the intensifying use of state-repression, punctuated by militant resistance of the organised popular classes – the working class, rooted in the tin-mines, initially led the resistance, but was later joined by a powerful wave of indigenous movements once the state betrayed its pact with the peasantry in the mid-1970s. The configuration of domestic bourgeois power changed, too, as the geographic fulcrum of capitalism in the country shifted from La Paz to Santa Cruz, but the dynamic of state-repression against the popular classes was maintained. Cycles of mobilisation and repression interacted and intensified, as the propertied classes remained inflexible to reform, on the one hand, and the labour-movement – and later the peasantry as well – went through a process of radicalisation, on the other. Worsening inequality and poverty over the course of this period fuelled this dynamic. As in earlier historical epochs, the fear and intransigence expressed by the ruling élite was accelerated and deepened by racist resentment and anxiety regarding the increasingly mobilised and overwhelmingly indigenous proletarian and peasant-majority.

The collective memory of worker-radicalism was sustained through semiclandestine networks during the moments of harshest crackdown, but also rose to the surface when there were brief openings in the political scene – such as in the Asamblea Popular (Popular Assembly, AP) in 1971, or the years of the democratic transition. Some peasant-organisations continued to organise independently of the state and seek alliances with labour and the Left even while the main peasant-federations became entangled in the snare of the PMC. When that pact broke down, radical indigenous traditions were given new life through the ideological and political consolidation of *katarismo*, and the formation of new, militant indigenous organisations. The peasantry and the working class managed to restore confidence in one another through their participation in the struggle for democracy after the collapse of the Bánzer régime in 1978. Sentiments of mutual solidarity during the democratic movement built on earlier common experiences of peasant- and worker-radicals who had been jailed and exiled together. Through the sustenance and renewal of various radical ideological currents and organisational adaptations, the traditions of worker-radicalism and indigenous liberation discussed in Chapter 2 were sustained and adapted to new conditions, helping later to feed and fire the left-indigenous cultures of resistance and opposition of the early twenty-first century.

3.1 The legacies of Barrientos

In mining, the 'modernisation' of COMIBOL initiated by the MNR through the Triangular Plan was deepened and intensified under General Barrientos, with layoffs and wage-cuts contributing to the overall strategy of labour-discipline. The sector was also increasingly opened up to foreign capital, so that, by 1968, the state controlled roughly 55 per cent of production to the private sector's 45.[3] Outside of the mining sector, the most important economic development in the 1960s and 1970s was the expansion of Bolivia's oil-economy, open to foreign capital. An American multinational, Gulf Oil Corporation, eventually came to control 80 per cent of Bolivia's total petroleum-production compared to a meagre 20 per cent for the state-enterprise, Yacimientos Petrolíferos Fiscales de Bolivia (YPFB). Minimal tax-obligations in the sector resulted in the repatriation of massive profits by the US-company.[4] As a percentage of GDP, agriculture and mining declined, manufacturing, energy, and transportation remained steady, and hydrocarbons, construction,

---

3. Dunkerley 1984, p. 127; Malloy and Gamarra 1988, p. 15.
4. Dunkerley 1984, p. 128; Malloy and Gamarra 1988, pp. 15–16.

commerce, finance, and housing increased.[5] Strengthening of parts of the domestic-capitalist class occurred in a number of these areas, such that the private sector as a whole controlled 'some 75 per cent of GNP and engaged some 85 per cent of the workforce' by 1968.[6] The state's absolute contribution to the economy continued to grow, however, accounting for considerable levels of new employment and 52 per cent of total investment in the country by the end of the 1960s.[7] The Barrientos régime managed to keep pace with average levels of growth elsewhere in Latin America during the period, and did so with low levels of inflation. International debt and social inequality continued to climb, however, while social spending decreased.[8]

The 'Bolivian military was still a rather tenuous force from a professional and institutional point of view', in the late 1960s. 'Barrientos increasingly was supported less by the military as an institution than by factions within the military'.[9] By the end of the decade, open rivalry within the armed forces and bids to replace Barrientos were clearly on display. The already uncertain pathway to presidential succession took a sharp turn in April 1969 when Barrientos was killed in a helicopter-crash. It was never shown conclusively whether the incident was accidental or homicidal.[10] Barrientos was briefly replaced by his vice-president, Luis Adolfo Siles Salinas. Siles then succumbed to the presidential aspirations of General Alfredo Ovando (September 1969 to October 1970). Ovando drew figures from the respectable civilian middle class into his cabinet, including Marcelo Quiroga Santa Cruz, later to become a martyr revered by Bolivian socialists. This was patently an attempt to distance himself from the legacy of Barrientos. Ovando's most momentous policy was the nationalisation of Gulf Oil on 7 October 1969; otherwise, he 'undertook very few positive measures'.[11] Vicious rivalries within the military continued to haunt the institution. Juan José Torres (October 1970 to August 1971) eventually climbed his way to office through a counter-coup on 6 October 1970.

5. Malloy and Gamarra 1988, p. 16.
6. Ibid.
7. Ibid.
8. Dunkerley 1984, p. 129.
9. Malloy and Gamarra 1988, p. 22.
10. Dunkerley 1984, p. 156.
11. Dunkerley 1984, pp. 165–6.

Crucial to his success was a general strike called by workers on 7 October because Torres enjoyed only marginal support within the military itself.[12]

3.1.1 *The working class, 1964–71*

The critical axis of violence and confrontation during the military dictatorship of Barrientos, as in the dictatorships that followed, was the relationship between the miners and the armed forces.[13] Repression began in mid-May 1965, when Juan Lechín was kidnapped by the military from his house in the middle of the night and forced into exile in Paraguay.[14] In response, a broad labour-front was organised under the umbrella of the COB, which included miners, teachers, factory-workers and construction-labourers. Together, they called for a general strike. The failure of the strike to materialise and sustain itself, though, revealed heightened divisions within the labour-movement.[15] The day after Lechín's coerced flight to Paraguay, the military concentrated its forces in the mining camps of Colquiri, Milluni, Catavi, Siglo XX, and San José.[16] Fierce battles between armed miners and the military left many dead and wounded. The same week, the Federación Sindical de Trabajadores Mineros de Bolivia (Trade-Union Federation of Bolivian Mine-Workers, FSTMB) and COB were declared illegal and many union- and political leaders were driven into exile or hiding.[17] *Co-gobierno* and *control obrero* were eliminated, worker-participation in decision-making in COMIBOL was abolished completely, wages were slashed by 40 to 50 per cent, and food-subsidies in the *pulperías* of the mining camps were cut, driving prices of basic goods into the clouds.[18]

---

12. Dunkerley 1984, p. 166.
13. On the political front, the second half of the 1960s witnessed the extreme fragmentation of the organised radical Left, under the weight of authoritarian repression. This had important consequences for the fate of the labour-movement, which still had the tin-miners as its principal force. During the Barrientos period, the Bolivian Trotskyists, for example, suffered serious internal fractionalisation and marginalisation from mainstream-politics, some of which spawned from the trying domestic political scenario, and some of which was derivative fallout from splinters in international Trotskyism within the Fourth International (Alexander 1973, pp. 137–54).
14. Dunkerley 1984, p. 123.
15. Malloy and Gamarra 1988, p. 11.
16. Nash 1993, p. 276.
17. Dunkerley 1984, p. 124.
18. Malloy and Gamarra 1988, p. 11.

In addition to exiling union- and leftist-political leaders, the Barrientos régime engaged in selective assassinations of its opponents. Among the casualties was César Lora, brother of Guillermo Lora, and leading figure of the POR in the mining regions. He was arrested and murdered by the army on 20 July 1965 in the department of Potosí.[19] Two months after Lora's killing, rebellion erupted in Siglo XX in an attempt by the miners to end the military occupation of their camps. In Catavi, the rank and file managed briefly to take control of the military barracks. The miners' advance was tragically short-lived. With reinforcements from the eastern lowlands, the military reasserted control through three bloody days of repression, leaving over two hundred dead and scores injured.[20] The next infamous mine-crackdown, known as the San Juan Massacre, occurred in June 1967, and left a minimum of 87 people dead, including women and children.[21] Because of the particularly vindictive and sadistic nature of that massacre, its legacy has been indelibly imprinted in the miners' collective memory of resistance and state-terror.[22]

The prolonged authoritarian period (1964–82) that Barrientos ushered in was overwhelmingly a dark one for labour, save for a brief respite under the military populism of Alfredo Ovando and Juan José Torres, and the remarkable if short-lived experiment in the extension of workers' power known as the Asamblea Popular (Popular Assembly, AP) in 1971.[23] Despite serious

---

19. Alexander 1973, p. 145.
20. Dunkerley 1984, p. 125.
21. Dunkerley 1984, pp. 148–9.
22. The San Juan massacre was emblematic of Barrientos's general repressive assault on the working class. It was meant to inspire fear, defeat hope, and crush resistance. Gathered in the town of Llallagua outside the Siglo XX mine on 23 June 1967, unionists and their families celebrated both the traditional indigenous festivities associated with the winter-solstice on the eve of San Juan, and the anticipation of a two-day illegal FSTMB congress. With the miners and their families still dancing in the streets and slowly making their way to their shacks at 4:30 in the morning, the military and national guard launched a surprise-attack, unleashing a cascade of machine-gun bullets, bazooka-shells, and mortar-fire on the unprepared, unarmed and, in good measure, inebriated miners. Grenades were thrown into the houses of mining families with the occupants asleep inside (Nash 1993, p. 278). While the official death-toll published in the newspapers was 87, Nash hints that the numbers may have been higher: 'An eyewitness at the funeral assured me there were many more; he told me that the number of caskets he saw going by looked like a stream of ants, and that there were burials in common ditches of bodies so destroyed by bazookas that they were no longer intact' (Nash 1993, p. 279).
23. In the latter years of the Barrientos period, Bolivia was extensively militarised. Barracks near mines were stocked with large numbers of military troops. Among these forces the infamous Boines Verdes tactical force stands out. It took its name from a

levels of repression, the Bolivian state never achieved the efficiency of co-ordinated, bureaucratic state-terror against the civilian populace as was soon to appear in the Argentine dictatorships (1976–83), the Pinochet nightmare in Chile (1973–90), or the genocidal horror of Guatemala in the early 1980s. While the years between 1964 and 1982 were mostly bleak and brutal, therefore, the working class – and in particular the miners – was able to maintain a semi-clandestine infrastructure of class-struggle, to hold illegal union-congresses occasionally, and to mount the odd general strike against their class-enemies, the state, and imperialism. These semi-clandestine networks and activities helped to sustain the popular cultures of resistance and opposition formed in earlier epochs that had been more hospitable for labour.[24]

Militants of the POR and PCB made advances in clandestine union-organising, although their activities came at a high cost. In addition to César Lora, the first three years of the Barrientos régime claimed the lives of César's close comrade from the POR, Isaac Camacho, as well as PCB organiser Frederico Escóbar.[25] The courageous underground-organising of figures such as these staved off the annihilation of the labour-movement but was unable to reverse brutal wage- and food-subsidy cuts, or stem the tide of attack on social-security benefits.[26] Women in the mining camps played a vital role in the survival of families whose fathers were imprisoned, in hiding, exiled, or unemployed. They used 'their skills in marketing', Nash points out, 'buying vegetables and fruits in Cochabamba or the Yungas, or manufacturing goods in La Paz and selling the products for a few cents' profit in Oruro'.[27] Others, 'bought illegally mined minerals from the jucos, those who scavenged for minerals in the abandoned shafts, and sold them at less than half of the legal

---

counter-insurgency squad in Vietnam and included Bolivian officers who were trained in the School of the Americas in Panama by American officers who had served in Vietnam (Nash 1993, p. 282).

24. 'Again and again', in the words of two insightful labour-historians, 'the FSTMB demonstrated its ability to survive direct repression and preserve its cohesion in the face of a disastrous collapse in living standards (dramatically increasing malnutrition), and in spite of substantial expansion of the private sector in mining' (Roddick and van Niekerk 1989, p. 154).

25. Lora 1977, pp. 355–6; Roddick and van Niekerk 1989, p. 155.

26. Ibid.

27. Nash 1993, p. 281.

price', using their *polleras* [traditional skirts] to hide the contraband on trips between mine and market.[28]

When General Ovando took office in September 1969, he had little popular support and therefore initially reached out to labour by reducing restrictions on union-organising and activities, announcing the forthcoming nationalisation of Gulf Oil, and facilitating a political relaxation that allowed for the return from exile of some union-leaders and leftist-political activists.[29] The FSTMB perceived the new political space, with all of its limitations, as an opportunity to re-emerge from the shadows. The miners were able to re-organise and held their confederation's 14th congress at the Siglo XX-Catavi mines.[30] By 1970, the militants of the labour-movement had had time to reflect on the extraordinary sequence of events since the 1952 Revolution, and in particular the nationalist-populist outcome of the Revolution, the limitations of *co-gobierno* and *control obrero*, the introduction of the far Right and repression beginning in 1964, and the legacy of the ephemeral guerrilla-adventure of Ché Guevara in 1967.[31]

At the FSTMB congress, major strategic questions were addressed; the congress itself was perhaps the most representative of its kind to be held in Bolivian history up to that point. Pensioners had representation, as did non-contracted workers in the mining zones, and women of the mining camps.[32] The political thesis adopted by the congress was one introduced by the POR.[33] It privileged direct action of the working class over parliamentary forms of political participation; rejected the experience of *co-gobierno* as reformist; criticised the nationalisation-process as having become excessively bureaucratised and for having reduced the role of workers to obeying commands from on high; and called for an anti-imperialist, socialist revolution. The thesis was

---

28. Ibid.

29. Nash 1993, p. 284; Roddick and van Niekerk 1989, p. 156.

30. Lora 1983, p. 209; Nash 1993, p. 284.

31. Guevara's guerrilla-campaign is beyond the scope of this study. However, its legacy in the Bolivian Left's popular cultures of resistance and opposition has carried on into the twenty-first century, and thus is referred to sporadically in later chapters.

32. Nash 1993, p. 284. This was only the latest evidence of the FSTMB's historical commitment to radical and expansive social-movement unionism of the type theorised in Chapter One.

33. Dunkerley 1984, p. 169.

subsequently approved by the fourth congress of the COB later that year, making it the political platform of the working-class movement as a whole.[34]

3.1.2 The Asamblea Popular, 1971

Under the régime of Juan José Torres, the working class was mobilised and organised to a much more significant degree than it had been under Ovando. Torres recognised the strength of the Left and thus responded politically to that strength, but his régime never espoused revolutionary socialism: 'He wanted to surprise and seduce [the Left] with friendly overtures but it was obvious that he was fundamentally afraid of it'.[35] His allegiance was ultimately to the military, rather than the masses. Torres offered the COB *co-gobierno* on quite generous terms, but the COB refused based on its analysis of the *co-gobierno* experience under the MNR and how it worked to circumvent the extension of workers' control throughout the economy rather than acting as a means toward that end. The workers in 1970 preferred militant class-independence. Right-wing colonels Hugo Bánzer and Edmundo Valencia soon carried out a coup-attempt against Torres on 10 January 1971. Again, Torres was indebted to the workers for their mobilisation and central role in preventing a right-wing overthrow. The experience of thwarting Bánzer's reactionary manoeuvre, moreover, increased the consciousness of the workers and the masses as they came to recognise to a greater and greater extent their potential power.[36]

In the massive May Day celebrations of 1971, the Comando Político announced that an Asamblea Popular would convene for its first meeting on June 22. The Asamblea – held in the Bolivian Congress with the sanction of Torres, but emphatically independent of the government – was made up of 218 delegates, 123 of whom were representatives of the labour-unions, compared to a mere 23 from peasant-confederations. The rest of the delegate-seats were filled by the traditional parties of the Left as well as two new parties formed in the immediate lead-up to the Asamblea: the Partido Socialista (Socialist Party, PS)

---

34. Lora 1983, pp. 209–10. Also at the COB congress, a Comando Político (Political Command) was established which brought together the major left parties, the unions, and the COB. All of this set the stage for the extraordinary Asamblea Popular (Popular Assembly, AP) under the Torres administration in 1971.
35. Zavaleta Mercado 1972.
36. Dunkerley 1984, pp. 183–4; Lora 1983, p. 205.

which based itself on 'an independent radicalism built upon a united front and anti-imperialism, couched in Marxist language but devoid of strict strategic limitations';[37] and the Movimiento de la Izquierda Revolucionaria (Movement of the Revolutionary Left, MIR), which '[i]n its early stages...proclaimed an unambiguous Marxist line, adopted extremely radical postures, and appeared to be set to displace the authority of the PCB and the POR with a bold and youthful politics that skirted the traditional stumbling-block of syndicalism'.[38]

The AP lasted but ten days and was consumed to some extent by fractious debate over procedure. However, its significance at the time and the legacy it bequeathed to later popular movements in the country is difficult to exaggerate. There was truly a sense in which the Asamblea was understood by its participants as embodying at least some characteristics of a soviet, and therefore the basis for the conquest of power and the establishment of a workers' state. Three principal ideological positions were visible in the Asamblea. The POR(L), the faction led by Guillermo Lora, determined that the existence of the assembly in its current form represented a situation of already-existing dual power and, specifically, the working-class wing within that dual power. Its position was the immediate invocation of that incipient power through mass-revolt. The PCB was theoretically inclined to take a more cautious approach toward the character of the Asamblea, but in practice tended to support the POR(L). Other groups on the far Left, including the MIR, the ELN, and PC(ML) considered the Asamblea as merely dual power in an embryonic form. For the Asamblea to sustain itself as the prefiguration of a workers' state would require the arming of popular militias of the grassroots, independent of, but allied with, the Torres government and army.[39]

The Right viewed the developing revolutionary process with palpable anxiety, concentrating its capacities, overcoming its divisions, and prepar-

37. Dunkerley 1984, p. 189.
38. Ibid. The PS had among its more famous members Quiroga Santa Cruz, while the MIR's regiment included René Zavaleta Mercado. Outside of the Asamblea, the Ejército de Liberación Nacional (National-Liberation Army, ELN), founded by Ché Guevara, remained active underground and had sympathisers within the Asamblea, particularly in the MIR. The Maoists of the PCML, in addition to their delegation within the Asamblea, were also active outside through their Unión de Campesinos Pobres (Poor Peasants' Union, UCAPO), whose members were staging land-occupations in northern Santa Cruz (Dunkerley 1984, p. 191).
39. Zavaleta Mercado 1972, p. 68.

ing a coup of its own.[40] By 21 August 1971, the neo-fascist Hugo Bánzer had fully ousted the Torres régime from power and installed himself in the presidency.[41]

3.1.3 *The indigenous peasantry, 1964–71*

The initial phase of land-reform in 1953 was highly valued by much of the peasantry because it quenched a thirst for land and abolished seigniorial obligations to overlords on the *haciendas*. However, the process was unequal from the start and, because it was also always intended to advance agrarian capitalism, its internal dynamics inevitably led to inequalities in land-holdings over time. Peasants were granted title to land during the agrarian reform based on the land they had held previously in usufruct; the plots held in usufruct varied in size prior to the Revolution, and therefore so did the plots after the agrarian reform. A small group of peasants who acquired larger plots were therefore able to lease sections of their land and/or hire poorer peasants and workers on their land.[42] The geographical differences in the processes and consequences of the agrarian reform were also vast. The Andean highlands and valleys were the regions that experienced the largest expropriations and redistributions, and where peasants obtained small plots and engaged in agricultural activities with low levels of productivity and technological advance. By contrast, in the relatively under-populated eastern lowlands, land-grants were much larger and the explicit objective of the state was to advance agrarian capitalism through large industrial farms. So, in 1967, 59 per cent of peasant-families had less than 5 hectares, while

---

40. Lora 1983, p. 206.

41. 'In the end', Zavaleta observes, 'it was a race against time, in which those with clear reactionary ideas won out over those who had only confused revolutionary aspirations' (Zavaleta Mercado 1972, p. 75). However confused the revolutionary aspirations of the 1971 Asamblea appeared to be in hindsight, the sense of possibility of a socialist revolution flowing from that process was real and powerful. These sentiments left residual materials in the popular cultures of resistance and opposition within the indigenous movements, labour-movement, and Bolivian Left more generally that managed to survive even through the crushing neoliberal restructuring of the country's political economy between 1985 and 2000. The idea of a popular assembly took shape once again in the left-indigenous struggles of the 2000–5 cycle of insurrection in the form of the demand for a revolutionary constituent assembly.

42. Eckstein 1983, p. 108.

by the end of that decade, 'the average size of new ranches in the lowland region of Santa Cruz was around 8,000 hecatares'.[43]

These were the material conditions in which Barrientos established the Pacto Military-Campesino (PMC) in 1966. In 'immediate power terms', suggest Malloy and Gamarra, 'the two pillars of the Barrientos régime were the peasants and the military...'.[44] The PMC created an institutional structure through which the military transformed the peasant-unions that had been controlled by the MNR into para-state structures controlled by the military itself. This helped to ensure peasant-loyalty to the state. Mechanisms of control were worked out through the military organisation Acción Cívica (Civic Action) and through military-bureaucratic handling of local mayoralties and departmental prefectures (governorships).[45] Barrientos, a *cochabambino*, naturally found his relationship with the peasantry most successful in the department of Cochabamba. As Xavier Albó points out, 'Barrientos spoke Quechua, drank *chicha* beer, hopped to any corner of the countryside in his helicopter, lavished small gifts, gave subordinate official posts to loyal peasants, and, with the motto of exchanging rifles for ploughs, set up the Armed Forces' Civic Action and Community Development Programme'.[46]

Of course, even in the mid- to late-1960s the PMC was not impermeable, and began to show signs of contradiction, fissures, and subterranean tensions. These underground-tensions surfaced first in December 1968 in Achacachi when an assembly of indigenous peasants staged a hostile reception for the visiting Barrientos.[47] Barrientos, following the advice of his American eco-

---

43. Eckstein 1983, p. 109. Many of the new large landowners subsidised by the state were in fact the prerevolutionary oligarchs whose land been expropriated in the revolutionary process of the 1950s. While they acquired huge tracts of new land in the east, the poor indigenous peasants from the Andean regions who were relocated to the same lowland areas through colonisation-projects in the mid-1960s, received only small pieces of property. With this dynamic in play, the bulk of the peasantry of the highlands was temporarily appeased through their acquisition of land – however small their plots – while agrarian capitalism took off elsewhere, especially in Santa Cruz.

44. Malloy and Gamarra 1988, p. 18.

45. Rivera Cusicanqui 1983.

46. Albó 1987, p. 386. In this way, the peasantry was largely pacified and transformed into a veritable conservative battering ram, available for periodic deployment against the rebellious miners. The unstable régime of Barrientos regularly mobilised the peasants through demonstrations or blockades near major cities in order to illustrate their social power and allegiance to the military dictator (Malloy and Gamarra 1988, p. 20).

47. Rivera Cusicanqui 1983, p. 137.

nomic advisors, had attempted to implement a new tax on peasants based on the size of their plots.[48] The protests that started in Achacachi spread throughout the rest of the department of La Paz, and eventually extended into Oruro. Peasant-opposition was detectable on a smaller scale in Santa Cruz and Potosí, and Barrientos was ultimately forced to renege on the tax-increase.[49] The tax-conflict, which marked the first serious confrontation between the peasantry and the Barrientos government, opened up a window for dissident peasant-leaders associated with the political Left, sympathetic to the COB, and in favour of peasant-union independence.[50] Dissidence expressed itself in the formation of the Bloque Campesino Independiente (Independent Peasant-Bloc, BCI), which was a small but important development under Barrientos.

After Barrientos's death, the tilt in Bolivia's political culture to the left under Ovando and Torres provided further space for nascent stirrings of independent peasant-unionism, and new political orientations. The rise in anti-officialist peasant-politics was especially advanced in La Paz and Oruro. These early challengers to the PMC reached their zenith in the Sixth National Peasant-Congress of the CNTCB, held on 2 August 1971 in Potosí. *Kataristas* won the presidency of the Confederation which was taken up initially by Raimundo Tambo, and later by Genaro Flores.[51] All of this was occurring as the revolutionary Left took charge of the opportunities under Torres, and called together the Asamblea Popular.[52] Outside of the BCI, whose project was primarily concerned with the indigenous peasantry of the *altiplano*, the Maoists in the PCML made some advances in the eastern part of the country with the formation of UCAPO in Santa Cruz. They focused on organising the

---

48. This struck peasants in the western *altiplano* in a particularly egregious manner, because while their plots were often somewhat larger than in the valleys, their land was also considerably less productive given the arid and hostile climate.

49. Albó 1987, p. 388; Rivera Cusicanqui 1983, p. 137.

50. Albó 1987, p. 388.

51. Ticona A., Rojas O., and Albó 1995, p. 41.

52. Relationships between the *kataristas* and the political Left and the COB were still strained, however. The *kataristas* were suspicious of the Left and the labour-movement because of their sometimes paternalistic and condescending attitude toward the indigenous peasantry. The *kataristas* in 1971 did not make an alliance with the COB a political priority. Likewise, the revolutionary Left and the COB often viewed the *kataristas* with scepticism because of the reactionary role the peasantry had played under the MNR since 1956 and, especially, since the advent of the PMC under Barrientos. As a result, they tended to prioritise the workers' vanguard-role in revolutionary transformation, as reflected in the meagre number of seats assigned to peasant-delegates at the Asamblea (Albó 1987, pp. 393–5).

mostly Quechua and Aymara migrant highland-peasants of the postrevolutionary colonisation-projects who had relocated to the lowlands.[53]

By and large, however, the PMC retained its hold on the peasantry throughout this period. The revolutionary Left either saw the indigenous peasantry as reactionary because of its recent history in the PMC and hostile orientation toward the miners, or they wedded themselves dogmatically to the idea of a workers' revolution, narrowly-conceived, that left little role for the agency of the indigenous peasantry. This short-sightedness failed to contend with the fact that the peasantry still represented a majority of the country's population. A combination of these attitudes was on display in the Asamblea Popular in 1971, when peasants were granted so few seats as delegates.

3.2   Political economy of Hugo Bánzer's dictatorship, 1971–8

Hugo Bánzer's *coup d'état* ushered in a pro-imperialist dictatorship which sought to eliminate the power of the workers' movement and the Left, slowly suck the life out of the indigenous peasantry, and build agrarian capitalism in the eastern lowlands through state-subsidisation, foreign credit, and attractive conditions for foreign capital. Narco-capitalism fused with legal bourgeois activities in the east and supplemented already vast concentrations of wealth in the hands of a few, as overall inequality in society increased. The model of accumulation envisaged by the régime unfolded with the support of authoritarian brutality, far in excess of that under Barrientos. Bánzer's domestic social base included the agro-industrial bourgeoisie of the lowlands, the military, the mining bourgeoisie, and the technocratic layer of the state-bureaucracy that controlled the extensive state-enterprises.[54] For the opening years of the régime, he also relied on the passivity of the peasantry. These social forces were expressed in the political coalition which backed the Bánzer régime. To consolidate its power, the President created the umbrella political party, the Frente Popular Nacionalista (Nationalist-Popular Front, FPN),

---

53. UCAPO began to organise direct land-occupations of the *haciendas* in the eastern lowlands. Leftists organising in the region theorised that the 'colonisers structurally constituted the sector in which it would be easiest to establish a bridgehead: they were more linked to the market and in closer contact with the dominant system's contradictions, through the issue of prices, and the contrasts with capitalist agro-industrial development of the Oriente (the eastern territory)' (Albó 1987, p. 389).

54. Mayorga 1978, pp. 110–11.

which consisted of the armed forces, the right wing of the MNR under Víctor Paz Estenssoro, the fascistic Falange Socialista Boliviana (Bolivian Socialist Phalange, FSB), and the ConFederación de Empresarios Privados de Bolivia (Confederation of Private Entrepreneurs of Bolivia, CEPB).[55]

Between 1971 and 1974, the FPN-administration displayed 'corporatist-fascist tendencies'.[56] The immediate post-coup strategy of the régime was a full-frontal violent assault on the organised working class and the political Left. After this, however, the MNR, within the FPN-coalition, played the role of securing small slivers of régime support from sectors of the petty bourgeoisie and working class. Bánzer sought to destroy completely the AP, the COB, and the FSTMB, while building a system of loyal unions to take their place.[57] Under an ideological cloak of national security and the threat of 'communist subversion', Bánzer led a sustained campaign of press-censorship, deportations, killings, and arrests. Students, liberation-theologians, union-activists, and leftist party-militants were detained in remote camps.[58] The tone of Bánzer's economic policy was set early on. IMF-backed shocks to the popular economy occurred on 27 October 1972 and 20 January 1974, in an attempt to decrease popular consumption and free-up capital for investment.[59]

The model of capitalist accumulation under Bánzer sought to maintain an important role for the state in the market by mediating between foreign capital and the domestic private sector. Excluding the peasant-agricultural sector, the state controlled approximately 70 per cent of the economy by the late 1970s. This marked the peak of the state's involvement in the market in the

---

55. US President Richard Nixon greeted Bánzer as a godsend. In his first year in office, military assistance from Washington was double that for the period 1968 to 1970. The Brazilian régime next door also provided backing (Dunkerley 1984, p. 205).

56. Mayorga 1978, p. 111.

57. Mayorga 1978, pp. 111–12. In 1974, Bánzer restructured the dictatorship into a 'New Order' by expelling the MNR from government; the social base was pared down to the CEPB (the mining and agrarian bourgeoisies) and the military (Mayorga 1978, p. 114), undergirded, of course, by the US-state, international financial institutions (IFIs), and Brazilian backing.

58. Malloy and Gamarra 1988, pp. 74–5. Between October 1971 and December 1977 (which excludes the earlier period of intense repression), human-rights organisations documented a minimum of 200 dead, 14,750 people imprisoned, and 19,140 exiled (on top of the roughly 780,000 Bolivians already living out-of-country for economic reasons). While these levels of repression did not match the horrors of state-terrorism in the Argentine and Chilean dictatorships later in the decade, it was nonetheless scarring in a country of only six million inhabitants (Dunkerley 1984, p. 208).

59. Malloy and Gamarra 1988, p. 86.

postrevolutionary period.[60] At the same time, the state played a vital role in subsidising and enriching the private entrepreneurs of the eastern lowlands whose economic and political power continued to surge. In spite of Bánzer's best efforts, Bolivia was unable to attract significant levels of foreign direct investment (FDI) in the 1970s, and therefore financed state-subsidisation of the eastern economy through burgeoning government-deficits and ever more astronomical levels of foreign debt.[61] When Bánzer was forced out of office in 1978, the relatively tiny populace of Bolivia owed $2.5 billion in debt.[62] Whatever the obvious long-term structural weaknesses of the economy in the 1970s, a commodities-boom on the world-market nonetheless provided a veneer of fairly rapid development, modernisation and success. Bolivia registered annual growth rates of 5 per cent in the mid-1970s. Agro-industry (with billions of dollars in capital siphoned through the state at concessionary interests rates to large capitalists), finance, commerce, hydrocarbons (natural-gas and oil), construction, and later, cocaine, were all sectors that experienced growth in this period. In terms of agriculture, cotton, sugarcane, soybeans and cattle were the four principal growth-sectors.[63] Favourable international commodity-prices under Bánzer's rule also favoured tin, although not as dramatically as other sectors. Between 1972 and 1978, the price of a pound of tin increased from $1.69 to $5.72, and the metal continued to account for 70 per cent of Bolivia's legal foreign-currency earnings.[64]

Processes of more rapid bourgeois class-formation in mining as well as inroads of the private sector into the industry were notable features of this period. Private entrepreneurs organised in the Asociación de Mineros Medianos (Association of Medium-Miners, ANMM) became increasingly sophisticated in their use of technology and mechanisation and managed to capture increasing shares of production in tin, antinomy, wolfram and zinc.[65] In mining, industry, finance, and construction, oligopolistic patterns emerged in which a few small firms dominated. These trends of concentration were accelerated

---

60. Malloy and Gamarra 1988, p. 100.
61. Eckstein and Hagopian 1983, pp. 73, 74, 79.
62. Malloy and Gamarra 1988, p. 101.
63. Gill 1987b, p. 50.
64. Dunkerley 1984, p. 225.
65. Eckstein and Hagopian 1983, p. 82. These Bolivian firms were almost invariably linked to American corporations such as US Steel, W.R. Grace, and IMPC (Dunkerley 1984, p. 226).

by the role of international financiers loaning most extensively and cheaply to the largest firms in the market.[66] While concentration in these capitalist sectors increased at the top of the social hierarchy, the share of the national income of the poorest 40 per cent of the population continued to erode.[67] Many of the contradictions of the development-model began to rise to the surface by 1978. That year, the economy grew at a rate of only 2.8 per cent, followed by 2.8 and 1.2 per cent in 1979 and 1980, respectively.[68]

3.2.1 *Santa Cruz and the new bourgeoisie*

'In search of profit and driven to compete', argues Neil Smith, 'capital concentrates and centralises not just in the pockets of some over the pockets of others but in the places of some over the places of others'.[69] In the Bolivian context, we have already seen the regional dimensions of the shift in economic dynamism from Sucre to La Paz at the outset of the twentieth century as the silver-economy was eclipsed by tin. In the 1970s, a pattern of concentrated growth in Santa Cruz, which had already begun in the 1960s, accelerated under the Bánzer régime.[70] Six of the ministers in Bánzer's first cabinet were from Santa Cruz. The loyalty of the Santa Cruz bourgeoisie provided a backbone to Bánzer's rule and a counterbalance to his early and open alienation of the labour-movement and steadily mounting hostility to the indigenous peasantry in the Andean highlands and valleys.[71] More than simply an economic strategy, state-largesse helped lubricate the lines

---

66. Eckstein and Hagopian 1983, pp. 82–4.
67. Eckstein and Hagopian 1983, p. 71.
68. Dunkerley 1984, p. 227.
69. Smith 2006, p. 189.
70. Endowed with abundant arable land and natural gas and oil (among other natural resources), and uniquely characterised by weak traditions of peasant- and worker-radicalism, Santa Cruz was a natural selection for the geographical fulcrum of Bánzer's state-led capitalist-developmental project. A new regional bourgeoisie was consolidated and the core basis of Bolivia's civilian and military right-wing political forces over the next several decades was secured.
71. International creditors and Bánzer alike shared a strategic inclination toward building an export-sector in response to the commodity-boom of the early 1970s. Large-scale commercial agriculture was promoted through the distribution of massive concessionary credit and large grants of frontier-land to capitalist entrepreneurs (Gill 1987, pp. 50–1).

of political patronage tying the loyalty of big-business interests in the east to Bánzer's government.[72]

The new regional bourgeoisie was constituted by a blend of traditional *cruceño*-landowners and, 'ex-hacendados and mine owners from the highlands and valleys, military officers, administrators, professionals, and a substantial number of foreigners'.[73] While initially making their fortunes in the commercial agricultural boom of the early 1970s, they subsequently reinvested their capital in urban businesses. Some also established new banks in the lowlands, made fortunes in real estate, and secured manufacturing licences from foreign multinational corporations (MNCs) to make their products – cosmetics, pharmaceuticals, and some electronic equipment – locally which they had previously imported.[74]

However, a combination of the fluctuating international price of cotton, increased cost of new machinery, inefficiencies in the credit-system, labour-shortages, and marketing problems made the Bolivian cotton-industry uncompetitive on the world-stage and ended the cotton-boom by 1974.[75] A recovery in the price of sugar partially compensated for the cotton-trend in the mid-1970s, but, in 1976 and 1977, sugar-prices plummeted internationally. In response to the dual crisis in cotton- and sugarcane-production, some of the agro-bourgeoisie turned to soybeans or cattle-ranching as alternatives. Many others moved to cocaine, which was experiencing a ferocious spike in value on the world-market by the mid-1970s.[76] Demand was soaring in Europe and North America and Santa Cruz was uniquely positioned to benefit. The region was connected by highway to the main coca-growing region in the country – the Chapare, in the department of Cochabamba –, hosted waterways with connections to the Beni lowlands and Brazil, and contained, 'vast tracts of remote, frontier land [which] were ideally suited for the creation of clandestine landing strips'.[77] Most important, however, was the fact

---

72. Gill 1987b, pp. 52–3.
73. Gill 1987b, p. 175.
74. Eckstein and Hagopian 1983, p. 82. Still others took advantage of the proximity of railroads to Argentina and Brazil to stake out control over contraband-trade in everything from automobiles to cigarettes (Gill 1987, p. 175). This buoyant economic power translated increasingly into local, regional, and national political power.
75. Gill 1987b, pp. 180–1.
76. Gill 1987b, pp. 182–3.
77. Gill 1987b, p. 183.

that the 'lowland bourgeoisie was one of the few groups with the capital and the connections to mount an international drug smuggling operation'.[78] Huge cocaine-profits in the late 1970s were deposited in untraceable offshore bank-accounts or laundered through legitimate businesses in Bolivia, substantially blurring the line between legal and illegal capitalist enterprises in the process. 'By the end of the decade', writes anthropologist Lesley Gill, 'returns from cocaine sales were estimated to be nearly double the annual value of all Bolivian exports, which did not exceed US\$850 million'.[79] Conspicuous consumption of imported luxury-items made the longstanding contrast between Bolivia's wealth and poverty even more starkly grotesque.

3.2.2 The working class, 1971–8

The Bánzer régime sought to wipe the labour-movement and other popular organisations off the map. This was a consequence in part of the general depth of fear among the propertied classes after what had occurred during the preceding administrations of Alfredo Ovando and Juan José Torres – when working-class struggle had reached new heights, particularly in the form of the Asamblea Popular. But the rhetorical stance of the régime and its quick forays into violent repression helped to conceal only momentarily a rather more complex underlying balance of social forces. Most important, the Banzer régime was unable to eliminate or replace the militant miners' unions and their rank-and-file traditions of resistance and opposition. Even when the workers' movement was more or less debilitated, it managed to survive in semi-clandestinity with sufficient strength to lead punctuated, powerful assaults on the dictatorship in defence of workers' rights and democracy for society as a whole. The Bolivian state was incapable of the brute liquidation of popular organisations, despite its open desire to follow the lead of Pinochet in Chile after that country's 1973 coup. If full-blown fascism was prevented, these were nonetheless dark years for workers. According to COB records, the purchasing power of wages and salaries declined by 36.3 per cent between

---

78. While direct evidence tying Bánzer's régime to narcotrafficking is unavailable, it is 'extremely improbable that the military was ignorant of the cocaine traffic', and numerous *cruceño* agro-capitalists and military personnel were subsequently arrested for their extensive involvement in the industry after Bánzer's administration came to its inglorious finish (Gill 1987, p. 184).

79. Gill 1987b, p. 187.

1971 and 1978. Meanwhile, the workers' share of national income declined from 47 to 31 per cent over the same period.[80]

Lacking sufficient arms, the workers' movement in the mining zones avoided immediate frontal confrontations with the amassed troops. Instead, militants retreated into the sinews of clandestine organising within the rank and file through *comités de base* [grassroots-committees], and prepared for future opportunities.[81] Such clandestine and semi-clandestine preparation, operating through an intricate infrastructure of class-struggle, allowed workers' to respond to the first IMF adjustment-package in October 1972 with resistance strong enough to ensure compensatory payment to workers of a 'patriotic bonus' at Christmas. The response to the second economic package in 1974 was more powerful. Spurred forward by a 36-hour strike by Cochabamba workers in the Canadian-owned Manaco shoe-factory, popular resistance soon spilled over into a national general strike including miners and bank-employees, as well as large peasant-mobilisations in Cochabamba.[82] The fact that the Banzer government now faced resistance from both the labour-movement and, increasingly, the indigenous peasantry, weakened its position considerably.[83]

Banzer's expulsion of the MNR from the ruling bloc in November 1974 was an attempt to shore up fascist resolve inside the state-apparatus and respond to the weakening of régime-capacity to rule over society. Radically authoritarian measures were decreed and more union-leaders were forced into exile.[84] But the effectiveness of the resistance of the *comités de base* is reflected in the fact that the COMIBOL was still forced to negotiate with the authentic union-representatives rather than state-appointed hacks. Moreover, working-class militancy actually increased after the 1974 internal re-organisation of the military administration. The FSTMB, for example, managed to stage its Sixteenth

---

80. Roddick and van Niekerk 1989, p. 158.

81. The dictatorship managed to make political work in left parties virtually impossible, but they failed dramatically in their attempt to replace the democratic union-movement with an official one appointed by the state (García Linera, Chávez Léon, and Costas Monje 2005, p. 59; Lora 1983, pp. 210–11). In spite of the formal illegality of the historic union-federations and confederations, the FSTMB managed to hold its Fifteenth Congress in which its exiled leaders were re-elected and loyalty to the COB declared openly (Roddick and van Niekerk 1989, p. 158).

82. Iriarte 1983; Roddick and van Niekerk 1989.

83. Roddick and van Niekerk 1989, pp. 158–9.

84. Lora 1983, p. 212.

Congress in May 1976. The entire popular movement surged forward after the news of the assassination of ex-president Torres on the streets of Buenos Aires on 1 June 1976. Protests swelled in the streets of La Paz and other major urban centres.

Moving into this window of opportunity, a strike of miners and factory-workers was declared later in June. However, in the event, the strike suffered from poor co-ordination and state-repression, and did not extend throughout all the COMIBOL-mines, never mind into other significant sectors of the economy.[85] The military had already re-occupied the mining camps, arrested the executive of the FSTMB, and exiled an additional 52 union-leaders in Chile in the aftermath of the pro-Torres demonstrations in the cities. When the strike was initiated, Banzer upped the ante, sealing electricity, food, and water from the mining camps where strikes continued. After enduring a month of these trying circumstances through the smuggling of goods under the cover of night, the strike was ended and the popular movement reached its nadir during the Banzer period. The pace and depth of repression reduced the room for manoeuvre further and depressed morale within the workers' movement.

And yet, the economic woes of the late 1970s quickly exposed the régime to new vulnerabilities as increasingly large sections of society came to be dissatisfied with the status quo. By the second half of 1977, the labour-movement was once again concentrating its forces and leading popular dissent. Between 28 December 1977 and January 1978, a small hunger-strike led by four wives of prominent FSTMB-leaders grew exponentially into a hunger-strike of more than 1,000 with thousands more supporting the action from different sectors of the society, including the Catholic Church. Despite its inauspicious beginnings, the hunger-strike took on a life of its own and proved critical, first, to restoring formal trade-union rights while Bánzer remained in power and, more profoundly, to compelling the end to Bánzer's criminal control of the state.[86]

---

85. Lora 1983, p. 213.
86. de Chungara 1978; Roddick and van Niekerk 1989, p. 160.

3.2.3 *The indigenous peasantry, 1971–8*

The most important development in indigenous struggle in twentieth-century Bolivian history was the ideological and political consolidation of *katarismo* in the rural *altiplano* and the city of La Paz during the Bánzer period. The phases of *active* and *subordinate* peasant-subordination to the state under the MNR, followed by the construction of the PMC under Barrientos, seemed to confirm the widespread belief that, once a peasantry's thirst for land has been quenched, it transmogrifies into a fundamentally conservative political force. However, the inadequacies and contradictions of the agrarian reform of 1953 inside an overarching model of state-led capitalist development became pronounced over time, creating specific contradictions and grievances in the countryside. The small plots of land that most peasants acquired in 1953 were subject to incessant subdivision over the next decades as the population grew. Intensification of production, ecological degradation, and disruptive alterations in the rotation-cycles of crops were also consequences of peasants' growing exposure to market-imperatives. Many peasants were therefore proletarianised in the decades following the 1952 Revolution. They were separated from their land and migrated to the cities with only their labour to sell.[87] At the same time, the officialist peasant-union bureaucracy grew more distant from the grassroots of indigenous communities, and was openly and visibly linked to corruption-riddled, patron-client networks. When Bánzer came to power, moreover, even the personalist charisma of Barrientos disappeared, leaving the blunt militarisation of peasant-state relations under the PMC more nakedly visible.

Precursors to the explosion of *katarismo* under Bánzer's administration reach back to the 1960s. Some members of a younger generation of Aymara peasants from La Paz were able to attend secondary school and university because of the educational opportunities opened up in the aftermath of the Revolution, and the challenge that the MNR's official ideology of *mestizaje* represented to the old patterns of racism.[88] Men such as Raimundo Tambo, from the commu-

---

87. Rivera Cusicanqui 1983, p. 134.

88. Clearly, the ideology of *mestizaje* introduced new forms of racial domination, predicated as it was on the assimilation of indigenous people into the dominant *mestizo*-culture, with the attendant abandonment of their own cultures and languages. It is nonetheless true that the postrevolutionary period challenged some of the most grotesque features of oligarchical racism established in the early 1900s.

nity of Ayo Ayo, and Genaro Flores, from Antipampa, migrated to La Paz and attended Villarroel secondary school where they were introduced to the ideas of the little-known Fausto Reinaga, a self-published author of books arguing for radical *indiunismo* in Bolivia and founder of the Partido Indio (Indian Party, PI).[89] At the high school, young *kataristas* formed the Movimiento 15 de Noviembre (Fifteenth of November Movement, M–15) whose name commemorated the date of the drawing and quartering of Tupaj Katari. Later, when many of these youth went on to university in La Paz and were joined by other like-minded activists, they formed the Movimiento Universitario Julián Apaza (Julián Apaza University-Movement, MUJA).[90] These urban foundations were the initial steps toward a recomposition of independent infrastructures of indigenous-peasant struggle in the countryside.

In 1969, Aymara residents of La Paz also formed the Centro de Promoción y Coordinación Campesina MINK'A (Centre for Peasant-Promotion and Coordination, MINK'A) which sought to educate and organise Aymara peasants in the *altiplano* on themes of *katarismo* and build effective networks linking rural and urban indigenous communities. Shortly after, in August 1971, Aymara peasants and residents of La Paz founded the Centro Campesino Tupaj Katari (Tupaj Katari Peasant Centre, CCTK) whose mandate was to produce and disseminate radio-programmes in the Aymara and Quechua languages, publish a journal, and find a market for peasant-produce in the cities.[91] In the late 1960s and early 1970s, therefore, there emerged the initial infrastructure of a *katarista* movement which was developing a critique of internally colonial race-relations since 1825, exposing the cultural, political and socioeconomic limits of the 1952 Revolution, and drawing inspiration from anticolonial struggles dating back to the eighteenth century.[92]

---

89. Reinaga 1970; Albó 1987, p. 391. Today, many of the kiosks in La Paz sell cheap copies of Reinaga and he is alluded to favourably, if often loosely and vaguely, in the political speeches of innumerable political currents on the Left and in indigenous movements. The Partido Indio never had a significant indigenous base and never became a significant party, despite the rising fortunes of Reinaga's personal political status with time.

90. Julián Apaza was the birth name of anticolonial hero Tupaj Katari.

91. Rivera Cusicanqui 1983, p. 140.

92. There were two major competing currents within early *katarismo*. One emphasised the necessity of focusing exclusively on indigenous rights and fighting racism and downplayed the interrelationship between class and ethnicity. Followers of this multifaceted sector of *katarismo* are often referred to as *indianistas* (Yashar 2005, p. 169). More important, however, were those groups who sought alliances with other social

It is essential to emphasise that *katarismo* was a phenomenon that quintessentially bridged the rural and urban worlds, linking together urban-Aymara teachers and students in the capital with the grassroots of the peasant-movement organised through *ayllus* (traditional communitarian structures), primarily in the rural provinces of the department of La Paz, but also extending into parts of Oruro. The coalescence of improved communications infrastructure and more educational opportunities meant that previously illiterate and monolingual populations in the *altiplano* were increasingly exposed to quite radically new ways of life through the proliferation of rural public schools and radio stations.[93] Young Aymara migrants to the city experienced in their daily lives the persistent racism of the dominant Bolivian culture, which called into question the integrity of the integrationist programme of the postrevolutionary MNR-project. In the face of precarious and exploitative work for the urban indigenous poor, and racist hostility from the white-*mestizo* upper and middle classes, the revolutionary message of equality under *mestizaje* often seemed little more than cliché and platitude.[94]

Whatever momentum the *kataristas* enjoyed in 1971, all immediate progress was cut short by the Bánzer coup. While some of the overtly 'cultural' initiatives of the *katarista* movement such as radio-shows and festival-activities were able to continue, open political contestation of the official peasant-union movement became immensely difficult. However, the Bánzer régime soon caused the most momentous break in peasant-state relations since the revo-

---

forces such as leftist-political parties and the COB. They strengthened and refined an analysis and praxis which linked struggles against indigenous oppression with militant class-action and socialist objectives. The hegemony of the latter groups within *katarismo* is revealed by the fact that they were known broadly as *kataristas*. In historical perspective, the roots of these newly flourishing debates are traceable to the popular cultures of resistance and opposition formed during labour-peasant alliances in the late 1920s and late 1940s.

93. Canessa 2000, p. 122.

94. Rivera Cusicanqui 1983, p. 155. Figures such as Flores and Tambo, who had been politicised in the city, moved back to their communities and began to rise through the ranks of the official union-networks at the local and departmental levels (Ticona et al. 1995, pp. 40–1). At the same time, in Oruro, Macabeo Chila became the most important dissident peasant-leader in that department, which is also Aymara and part of the *altiplano*; representing a political current initially outside of *katarismo*, Chila and other peasant associates had blended left-wing critique of the socio-economic order, drawn from the labour-movement and revolutionary parties, with historical and cultural pride in Aymara language and tradition, influenced by the encouragement of the Oblatos fathers, Quebecois priests who apparently taught about and practised sensitivity to the region's cultural and linguistic particularities (Albó 1987).

lution in 1952. In response to the January 1974 economic-adjustment pack-age, 20,000 peasants in Cochabamba joined the striking factory-workers of Manaco and blocked the roads connecting Cochabamba with Santa Cruz, the Chapare, Oruro, and Sucre. At the same time, in an act of solidarity, indig-enous peasants in the Aroma province of La Paz paralysed traffic between La Paz and Oruro.[95] On 29 January, the peasants demanded that the presi-dent meet the protesters in face-to-face negotiations and that Colonel Alberto Natusch Busch, Minister of Peasant and Agricultural Affairs, be replaced with a peasant-representative. That evening, rather than a negotiating team, the government sent troops to repress the peasants, leading to the death or 'dis-appearance' of at least 80 according to La Comisión de Justicia y Paz (Peace and Justice Commission, CJP). The killings came to be known as the Masacre del Valle (Massacre of the Valley). The massacre was the most crucial event in the discrediting of the PMC and contributed to massive support for indepen-dent peasant-unionism.[96]

At first glance, it appears paradoxical that the renewed drive for an autono-mous peasant-union movement after 1974 came from the *kataristas* in the *alti-plano* rather than from the Cochabamba Valley, where the massacre occurred. However, the different regional trajectories of the peasant-movement at that time had to do with the deep historical legacies of each area. In Cochabamba, the integrity of free indigenous communities had been deeply compromised by capitalist development, extensive proletarianisation of the peasant-pop-ulation, and more profound processes of cultural *mestizaje*. In this historical context, peasant-subordination to the MNR, and, subsequently, to the PMC, was always more advanced and difficult to overcome than in the *altiplano*.

By contrast, in many of the rural areas of the departments of La Paz and Oruro, where indigenous peasants tended to be less integrated into the mar-ket and more deeply engaged in subsistence-farming, the PMC was perceived as an imposition on previously established *ayllu*-state relations.[97] The relative historical distance from the PMC, in conjunction with the presence of pre-existing *katarista* infrastructures from the 1969–71 period and persistence of *ayllu* community-networks, provided a basis from which to launch a more

---

95. Rivera Cusicanqui 2003 [1984], p. 156.
96. Rivera Cusicanqui 2003 [1984], p. 158.
97. Yashar 2005, p. 171.

decisive critique of peasant-subordination to the state, even in the hostile political climate of Bánzer's dictatorship. Bánzer eventually responded to the growing peasant-unrest by clamping down on the electoral processes within the CNTCB, and engaging in open coercion, such as when paramilitaries were unleashed on *katarista* supporters in the province of Aroma in 1976. While the régime was temporarily able to prevent the ascension of *kataristas* in the official ranks of the indigenous-peasant movement nonetheless continued to make their presence felt at the peasant-union congresses at all levels.[98]

By the late 1970s, when the economy began to crash and the labour-movement was picking up steam, the *kataristas* expanded their links with the working class and began to make building an alliance with the COB a much clearer priority. In 1976, *katarista* militants were present in multiple protest-events at the universities and in workers' congresses as representatives of the peasantry. They supported the miners in their 1976 strike, supplying food and supplies for their comrades who had been cut off from basic necessities by the military occupation of the mining zones. In the escalation of repression that followed, *kataristas* were among the many dissidents incarcerated or sent into exile.[99] Again, the collapse of the PMC allowed the slow rearticulation – in a very new historical period – of indigenous-peasant/proletarian alliances that characterised the Chayanta uprising in 1927, and the indigenous-peasant/labour insurrections of 1946 and 1947 during the authoritarian *sexenio* period.

The time in jail and exile actually served as an incubation-period for political development and co-operation between the *kataristas* and the labour-movement in their joint fight against the dictatorship. In the prisons and expatriate networks in neighbouring countries, *katarista* peasant-leaders met with miners, unionists, leftist party-militants, and student-radicals, each having an influence on the other, as projects of indigenous liberation bled into projects predicated on class-struggle and socialist emancipation.[100] Such underground-camaraderie improved relations between the emergent independent indigenous-peasant movement and the workers' struggle organised through its key-organisation, the COB.[101]

---

98. Rivera Cusicanqui 1983, p. 148.
99. Rivera Cusicanqui 1983, p. 149.
100. Rivera Cusicanqui 1983, p. 150.
101. By the second half of 1977, when the workers' struggle has picked up its pace once again, exiles began to return, rejuvenating the COB's activities and injecting a

At the Fifth Congress of the COB in May 1979, the *kataristas* were invited to attend. Out of that meeting, it was decided that a congress of peasant-unity would be held to determine the basis of new peasant-union federation affiliated with the COB. Invitees included the CNTCB-Túpaj Katari (CNTCB-TK), the Julián Apaza Confederation and the Independent Peasant-Confederation. The peasant-congress agreed to peasant-unity and created the Confederación Sindical Única de Trabajadores Campesinos de Bolivia (Bolivian Peasant Trade-Union Confederation, CSUTCB), and Genaro Flores was elected as the new body's first general secretary.[102] The CSUTCB has from that date forward been the unparalleled representative institution of the peasantry, and has affiliated to the COB. The creation of the CSUTCB marked a high-water mark for the *katarista* movement and signalled the definitive end of the PMC.

3.3 The struggle for democracy, 1978–82

Cleavages in labour-state and peasant-state relations expanded into veritable chasms by the late 1970s. In conjunction with the deteriorating economic performance of the Bánzer administration in the midst of falling commodity-prices, the institutional arrangements of authoritarian control that had been established in the wake of the coup of 1964, and re-established through the coup of 1971, began to fall apart. A new period opened, characterised by the struggle for democracy.

The transition-years were phenomenally unstable, witnessing three elections, five presidents, and a series of coups, counter-coups, and failed coups between 1978 and 1980. When Hugo Bánzer attempted to open up a process

---

greater plurality of revolutionary perspectives into the organisation. This new openness, in addition to the impressive independent actions of the *kataristas* and their penetrating contributions to debates within the COB, forced the workers' organisation by the end of the 1970s to open its eyes to the authenticity of the *katarista* movement as the organic representative of the most dynamic of various political forces within the peasantry (Albó 1987, p. 403). The plausibility of incorporating the *kataristas* as peasant representatives within the COB was dramatically increased by the fortuitous decision of the PCML to align with the MNR of Paz Estenssoro in the 1979 elections. In so doing, the PCML lost all credibility within the labour-movement and the COB in particular. The PCML was hitherto the main proponent of excluding all peasant-groups from the COB except the Bloque Campesino Independiente and the Federacion de Colonizadores in which it enjoyed preponderant influence. When the party abandoned the COB, the most hostile opposition to *katarista* inclusion therefore disappeared.

102. Albó 1987, p. 403.

of controlled electoral transition in November 1977, he underestimated the strength of his civilian and military opponents. In addition to opposition from human-rights groups, the Catholic Church, the *kataristas* and the labour-movement by 1977, different factions within the military were also conspiring to overthrow the president.[103] Bánzer wagered that a limited democratic opening on his terms would 'deprive these dissidents of the excuse to conspire' and facilitate his ongoing control of the country under the pretence of democracy.[104] The situation quickly escaped his command. The hunger-strike initiated by miners' wives gathered tremendous momentum between December 1977 and January 1978. By the end of January, the strikers and their supporters had achieved unrestricted amnesty for those imprisoned and exiled and the legal recognition of the independent labour-movement. It was immediately evident that the controlled transition envisioned by Bánzer was transforming into a fundamental challenge to authoritarianism in the country. In the July 1978 elections, Bánzer appointed General Pereda Asbún as his presidential nominee – Bánzer planned to control the subsequent government from behind the scenes. Their ticket was registered under the party-name Unión Nacionalista del Pueblo (Nationalist Union of the People, UNP). The elections were tainted by unmitigated fraud resulting in Pereda's precise victory of 50 per cent of votes cast, the smallest number required to bypass any congressional debate as to who becomes president.[105] Despite the fraud, UDP-leader Siles Zuazo still received 24.6 per cent of the popular vote, registering his biggest gains in La Paz, the mining zones, and the rural Aymara and Quechua population of the *altiplano*.[106] Popular uproar denouncing fraud initially led Pereda to promise new elections within six months, but rivalries in the military outpaced the elections.

Pereda's régime was quickly disbanded after a successful coup orchestrated by General David Padilla on November 24, 1978. Padilla then announced another round of elections for July 1979. In the 1979 elections, there were three main contenders: Siles Zuazo led the UDP – which consisted of an alliance between the Movimiento Nacionalista Revolucionario de Izquierda (Left Revolutionary Nationalist Movement, MNRI), the MIR and the PCB;

---

103. Malloy and Gamarra 1987, pp. 93–119.
104. Whitehead 1986, p. 58.
105. Whitehead 1986, p. 59.
106. Whitehead 1986, p. 60.

Paz Estenssoro led a coalition of right-wing factions of the MNR called the Movimiento Nacionalista Revolucionario Histórico (Historical Revolutionary-Nationalist Movement, MNRH); and Bánzer led the new right-wing party, Acción Democrática Nacional (National-Democratic Action, ADN). The 1979 elections were less fraudulent than those of 1978, and Siles Zuazo garnered 35.9 per cent of the popular vote. It was also significant that Quiroga Santa Cruz, running to the left of Siles as leader of the PS–1, won over 100,000 votes as a consequence of his eloquent criticisms of the Bánzer dictatorship.[107] The results of the 1979 elections were nevertheless indecisive, and resulted in an agreement in congress to allow the long-standing MNR-figure, Wálter Guevara, to act as interim president for one year.[108] With no discernible mandate, Guevara's weak administration was predictably faced with a coup challenge in a matter of months. In November 1979, Colonel Alberto Natusch Busch launched a coup which lasted sixteen days and left over 200 dead.[109]

What was special about the Natusch coup was that it motivated the most impressive popular mobilisations based on a worker-peasant alliance since the 1952–3 period. When Natusch made it clear that he was seeking the total destruction of the transitional process to electoral democracy in Bolivia, the COB immediately responded by calling for a general strike in defence of representative democracy.[110] The COB once again openly assumed its position as the 'soul of civil society', becoming the undeniable epicentre through which all popular opposition to the dictatorship was channelled.[111] The primarily Aymara indigenous peasantry of the *altiplano* responded *en masse* to the COB's call for a general strike, and employed a broad array of mobilisational techniques drawn from the classical repertoire of Andean indigenous insurgency. They blocked roads, occupied land, and took over the territory surrounding the vulnerable valley city of La Paz.[112] The *kataristas'* principal leader, Genaro Flores, assumed the role of second-in-command within the COB. The PMC was definitively ruptured during the November uprisings against the Natusch Busch coup. For Zavaleta Mercado, it was a late

---

107. Zavaleta Mercado 1983b, pp. 54–6.
108. Malloy and Gamarra 1987, p. 111.
109. Whitehead 1986, pp. 64–5.
110. Zavaleta Mercado 1983a, pp. 236–7.
111. Zavaleta Mercado 1983b, p. 21.
112. Zavaleta Mercado 1983a, p. 237.

twentieth-century conjoining of the 1952 Revolution, which was led by workers, and the 1781 siege of La Paz, which was led by Aymara peasants under the command of Túpaj Katari.[113]

In the 1980 elections, the popular sentiments expressed in extra-parliamentary form through the COB in November 1979, were essentially translated into electoral support for the UDP. Siles won 39 per cent compared to Paz Estenssoro's 20, and Bánzer's 17. The rise of the UDP, the recent memory of the 1979 mass-mobilisations of workers and peasants, and a fear of the Left's possible legal recriminations against military leaders for their part in past abuses of human rights, proved too much to bear for sections of the armed forces. In addition to these defensive impulses, coupists in the military were positively motivated by the possibilities of employing control of the state-apparatus to corral obscene personal profits from the cocaine-trade.[114] Luis García Meza Tejada carried out a coup on 17 July 1980 with the explicit intention of quashing any and all advances toward democratisation that had been achieved up to that date. García Meza, and the sections of the military from which he enjoyed support, understood that in order to crush a highly mobilised civil society the brutality they unleashed would have to be exponentially more severe than that utilised by the military in its unsuccessful 1979 bid at reinstating dictatorship under Natusch Busch.[115] A number of domestic and international challenges to García Meza's rule emerged almost immediately, and he was only able to stay in power for a little over a year.[116] At home, the

---

113. Zavaleta Mercado 1983b, p. 22. The tragedy of the culmination of this situation in November 1979 was that the COB displayed at one and the same time its historic capacity to bring together the popular classes in revolt *and* its historic impotence in carrying through a revolutionary transition and providing an alternative socialist project to the revolutionary nationalism of the MNR (Zavaleta Mercado 1983a, p. 239). In the event, the Natusch Busch coup was circumvented, but the end result was the rise to power of MNR-stalwart, and Bolivia's first female president, Lydia Gueiler (Malloy and Gamarra 1987, p. 111). In her short period in office, Gueiler attempted to introduce an economic-adjustment plan backed by the IMF, but this was strongly rejected by the COB and other popular organisations. New elections were scheduled for June 1980 (Whitehead 1986, p. 65).

114. Gill 1987b, p. 196.

115. Whitehead 1986, p. 67.

116. Despite his ongoing support for authoritarian régimes in places such as South Korea, the Philippines, Indonesia, Nicaragua, and El Salvador (Cumings 1997, p. 375; Chomsky 1979, pp. 18–20; Chomsky 1982, p. 291; Chomsky 1987, pp. 33–4), American President Jimmy Carter was putting pressure on some South-American dictatorships to limit their most flagrant human-rights abuses and perform at least small complacent steps towards moderate liberalisation (Dunkerley 1984, p. 237). In the Bolivian case,

Bolivian régime was little more than a narco-state with no long-term development-project other than the unyielding display of state-terror against the civilian population. The domestic economy, made a rapid transition from bad to worse. García Meza's pariah-status made foreign credit increasingly unavailable, traditional exports were suffering serious decline, the foreign debt accrued by Bánzer was of monumental proportions and due to be repaid, and state-owned enterprises were ailing after years of neglect.[117]

Given this scenario, the military entered a period of even more intense factionalism with numerous coup-attempts during García Meza's short term in power. Capitalist entrepreneurs outside the narco-network turned against the dictatorship, and the popular movement led by the COB reignited its mobilisations against the régime. García Meza was eventually forced to hand over power to a temporary junta of commanders in August 1981.[118] The crisis of authoritarianism nonetheless endured through a new series of extremely weak and ephemeral military presidents. It was increasingly evident, though, that the die had been cast.

In 1982, it was obvious a transition to civilian rule would occur, but there was some dispute as to whether or not there would be new elections – in which the UDP would have done well – or whether the Congress elected in the 1980 elections would be simply reinstated, and civilian rule instituted immediately. The latter course turned out to be the one taken, and Siles Zuazo assumed the presidency on 10 October 1982 as leader of the UDP. The UDP-government consisted of a loose coalition between the MNRI, the PCB, and the MIR. In economic terms, the first democratic government to come to power after decades of authoritarian rule found itself in the most inauspicious of circumstances. Latin America was falling headfirst into its lost decade. Mexico's moratorium

---

the Carter administration had played up the 1980 elections and therefore was deeply embarrassed by the García Meza coup. Indeed, there were only sixteen states that recognised the new government, including apartheid South Africa, Israel, and a series of Latin-American dictatorships (Gill 1987, p. 196). The neo-fascist régime in Argentina provided financial and technical assistance to García Meza, apparently including more than two hundred advisers (Dunkerley 1984, p. 299).

117. Despite the fact that the cocaine-trade provided more income than the rest of Bolivia's exports combined, it was insufficient to overcome the overall crisis in the economy. Moreover a significant share of narco-dollars tended to be siphoned into the foreign bank-accounts of private drug-lords rather than going to the state or being invested into productive activities in the national economy (Gill 1987, p. 197).

118. Gill 1987b, pp. 197–9.

on debt-payments had shutdown credit-lines to the region just as international commodity-prices for Bolivia's primary mineral exports were in serious decline.[119] Foreign investment was similarly diminishing at the same time as financial burdens rooted in international debt were squeezing countries throughout Latin America.[120] Bolivia did not buck the regional trend of newly democratic governments emerging from dictatorships saddled with massive and unmanageable debts.[121] The situation was intensified by a climatic crisis in the *altiplano* (high plateau) causing serious droughts, the falling price of tin on the international market, and the inability of the state to collect sufficient revenue to meet even partially the pent up demands for better wages and jobs coming from the working class.[122] Fiscal accounts were therefore in serious deficit, while debt-servicing requirements constrained the state's capacity to invest capital in productive investments. On a per capita basis, the external debt, accrued mainly under Bánzer's administration (1971–8), was worse even than Brazil's or Mexico's.[123]

The UDP was a quintessentially populist government which attempted to maintain a balance between the incompatible demands and interests of the popular classes, and domestic capital and imperialism, the latter channelled most directly through the IMF in this instance. The UDP followed a deeply inconsistent economic path defined in no less than five distinct economic packages. These were designed to stabilise the economy while alienating neither the IMF nor the ConFederación de Empresarios Privados de Bolivia (Confederation of Private Entrepreneurs of Bolivia, CEPB) to the UDP's right, nor the COB to its left.[124]

Hyperinflation became by far and away the most critical issue of the abysmal overall economic scenario. It reached the astonishing level of 27,000 per

---

119. Conaghan 1994, pp. 244–5.
120. Conaghan, Malloy, and Abugattas 1990, p. 3.
121. Arze and Kruse 2004, p. 24.
122. Ibid.; Crabtree, Duffy, and Pearce 1987; Medeiros 2001, p. 407.
123. Veltmeyer and Tellez 2001, p. 73.
124. Dunkerley 1992, p. 190; Malloy 1991, p. 49. The UDP's balancing act between competing class-forces was untenable even in the medium term, and the economic consequences of the five economic packages were eloquent demonstrations of this fact. GNP decline began in 1981, prior to the UDP's coming to office, but it intensified under the new administration. In 1982, GNP fell by six per cent, followed by a further three per cent decline in 1983, zero growth in 1984, and a further three per cent decline in 1985. External debt was increasing while GNP per capita suffered a tumble from US$590 in 1981 to US$440 in 1985 (Grindle 2003, p. 323).

cent in 1984–5. Apparently, this garnered for Bolivia the dubious distinction of seventh most severe incidence of inflation in human history, and most severe ever in Latin America.[125] During hypinflationary cycles, the popular sectors suffer the most because they lack 'the means to shield their incomes by purchasing durable assets, holding foreign currency, or locating capital abroad'.[126] In the Bolivian case, hyperinflation 'devastated the finances of the urban working classes, whose meagre savings were wiped out overnight'.[127] The remodelled right-wing MNR, under the leadership of Víctor Paz Estenssoro, was then able to play 'on this traumatic experience to gain and sustain support for the neoliberal reforms forcefully backed by creditors that he touted as the country's only salvation'.[128]

Because the UDP never took up the popular project of the mobilised indigenous working class and peasantry – even as it failed to satisfy right-wing opposition within Congress – it faced considerable resistance from the Left. It was precisely these forces on the radical Left that sowed fear in the ranks of the bourgeoisie and which played an important part in eventually solidifying the various fractions of the capitalist class into a more or less unified bloc behind the neoliberal project. The labour-movement was intent on pushing forward the radicalisation and deepening of the democratisation-process, beyond the political arena and into social and economic spheres, under the new UDP-government.[129] Between 1971 and 1982, average real wages had plummeted

---

125. Malloy 1991, p. 38; Sachs 1987, p. 279. It is widely understood that hyperinflation, defined as inflation that exceeds 50 per cent per month, inflicts its most pernicious damage on the urban working classes, while it negatively affects the majority of the population. In Latin American opinion-polls it has been found that intense bouts of inflation outweigh any other problems in the public's perception (Weyland 1998, p. 554).

126. Roberts 2002, p. 6. Radical neoliberal adjustments in Argentina, Peru, Brazil and Bolivia were implemented during, or in the immediate lead up to, hyperinflationary cycles. To the extent that the neoliberal reforms in these countries received initial popular backing, it is plausible to assume that it was because they 'promised to end incipient hyperinflation and thus recuperate sizeable past losses and avert high future costs' (Weyland 1998, p. 552).

127. Arze and Kruse 2004, p. 24.

128. Ibid.

129. Recall the extraordinarily rich and radicalising peasant-worker alliances that developed at the end of the 1970s and beginning of the 1980s, as the struggle for democracy gained momentum. Key peasant- and worker-and-peasant organisations involved sought to make the transition to democracy a simultaneous transition to socialism. This radicalisation helped to stimulate fear in the bourgeoisie, and allowed

by 17.2 per cent. By the end of 1982, the decline had worsened to 39 per cent.[130] In light of this, the exercise of radical rhetoric by the UDP, without substantive real action, proved insufficient. While the PCB controlled the ministries of labour and mines, it had little political or ideological leverage over the majority of the leadership of the COB who were independents, and a rank and file renowned for its militancy.[131] Meanwhile, even though the POR had by and large degenerated into sectarianism, the wider Trotskyist legacy left its imprint on militant activists who saw in the COB the only vehicle through which to defend the working class and counteract what they saw as the class-collaborationism of the PCB. The PCB, then, failed to win over the rank and file within the mines and the labour-movement more generally and faced 'a radical critique of the contradictions of managing a capitalist slump under a proletarian banner'.[132]

The COB proved to be a formidable opponent of the UDP's populism.[133] The mounting tension culminated with the dramatic strike of March 1985, including a 'week-long occupation of La Paz by miners'.[134] The march was, 'unparalleled in its scale and appeared to promise a decisive settling of accounts amidst incessant discharges of dynamite that traumatised the middle class'.[135] In the end, however, the COB could not project an alternative, coherent, revolutionary project to replace the UDP, and it was only the tenacity of the rank and file which kept the strike alive for as long as it was. Troops were deployed after two weeks by the Siles Zuazo government with little opposition or violence ensuing. This was a crushing defeat for the radical Left.[136]

Conclusion

The legacies of General Barrientos's armed rise to power in 1964 were multiple. Most dramatic, of course, was the fact that not until 1982 would electoral

---

for its various fractions to solidify into one relatively unified bloc behind the project of neoliberalism by the mid-1980s.

130. Conaghan 1994, p. 245.
131. Dunkerley 1992, p. 187.
132. Dunkerley 1992, p. 200.
133. Ibáñez Rojo 2000.
134. Dunkerley 1992, p. 201.
135. Ibid.
136. Dunkerley 1992, pp. 201–2.

democracy be restored. Barrientos introduced more layoffs and militarised labour-discipline in the mines. He opened the country's doors to foreign capital. The latter was evident in the oil-sector, where US-capital's control was almost total. The private sector's contribution to the economy as a proportion of the GNP increased, even as the absolute role of the state continued to grow in terms of public investment and rising rates of state-employment.

The organised political Left suffered internal fragmentation and marginalisation from the wider terrain of politics. In 1967, the dictatorship outlawed all leftist parties of significance. The critical cleavage of the era, though, was most certainly relations between the labour-movement and the state. Trade-union activists in the mines suffered repression, exile, imprisonment, selective assassinations, and even full-scale massacres, such as that of San Juan in 1967. Nonetheless, state-repression was not as severe or well-coordinated as it would later prove to be in the fierce dictatorships of neighbouring Argentina and Chile. The labour-movement and the Left were not as systematically annihilated in Bolivia. As a result, miners maintained a semi-clandestine infrastructure of class-struggle that helped to sustain popular cultures of resistance and opposition.

Four characteristics of the Bánzer dictatorship proved profoundly important for the country's political and economic trajectory over the coming decades. First, the bourgeoisie of Santa Cruz, which played an instrumental role in Bánzer's coercive rise to power, grew and consolidated itself still further.[137] This marked a lasting shift in the dynamic pole of Bolivian capitalism from La Paz to Santa Cruz, the latest turn in the country's uneven development. Second, Bánzer's economic betrayal and military repression of the indigenous peasantry rang the death knoll of the Pacto Militar Campesino (Military-Peasant Pact, PMC) by 1974. The newly-independent peasantry subsequently forged the Aymara and Quechua *katarista* indigenous movement in the *altiplano* and the city of La Paz. The legacy of this movement is clearly discernible in the popular cultures of resistance and opposition that characterised the left-indigenous struggles of the early twenty-first century. The break between the military and the peasantry, and the rise of the *katarista* movement, are among the most important features of the Bánzer period. They had a decisive impact on the balance of racialised class-forces in society.

---

137. Gill 1987b, p. 50.

Third, the Bánzer régime's unsuccessful attempt to permanently wipe out the workers' movement had the unintended consequence of spurring the organised working class to play a leading role in the struggle for electoral democracy. That struggle was ultimately successful in 1982. Labour-state relations, in this respect, played a key part in breaking the historical sequence of authoritarian rule. Fourth, the foreign debt accumulated by Bánzer set the stage for the debt-crisis and hyperinflationary conditions of the early 1980s. These developments in the country's political economy were the pretexts through which orthodox neoliberal restructuring was implemented and justified between 1985 and 2000.

Overall, changes in the balance of racialised class-forces – the ability of the labour-movement to continue to resist authoritarian rule, and the new weight of an independent indigenous-peasant movement – intersected with contradictions in capitalist development – a commodities-boom in the early- to mid-1970s, followed by falling prices near the end of that decade, and soaring levels of debt – to cause the gradual decomposition of military authoritarianism. This set the stage for the popular battle to restore democracy between 1978 and 1982. This struggle saw radical movements of the working class and the peasantry unite, as well as the electoral victory of the centre-left Unidad Democrática Popular (Popular-Democratic Unity, UDP). Ultimately, however, the period ended in hyperinflationary crisis. The Right was soon in a position to present itself as the only alternative to the chaos of the UDP and the revolutionary-socialist threat of the COB and other popular forces.[138] 'Circumstances in Bolivia prior to the installation of the neoliberal project closely resembled' a 'crisis of social domination', or a 'situation in which the threat from below menaces the viability of the capitalist system as a whole'.[139] As will be demonstrated, this crisis scenario forged an unprecedented united front on the part of the Bolivian capitalist class, in alliance with external imperialist powers. On this basis, a profoundly regressive neoliberal model of accumulation was introduced, beginning in 1985.

---

138. Conaghan 1994, p. 247.
139. Conaghan, Malloy, and Abugattas 1990, p. 18.

Chapter Four

Neoliberal Counter-Revolution, 1985–2000

In Bolivia, the speed, breadth and depth of neoliberal restructuring in the mid-to-late 1980s depended
upon the particularities of the shifting domestic balance of racialised class-forces in a period of extreme
economic and institutional crisis.[1] This balance
shifted away from the rural and urban indigenous
popular classes and toward a deeper domination
by the white-*mestizo* capitalist class, especially the
internationally-oriented fractions allied with foreign
capital. The new political coherence and relative
unity of the different fractions of the Bolivian bourgeoisie in the face of left-wing threats to the status
quo in the early 1980s made the first phase of the neoliberal project (1985–93) possible to implement on the
ground. The imposition of neoliberal restructuring
domestically required a coherent ruling-class *political*
as well as *economic* project of dismantling the infrastructures of popular class-power – in this period, the
destruction of the tin-mining unions was the most
important facet of this effort. The strategy was rolled

---

1. I pay special attention to dynamics occurring within the country, although, clearly,
this balance of social forces was in turn influenced by external imperialist pressures
from international financial institutions and imperial states, and in particular the US-
state. Imperial leverage over Bolivian domestic policy was heightened at this juncture
because of the unfolding debt-crisis throughout Latin America. Bolivian neoliberalism
also depended upon a generally favourable international and regional environment in
which neoliberal ideology reigned supreme and imperialist powers used their leverage to demand economic restructuring.

out through shifting emphases and combinations of coercion and consent, enacted through polyarchic institutions but with clear inclinations toward outright authoritarianism at several junctures and in various spheres of policy-implementation. Still, localised struggles from below endured. The *cocaleros*, or coca-growers, in the Chapare region of Cochabamba replaced the tin-miners as the leading social force resisting imperialism and neoliberalism. Elsewhere in the country, small indigenous movements began to emerge in the wake of *katarista* hegemony by the early 1990s. Thus, while clearly taking on new forms, the cycles of repression and resistance common to the authoritarian period (1964–82) were sustained in Bolivia's neoliberal era. The new forms of struggle were strengthened by novel combinations and re-adaptations of long-standing popular cultures of resistance and opposition. The evolving ideology of the *cocalero*-movement, for example, involved the interpenetration of revolutionary-Marxist traditions associated with the ex-miners who relocated to the Chapare, and indigenous liberation-traditions associated with Quechua peasant-communities. These traditions were able to crystallise to the extent that they did because of the presence of a pre-existing rural infrastructure of class-struggle – a dense network of peasant-*sindicatos*.

In 1993, Gonzalo Sánchez de Lozada, leader of the Movimiento Nacionalista Revolucionario (Revolutionary-Nationalist Movement, MNR), was elected as the country's new president. A second phase of Bolivian neoliberalism (1993–2000) was initiated. The state adopted the political and ideological framework of neoliberal multiculturalism (see Chapter 1), in an attempt to co-opt indigenous-liberationist demands from below. This involved separating cultural recognition of indigenous peoples by state-institutions from the material reality of racialised class-exploitation under neoliberal capitalism. Some indigenous cultural rights were recognised by the state, but this recognition was accompanied by the generalised deepening of neoliberal economic restructuring, the results of which ran against the objective interests of the indigenous proletarian and peasant-majority. The core of the second phase of neoliberalism was characterised by the privatisation of most state-owned enterprises and the concomitant penetration of Bolivian markets by foreign capital. Neoliberalism in the second phase continued to witness the radical concentration of political and economic power in the hands of foreign and domestic capital. The world of work was profoundly reorganised, as the informal sector grew to include almost 70 per cent of the urban work-force and public-sector employment declined substantially. Unionisation became more difficult. Workers' struggles tended to be more improvisational, local, defensive, and reactive than they had been in the past.

After years of moderate economic growth in the early- to mid-1990s, the Bolivian economy entered a sharp recession in 1999. The contradictions of neoliberal-capitalist development and neoliberal multiculturalism converged to shift the balance of racialised class-forces slowly back towards the indigenous proletarian and peasant-majority. A profound crisis of the state consequently erupted by the end of 1999. The state's capacity to reproduce the social relations of neoliberal domination was increasingly called into question, both ideologically and politically. Sections of the labour-movement – especially in El Alto, La Paz, and Cochabamba – adopted an orientation of social-movement unionism, and were able to start to rebuild a new infrastructure of class-struggle in major cities, drawing on long-standing popular cultures of resistance and opposition from the Bolivian labour-movement, adapted to the new world of work.

4.1 From state-led developmentalism to neoliberalism

The accumulation-régime established in Bolivia following the 1952 National Revolution was characterised by state-led capitalism and a host of limited yet real social-citizenship and welfare-rights guaranteed by the state. Collectively, this 'State of '52' was brought to its knees in 1985 with the assumption of power by Víctor Paz Estenssoro and the implementation of the harshest orthodox-neoliberal stabilisation-programme in Latin America since the Pinochet counterrevolution in neighbouring Chile. While newly democratic Hugo Bánzer, of Acción Democrática Nacionalista (Nationalist-Democratic Action, ADN), ended up winning a plurality in the 1985 elections with 32.8 per cent of the popular vote, Congress nonetheless selected Paz Estenssoro of the MNR, who had received 30.4 per cent, to be the country's next president. The MNR's determination to reverse the socioeconomic foundations of the State of 52 required the adroit formation of a 'political pact' with the ADN, termed the Pacto por la Democracia (Pact for Democracy), in combination with authoritarian manoeuvrings of an insulated economic team of techno-crats and representatives of the capitalist class. Such authoritarian features of economic policymaking, it should be recognised, were hardly unique to Bolivia within the larger Latin-American context in this period.[2]

Within 23 days of taking office, on 28 August 1985, Paz Estenssoro inaugurated his 'neoliberal revolution' with Supreme Decree DS21060, which outlined the country's Nueva Política Económica (New Economic Policy, NEP).[3] The NPE had as its ostensible aims an anti-inflationary shock to overcome hyperinflation, dramatic internal and external liberalisation, and the fundamental uprooting and downsizing of the public sector.[4] The economic programme was designed to liberalise the economy and push the private sector to front-stage as the engine of economic growth, replacing what was understood to be a decrepit and overextended populist state which had survived since the 1950s. The NPE contained the central components of orthodox stabilisation as well as an orientation toward a more fundamental and long-term restructuring of the economy.[5] In employing the precise language used by international financial institutions, DS21060 was designed to win the backing of the International Monetary Fund (IMF), the World Bank, the Inter-American Development Bank (IDB), and the United States.[6]

Whatever the immediate, medium- and longer-term tasks of the NPE, however, it must be understood that, at heart, the economic programme was the first step in a ruling-class project to aggressively reconstitute capitalist class-power over the indigenous proletarian and peasant-majority.[7] Sánchez de

---

2. Centeno and Silva 1998; Teichman 2001. In exchange for rubberstamping the decisions made by the executive and his team of technocrats in the economic sphere, the ADN received a share of the patronage-pie, assuming control of several state-owned enterprises (Gamarra 1996, p. 74). Additionally, a secret addendum to the agreement in May 1988 ensured that the MNR would support Banzer's run for the presidency in the elections of 1989 (Gamarra 1994, p. 107). By 1986, Juan Cariaga had taken over the Finance Ministry, and, most importantly, Sánchez de Lozada had assumed the position of Minister of Planning. With legislative opposition under control, these two men, Jeffrey Sachs as foreign advisor, and Paz Estenssoro in the presidency, were representative of an enormous concentration of power.

3. The infamous decree, then as now, is referred to on Bolivian streets simply as 'twenty-one, zero, sixty'.

4. Gray Molina and Chávez 2005, p. 93.

5. Gamarra 1994, p. 105; Mann and Pastor Jr. 1989, p. 171.

6. Kohl and Farthing 2006, pp. 65–6.

7. Finance and mining segments of the capitalist class dominated the CEPB and played an instrumental role in the implementation of the neoliberal model. Juan Cariaga, an executive in the Banco de Santa Cruz, and Gonzalo Sánchez de Lozada, a millionaire and large stockholder in one of the most important Bolivian mining companies, COMSUR, were the most important ministers (finance and planning) in the cabinet of

Lozada, quoted here, perhaps best conveyed the broad neoliberal project of transforming the state into a more effective instrument with which to crush the interests of the indigenous popular classes, in favour of the ruling class:

> One comes to the conclusion that the state is practically destroyed. The fundamental institutions of the state's productive apparatus have been feudalised, corruption has been generalised and is being institutionalised, and the mechanisms of control and oversight have stopped operating. In this context, the state is unarmed and lacks the capacity to execute and implement any economic policy that the government proposes to put into practice. Therefore, the first political goal consists of re-establishing the authority of the state over society.[8]

The medicinal potpourri providing the basis for neoliberal shock-therapy in 1985 included the reduction of fiscal deficits, freezing of wages and salaries, devaluing and stabilising the currency, slashing public-sector employment, implementing a new regressive tax-system, liberalising trade-barriers through across-the-board tariff-reductions, deregulating labour-markets and restrictions on foreign investment, eliminating subsidies on basic food-items and other necessities, and letting prices float while at the same time eliminating price-ceilings.[9] The impact of restructuring in the public sector was enormous. During the first year of the new administration, public-sector employment decreased by 24,600 people, and by a further 8,550 people the following year. By 1988, there had been a reduction of 17 per cent of the public-sector workforce.

---

the first neoliberal government in the mid-1980s (Conaghan, Malloy and Abugattas 1990, pp. 14–15). Because industrial capitalists dependent on the development-model of import-substitution constituted a smaller part of the economy than in neighbouring Latin-American countries, there was significantly less intra-class dispute between fractions of capital concerning the introduction of neoliberalism. The unprecedented unity of the Bolivian bourgeoisie in the mid-1980s was made more powerful by the threat the radical Left constituted at the end of the 1970s and early 1980s. As anthropologist Harry Sanabria observes, 'While not all dominant class factions gained or lost equally in the short run, neoliberalism has enhanced the viability of the existing social order' (Sanabria 1999, p. 538).

8. Conaghan, Malloy, Abugattas 1990, p. 18.

9. Conaghan, Malloy, Abugattas 1990, p. 4; Dunkerley 1992, p. 211; Gamarra 1994, p. 105; Grindle 2003, pp. 319–23; Veltmeyer and Tellez 2001, p. 76.

The NPE successfully reduced inflation from the astronomical rate of 27,000 per cent in 1984–5, to around 10 per cent in 1986.[10] Basic macro-economic indicators were far from uniformly positive, however. In 1986, the year after the sharp adjustment, GDP sunk by almost 3 per cent to between 2 and 3 per cent overall, while the per capita GDP rate fell by close to 6 per cent in the same year. Per capita GDP growth was negative again in 1987 and barely inched above zero in 1988. Levels of unemployment and underemployment reached 20 per cent and 60 per cent respectively.[11]

4.1.1 Privatisation of the tin-mines

The most dramatic initiative occurred in September 1985, when the government declared a state of siege in order to arrest and banish to internal exile key-figures in the labour-movement so as to avoid popular unrest as it laid off of at least 23,000 workers from the state-owned mining corporation, COMIBOL.[12] The backers of the neoliberal state were well aware that they had to eliminate the threat of opposition from the tin-miners, organised both through the FSTMB and the COB.[13] The miners, as we have seen, had played the vanguard-role in the Bolivian Left for the better part of the twentieth century. A dramatic fall in the international price of tin proved a fortuitous opening for the neoliberal state-makers, and devastating for the miners and the indigenous popular classes more generally.

Bolivia's tin-economy had already been in quite serious decline by the time the international price dove dramatically in October 1985. Company-losses increased from $US30 million in 1980 to $US165 million in 1985. Within the legal export-economy, tin's contribution to earnings fell monumentally from 62.3 per cent in 1980 to 21.7 per cent in 1986.[14] Compared to competi-

---

10. Gamarra 1994, p. 105. This dramatic turn away from hyperinflation was one facet of the social construction of Bolivia's NPE in the international sphere as an economic miracle of the Third World, one which pundits proclaimed ought to be emulated by other developing countries. International financial institutions, foreign governments, world-renowned economists, and the business-press lavished praise on the Paz Estenssoro administration (Malloy 1991, p. 38).
11. Dunkerley 1992, p. 213; Gray Molina and Chávez 2005, p. 96.
12. Grindle 2003, p. 324. As indicated later in this chapter, the figure rises to roughly 27,000 when miners who lost jobs in the private sector over this period are included.
13. Hylton and Thomson 2007, pp. 95–7; Medeiro 2001.
14. McFarren 1992, p. 134.

tors in the tin-economy globally – Malaysia, Indonesia, and Brazil – Bolivia's extraction-costs were much higher. The crash sunk the per-pound price of tin from \$US6 in 1985 to \$US2.50 in 1986.[15] Decree 21060 had already introduced a programme to shutdown marginal mines, 'cooperativise' others, and sell-off profitable mining sites to private corporations.[16] The tin-crash of October, however, sped up the process by threatening the sustainability of the wider NPE through the destabilisation of the economy, and, at the same time, providing a useful entry-point for a frontal assault on the miners.[17] The price-collapse helped destroy the material basis for the economic and political strength of the mining unions and was therefore fundamental to their demise.[18]

The government's plan was remarkably successful. Most state-mines were shut down and privatised, through co-operativisation or sale to private mining companies. According to one analyst, 'By the end of 1986, over eighty per cent of miners employed in state mining (and virtually all members of the miners' union) were jobless and widespread hunger, poverty, and despair pervaded former mining camps'.[19] Taking the number of workers who lost their jobs in the public and private mining sectors together, over 27,000 of 30,000 miners had lost their jobs by the beginning of 1987.[20] State-promises of 'relocation', understood incorrectly by many miners as guaranteed jobs in the cities, set off a large wave of migration from mining communities to major urban centres such as La Paz and Cochabamba. Others went to the Chapare region, where many would become coca-growers in the burgeoning coca-cocaine industry.

Miners in the FSTMB were quick to mount defensive strikes and the occupation of mines, by now a traditional part of the arsenal of collective action against the state. In response to the miners' resistance, the coercive apparatuses of the state were deployed to guard the striking workplaces of miners and the

---

15. Crabtree, Duffy, and Pearce 1987.
16. Nash 1992, p. 277.
17. Sanabria 2000, p. 66.
18. Sanabria 1999, p. 544. On the importance of the relative weight in the national economy of the sector around which labour-unions or popular movements are struggling in determining the leverage of popular classes vis-à-vis capital and the state, see Spronk and Webber 2007, and Bergquist 1986.
19. Sanabria 1999, p. 544.
20. McFarren 1992, p. 131.

occupied mines, while foodstuffs, wages, electricity, natural gas, and other basic necessities were cut off from mining communities.[21] A general strike in July 1986, called by the FSTMB, was equally incapable of reversing, or even slowing, the neoliberal assault. The failure of strikes, occupations, and a general strike initiated by the FSTMB, eventually led to a new strategy. The Marcha por la vida (the March for Life), began in the city of Oruro on 22 August 1986 with a coalition of miners, mining housewives, peasants, teachers, and students. The marchers, who at their peak numbered around 10,000, planned to march from Oruro to La Paz over a one-week period.[22] Ultimately, though, the March for Life failed to achieve even the most minimal objectives of the protesters and poignantly marked the last major attempt from the miners to collectively resist the restructuring process for some years to come.[23]

4.1.2 *The new world of labour*

In addition to the layoffs in the state-mining sector after privatisation, it should also be recalled that, in the first two years of the NPE (1985–7), hundreds of thousands of additional workers from other sectors were forced into the reserve-army of the unemployed, including 6,000 from the private mining sector, 10,000 from public administration, and 2,000 from banking. In addition, over 110 factories were shut down in this period.[24] As the neoliberal project advanced and consolidated itself throughout the 1990s, the decomposition of the traditional infrastructure of working-class power continued to accelerate. Paradoxically, this did not take shape through a new neoliberal labour-code, but, rather, through the state's systematic failure to implement the existing protections for employees in the labour-code as well as a confluence of other factors: the addition of presidential decrees and ministerial resolutions which rendered sections of the labour-code favourable to workers ambiguous or contradictory; selective repression by the state when worker-resistance threatened the interests of capital; and, most importantly, capital's all-out offensive to reorganise the production-process in order to

---

21. Sanabria 2000, p. 67.
22. Nash 1992, p. 278.
23. Sanabria 1999, p. 545; Nash 1992, pp. 289–90.
24. Kruse 2002, p. 225.

reduce labour-costs and increase profits and competitiveness.[25] In addition to the overall lackadaisical approach to implementing the labour-code, DS21060 made hiring and firing easier, allowed for short-term contracting, and facilitated employer-abuse of probationary periods, home-work, subcontracting, and the establishment of phony microenterprises which allowed for the circumvention of laws on unionisation.[26] Therefore, while neoliberal reforms were never in fact enshrined in a new labour-code, neoliberalism nonetheless fundamentally transformed the production-process and the world of work.

The privatisation of the main state-owned enterprises was the most dramatic change to the structure of production on a national level. In addition to the case of the state-owned oil- and gas-company, Yacimientos Petrolíferos Fiscales Bolivianos (Bolivian National Petroleum-Company, YPFB) – to be addressed at length momentarily –, were the privatisations of the state-airline, Lloyd Aero Boliviano (LAB), the Empresa Nacional de Energía (National Energy-Company, ENDE), the railroad-company, and the long-distance telephone-enterprise (ENTEL), among others. With the privatisation of these state-enterprises, there was a general process of 'rationalising' and 'flexibilising' their labour-forces. This meant the restructuring of the enterprises in ways that maintained or reduced the number of employees, subcontracted out certain activities to non-union labour, and created obstacles to the unionisation of these new sectors.[27] At a tier lower in the economy, the largest 100 foreign and local enterprises in industry, mining, commercial agriculture and banking also saw an augmentation of subcontracting and the 'informalisation' of production-processes. This level of the economy was increasingly integrated into the informal economy by way of utilising small, non-unionised production-units which contributed various small parts to the final product during the production-process. This almost invariably meant increased use of non-unionised female, teenage, and child-labour.[28] Below the

---

25. By the end of the 1990s, the labour-code in Bolivia had not undergone substantial revision since it was established in 1939. However, an astronomical 4,200 legal dispositions had been added to the code in the years between. These dispositions – in the form of laws, decrees, regulations, and ministerial resolutions – sought to adapt the labour-code to novel labour-relations and/or inscribe exceptions to various rules therein. As one labour-analyst points out, 'The result was a confusing and contradictory mass of labour regulation, much of which was ignored' (Cook 2007, p. 177).

26. Cook 2007, pp. 180–1.

27. Kruse 2002, p. 228.

28. Kruse 2002, pp. 229–30.

Table 4.1   Employment by segment of the labour-market

Year	Public Employ.	Private Business Employ.	Informal Private Employ.
1985	24%	16%	60%
1995	13%	19%	68%

Source: (Kruse 2002, p. 232).

key privatised state-enterprises and the 100 main firms of the next tier, there were an estimated 500,000 microenterprises by the late 1990s in agriculture, commerce and artisanal activities.

In the decade between 1985 and 1995, public-sector employment in urban areas shrunk quite dramatically from 25 per cent of the workforce to 13 per cent.[29] The real growth as a proportion of the work-force occurred in the informal sector, which expanded from 60 per cent in 1985 to 68 per cent in 1995 (see Table 4.1). One of the key benefits for employers in the expansion of the informal sector is the fact that this is non-union work, and that unionisation is actually illegal in enterprises that employ under 20 individuals.[30] The obstacles to forming new unions are consequently extremely difficult in the informal sector.

Advocates of the neoliberal model point to official unemployment-rates below five per cent during the late 1980s and into the late 1990s, with the exception of a level of 10.4 per cent in 1989. However, by some estimates, *underemployment* reached 53 per cent of the economically active population (EAP) in 1997.[31] Work became dramatically more precarious. More and more young workers between the ages of 10 to 24 with no union-experience or knowledge of their rights were employed. There were increasing numbers of female workers who also had less union-experience and were more vulnerable to intimidation and sexual harassment on the work-site. Finally, there

---

29. Neoliberal theory held that these job-losses would be compensated with new formal jobs in expanding private businesses. However, the formal private sector accounted for only 18.4 per cent of the work-force in 1995, up barely more than two points from 16 per cent in 1985.
30. Arze Vargas 2000, p. 45.
31. Arze Vargas 2000, p. 30.

was a marked decline of permanent contracts and the increase of short-term contracts, day-labourers, and part-time work with no benefits.[32]

Across different sectors of the economy there was an amplification of the number of hours worked per individual at lower rates of pay, as people were increasingly forced to take on second jobs.[33] The number of workers taking home salaries without any complementary benefits increased significantly between 1982 and 1992 in various sectors: from 40 to 55 per cent in industrial manufacturing, 71 to 82 per cent in construction, 49 to 55 per cent in transportation, 42 to 61 per cent in commerce, and in services, 22 to 38 per cent.[34] The fragmentation of the production-process into smaller and smaller units means that workers were no longer concentrated in large groups, as factories were displaced by smaller workshops. External subcontracting by large enterprises of various tasks that contribute to the overall production-process meant that a growing sector of subcontracted workers laboured in small workplaces with deteriorating working conditions and environments, no unions, lower wages, and worse quotas than the older, formal employees of the main firms. In other cases, different production-stages were subcontracted to 'one-person' firms or 'family-enterprises' the employees of which are sometimes referred to as 'micro-entrepreneurs' in the economics-literature. They are better thought of as informal proletarians frequently working under awful conditions without protection, doing the tasks 'once done by a regular worker enjoying social security, health benefits, and bonuses'.[35]

The combined consequences of the new precariousness of work, the dis-articulation of the COB as an effective organising body of the working class, the structural heterogeneity of the work-experiences of the new urban working class, and the boldness of a capitalist class relatively unified behind the project of political and economic neoliberal transformation, together worked against the collective capacities of working-class resistance in the late 1980s and throughout the bulk of the 1990s. Union-strategies and the strategies of rank-and-file workers tended to be more improvisational, defensive and

---

32. Arze Vargas 2000, p. 31. A good deal of new hiring was made through temporary contracts. Only 14 per cent of the formal private-sector contracts registered with the government in 1994 were 'indefinite' contracts, as compared to 68 per cent fixed-term contracts, and 18 per cent short-term specific job-projects (Cook 2007, p. 181).

33. Arze Vargas 2000, p. 32.

34. Arze Vargas 2000, p. 34.

35. Olivera and Lewis 2004, p. 123.

reactive, and less political, than they had been in the past.[36] However, there were also notable exceptions, as the Bolivian rural and urban working classes and the peasantry began to experiment with new forms of organising and doing politics by the end of the 1990s. Sectors of the urban union-movement in Cochabamba, El Alto, and La Paz began to forge novel ties with informal proletarian community-organisations and to bring the issues and needs of non-unionised workers directly into their struggles. They also began to build new connections with rural movements. This sort of social-movement union-ism (see Chapter 1) was growing in a number of different regions of the coun-try, but was especially evident in Cochabamba and El Alto-La Paz, the two epicentres of urban insurrection in the period between 2000 and 2005.[37] Thus a complex process began in the late 1990s through which the urban and rural infrastructure of class-struggle began to be rebuilt after fifteen years of neo-liberal onslaught. The result, as we will see in subsequent chapters, was the most important surge in left-indigenous popular mobilisation in the continent between 2000 and 2005.

4.1.3 Formation of the cocaleros' movement

If, on the one hand, the tin-mining industry was in calamitous decline, the world of work was being structurally transformed in ways that made col-lective action more difficult, and the historic vanguard of the Bolivian Left had suffered a slide into seeming oblivion, the coca-cocaine industry was booming by the mid-1980s. This newly dynamic industry – rooted primar-ily in the Chapare region, but also in the Yungas – became the spawning ground of left-indigenous renewal and conflict with the neoliberal state and US-imperialism. The cocaleros, or coca-growers, had replaced the miners as the most dynamic sector of popular struggle by the late-1980s. Between 1967 and 1981, permanent migration to the Chapare had increased from 24,000 to 68,000 people. As the international cocaine-market began to heat up, the numbers increased. Between 1981 and 1982, for example, 'as many as 420,000

---

36. Kruse 2002.

37. The role of social-movement unionism in the political organising done by the factory-workers' union in Cochabamba and the FSTMB, the COB, and COR-El Alto in La Paz and El Alto, are addressed in subsequent chapters.

people – 7% of Bolivia's total population – travelled to the Chapare to work in coca cultivation or cocaine production'.[38]

Between 1982 and 1986, a 50 per cent collapse in real wages, combined with the elimination of roughly 60,000 jobs in the wake of neoliberal shock-therapy, created a reserve-army of labourers seeking employment.[39] Displaced miners and other workers formerly employed by the state, as well as landless peasants and those engaged in less lucrative agricultural commodity-production, were attracted to the Chapare region in large numbers.[40] As GNP contracted by almost a quarter between 1981 and 1986, coca-cultivation approximately doubled.[41] Official exports of legal commodities declined by almost 25 per cent between 1984 and 1986, while, in 1987, illegal coca-exports 'generated $1.5 billion', of which 'an estimated $600 million stayed in the country – equivalent to all legal exports combined'.[42] Income from coca-producing peasants provided livelihoods for roughly 50,000 families – between 120,000 and 500,000 individuals were employed in some form of coca-cultivation between the mid-1980s and the late 1990s.[43] It has been estimated that another 300,000 people were employed in jobs indirectly dependent on the drug-trade.[44]

In the mid-1980s, the US and the IMF insisted on Bolivia's strict adhesion to neoliberal restructuring, and simultaneous state-intervention against the proliferating coca-cocaine industry. But, of course, the coca-cocaine industry was intricately intertwined with the emergence of Bolivian neoliberalism. The Paz Estenssoro government, therefore, was made to play 'a delicate game of drug diplomacy'.[45] Initially, largely symbolic gestures 'such as occasional high-profile drug seizures and arrest of traffickers' which had 'little impact on the illegal trade', were tactics employed by the Bolivian state to appease

---

38. de Franco and Godoy 1992, p. 383.
39. de Franco and Godoy 1992, pp. 383–5.
40. Sanabria 1997, pp. 171–2. It is not difficult to see the attraction. Unskilled labourers in cocaine-production could earn 20 times the pay of public employees, while migrant landless rural workers employed in the drug-industry could make between three and five times what they could in legal activities in the regions from which they came (de Franco 1992, p. 386).
41. Léons and Sanabria 1997, p. 14.
42. Andreas 1995, p. 79.
43. Farthing 1995; Kohl and Farthing 2006, p. 74.
44. Andreas 1995, p. 79.
45. Andreas 1995, p. 77.

US foreign policy.[46] However, Washington soon tightened its grip, forcing a response. Since the end of the Cold War, the US 'drug-war' throughout Latin America has effectively replaced the menace of 'communism' with the menace of 'narcotrafficking' as a useful ideological device to ensure ongoing US-manipulation of the internal affairs of countries in the region. The drug-war has 'disguised Washington's repressive and exploitative policies behind a high moral purpose', allowed it, 'to penetrate the internal security forces of Latin America and establish its own political agenda', and to gain 'direct access to the society in order to push its economic and counter-insurgency agenda'.[47] As the 1980s progressed, the cocaleros in Bolivia were becoming a potentially insurgent movement and the necessity of confronting them was similar to the prior necessity of tackling the 'problem' of the miners.

In the Chapare region, utilising a basis of pre-existing agrarian union-networks as a new rural infrastructure of class-struggle, the cocaleros were developing the capacity to confront neoliberal and imperialist policy. By the 1960s, the first peasant-federation of sindicatos, or unions, had been established in the Chapare.[48] Around 85 per cent of the Chapare sindicatos fell under the Federación Especial de Trabajadores Campesinos de Trópico de Cochabamba (Special Federation of Peasant-Workers of the Tropics of Cochabamba, FETCTC) or the Federación de Carrasco (Federation of Carracaso).[49] These sindicatos represented the primary pre-existing infrastructure of class-struggle in the local context. Their ties with the national setting were equally important in enhancing the organisational capacity of the cocaleros. The FETCTC increased the status of the cocaleros within the national peasant-union, the Confederación Sindical Única de Trabajadores Campesinos de Bolivia (Trade-Union Confederation of Bolivian Peasant-Workers, CSUTCB), on a number of fronts. By the mid-1980s, the Chapare federation of peasants had replaced the Aymara katarista movement as the most important focal point of peas-

---

46. Ibid. While rhetorically aligning itself with US drug-policy, the Paz Estenssoro administration tacitly legalised the 'laundering of cocaine profits by allowing US dollar accounts at the central bank, no questions asked'. This facilitated the repatriation of 'a quarter of the estimated US$2 billion which had fled the country between 1980 and 1985' (Kohl and Farthing 2006, p. 73).
47. Petras and Veltmeyer 2001, 140. After 9/11, the drug-war has been incorporated into the so-called 'war on terror' through the catch-all concept of 'narcoterrorism'.
48. Healy 1991, p. 89; Healy 1998, p. 107.
49. Healy 1991, p. 89.

ant-activism in terms of ability to collectively mobilise its membership. This dynamism underwrote its newly hegemonic role inside the CSUTCB.[50] Mobilising around the coca-leaf as a symbol of indigenous identity, the Chapare federation 'adopted the argument that protecting coca protects Bolivian culture in order to convince those CSUTCB delegates and leaders from non-coca-growing regions to support their position that coca cultivation should continue and efforts to eradicate it should be opposed'.[51]

US counter-narcotics policy has long focussed on supply-side, punitive and repressive tactics, rather than investment in solutions aimed at controlling domestic demand.[52] By the late 1980s, in response to US-pressure to more seriously confront the *cocaleros*, the Bolivian state adopted increasingly repressive campaigns of coca-eradication.[53] Against such developments, the *cocaleros* mounted popular resistance. At the micro-level, they engaged in 'sabotage and hit-and-run attacks, slowing down the work of eradication teams; 'voluntary' destruction of unproductive coca-fields, and the use of compensation funds to plant new coca-crops elsewhere; relocation of tiny coca-fields deep in the forest (thus taking advantage of the cover provided by dense tropical foliage against surveillance); and massive yet sporadic confrontations with security-forces.[54] On a larger scale, the *cocaleros* organised mass-rallies, marches, hunger-strikes, road-blocks, cultural events, alliances with other sectors of popular civil society, occupation of government-offices, and tactical negotiations with government-officials.[55]

The struggle of the *cocaleros* added new layers of complexity and creativity to popular cultures of resistance and opposition within the popular classes. Re-located ex-miners brought with them potent organisational and ideological capacities, even if they had to be reconfigured to meet a new cultural and

---

50. Healy 1991, p. 93.
51. Ibid.
52. Léons and Sanabria 1997, p. 41.
53. Sanabria 1999, p. 551. One example of this process was Law 1008, passed in 1988. The law criminalised coca-growers by restricting the civil rights of those accused of drug-trafficking, in the main, 'low-level drug industry workers caught smuggling small quantities of paste' (Gill 2004, p. 169). Law 1008 was also responsible for the establishment of the Fuerza Especial para la Lucha Contra el NarcoTráfico (FELCN), an élite, militarised anti-narcotics police-force 'shaped by the U.S. Drug Enforcement Agency' (Gill 2004, p. 169).
54. Sanabria 1999, p. 552.
55. Healy 1991, p. 112.

socioeconomic terrain.[56] James Petras argues that class-conscious ex-miners who were transformed into peasants were 'able to disseminate an ideology and form of leadership among the wider peasantry that provid[ed] a qualitatively different perspective to the struggle'.[57] The exchanges of popular cultures of resistance and opposition also flowed the other way in peasant-ex-miner relations. As ex-miners settled in the Chapare region, populated with coca-growing Quechua indigenous communities, 'their acculturation into the traditional spiritual discourses and practices associated with the coca leaf and...demands for greater Indian autonomy' took form and deepened. In terms of these oppositional cultures, then, we can conclude that the 'politics of the coca growers involve[d] harnessing ancestral spiritual beliefs to modern forms of class and anti-imperial struggle. Marxist analysis [was] linked to pre-European values'.[58] What makes the *cocaleros* so important is, first, the fact that they were for a period the *only* radical force of resistance with any capacity to confront the state, and, second, that they later became the principal social base of the Movimiento al Socialismo party.

The *cocaleros* constructed a thoroughgoing anti-imperialist, anti-neoliberal and eclectically indigenous-nationalist critique of the status quo. They demanded the reassertion of popular-collective control over privatised natural resources then in the hands of transnational capital, the recognition of indigenous land and territory, and the free trade and industrialisation of the coca-leaf. They also sought deeper democracy and social justice, human rights for the indigenous population, popular sovereignty, and the re-nationalisation of privatised state-enterprises. Overall, their protests and visions of change were rooted in a general rejection of the neoliberal-economic model.[59]

4.1.4 Formation of the Movimiento al Socialismo (MAS)

It was directly out of the social and political milieu of the *cocaleros* in the Chapare that the Movimiento al Socialismo (Movement Towards Socialism, MAS) party created in the late 1990s.[60] As early as 1992, the *cocaleros* and

---

56. Gill 1997; Stefanoni and Do Alto 2006, p. 39.
57. Petras 1997, p. 28.
58. Petras 1997.
59. Orozco Ramírez 2005, pp. 20–1.
60. Gill 2004, pp. 163–78; Orozco Ramírez 2005, p. 17; Stefanoni 2003.

indigenous-peasant organisations in the *altiplano* began to recognise the limitations of community- and peasant-union mobilisation in confronting the tremendous obstacles facing the popular movement. At the Asamblea de los Pueblos Originarios (Assembly of Indigenous Peoples), held on 12 October 1992 under the umbrella of the CSUTCB, the necessity of a *brazo político*, a political arm, for the peasant-union movement was put on the table. The diverse currents and organisations attending the assembly were too internally fractious, however, to determine anything about the shape and content of that political arm.[61] Gradual steps toward the formation of an *instrumento político*, or political instrument, nonetheless proceeded over the next few years. In the First Land- and Territory-Congress in Santa Cruz in 1995, the main peasant- and indigenous organisations of the country met and reaffirmed the objective.[62] This set the stage for the Seventh Ordinary Congress of the CSUTCB in March and April 1996 in Santa Cruz, where the move to consolidate a new political instrument was ratified.

Thus was born the Asamblea por la Soberanía de los Pueblos (Assembly for the Sovereignty of the Peoples, ASP). Peasant-leader Alejo Véliz was elected as head of the party. Due to legal technicalities in the electoral system, the ASP was unable to gain recognition as a registered party in the 1995 municipal elections, but, through a tactical electoral agreement, the new party ran jointly with the Izquierda Unida (United Left, IU), and won 49 town-council seats and ten mayoralties, all in the department of Cochabamba.[63] The ASP described its basis in 1995 as a struggle for a communitarian, multinational, socialist Bolivia, in which the class-struggle and the national struggle would be combined.[64] In the 1997 presidential elections, the ASP-candidates again ran under the IU-banner with Alejo Véliz as their presidential contender. However, by 1998, disputes between the three main indigenous leaders in the country – Felipe Quispe, Alejo Véliz, and Evo Morales – led to the eventual disintegration of the ASP. In its place, two new parties eventually emerged, the Movimiento Indígena Pachakuti (Pachakuti Indigenous Movement, MIP),

---

61. Stefanoni and Do Alto 2006, p. 57.
62. In attendance were the Central Sindical de Trabajadores Campesinos de Bolivia (CSUTCB), the Confederación de Colonizadores (CSCB), the Central Indígena del Oriente Boliviano (CIDOB), and the Federación Nacional de Mujeres Campesinas de Bolivia-Bartólina Sisa (FNMCB-BS), among other indigenous-peasant organisations.
63. Orozco Ramírez 2005, pp. 17–18.
64. Stefanoni and Do Alto 2006, p. 61.

led by Felipe Quispe and primarily appealing to the Aymara indigenous radicalism of the *altiplano*, and the Instrumento Político por la Soberanía de los Pueblos (Political Instrument for the Sovereignty of the Peoples, IPSP), led by Evo Morales and appealing to a much broader, inter-ethnic and cross-regional social base.[65] Again, due to technicalities, the IPSP was unable to establish status as an official party in the electoral arena and therefore assumed the name of an officially registered but defunct political party, the Movimiento al Socialismo (MAS). Under this banner, in the 1999 municipal elections, the IPSP-MAS ticket garnered 3.27 per cent of the national vote, 10 mayoralties, and 79 municipal-council seats.[66] A great deal of the new party's appeal resided in its grassroots-nature.[67] During the late-1990s, the MAS was rooted in extra-parliamentary political action, deeply responsive to its *columna vertebral* (backbone), the *cocaleros* of Chapare, and functioned as a radically anti-neoliberal and anti-imperialist party. The party also helped to 'indianise' Bolivian nationalism, bringing indigenous issues to the centre of political life by drawing on the legacy of the *katarista* indigenous movement of the 1970s.[68]

4.1.5 *Other indigenous-peasant struggle in the late-1980s*

Within the sphere of rural indigenous political activism, there was also extensive displacement and realignment within older movements as well as the emergence of new ones. Between 1979 and 1982, the Aymara *katarista* move-

---

65. The MAS-leader was born Juan Evo Morales Ayma on 26 October 1959, in the province of Sud Carangas in the department of Oruro. Four of his seven Aymara indigenous siblings died from illnesses related to poverty and the absence of an adequate health-infrastructure in the region. His family, like many others, migrated to northern Argentina in search of work. In Argentina, Morales dropped out of school because of difficulties with the Spanish language. He was raised exclusively in Aymara. He would eventually return to school in Oruro, working at various points as a baker and a trumpeter in the well-known Banda Real Imperial. At the outset of the 1980s, his family was forced to migrate to the Chapare due to a massive drought in the *altiplano* (Stefanoni and Do Alto 2006, pp. 53–6). Today, his primary language is Spanish, and while he is also relatively fluent in Quechua (from his time spent in the Chapare), he no longer speaks confidently in Aymara. In the Chapare, Morales began his gradual ascent through the ranks of *cocalero* peasant-unions, becoming secretary-general of the Six Federations in 1988. Ten years later, he was elected leader of the MAS and has maintained this post ever since. By 2002, he was a serious candidate in presidential elections.

66. Van Cott 2005, p. 86.

67. Albro 2005a, pp. 440–1.

68. Stefanoni and Do Alto 2006, pp. 64–9.

ment had enjoyed hegemony over the peasant-indigenous movement at a national level, principally through its predominant position in the CSUTCB. In the second congress of the CSUTCB in 1983, the *kataristas* and more class-based peasant-movement sectors closely aligned with the COB and left-wing parties were able to rally behind a joint position of peasant class-struggle as well as the denunciation of racism and the demand for a plurinational Bolivian state. However, indigenous struggle suffered a similar disorientation and fragmentation as the Left experienced in the fallout from the UDP-period.

At the third congress of the CSUTCB in 1985 divisions arose between the Movimiento Campesino Base (Grassroots Peasant-Movement, MCB), a close ally of the COB, and the *kataristas*. A unified political position proved impossible.[69] Internal divisions within the *katarista* movement multiplied to such an extent that there were ten separate political parties claiming a common *katarista* lineage. The sector of the MRTK led by Víctor Hugo Cárdenas was the most powerful of the tiny parties and thus was able to lay claim to the *katarista* name. At the fourth congress of the CSUTCB, however, the fact that none of the peasant-leaders identified themselves as *kataristas* signalled the organisational crisis of the movement.[70] Some of the potential bases of *katarismo* in the largely indigenous populations of El Alto and the poorer neighbourhoods of La Paz lent their electoral support in the late 1980s to a new populist party, Conciencia de Patria (Conscience of the Fatherland, CONDEPA), which identified explicitly with the urban-Aymara population, using a discourse that counter-posed the interests of *el pueblo* (the people) with those of the oligarchy.[71] CONDEPA was led by Carlos Palenque, a popular Aymara television- and radio-host known to his supports as *el compadre*. Palenque

---

69. Albó 1995, pp. 59–60.

70. Albó 1995, p. 60. Despite the organisational decline of *katarista* political parties and the movement's diminishing weight within the CSUTCB, however, the ideas of *katarismo* had already penetrated the public sphere and changed the parameters of indigenous and leftist politics, as well as public opinion more generally on the indigenous question in Bolivia. The survival of *katarista* ideas within popular movement milieus became evident in the early 2000s as left-indigenous activists grappled in similar ways with the interconnections between race and class, while *katarista* influence on public opinion was reflected in the fact that even mainstream-parties were forced to incorporate some indigenous components to their political agendas, even if they tended to do so in the tokenistic fashion associated with neoliberal multiculturalism.

71. Tapia 2004, p. 160.

won the mayoral elections in La Paz and El Alto between 1989 and 1991, and CONDEPA 'became the leading political force in the country's largest urban center and in the surrounding department'.[72]

While the organisational vacuum created by the decline of mainstream-*katarismo* was partially filled by CONDEPA in El Alto-La Paz and the surrounding countryside, it is important to remember as well the formation in the late 1980s and early 1990s of a revolutionary wing to the *katarista* movement, despite the fact that its numbers were few. At the extraordinary Congress of the CSUTCB in 1988 a new militant organisation, Ofensiva Roja de Ayllus Kataristas (Red Offensive of Katarista Ayllus, also known as Ayllus Rojos, Red Ayllus), first made its presence known. The Ayllus Rojos were an eclectic amalgamation of Marxist-indigenous activists, bringing together *indígenista* Aymaras, miners, and urban Marxists.[73] While influenced by the writings of *indianista* Fausto Reinaga, the Ayllus Rojos nonetheless transcended Reinaga's thesis of a racially bifurcated 'two Bolivias', one indigenous and one *q'ara*.[74] Instead, the group sought to build alliances between indigenous struggle and other popular, collective actors in Bolivian society, notably urban workers.[75] In 1991–2 an armed wing of the Ayllus Rojos emerged called Ejército Guerrillero Tupaj Katari (Tupaj Katari Guerrilla-Army, EGTK). Felipe Quispe was a leading figure in this guerrilla group, as were Álvaro García Linera and Raquél Gutiérrez, a Mexican who was the only non-Bolivian member of the group. The EGTK focused on small insurgent actions which included exploding high tension towers and oil- and gas-pipelines.[76]

---

72. Albó 1995, p. 64. The other major outsider-party to arise in the late 1980s was the Unidad Cívica Solidaridad (Solidarity Civic Union, UCS), which was led by beer-industry magnate Max Fernández (Mayorga 2002, pp. 212–16). Fernández was less of a traditional populist than Palenque. While it is true that he ran the UCS 'in an authoritarian manner, and, in classic populist style, control over his political party [was] determined by his capacity to deliver prebends', (Gamarra 1996, p. 77) he was much more of an élite business-politician than Palenque, and one who engaged in clientelistic handouts and financed targeted public works for poor communities, but who eschewed the more radical rhetoric of classical populism that was a staple in Palenque's discourse. The UCS did not participate in the 1989 elections, but the party won 14.02 per cent in the June 1993 elections.

73. Albó 2002b, p. 80.

74. Reinaga 1970.

75. García Linera 2005b, pp. 10–11.

76. Albó 2002b, p. 80. The movement that Quispe and García Linera were helping to build had two wings, according to Quispe, one left-wing Marxist and the other *túpajkatarista*, or indigenous-liberationist, in the tradition of the anticolonial hero of

In the late 1980s, as the mainstream *katarista*-movement was eclipsed by populists and low-level guerrilla-activity, a new set of indigenous organisations arose out of the tropical lowlands of eastern Bolivia. Various indigenous groups coalesced in the Confederación Indígena del Oriente, Chaco y Amazonia de Bolivia (Idigenous Confederation of the Bolivian East, Chaco, and Amazon, CIDOB). The Asamblea del Pueblo Guaraní (Assembly of Guaraní People, APG) was also formed around the same time, in 1987.[77] The new indigenous movements made their inaugural debut by staging an historic Marcha por el territorio y la dignidad (March for Territory and Dignity), in 1990 – a 35-day procession of approximately 700 men and women from lowland-indigenous groups, beginning in the northern-lowland city of Trinidad and ending over 400 miles away in the capital of La Paz.[78] The march resulted in the legal recognition of over seven million acres of indigenous territory.[79] Most significant, however, was the fact that the march marked a new beginning of indigenous resistance from the lowlands and hence broadened the field of indigenous resistance across the country which had hitherto been rooted primarily in Aymara movements of the *altiplano* and Quechua *cocalero*-struggles of the Chapare.[80]

---

the 1781 insurrection against the Spaniards, Túpaj Katari. García Linera was in the Marxist wing, while Quispe located himself in that of the *túpajkataristas*. In 1988, the group released a political communiqué and ideological document proposing to move forward with an armed struggle in the form of the EGTK. According to Quispe, they believed this was the only way forward in the struggle against the 'capitalist, colonialist, racist and imperialist system' (Quispe 2006). The EGTK, never more than 200 members strong, started its activities in 1988. García Linera, Quispe, Gutiérrez and other comrades were eventually captured, tortured and imprisoned in 1992, denied trial, and kept in jail for the next five years (Bigio 2006).

77. Albó 1995, p. 62.

78. The marchers, who were protesting logging activity in indigenous territories and demanding legal recognition of those territories, were met in solidarity just outside La Paz by Aymara indigenous activists who accompanied them in huge numbers to downtown La Paz.

79. Albó 1996, pp. 15–16.

80. It should also be understood that the international and regional context in the early 1990s was favourable to the domestic emergence of new indigenous movements (Dunbar Ortíz 2007). In 1992, the Guatemalan-indigenous activist and recipient of the Nobel Peace Prise, Rigoberta Menchú, helped to initiate a number of continental pan-indigenous meetings throughout Latin America behind the theme of 500 Years of Resistance to counter official celebrations of the Columbian quincentenary (Brysk 2000, p. 3). In the case of Bolivia, after activists returned from one of the continental meetings in Quito, demonstrations embracing the '500 Years of Resistance' framework were launched with success on 12 October 1992 in almost every city (Albó 1995, p. 63).

4.1.6   *The* Acuerdo Patriótico

Returning to the sphere of formal politics, the 1989 elections witnessed acrimonious, partisan-divisions within the ruling class as the dominant, ideologically indistinguishable parties – the MNR, ADN and MIR – vied for government-control. Sánchez de Lozada, presidential candidate for the MNR, reneged on the secret deal of the Pact for Democracy in which the party had agreed to back Bánzer's presidential bid in the 1989 elections.[81] The election-results demonstrated a three-way split between the mainstream-parties. Sánchez de Lozada of the MNR won a small plurality with 23.07 per cent, Bánzer of the ADN came a close second with 22.7 per cent, and Jaime Paz Zamora of the MIR won 19.64 per cent. Bánzer and Paz Zamora were equally disinclined to deal with Sánchez de Lozada, and thus conspired in Congress to prevent him from becoming president despite his plurality-showing at the polls. The resolution of the three-way tie in the period following the elections, 'could only be managed by electoral malpractice and a twelve-week circus of offers and counter-offers over the spoils of the state in an effort to secure the presidency through a vote in congress'.[82]

While distinct in some ways from the agreement ending in the Pact for Democracy in 1985, the resolution of the intra-élite struggle for governmental power in 1989 nonetheless took the form of a political pact, this one called the Acuerdo Patriótico, or Patriotic Accord. Under the arrangement, constructed by the ADN and the MIR, Paz Zamora took the presidency while Bánzer became head of the newly formed Consejo Político del Acuerdo Patriótico (Political Council of the Patriotic Accord, COPAP), a bipartisan-committee designated to running the day-to-day affairs of the new governmental coalition.[83] The ADN-MIR government's defining character was the continuation and deepening of the NPE between 1989 and 1993.

The continuation of neoliberal policy throughout the late 1980s and into the early 1990s was both cause and consequence of a dilapidated and diffused Left operating in new and uncharted social and demographic waters. Likewise popular-indigenous movements were taking on new and unpredictable organisational and ideological forms. In Bolivia, the union-Left had always

---

81. Gamarra 1994, pp. 109–10.
82. Dunkerley 1992, p. 178.
83. Gamarra 1996, p. 75.

superseded in importance the organised political Left, even if the two spheres cannot be neatly separated from one another. Therefore, the impact of the collapse of the COB for the prospects of the Left generally is difficult to exaggerate. The COB diminished in stature from the undisputed leader in popular organisation in Bolivia until the mid-1980s, to a fundamentally withered and disoriented shadow of its former self. Apart from the organisational rupture it suffered with the 're-location' of miners throughout the country, the COB had lost a great deal of its moral and political credibility among popular forces after it was unable to slow, much less reverse, the onslaught of the NPE restructuring process. Extra-electoral politics shifted from radical political unionism, towards sector-based unionism, and, more generally, towards clientelism and civic-municipal politics where neoliberal forces generally prevailed.[84] Moreover, individuals formerly involved in leftist politics were increasingly attracted to the proliferating NGO-sector, where the potential bases for a confrontational social-movement politics were redirected towards localised, individualised, technical, and apolitical solutions to problems of poverty and unemployment. These local-level 'solutions' presumed the continuity of the neoliberal model at the macro-level.[85]

4.2 State-multiculturalism and phase II of neoliberal restructuring, 1993–2000

In the elections of 6 June 1993 Gonzalo Sánchez de Lozada of the MNR won 35 per cent of the popular vote, defeating the Acuerdo Patriótico (Patriotic Accord, AP). Perpetuating the 'pacted democracy' of the 1980s, the MNR quickly established a Pacto de la Gobernabilidad (Governability-Pact) with Max Fernández and his Unidad Cívica Solidaridad (Solidarity Civic Union, UCS), as well as a Pacto por el Cambio (Pact for Change) with the Movimiento Bolivia Libre (Free Bolivia Movement, MBL), both of which assured Sánchez de Lozada victory in the presidential vote in Congress. He became president on 6 August. Sánchez de Lozada's Aymara running mate Víctor Hugo Cárdenas of the Movimiento Revolucionario Tupaj Katari (Tupaj Katari Revolutionary Movement, MRTK) became the first indigenous Vice-President of Bolivia. The

---

84. Dunkerley 1993, p. 124.
85. Arellano-López and Petras 1994.

new government (1993–7) deepened the neoliberal economic and political ruling-class project even while it embraced a sophistry of social solidarity with the poor and a multicultural sensibility toward the indigenous majority. When ex-dictator Hugo Bánzer, of the Acción Democrática Nacionalista (Nationalist-Democratic Action, ADN), was elected president in 1997, some of the multicultural state-discourse subsided, but the economic trajectory introduced by Sánchez de Lozada was strengthened and extended.

After having been blocked from assuming the presidency in 1989, despite having won a plurality at the polls, Sánchez de Lozada apparently 'entered a period of deep depression'.[86] He soon recovered, however, and founded the right-wing think-tank Fundación Milenio (Millennium-Foundation). In addition to a number of Bolivian associates, the foundation was supported by an international advisory board of political scientists, including Juan Linz of Yale University, Arturo Valenzuela of Georgetown University, Carlos Nino of Argentina, and Bolivar Lamounier of Brazil. The group produced policy-programmes on political, market-, and state-reform, meeting five times between 1991 and 1993.[87] The Foundation eventually produced the MNR-electoral campaign-platform, El Plan de Todos (Plan for Everyone), which offered the following as its seven pillars: attracting foreign investment; creating jobs; maintaining economic stability; improving health-care and education; facilitating popular participation; reforming the role of the government; and restricting corruption.[88]

To distinguish it from the hard-nosed neoliberalism of the Nueva Política Económica, the Plan de Todos was pitched as a social-market solution to the development-problems facing Bolivia. Enduring troubles of unemployment, low wages and corruption were going to be resolved through the privatisation of inefficient state-owned enterprises. Education, health and other basic social services were to be improved. Local communities, especially indigenous ones in poor rural areas, were going to have greater participation in development planning and decision-making at the local level.[89] Sánchez de Lozada claimed that the privatisation of state-owned enterprises, and the foreign investment

---

86. Grindle 2000, p. 113.
87. Grindle 2000, pp. 113–14.
88. Gamarra 1996, p. 81.
89. Grindle 2003, p. 330.

this would attract, would create 500,000 new jobs and a GDP growth-rate of between 4 and 10 per cent annually.[90]

Pre-electoral polls demonstrated the popular resonance of indigenous issues among much of the Bolivian public. The MNR adopted an opportunistic approach to ethnicity in order to attract indigenous voters, a common practice of most political parties by the early 1990s.[91] The MNR promised in its campaign-literature and election-billboards a New Bolivia, La Bolivia Nueva. The New Bolivia that the MNR was projecting, rejected the culturally integrationist nationalism of the post-1952 revolutionary period, and, instead, embraced a politics of constitutional recognition of the pluricultural and ethnically heterogeneous nature of Bolivia, as well as recognition of gender-inequality as a problem to be overcome.[92] This multiculturalism and gender-consciousness, however, were attached to a fundamental commitment on the part of the MNR to deepen and spread the neoliberal-economic restructuring initiated in 1985. Indeed, Sánchez de Lozada himself had played a key role in the initial neoliberal assault on the popular economy as Minister of Planning under President Víctor Paz Estenssoro.

The selection of Cárdenas as Sánchez de Lozada's vice-presidential running mate was a key facet of the indigenous-multicultural inflection to MNR-neoliberal strategy in 1993. Cárdenas enjoyed credibility among the Aymara population, especially in the city and department of La Paz, for his role as a *katarista* movement-leader.[93] The MNR made a concerted effort to attract social sectors that had previously identified with the party, but which had left in response to the neoliberal turn it took in the mid-1980s. Especially important in this regard was the indigenous peasantry that had supported the MNR for much of the postrevolutionary period. The MNR-campaign in 1993, therefore, portrayed both Cárdenas and Sánchez de Lozada as 'children of the revolution', and in the event of the 1993 elections, Cárdenas was able to deliver a 'huge voting bloc of mainly rural Aymara *campesinos* to the MNR'.[94] After the victory, Cárdenas explicitly linked his well-developed conceptualisation of Bolivia as a 'plurinational' state to the MNR's new project under Sánchez

---

90. Kohl 2002, p. 456.
91. Medeiro 2001.
92. Healy and Paulson 2000, pp. 2–5.
93. Albó 1995, p. 66.
94. Gamarra 1996, p. 79.

de Lozada, and reinforced the indigenous symbolism of the pact between the MNR and the MRTK through publicly speaking in Aymara without translators, and appearing publicly with his wife, who wore traditional indigenous dress.[95]

Neoliberal multiculturalism in Bolivia was institutionalised under Sánchez de Lozada through a series of carefully constructed laws and reforms. Most significantly, in 1994, the new administration amended the constitution such that its first article now defines Bolivia as multiethnic and pluricultural.[96] Article 171 recognises the right to limited self-government for indigenous communities, although the state's commitment is vaguely worded.[97] Another visible change in the institutional apparatus of the state occurred when the former Ministry of Peasant- and Agrarian Affairs was transformed into the Ministry of Ethnic and Indigenous Affairs.[98] In the MNR's Plan de Todos, indigenous cultural issues were integral components to the justification and legitimisation of educational reform, land-reform, and decentralised popular participation. All of these reforms were built on the contradictory foundation of culturally 'liberating' the indigenous working-class and peasant-population through recognition of certain linguistic and traditional rights by the state, while simultaneously reinforcing the neoliberal mechanisms responsible for the dramatic increases in their exploitation and suffering over the previous decade.[99] Perhaps the starkest contradiction between the multiculturalism espoused in the platform of the MNR in the 1990s and the material reality of the party's actual reforms to Bolivian political and economic structures was expressed in the rapid transfer of community-owned and state-owned natural resources to foreign multinational corporations. Indeed, privatisation of this sort was a defining feature of the Sánchez de Lozada's, and later Hugo Bánzer's, governments.

95. Albó 1995, p. 68.
96. Healy and Paulson 2000, p. 11.
97. Kohl 2003, p. 341.
98. Gustafson 2002, p. 268.
99. Albó 1995, p. 70; Arellano-López and Petras 1994; Gill 2000, pp. 135–54; Gustafson 2002, pp. 276–82; Kohl 2002, p. 465; Kohl 2003, pp. 342–5; Kohl and Farthing 2006, p. 132; Lora 2006; McNeish 2002; Medeiro 2001, pp. 410–11; Quispe 2004.

4.3 Privatisation

4.3.1 *Natural gas*

The centrality of natural gas in Bolivia's economy is comparable to silver and tin in earlier historical epochs.[100] New discoveries since 1997 put Bolivia's natural-gas reserves at the second largest in South America, after Venezuela. Proven and probable natural-gas resources grew to 48.7 trillion cubic feet by 2005, and future discoveries were highly probable.[101] Demand for natural gas in neighbouring Argentina, Brazil, Chile and Uruguay was already high by 2000, and was projected to continue to increase into the future. The combination of large reserves and growing regional demand meant that Bolivia was one of the only countries with the capacity to serve the growing Southern-Cone market.[102]

Under the first administration of Sánchez de Lozada (1993–7) the hydrocarbons-sector was privatised through the Law of Capitalisation and the Hydrocarbons-Law of 1996. These measures effectively returned the hydrocarbons-industry to the regulatory régime of the 1920s.[103] The Sánchez de Lozada government was fervently committed to deepening the neoliberal project in Bolivia through extensive privatisations, while the World Bank and the International Monetary Fund (IMF) were the source of high-level pressure from outside.[104] As in the railroad-, airline- and telecommunications-sectors, the Bolivian government preferred to describe the privatisation of hydrocarbons as 'capitalisation' in an effort to dampen popular criticism of the initiative. The capitalisation of YPFB entailed the sale of 50 per cent of the state-company – divided into three enterprises – to various petroleum-multinationals.

The privatisation-process was fraught with corruption and fraud.[105] Prior to its privatisation, YPFB had been 'on the verge of completing a contract to build a pipeline to connect Bolivian gasfields to Brazilian markets', which would have increased its profits 'by at least $50 million a year for 40 years. These

---

100. Chávez and Lora 2005.
101. EIU 2006, pp. 28–30.
102. Villegas Quiroga 2004, pp. 25–9.
103. Miranda Pacheco 1999; Shultz 2005, p. 16.
104. Hindery 2004, pp. 288–91.
105. For a theoretical argument on how the privatisation-process in Bolivia mirrors David Harvey's (2003) concept of 'accumulation by dispossession', see Spronk and Webber 2007.

earnings, instead, were largely transferred to private firms that borrowed capital from the same international institutions that had previously offered loans to YPFB'.[106] The new hydrocarbons-legislation also reduced wellhead-royalties owed to the state by transnationals from 50 per cent to 18 per cent in all 'new' discovery-sites. There was gross manipulation of the new law concerning 'existing' and 'new' fields of natural gas in 1996, which resulted in straightforward giveaways to foreign petroleum-companies. Hydrocarbons-Law No. 1731, passed on 26 June 1996, altered Hydrocarbons-Law No. 1689 of 30 April 1996 (just two months earlier). The new law changed the definitions of the largest fields from 'existing' to 'new' and therefore subjected the companies operating in these fields to dramatically reduced royalties.[107] The new law primarily affected the major natural-gas deposits of San Alberto and San Antonio. Each was moved from existing (according to the April law) to new and therefore subject to the lesser royalty.[108] In geographer Benjamin Kohl's estimation, this constituted 'a giveaway that could cost the nation hundreds of millions, if not billions, of dollars over the next 40 years'.[109]

Privatisation of hydrocarbons led to a declining proportional take of the Bolivian state in this sector's revenue over time as production in new reserves (at 18 per cent royalty-rates) increased relative to existing reserves (at 50 per cent royalty-rates), and the international prices of oil and gas accelerated. Absolute state-revenues accrued through royalties and taxes rose by 198 per cent between 1999 and 2004, but the state's share of the sector's turnover systematically declined.[110] What is most damning to the neoliberal model in hydrocarbons are the figures showing how much the YPFB contributed to the Treasury between 1990 and 1996, prior to privatisation, compared to what the private companies contributed between 1999 and 2004, after privatisation and before the moderate reforms to the neoliberal model in 2005 and 2006. Between 1990 and 1996, the YPFB contributed $US1,790.6 million to the Trea-

---

106. Kohl 2004, p. 904.
107. Reducing the royalties owing to the state in new camps from 50 to 18 per cent is designed to compensate a company for risks assumed in exploration, and more foreign capital, it is maintained, will consequently be attracted to the sector. In the case of the June 1996 Hydrocarbons-Law, however, no new risk was being assumed by the benefiting companies.
108. Villegas Quiroga 2004, pp. 84–5.
109. Kohl 2004, p. 904.
110. McGuigan 2007, p. 35.

sury, compared to US$1,238.6 million contributed by the companies between 1999 and 2004, a difference of $US552 million.[111]

4.3.2 *Cochabamba's water*

The privatisation of water in the city of Cochabamba grew naturally out of the earlier stages of economic restructuring. Through pressure from the International Monetary Fund and the World Bank and violation of Bolivian legal procedures and regulations, water that had been under the control of a public water-utility or, in some areas, communal water-systems, was transferred to private ownership.[112] Beginning in 1994, the Bank repeatedly demanded that SEMAPA, Cochabamba's municipal water-system, be auctioned off as a condition for new or renegotiated credits.[113] In the mid-1990s it extended a US$4.5 million loan in order to improve public water- and sanitations-facilities. The idea here was to make the public utilities more attractive for private investment.[114] Two critical acts by the Hugo Bánzer government (1997–2001) during this process set the stage for future conflict over the commodification of water. First, in September 1999, a 40-year concession to control the Cochabamba water-system was granted to the international consortium Aguas del Tunari, a consortium legally registered as International Water in the Cayman Islands. The Italian multinational Edison SpA and the American giant Bechtel owned 50 per cent of International Water, while 25 per cent was owned by Abengoa of Spain. The remaining 25 per cent was divided between 4 different Bolivian investment-groups, all with ties to parties in the government.[115] The auction for SEMAPA drew one bidder, and the terms of the contract reflected the lack of competition. Aguas del Tunari was guaranteed an annual return of 15 per cent on its investment, to be adjusted to the consumer price-index in the United States, for 40 years.[116] The concession, in this respect, failed to comply with existing Bolivian legislation according to which three proposals were required for a valid auction.[117] The

---

111. McGuigan 2007, p. 52.
112. Albro 2005b; Finnegan 2002; Spronk 2007b, p. 15.
113. Arze Vargas 2000.
114. Spronk and Webber 2007, p. 39.
115. Arze Vargas 2000.
116. Finnegan 2002.
117. Crespo 2000.

characteristics of fraud and legal manipulation common in other privatised sectors were also visible, then, in the case of water.

Second, in October 1999, the government passed the Ley de Servicios de Agua Potable y Alcantarillado Sanitario (Law 2029 on Potable Water and Sanitary Drainage) which legalised the concession granted in September. This law facilitating the privatisation of water passed through Congress at breathtaking speed with little to no consultation with those who would endure its consequences.[118] Theoretically, Law 2029 could grant concessions and licenses for water management to any legally recognised institution. In practice, however, the conditions for obtaining concessions and licences were heavily biased towards large enterprises which operated according to market-criteria. Further, the law stipulated that once concessions were granted concessionaires had exclusive right over the concession-area, meaning pre-existing communal forms of water-governance – in both rural and urban areas – would be forced to enter into contracts with the concessionaires, likely large enterprises operating within market-logic.[119] This indicated, in other words, the unmitigated transition from communal property to exclusive private property through a secretive state-process with the backing of powerful international financial institutions and interested multinational water-corporations. Because the contract granted to Aguas del Tunari awarded the company a guaranteed rate of return, and because the World Bank had stipulated to the Bolivian government that state-revenue could not be used to generate this money, the obvious source was the water-consuming residents of Cochabamba. Aguas del Tunari skyrocketed water-tariffs accordingly.[120] The working-class and lower-middle-class residents of the city and peasants in the surrounding countryside did not take this lightly. Tariff-increases were the catalyst to the Cochabamba Water-War of 2000, the opening act of a five-year left-indigenous insurrectionary cycle throughout Bolivia's countryside and major cities.

4.4 Recession and state-crisis at the end of the 1990s

Between 1989 and 1996, average annual growth in Bolivia was just over 4 per cent, reaching a high of 5.27 per cent in 1991, a low of 1.65 per cent in

---

118. Crabtree 2005.
119. Assies 2003.
120. World Bank 1999; Spronk and Webber 2007, p. 39.

1992, and a new peak of 5.03 per cent in 1998. Agriculture was the fastest growing sector between 1992 and 1997, but hydrocarbons and minerals still accounted for more than half of legal exports.[121] Soybean- and vegetable-oil exports from the eastern lowlands had grown to ten times their size since 1990 attracting significant amounts of Brazilian investment into commercial agricultural enterprises.[122] As a result of overall growth in the economy, between 1993 and 1999, the World Bank claims urban poverty declined from 52 per cent to 46 per cent.[123] However, contradictions in neoliberal capitalism at the global, regional, and national levels struck Bolivia hard in 1999. GDP-growth plummeted to 0.43 per cent that year, rose only to 2.28 per cent in 2000, and declined again to 1.51 per cent in 2001. Between 1999 and 2003 the average growth-rate was 1.9 per cent, which measured out to roughly 0 per cent in per capita terms. As a consequence, World-Bank figures suggest that, between 1999 and 2002, overall poverty-rates in the country increased from 62 per cent to 65 per cent, and extreme poverty also experienced a slight increase. Income-inequality also increased during this period.[124]

The national economic crisis was deepened further by the loss of state-revenue as a result of the massive sell-off of valuable state-owned enterprises, particularly YPFB. State-revenue from hydrocarbons and the mining sector which used to trickle down to poor rural municipalities dried up almost completely, sewing widespread discontent.[125] The effect of privatising hydrocarbons was indeed a catastrophic contribution to the budget-crisis suffered by the state.[126] From 1997 to 2002, Bolivia's budget-borrowing increased from 3.3 to 8.6 per cent of its Gross National Income (GNI).[127] This gave international financial institutions and the US-state even more leverage over the Bolivian

---

121. Natural-gas exports increased significantly in 1999 when the new gas-pipeline to Brazil was finished, making hydrocarbons much more important to the Bolivian economy.
122. Kohl and Farthing 2006, p. 121.
123. World Bank 2005, p. 1. It should be indicated that many scholars have called into question the veracity of World-Bank figures on poverty. Just as important, poverty-figures say nothing about the rate of exploitation of labour by capital.
124. World Bank 2005, pp. 1–3. It should be recalled that Bolivia was already the poorest country in South America, and one of the most unequal countries in the most unequal region of the world. By 2000, out of all Latin-American and Caribbean countries, only Brazil and Chile registered worse Gini coefficients.
125. Kohl and Farthing 2006, pp. 151–2.
126. Kohl 2003, p. 346.
127. Schultz 2005, pp. 16–17.

government's policy-response to the crisis.[128] As others have pointed out, privatisation of the hydrocarbons-sector was a key component in the World Bank's and IMF's overall plan for Bolivia. In a cruelly ironic twist, when that privatisation helped to worsen the economic crisis by sapping the state of a key-source of revenue, the IMF demanded that the budget-shortfall be made up through cuts in social spending and increases in regressive taxes that hit poor Bolivians the hardest.[129]

As can be seen in Table 4.2, the economic crisis at the end of the 1990s reinforced the coalescence of class- and racial inequalities. While the urban population as a whole suffered a poverty-rate of 51.5 per cent in 1999, Quechua-speaking indigenous residents of urban areas suffered a poverty-rate of 55.87 per cent, Aymara speakers 61.45 per cent, and Guaraní and other indigenous language-speaking peoples 92.9 per cent. In rural areas, the situation was worse still. The total rate of rural poverty was 81.58 per cent in 1999, while the rates were 87.5, 89.08, and 78.85 per cent for Quechua, Aymara, and Guaraní (and other indigenous peoples) respectively. The poverty-rate for the country in its entirety was 62.64 per cent in 1999, but 80.19, 78.29, and 83.84 per cent for Quechua-speaking, Aymara-speaking, and Guaraní- and other indigenous-language-speaking indigenous peoples in 1999.[130]

Popular discontent with the social consequences of neoliberalism began to grow quite dramatically in the late 1990s and early 2000s. This can be seen through a number of different indicators. By 2001, according to polls conducted by Latinobarómetro, over 90 per cent of the Bolivian population reported that they thought the income-distribution in the country was 'unfair' or 'very unfair'.[131] Data compiled by the Bolivian Ministry of Labour between 1982 and 2000 attempts to track episodes of strikes or slowdowns as reported in national newspapers.[132] Under Paz Zamora (1989–93) there were 968 strikes

---

128. Fernández Terán 2003, pp. 112–39.

129. Schultz 2005.

130. The relationship between ethnicity and poverty is imperfectly captured by relying exclusively on language-figures. Some of those who do not speak an indigenous language, particularly urban residents, could nonetheless identify themselves as indigenous given the option, for example. Nonetheless, these are the best figures available.

131. World Bank 2005, p. 3.

132. Gray Molina and Chávez 2005, p. 86. While this method tends to bias occurrence of these sorts of contentious episodes in capital-cities, the data nonetheless act 'as a useful proxy for social discontent with the policies of the state or with political actors of different time periods' (Gray Molina and Chávez 2005, p. 86).

Table 4.2   Poverty according to ethnicity and urban/rural geography, 1999

Area/Ethnicity	Poverty-Indices	Extreme-Poverty Indices
Urban Area		
Quechua	55.87	28.04
Aymara	61.45	36.08
Spanish	48.86	21.08
Guaraní and other native language	92.90	69.05
Foreigner	11.44	3.02
None of the above	64.90	23.63
Urban population	51.50	23.63
Rural Area		
Quechua	87.50	68.67
Aymara	89.08	70.43
Spanish	65.84	35.20
Guaraní and other native language	78.85	49.12
Foreigner	50.00	0.00
None of the above	86.62	65.23
Rural population	81.58	59.06
Total		
Quechua	80.19	59.28
Aymara	78.29	57.02
Spanish	51.80	23.53
Guaraní and other native language	83.84	56.19
Foreigner	13.32	2.87
None of the above	74.67	46.43
Population	62.64	36.73

Source: Gray Molina and Chávez 2005, p. 91.

and slowdowns; under Sánchez de Lozada (1993–7) 631; and under Bánzer (1997–2001) 1,364. Clearly, there was a discernible expression of discontent from the population as a response to the social consequences of neoliberalism. The reproduction of the neoliberal form of state-power in Bolivia was increasingly undermined by changes in the balance of racialised class-forces, economic recession, and the declining legitimacy of neoliberalism.

Conclusion

This chapter sought to trace the historical sequences and events that defined the racialised class-struggle and developments of capitalism in its neoliberal form within the Bolivian context. It began by explaining the transition from state-led capitalism to neoliberalism in broad strokes, explaining how Víctor Paz Estenssoro was able to introduce such a radical programme of political economic transformation in 1985. We explored the new political coherence of the Bolivian bourgeoisie and how this allowed the Right to take advantage of hyperinflationary crisis. We also examined the transition in the fulcrum of popular class-struggle from the tin-mines to the coca-plantations, the new world of labour borne of neoliberal restructuring, the formation of the MAS, and various modes of lowland-indigenous resistance that emerged over the neoliberal epoch.

We looked at the dynamics of élite 'pacted democracy' throughout the first and second phases of Bolivian neoliberalism between 1985 and 2000. While consent was tactically employed by the state in its relations with popular organisations of the working class and peasantry over these fifteen years, the frequent recourse to coercion clearly demonstrated that patterns of state-repression introduced in the preceding era of authoritarianism had not entirely been abandoned. Indeed, the neoliberal period showed remarkable continuity of the old scenario, whereby bouts of coercion are interrupted periodically by popular mobilisation of the working classes and the peasantry in defence of their rights.

Finally, it was shown how between 1989 and 1998, Bolivia experienced moderate economic growth. A confluence of external and internal contradictions in the neoliberal model altered that situation quite dramatically in 1999 as the country entered a serious recession. Poverty and inequality shot up, and these increases hit the indigenous working-class and peasant-majority most severely. The privatisation of what had been revenue-generating state-owned enterprises – especially YPFB – amplified the budget-shortfalls experienced by the state during the economic crisis. Dependence on foreign assistance consequently increased. This, in turn, had the effect of further increasing the leverage of international financial institutions and the US-state over domestic Bolivian policy. Their prescription to the crisis was more neoliberalism.

Within much of the Bolivian population, however, a myriad of empirical indicators illustrated that there was growing discontent with the neoliberal-economic programme and the ostensibly democratic, but frequently repressive, régime responsible for its enforcement. Utilising a new infrastructure of class-struggle, social-movement unionism, and variations of Bolivia's entrenched popular cultures of opposition and resistance, the indigenous peasantry and working classes of the department of Cochabamba soon displayed this discontent in dramatic forms of urban and rural rebellion.

Chapter Five

Left-Indigenous Insurrectionary Cycle, 2000–3

The Cochabamba Water-War of 2000, Aymara peasant-insurrections of the western *altiplano* (high plateau) in 2000 and 2001, and proletarian anti-tax revolt
in La Paz and El Alto in February 2003, constituted
the opening acts of what developed into a five-year
cycle of left-indigenous insurrection in Bolivia. This
gradual extension of popular class-power from below
helped shift the balance of class-forces in society and
opened up a crisis within the ruling class by 2003, as
well as an extended crisis of the Bolivian neoliberal
state. The reactive sequences of popular mobilisation
and state-repression over these five years provided
the basis for an escalating scale of radicalism. Anticapitalist and indigenous liberationist demands of
protesters broadened in scope, and the repertoires of
struggle became more confrontational with time.

In the Cochabamba Water-War and the Aymara
peasant-insurrections, dense infrastructures of class-
struggle strengthened the capacities for revolt and
provided an organisational base and political space
for the development of a collective oppositional
consciousness rooted in the politics of indigenous
liberation and class-struggle simultaneously. This
emergent oppositional consciousness defended longstanding indigenous traditions of communal land-
and water-management against market-penetration,

incorporated strategic lessons and ideological visions from hundreds of years of experience in indigenous and worker-radicalism, and made new demands for a constituent assembly and an alternative to neoliberalism. Increasingly, for worker- and peasant-radicals alike, that alternative was seen to be a new variant of socialism adapted to the particularities of Bolivia's social formation. The anti-tax rebellion of February 2003 revealed the depth of the state-crisis, as the military and rank-and-file police-forces turned on each other with arms in the midst of urban working-class rioting. The February uprising was more spontaneous than the other two episodes of contention considered in this chapter, and relied less on the existing infrastructure of class-struggle – although these also played a part. The February rebellion, more than anything, added a strong urban working-class component to the unfolding left-indigenous insurrectionary cycle, and deepened the critique of neoliberalism as protesters explicitly targeted symbols of right-wing political parties, and domestic and foreign capital, during the revolt. In each of the three rebellions, state-repression, employed with the intent of dampening the scale and intensity of protests, had the contrary effect of fuelling the fires of resistance. The legitimacy of the neoliberal order and the expressions of coercive state-power in its defence were increasingly called into question as the number of dead civilians continued to climb.

5.1 The Cochabamba Water-War, 2000

5.1.1 Usos y costumbres *and oppositional consciousness*

The drive to privatise water in the city of Cochabamba and its surrounding countryside acted as the initial catalyst for the emergent left-indigenous struggle in twentieth-first century Bolivia. The Water-War consisted of an anti-neoliberal popular movement, struggling against the commodification of perhaps the most important of public goods.[1] Social-movement actors articulated a powerful understanding of the rebellion, wedded to *usos y*

---

1. For an argument on how the commodification of water in Cochabamba can be usefully theorised in terms of David Harvey's (2003) concept of 'accumulation by dispossession' see Spronk and Webber 2007. McNally 2006 has enlightening things to say regarding the processes of commodification and enclosure of the commons throughout the history of capitalism, and the popular forms of resistance these processes have spawned.

costumbres, or the customary use of commonly governed water-supplies of the Quechua indigenous communities, dating back centuries in rural areas surrounding Cochabamba, and decades in some poor neighbourhoods in the city. The privatisation of water was a fundamental violation of these *usos y costumbres*. Activists also emphasised the notion that water is a resource that is biologically and socially critical for life itself. To privatise water would be to privatise life itself. Water-scarcity and the threat posed by privatisation in the Cochabamba context fundamentally impacted a multi-class, rural and urban layer of the population simultaneously.

The role of the international financial institutions and a consortium of multinational corporations fueled the revitalisation of a rich Bolivian tradition of anti-imperialism. The formation – through collective action and confrontation with the state – of a deepened oppositional consciousness, a stronger sense of solidarity, and a heightened awareness of the power of collective mass-action, contributed to the radicalisation of measures and demands as the protest developed.[2] The Cochabamba Water-War was of fundamental importance in part because it represented the first left-indigenous popular victory following fifteen years of relatively weak and impotent popular resistance on the part of the popular sectors of Bolivian society. The indigenous-peasant and proletarian classes of Bolivia were perceived to have won, if perhaps only temporarily, in a battle against the Bolivian ruling class, the neoliberal state, the World Bank, and a transnational water-consortium led by American transnational Bechtel.

We cannot begin to understand the popular struggle against the commodification of water in the city and region of Cochabamba without first coming to terms with the conflict's position within the greater project of neoliberalism in Bolivia initiated first in 1985. One of the principal leaders of the Water Water, Omar Fernández, reminded me of this when I asked him about the importance of the Water-War, how it started, and how it was associated with the movements that followed throughout the country:

> First, in 1985 a new model was implanted in the country, a neoliberal model based in two fundamental points: the privatisation of the entire economic system and the handing over of natural resources to transnational corporations.

---

2. Tapia 2000.

This model... worsened the economic situation of the country.... One could see, little by little, how the communities, how the people were being left without their natural resources, how the state companies were transferred to private transnational corporations, and how there were no benefits to the population. Rather, there was more unemployment.... The capital disappeared because... this was an economic system that functioned like a vacuum cleaner; that is, the only thing the transnationals did was to take the profits outside the country.[3]

Fernández goes on to link the neoliberal-economic model to the specific situation of water in Cochabamba:

In Cochabamba, we can see clearly that this system also tried to privatise water, tried to take water from peasant communities and give it to a transnational. The transnational tried to raise the tariffs in Cochabamba which caused this mobilisation. It was in Cochabamba, where a situation emerged that extended throughout the entire country, in which the people were no longer prepared to continue with the [neoliberal] model.[4]

He notes how the Water-War was about more than simply water, and how the popular mobilisation set an example for other movements throughout the country in the years to come:

In this sense, the people did not only want to reclaim the water, the people said that they had to reclaim all that had been given to the transnationals. The people also realised that through mobilisations, through the unity of different sectors we can win important victories like the Water-War. It's because of this that in October 2003 there was a mobilisation in this country [the first Gas-War], above all in El Alto, where the people were ready to reclaim hydrocarbons for the benefit of the Bolivian people.[5]

5.1.2 Infrastructure of class-struggle

The success of the Cochabamba Water-War depended on the recomposition of rural and urban infrastructures of class-struggle. These infrastructures took

---

3. Fernández 2005.
4. Fernández 2005.
5. Fernández 2005.

novel forms, adapting to the changes in the country's class-structure that grew out of neoliberal-economic restructuring in the 1980s and 1990s. The infrastructure of class-struggle in the case of the Cochabamba Water-War is illustrated in Figure 5.1. As indicated there, the central organisational actor was the Coordinadora, integrated by five organisations. There was no formal hierarchy between the organisations of the Coordinadora, but the larger circles above, encompassing the Federación de Fabriles de Cochabamba (Federation of Factory-Workers of Cochabamba, Fabriles), the Federación Departamental de Regantes (Departmental Federation of Peasant-Irrigators of Cochabamba, FEDECOR), and the Coordinadora de las seis federaciones del trópico de Cochabamba (Coordinator of the Six Coca-Grower's Federations of Tropical Cochabamba, CSFTC) indicate the more prominent role these organisations played in practice relative to the less significant organisations encompassed in the smaller circles below, the Central Obrera Departamental (Departmental Workers' Central of Cochabamba, COD-Cochabamba), and the Federación de Maestros Urbanos de Cochabamba (Urban Teachers' Federation of Cochabamba, FMUC). Table 5.1 summarises the grievances, demands, protest-repertoires, and geographical scope of this infrastructure of class-struggle over the course of the Water-War.

The key foundation of the Coordinadora was the Fabriles, led by Oscar Olivera – the grandson of a miner, the son of a carpenter, and himself a shoe-factory worker who became the most important popular leader in the entire Water-War (see Figure 5.1). The Fabriles were important because they adopted a politics of social-movement unionism. Their organising techniques, driven by this political orientation, helped to rebuild a popular infrastructure of class-struggle in the rural and urban areas of the department of Cochabamba. This infrastructure then reached its zenith in the form of the Coordinadora. The dank offices of the Fabriles are situated in the central plaza of Cochabamba. Over a number of years preceding the Water-War, they had become a central locale for activists organising in the city, a place where the complaints of unorganised workers could be voiced and addressed. The Fabriles were the most adept of any unions in Cochabamba at navigating the new terrain of the informalised neoliberal labour-market, after the devastation of union-power throughout the 1980s and 1990s. The union made an explicit effort to join in various community-struggles, and to organise unorganised, temporary, subcontracted, and precariously-situated workers, especially women and young people.

Table 5.1 Cochabamba Water-War, January–April 2000

Infrastructure/Forces	Grievances	Demands	Protest-Repertoires	Geographical Scope
Coordinadora (Leadership – Oscar Olivera and Omar Fernández)	Accumulated social consequences of Neoliberalism	Reversal of water-privatisation	Street-Clashes with armed forces and police	Department o[f] Cochabamba
Federation of Factory-Workers of Cochabamba (Fabriles)	State-repression Water-privatisation	Alternative to neoliberalism Constituent assembly	Mass-assemblies Road-blocks	
FEDECOR	Violation of *usos y costumbres* – communal traditions of water-management	Deepening of democracy in all spheres of social life	Mass-occupations of public urban spaces	
CSFTC				
(Leadership – Evo Morales)			marches	
COD-Cochabamba				
FMUC				
Residents of peripheral urban slums/poor water-consumers				
Street-kids				
International activists				

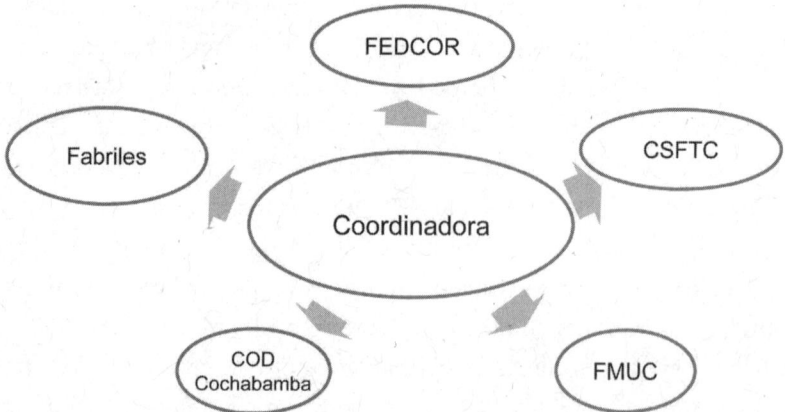

Figure 5.1 Coordinadora

The Fabriles also hosted educational forums on the new situation facing the working class, and attempted to foster and rebuild a culture of working-class solidarity that had been stunted severely by years of economic restructuring.[6] The efforts to rebuild working-class power through education and organisation on the part of the Fabriles are perhaps best expressed in a speech delivered by Olivera at the Eighteenth Congress of the Confederation of Bolivian Workers in September 2000:

> The only effective way to defend ourselves and launch a real campaign of resistance is to build organisational links to 'irregular' workers (and this includes temporaries, sub-contracted workers, piecework laborers, and seasonal employees). This strategy needs to encompass every factory, every mine, every enterprise – whether or not it is privatised – and the hundreds of little subcontracting workshops.... At the moment, because of the bosses' manipulations, it looks like these workers are our competitors. But we are all workers who produce wealth that ends up in the hands of the same bosses.[7]

Because of the moral authority gained through a long history of organising along the lines of social-movement unionism, and the leadership-qualities of Olivera, the offices of the Fabriles also became the headquarters of the Coordinadora, and Olivera became the President of the Coordinadora.[8]

FEDECOR, led by Omar Fernández, is widely recgonised as the other foundational backbone of the Coordinadora, alongside the Fabriles.[9] FEDECOR was officially founded on 3 October 1997 in the community of Tiquipaya, after a lengthy organising process of seminars and workshops that brought together different indigenous peasant-movements.[10] The indigenous-peasant resistance-movements from which FEDECOR emerged had been battling with

---

6. Gutiérrez Aguilar 2008.
7. Olivera 2004c, pp. 124–5.
8. García Linera 2004b, c, p. 80.
9. García Linera, Chávez Léon, and Costas Monje 2005, pp. 623–6. Fernández was the Coordinadora's first vice-president.
10. Vargas and Kruse 2000. It is also important not to obscure a much longer history of popular organising and Quechua indigenous traditions of communal water-governance. According to many analysts, the organising infrastructures of governance and regulation around water and irrigation in the Cochabamba Valley have, with some modifications, existed since precolonial times (García Linera 2005a). See, also, Larson 1998.

the city of Cochabamba over water-resources since the 1970s.[11] Between 1994 and 1996, various community irrigating organisations joined together in these struggles, transcending the limitations of localised resistance. Eventually, a number of communities in the Central Valley came together to forge a united front against escalating city-consumption of scarce water-supplies.

A third social force in the Water-War were the *cocaleros*, led by Evo Morales, and organised through the CSFTC.[12] The *cocaleros* constituted a cohesive presence within the Coordinadora as well as participating directly in marches and confrontations with state-authorities, before and during the Water-War. They were able to forge rural linkages with the *regantes*, urban alliances with the popular classes of Cochabamba, and even overcome some of the middle-class distrust of their struggles over the coca-leaf through their valiant participation in the Water-War. As others have noted, the compact and disciplined presence of the *cocaleros* during the Water-War renewed the life of the protest at critical junctures.[13] As Figure 5.1 illustrates, the COD-Cochabamba, and the FMUC were also integrated into the Coordinadora and played a secondary role in organising and carrying out demonstrations during the Water-War.

Apart from these more formally-organised actors, a host of other social groups that cut across different classes intervened in secondary ways. For example, the privatisation-law threatened the local water-associations of residents of the peripheral neighbourhoods of the city. They had, through sheer ingenuity, created forms of water self-governance over the years in lieu of public systems that would service their neighbourhoods. These poor urban residents became a key social force in the road-blockades and confrontations of the Water-War. Important, too, were those water-consumers who had access to the SEMAPA (the public water-utility) network which was taken over by Aguas del Tunari. By January 2000, after the takeover, the increase in tariffs for some water-consumers exceeded 200 per cent. According to some estimates, the new tariffs raised rates to 'approximately $35 American per family per month, in a city where the minimum wage is around $60'.[14]

---

11. Confrontations intensified considerably in the mid-1990s, as SEMAPA dug deep wells in the countryside to service growing demands for water in the city. In 1994, for example, such activities spawned a large-scale peasant-mobilisation against well-drilling, mobilisations that would continue throughout the 1990s (Crespo 2000).
12. Gutiérrez Aguilar 2001.
13. García Linera, Chávez León, and Costas Monje 2005.
14. Vargas and Kruse 2000.

Consumers across the working and middle classes were incensed by the tariff-hikes and displayed their discontent in the streets. Sections of the middle class and university-students supported the protests of the Water-War, especially as their momentum increased.

Without doubt the most heroic unorganised sector of the rebellion were the street-kids, or the self-identified 'guerreros del agua [water-warriors]'. In the most furious zones of police-repression and activist-resistance, it was no coincidence that the strongest presence was that of the water-warriors. The dispossessed were transformed in the course of struggle into water-warriors, 'nobodies' became giants. The insurrectional process itself gave those with the least to lose, in some senses, a renewed sense of life, even as they were, paradoxically, the most willing to die.[15]

Less important, but still worth mentioning, were groups of professionals who intervened in dealings with the technical aspects of the law and the contract with Aguas del Tunari.[16] For example, the Sociedad de Ingenieros Bolivianos (Society of Bolivian Engineers, SIB), while having supported well-drilling in the past, expressly came out against it by the end of 1990s, and joined forces with FEDECOR and other organisations in formulating technical alternatives.[17] Finally, the Cochabamba Water-War became a powerful symbol at the international level, an inspiration for social movements around the world fighting against privatisation and for social justice. In particular, Oscar Olivera became a world-renowned figure in the global-justice movement. In mid-April 2000, on his first trip outside of Bolivia, he flew to Washington DC to participate in demonstrations against the IMF and World Bank. Essential to this undertaking, as well as to the wider-scale publicity-efforts within

---

15. Orellana Aillón 2004.
16. Gutiérrez Aguilar 2001.
17. Assies 2003. Another example of professional involvement is the Comité de Defensa del Agua y la Economía Familiar (Committee in Defence of Water and the Family-Economy, CDAEF), an organisation formed by environmentalists, technical advisors, and neighbourhood-representatives in June 1999 to study the possible consequences of a new water-law on privatisation (Crespo 2000). Advisers from non-governmental organisations also played an important role. Peasant-organisations, indigenous peoples, and colonists, interacting with NGO-organisers, reacted to an executive draft-law on water-resources in August 1998, for example: 'They came together as a national technical water board to develop a counterproposal inspired by the International Labor Organization's (ILO) Convention 169, and Article 171 of the Bolivian Constitution, which recognise the social economic, and cultural rights of indigenous peoples' (Assies 2003).

progressive media-networks internationally, was a group of expatriate Americans living in Bolivia and active in local and international social-movement networks. Most important among these activists were Jim Shultz and Tom Kruse.[18] This appearance by Olivera in Washington brought a new level of international exposure to left-indigenous struggles in Bolivia.

All of these organisations and less-organised participant-groups – the rural and urban infrastructure of class-struggle – were tied together through the Coordinadora. The Coordinadora had its origins in FEDECOR and the Fabriles who, in the face of Law 2029, began to work seriously at building a network of allies, a major part of this effort being a series of meetings and assemblies held in the offices of the Fabriles in late 1999. On 12 November of that year, the Coordinadora was officially constituted with over twenty participating social-movement organisations.[19]

The deeply democratic nature of the Coordinadora also contributed to its successes. Assemblies of urban water-committees, peasant-irrigators, poor urban *barrios*, unions, and other local spaces facilitated the collective process for resolving problems, and linked immediate needs facing communities with larger-scale political and economic structures of domination and exploitation. The Coordinadora functioned with rotational delegations from all of the participating local associations, unions and committees. In intense moments of struggle, such as in April, this popular parliament governed daily. There were also *cabildos*, or open gatherings, in which crowds from between 5,000 and 100,000 made collective decisions to block roads, declare general strikes, and engage in other collective actions. Finally, the Coordinadora had an executive committee headed by Olivera and Fernández. This committee was regularly held to account through the *cabildos*.[20] As its name suggests, therefore, the Coordinadora was a flexible co-ordinator of various social movements and infrastructures of rural and urban popular class-struggle.[21]

These characteristics of participatory and assemblyist styles of revolutionary democracy in the streets were critical to the emergence of extraordinary,

---

18. Albro 2005b.
19. Founding participants included FFEDECOR and other irrigators' associations, civic committees from the rural provinces of the department of Cochabamba, the COD-Cochabamba, the Fabriles, and the FMUC, among others. See Figure 5.1.
20. Gutiérrez, García, and Tapia 2002, pp. 174–5.
21. García Linera, Chávez Léon, and Costas Monje 2005, p. 634.

if localised, expressions of popular power. García Linera writes, 'A number of times in 2000 (February, April, and September–October), this dense web of assemblies and plebeian democratic practices not only demanded rights from the state with its system of parties and parliament, but also replaced the state as the mechanism of government, as the system of mediation, and as the culture of obedience'.[22]

5.1.3   Three battles and state-crisis

Over the last several decades, demographic change, capitalist development, and rapid urbanisation in a region of natural water-scarcity primed the department of Cochabamba for the emergence of serious public contention over water-resources. In the decades following the National Revolution, manufacturing, construction-, and service-sector expansion in the city of Cochabamba drew in rural migrants. The closure of the tin-mines in 1985 also fed population-growth in the city. A succession of droughts in the 1980s played an additional role in pushing peasants to migrate. The city's population grew from 205,000 to 414,000 between 1976 and 1992.[23] Urban infrastructure did not keep pace. In 2000 the public potable-water and sewerage-system reached scarcely half the population of the city, and even this service was rationed and irregular.[24] In the Central Valley, small-holding indigenous peasants were intensively farming their *minifundia*, producing carrots, peaches, peas, corn, wheat, and barley for the burgeoning urban markets. Pig- and dairy-farming were also accelerating.[25]

All of this commercial activity in the rural areas heightened demand for irrigation, while the rapid population-growth simultaneously spiked levels of water-consumption in the cities. This scenario created serious water-conflicts dating back to the 1970s. Conflicts intensified in the 1990s with the expansion of well-drilling under the guidance of SEMAPA. With the concession to Aguas del Tunari and the passing of Law 2029 in 1999, the Water-War began in earnest. The height of the conflict, however, can be distilled to three intense

22. García Linera 2004c, p. 81.
23. Assies 2003.
24. Laserna 2000.
25. Orellana Aillón 2004.

episodes in January, February, and April 2000, remembered by participants as the three 'battles' of the Water-War.

Water-consumers streamed into the offices of the Coordinadora displaying with anger paper-slips demonstrating their inflated tariffs. The Coordinadora called a public meeting on January 10 in response. Water-consumers, urban water-committees, professionals, environmentalists, trade-unionists, FEDE-COR, and the Fabriles rallied to the Coordinadora's call to assemble. At the assembly, an indefinite blockade of the city was ratified, to begin the next day.[26] In the following days, marches proliferated throughout the city, block-ades were strong in the peripheral urban *barrios* and in rural areas, and the Manaco shoe-factory workers launched an important parade of bicycles, link-ing the issue of water-access to their workplace-resistance over the firing of 60 workers. A ministerial delegation was sent to Cochabamba and on 14 January a temporary truce was reached with the government.[27]

The truce was short-lived, however. With demands unfulfilled and the government not proceeding seriously with negotiations, on 4 February, the Coordinadora launched a 'toma pacífica', or peaceful takeover, of the Plaza de Armas, the symbolic heart of power in the city. Their demands included the repeal of Law 2029 and presidential decrees that had facilitated the con-cession. They also called for the revocation of the Aguas del Tunari contract, the annulling of the Superintendency of basic services, and the building of a consensus with popular forces around the Water-Resource Law still being passed through Congress at the time.[28] The state responded by sending the infamous *dálmatas* (dalmations – a motorcycle police-section) from La Paz and Oruro. Days earlier the Grupo Especial de Seguridad (GES, Special Security-Forces) had been deployed in the city. Repression began on the morning of 4 February, with tear-gas and police-clubs being used against protesters.[29]

That day and the next there were ferocious street-battles between protest-ers and the repressive arms of the state, the latter reduced to defending a four-block perimeter surrounding the plaza, while the crowd in rebellion con-trolled the rest of the city, and indeed the rest of the region with roadblocks and a general strike. Even control of the plaza passed to the people late in

---

26. Gutiérrez 2000.
27. Assies 2003.
28. Crespo Flores 2000.
29. Olivera 2004d, p. 34.

the evening of 5 February.[30] The city was entirely paralysed, with vehicular transit impossible. Again, after 22 protesters were injured and 135 detained, a fragile truce was declared, mediated by the Catholic Church and the Human Rights Ombudsperson.[31] The truce was based on the government's promise to revise the Aguas del Tunari contract, to modify Law 2029 with the participation of civil society, and a suspension of the tariff-rate increases.[32]

By the end of February, negotiations had once again reached a deadlock. In March, the principal spokespeople for the Coordinadora announced that a revision of the contract was insufficient, and that a continued truce would require instead the cancellation of the contract in its entirety. The Coordinadora steered itself out of state-negotiations and at the end of March launched a 'consulta popular', or popular referendum, through which the population was asked to respond to three questions concerning the tariffs, the contract with Aguas del Tunari, and the law on water-privatisation. Over 50,000 people responded to the referendum on 26 March which had been organised in an incredibly brief period of ten days. One reporter captures the government's response: 'In March, the Coordinadora held an unofficial referendum, counted nearly fifty thousand votes, and announced that ninety-six per cent favored the cancellation of the contract with Aguas del Tunari. "There is nothing to negotiate", the government replied'.[33]

The stage was set for the 'Last Battle'. Popular mobilisations had spread to other parts of the country. By the end of March, the Confederación Sindical Única de Trabajadores Campesinos de Bolivia (Trade-Union Confederation of Bolivian Peasant-Workers, CSUTCB) began blockading roads with its own list of demands, particularly in the rural districts of the department of La Paz, while FEDECOR erected road-blocks in the department of Cochabamba. On 4 April, the third and final phase of the Water-War was launched with a general strike in Cochabamba city and a general blockade of highways in the entire department. Rotating groups of families and communities monitored the blockades for a given set of hours, replaced methodically by the next rotation. The communities ensured that the activists in the streets and blockades were

---

30. Vargas and Kruse 2000.
31. Assies (2003, p. 26), citing the national daily *Presencia*, presents different figures: 70 civilians and 51 policemen wounded, 172 people arrested.
32. Crespo Flores 2000.
33. Finnegan 2002.

regularly nourished with food and beverages.[34] The next day, over 15,000 people convened in the plaza. Present in abundance were the multicoloured *polleras* (skirts) of indigenous-peasant women. The *wiphala* indigenous flag was another important symbolic component of the protest. The *wiphala* had already come to symbolise multinational-indigenous resistance, but later gained even greater force as the centre of mobilisations shifted to the *altiplano* and the cities of El Alto and La Paz in the following months and years. These symbols tie the Water-War directly to the whole cycle of social movements contributing to left-indigenous resurgence over the following five years. An oppositional consciousness, adapting traditions of the past to new rural and urban settings, began to congeal. It combined expressions and desires of indigenous liberation with class-politics.[35]

Late in the evening of 6 April, delegates of the Coordinadora were arrested by police as they attended negotiations with ministerial representatives of the government. The next day, protests reached an unprecedented scale. Radio-transmissions in Quechua notified the peasantry of the arrests, and a generalised mobilisation of the countryside began immediately. Urban radio and television transmitted the news to *Cochabambinos*, as residents of Cochabamba are called, with parallel effect. The teenagers, men, and women who constituted the rank of file of the water-committees of each urban *barrio* carried their banners, clubs, bottles, molotovs, rocks and knives into the plaza ready to confront the state. Roughly 60,000 poor urban dwellers and peasants gathered by midday marching through the city's central streets.[36]

Bánzer's government declared a state of siege, suspending constitutional rights and facilitating mass-arrests. The depth of social discontent revealed itself still more profoundly. On the day the siege was declared, 880 low-paid police mutinied in La Paz, taking advantage of the government's vulnerability to push for wage-demands. Simultaneously, *cocaleros* in the Yungas region of La Paz erected blockades, while students joined protests in the streets of Bolivia's capital.[37] Meanwhile, in Cochabamba, the streets came alive once again with the state of siege precipitating another wave of protests, assemblies

---

34. Gutiérrez 2000.
35. In Chapter 8, I analyse at length the various facets of what I call the 'combined-oppositional consciousness' that developed at the height of the left-indigenous insurrectionary cycle.
36. Gutiérrez 2000.
37. Assies 2003.

and barricades, now amidst a torrent of tear-gas and the use of live ammunition by the state's repressive apparatuses. The street-kids took a leading part in the confrontations. Seventeen-year-old Victor Hugo Daza was shot in the face by the military. Protesters soon after carried his dead body to the plaza.[38]

On 10 April, the Coordinadora and the government signed an agreement that annulled the contract with Aguas del Tunari, and ensured the reassertion of SEMAPA as the public water-system although now with representatives from the Coordinadora on its board. Detainees were released and the wounded were cared for at the expense of the government.[39] Oscar Olivera declared victory to a suspicious crowd, and the Water-War wound its way to a close, with social movements soon declaring it a major conquest over neoliberalism. In the words of Olivera:

> They tossed a foreign corporation out of the country. Even better, they briefly replaced the government, the political parties, the prefects, and the state itself with a new type of popular government based on assemblies and town meetings held at the regional and state levels. For one week, the state had been demolished. In its place stood the *self-government* of the poor based on their local and regional organisational structures.[40]

That the Water-War had developed into something much broader in scope than its initial protagonists intended became clear in September 2000. At a mass-assembly that month, the Coordinadora leadership publicly demanded a constituent assembly to remake the country in the interests of the indigenous proletarian and peasant-majority. The constituent assembly they envisaged would bring together 'urban workers, irrigation farmers, villagers, *cocaleros*,

---

38. As Assies points out in a footnote, 'A few days later PAT-TV made public a video film showing a sniper in civilian clothes, later identified as Captain Iriarte, kneeling behind a line of soldiers, who clearly offered him cover, and then taking aim and firing into the crowd. Though what happened was clear for all to see, government officials invented lie after lie to deny any government or army responsibility. Human rights groups in Cochabamba registered 59 wounded, 24 of whom had bullet wounds' (Assies 2003, p. 35). The injustice went beyond lying as, 'Captain Robinson Iriarte, who graduated from the US School of the Americas, the training center for state terrorists in Ft. Benning, Georgia, was later acquitted of any wrongdoing by a military court and reinstated in his post' (Olivera 2004, p. 43). Relying on documents of the Asamblea Permanente de Derechos Humanos de Cochabamba, Albro writes that, by the end of the Water-War, 'six people had died nationwide, with hundreds more injured and dozens forcibly detained by the police authorities' (Albro 2005, p. 252).
39. Assies 2003.
40. Olivera 2004c, p. 125.

Aymaran communities, landless peasants, and beyond'.[41] It was to be, 'a new type of political action born out of civil society as a means to discuss and to decide collective matters'.[42] Olivera emphasised that the constituent assembly 'should be understood as a great sovereign meeting of citizen representatives elected by their neighborhood organisations, their urban and rural associations, their unions, their communes'.[43] These organic representatives of the popular classes, 'would decide upon the modes of political representation, social control, and self-government that we should give ourselves for the ensuing decades'.[44]

It is important to note that the Water-War initiated a cycle of left-indigenous protest that spread throughout the country. It proved to be the spark of Bolivia's most recent left-indigenous cycle of revolt: Olivera expressed this dynamic to me in a powerful fashion:

> The people realised that its possible to defeat the system, that it's possible to defeat the transnationals and that it's possible to dispense with the political parties of the institutional state-system that up until that moment had been privatised by the political parties. They had privatised the right to speak and to make decisions. Therefore, I think that we broke not only the monopoly of the transnationals and their plundering of our natural resources, but the monopoly on the right to speak and make decisions held by the political parties. The people, since 2000, since the Water-War, began a process of self-organisation, a process of mobilisation, a process of proposals and demands that culminated, I would say, in the great popular uprising of October 2003 which threw out...the most symbolic, the most emblematic figure of neo-liberalism, Gonzalo Sánchez de Lozada.[45]

5.2 The insurrectionary Aymara peasantry

If the Water-War in Cochabamba was one regional axis of the emergent insurrectionary cycle in 2000, another critical zone was the western *altiplano* of the departments of Oruro and La Paz, as well as the northern valleys of

---

41. Olivera 2004a, p. 136.
42. Ibid.
43. Ibid.
44. Olivera 2004a, p. 137.
45. Personal interview, July 2005.

the latter.[46] In April and September–October 2000, as well as in June–July 2001, the Aymara peasantry in these regions, organised through the CSUTCB and led by Aymara radical Felipe Quispe, orchestrated wide-scale mobilisations with massive road-blockades. The protests marked the historic re-emergence of the Aymara peasantry, which had not made a political intervention of this magnitude since the rural component of the 1979 struggles for democracy, led by Genaro Flores.

5.2.1 The CSUTCB and rural infrastructure of class-struggle

Deborah Yashar's emphasis on the importance of pre-existing transcommunity-networks for the emergence of indigenous social movements in Latin America corresponds tightly with Bolivian reality.[47] At the macrostructural level in the *altiplano*, the CSUTCB and the web of rural unions-*ayllus* whose current structures date back to the 1953 postrevolutionary land-reform processes are key. The structure of the CSUTCB is illustrated in Figure 5.2. At the micro-structural level, the reassertion of traditional Aymara organisational repertoires of social, political, economic, and insurrectional life also played a determining role in the rebellions of 2000 and 2001. Table 5.2 indicates the infrastructure of struggle, grievances, demands, protest repertoires, and geographic scope of the Aymara insurrections, only the highlights from which are discussed in the text. The CSUTCB was formed in 1979 at a congress for peasant-unity convoked by the COB. The formation of the CSUTCB brought a definitive end to conservative Pacto Militar Campesino, and represented the beginning of an independent indigenous-peasant movement. While, technically, the CSUTCB remains a part of the COB, in practice, it acts as an autonomous body with its own complex infrastructural web extending to all nine departments of the country. An executive committee stands above nine departmental federations in the organisation's hierarchy (see Figure 5.2).[48]

The infrastructure of indigenous-peasant class-struggle provided by the CSUTCB was critical to the mobilisations of 2000 and 2001. For April

---

46. García Linera 2002a; Gutiérrez and García Linera 2002; Kohl 2006.
47. Yashar 2005, pp. 71–5.
48. From here the CSUTCB's structure descends into increasingly smaller geographically representative structures, from provinces, to cantons (with their own centrals), to sub-centrals, and, finally, to small indigenous communities, and base-level agrarian unions, *sindicatos comunales*, and *ayllus*.

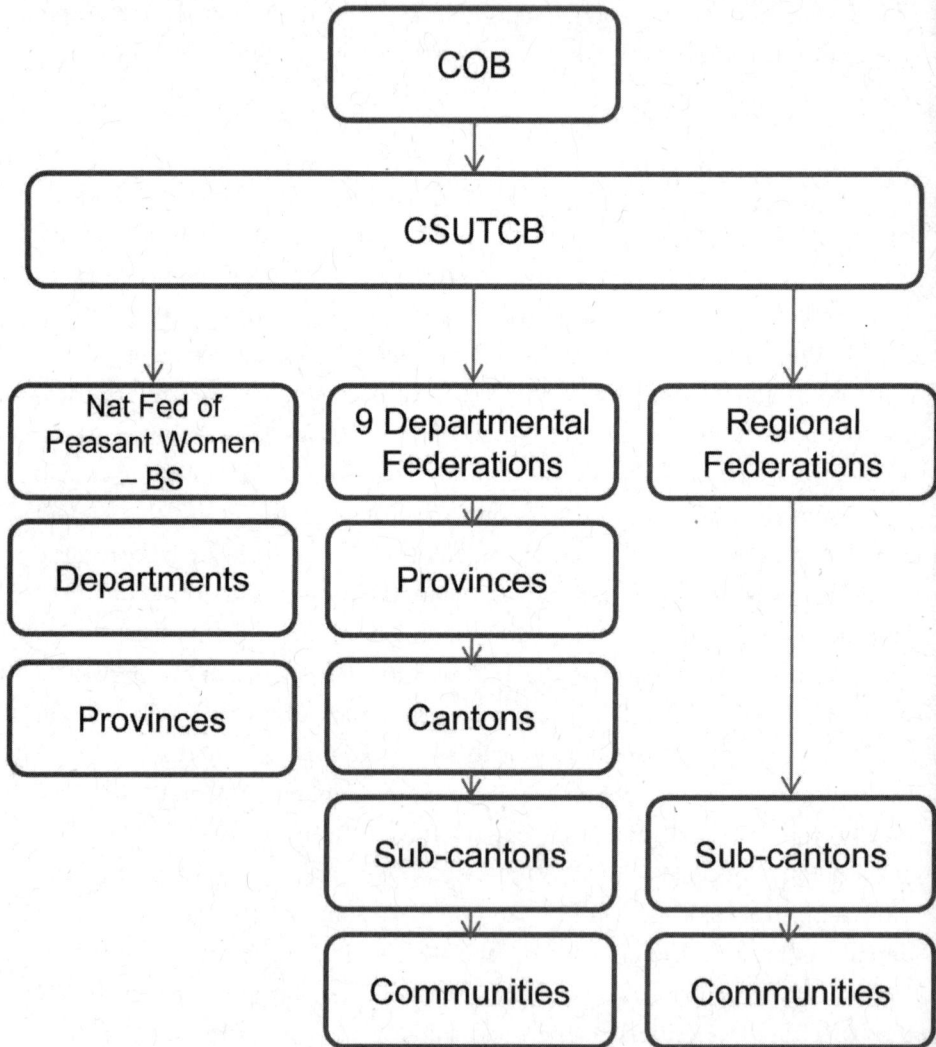

Figure 5.2   CSUTCB

Table 5.2   Aymara peasant-insurrections, April–September 2000
and June–July 2001

Infrastructure/ orces	Grievances	Demands	Protest-repertoires	Geographical scope
SUTCB Leadership-Felipe Quispe)	Accumulated social consequences of neoliberalism	Regional indigenous self-governance in the western *altiplano* – Aymara nationalism	Road-blocks	*Centre*
	State-repression		Destruction of state-offices and institutions	Rural sectors of departments of Oruro and La Paz
	Water-privatisation	End to coca-eradication	Liberation of political prisoners	*Periphery*
	INRA land-law			
	Coca-eradication	Reversal of water-privatisation plans	Marches	Rural sectors of departments of Cochabamba, Chuquisaca, Beni, Pando, and Tarija
	Violation of *usos y costumbres* – threat to communal management of land and water by market- and state-forces	Abolition of INRA	Clashes with armed forces in rural communities and rural highways	
		Agricultural subsidies for poor-peasant communities		
		Access to agricultural technologies for poor-peasant communities	Establishment of general headquarters of Qalachaka	
	Violations of indigenous autonomy in the western *altiplano* by market- and state-forces	Communitarian socialist system rooted in *ayllus* and indigenous communities	Symbolic use of *wiphala* and other indigenous representations of resistance and power	
		Democracy in all spheres of social life		

and September–October 2000 and June–July 2001, the leadership of Felipe Quispe within the executive committee was also a key factor, as we will see. Below the executive, however, the role of the federation in the department of La Paz, as well as all the smaller units of the CSUTCB hierarchy within the department, facilitated the rebellions. It is important to point out that, while there is an elaborate formal hierarchy within the CSUTCB, in practice the hierarchy is often disrupted. So, for example, each departmental federation enjoys substantial autonomy in the development of its politics, practical decisions, and general political subculture. Similarly, provincial federations often enjoy autonomy in relation to the departmental federations above them. The loose nature of the network in this sense frequently has important consequences for the dynamics of rural peasant-struggle in Bolivia. Rather than declarations or orders for mobilisation being issued from the executive committee, for example, it is often the case that mobilisations swell up from below through provincial and departmental federations, obligating the executive committee to subsequently take up the cause and co-ordinate actions at a more macro-level. This was precisely the chain of command during the September–October 2000 events.[49]

Some of the general features of the CSUTCB can be teased out if we look at the relationship between the executive committee of the CSUTCB and the Federación Departamental Única de Trabajadores Campesinos de La Paz – Tupaj Katari (Departmental Federation of Peasant-Workers of La Paz – Tupaj Katari, FDUTCLP-TK). In general, if the executive committee decides to support a mobilisation-effort, the leadership of the FDUTCLP-TK, representing all of the provinces of the department of La Paz, will immediately convene to decide whether or not the department is going to participate in the collective action, and, if so, how it will participate. During the actual process of mobilisations and road-blockades the federation is obliged to hold regular meetings to evaluate the dynamics of the situation as they unfold. Furthermore, the federation has to maintain fluid lines of communication and consultation with provincial-level representatives, both to explain the motivations behind the mobilisation and to assess the popular sentiments of the rank and file. These rituals of constant meetings between the departmental and provincial federations, and, in turn, between provincial federations and community-bases through wider assemblies on the ground, are fundamental to the socialisation and politicisation of the bases. Only through these mechanisms do the themes around which the peasantry is mobilising gain social legitimacy. The deliberative rituals go a long way towards explaining the tremendous social capacity of mobilisations in the *altiplano*.[50] At the same time, without the extensive and layered infrastructure, provincial protests would remain parochial affairs. The capacity literally to shut down the country, as in September–October 2000, depended on the vitality of the infrastructure as a whole, even if there are different levels of politicisation, radicalisation, and mobilising capacity from province to province, and department to department.[51]

---

49. García Linera, Chávez Léon, and Costas Monje 2005, p. 136.
50. García Linera, Chávez Léon, and Costas Monje 2005, pp. 138–9.
51. Sub-centrals and agrarian-communal unions (*sindicatos comunales*), play a determinative role in the basic logistics of mobilisation in the Bolivian countryside. The sub-centrals act as intermediaries between the *sindicatos comunales* and the centrals of

Since the 1953 land-reform, the population in the countryside of the *alti-plano* has been organised formally into *sindicatos agrarios*, or agrarian unions. In practice, however, the ways in which these union-apparatuses have inter-mixed and blended with indigenous patterns of cultural and political organi-sation vary widely from region to region.[52] In some regions, the indigenous names of traditional authorities persist, and, in others, they have re-emerged with the politicisation of indigenous identities since the 1970s. For example, within various Aymara areas of the Bolivian countryside, the figures of *Mallku* and *T'alla* remain central to local self-governance.[53] Several *ayllus* organised together constitute *markas*, which are, in turn, divided organisationally into two parts, one higher (*aransaya*), and one lower (*urinsaya*). The Mallku is, therefore, the most important figure within a grouping of *ayllus*, called a *marka*. The Mallku governs in collaboration with *jilaqatas*. The latter function as the most important authority in each *ayllu*.[54]

These indigenous authority-structures, sometimes in combination with agrarian union-structures, represent the micro-level infrastructures of indig-enous class-struggle in the countryside, the cultural and institutional bases of the CSUTCB. Just as these ways of governing determine the organisation of daily life in many areas, they also have effects in the form of indigenous-peasant class-struggle. One example is the function of communal discipline [*disciplina communal*], with its dual components of obligation and rotation. During a road-blockade, for example, within a collective logic, each commu-nity, or sections of a community, takes a turn blocking roads and participating in marches or other forms of protest – for hours or days depending on the sce-nario. The communities or sections of communities then rotate, such that those

---

each canton. The dynamic interaction between these three levels precisely determines the timing, assignments of tasks, and all the functions of the different players in rural collective action (García Linera, Chávez Léon, and Costas Moje 2005, p. 142).

52. In general, it is not individuals who are incorporated into the unions on the basis of employment. Instead, entire communities are members of a union. In many regions, union-positions fulfill the role traditionally played by indigenous authorities, and are still elected either through assembly-style consensual democracy in the communities or by one-year leadership rotation based on possession of land within the community. In the latter case, leadership of the community rotates from the occupiers of different parcels of land annually.

53. Mallku, a male figure, and T'alla, the wife of Mallku, together act as political, social, religious, and territorial leaders of multiple *ayllus* at once.

54. Mamani Ramírez 2004, pp. 100–1.

at the blockades return to their land to watch the animals and attend to crops.[55] The same system of rotation dictates the provision of food and water to those on the blockades and protesting, which helps to explain how extremely poor communities have been able repeatedly to engage in such impressive periods of sustained mobilisation. In terms of obligation, it is understood within communities that just as with other obligations owed to the community in the routines of daily life, when, through assemblies, the community decides to mobilise it is obligatory that community-members participate.[56]

5.2.2 Blocking roads: April, September–October 2000 and June–July 2001

While the Water-War was raging in Cochabamba in April 2000, the Aymara peasantry instigated another set of actions in the western Andes of Bolivia. The immediate causes of the Aymara regional uprising were similar to those that ignited protest in Cochabamba. Fundamental as a spark to the insurrection in the *altiplano* was a bill before Congress that would have privatised access to water in the region. Just as the Quechua *regantes* had appealed to *usos y costumbres* in Cochabamba to contest water-privatisation, Aymara peasants in Oruro and La Paz demanded that the new water-bill not be passed because it violated communal indigenous understandings of water: '... in the logic of the ayllus, water cannot be bought or sold, or subjected to market logic because water is a vital part of life: it is the blood of the pachamama.... Mother earth, pachamama, would die if it [water] became a commodity with market value'.[57]

---

55. Patzi 2005a, p. 213.

56. García Linera, Chávez Léon, and Costas Monje 2005, pp. 164–5. Radio has also made a tremendously important contribution to the rural infrastructure of peasant class-struggle. It was vital for the transmission of ideas and the participation of leaders and rank and file alike in recent insurrections within the *altiplano*. Radio-transmissions in indigenous languages were crucial, at a practical level, in terms of publicising decisions made at meetings of leaders at various levels, and, at a political level, in terms of raising political consciousness in otherwise fairly isolated communities. Radio contributes enormously to the construction of a wider sense of collective solidarity. Indigenous community-members called into radio-shows as much as they simply received notices from their leaders. Radio San Gabriel, a station that transmits its programmes in Aymara, is a defining component of the political culture of the Aymara countryside (García Linera, Chávez Léon, and Costas Monje 2005, pp. 146–8; Espinoza 2004, pp. 33–5).

57. Mamani Ramírez 2004, p. 81.

The Aymara insurgents also demanded the annulment of the law of the Instituto Nacional de Reforma Agraria (National Agrarian-Reform Institute, INRA), promulgated by the Sánchez de Lozada government in 1996 as part of its Plan de Todos (Plan for Everyone). The Aymara peasants saw the law as a threat to their traditional *ayllu*-systems of land-governance in the *altiplano*, especially as the INRA-process increasingly emphasised land-titling and individual property-rights, a response to pressures from the World Bank and large-landholding lobbyists.[58] Protesters were also motivated to act on a host of other short-term demands, including the need for agricultural subsidies and access to new agricultural technologies, the creation of rural indigenous universities, and an end to the eradication of coca-crops in the Yungas.

The CSUTCB initiated its road-blockade on April 3, 2000. Roadblocks were concentrated in La Paz and Oruro, but also extended to the departments of Cochabamba, Chuquisaca and Tarija. Over the next few days, blockades were extended throughout the departments of Beni and Potosí.[59] Between 5 and 9 April, roads were blocked at a national level. Aymara peasants from the communities of Huatajata, Juarina and Achacachi in the province of Omasuyos, in the department of La Paz, were the pivotal social force behind the rebellions. Roads leading from the capital of La Paz to Copacabana and to northern areas of the department of La Paz were shutdown. The principal highway-corridor between the cities of La Paz and Oruro was blockaded with peasants from Patacamaya, Sica Sica, and Caracollo taking to the streets. In addition, the highways connecting the cities of Oruro and Cochabamba, and Sucre to Monteagudo, Potosí, and Cochabamba were all impassable. Finally, the major highway connecting Cochabamba and Santa Cruz was blockaded by the *cocaleros* of the Chapare community Villa Tunari.[60] Achacachi, the capital of the La Paz province Omasuyos, a community situated on the edge of Lake Titicaca, a short distance northwest of Bolivia's capital-city, represented the political heartland of all this activity.

The Bánzer government, having already declared a state of siege to deal with the mounting problems in Cochabamba, militarised the city of Achacachi as well as many surrounding towns and villages, notably Axllata Grande, on

---

58. Crabtree 2005, p. 79.
59. García Linera, Chávez León, and Costas Monje 2005, p. 122.
60. Patzi 2005a, p. 204.

9 April. Felipe Quispe and other leaders were arrested and shipped off to remote prisons within the country.[61] In the following confrontations between the military and mobilised peasants, two Aymaras were killed: Ramiro Quispe Chambi and Hugo Aruquipa.[62] Throughout Omasuyos, protesters destroyed state-offices and institutions, such as the Palace of Justice and the offices of the Sub-Prefect. The insurgent peasants managed also to liberate prisoners from the jail in Achacachi. State-repression intensified further, with over a thousand new troops deployed to the area by land and air, raiding houses in the early morning hours and torturing some of their occupants. Battles between Aymara peasants and the coercive apparatuses of the state extended into other provinces of La Paz.[63] Negotiations were initiated with the government, and by 14 April 2000 this round of Aymara protest wound down.

The lull in activity was short-lived. April's mobilisations in the *altiplano* were followed by a massive wave of blockades and protests over many of the same issues, starting on 11 September and lasting until 7 October 2000. Tens of thousands of peasants blocked the central highways connecting Cochabamba and Santa Cruz and Oruro and Potosí. They also occupied all the roads and highways connecting the city of La Paz with the rest of the provinces, as well as the main thoroughfares to the other departments in the country. The blockades were so effective at shutting down the flow of goods that basic supplies for the city of La Paz had to be flown in under the order of President Bánzer and the Prefect of La Paz.[64] Peasants from the valleys of Inquisivi and Loayza occupied the La Paz-Oruro highway. Over 50,000 assembled in Achacachi from provinces throughout the department of La Paz to decide on further actions. Talk of an Aymara nation, civil war, and a march on La Paz were in the air.[65]

Forrest Hylton and Sinclair Thomson note, 'By September–October 2000, the road-blockades organised by the CSUTCB and their calls for a march on the capital raised the revolutionary spectre of 1781. Food shortages started

---

61. Mamani Ramírez 2004, p. 46.
62. Mamani Ramírez 2004, pp. 26–42.
63. Patzi 2005a, pp. 207–8.
64. During conflicts between peasants and the state over this period, nine peasants were killed between the *cocaleros* of the Chapare and the Aymara highland road-blockers, while approximately 127 were injured (García Linera, Chávez León, and Costas Monje 2005, p. 123).
65. Patzi 2005a, p. 212.

to affect La Paz'.[66] During the September–October actions, discussion circulated throughout many of the rural provinces of La Paz of more fully realising indigenous self-governance in the region. This sentiment found its expression in the establishment of the *cuarta general indígena of Qalachaka* (the General Headquarters of Qalachaka, located near Achacachi). All the while, the Aymara peasantry of the *altiplano* engaged in what Quispe termed Plan Pulga, or Operation Flea, whereby peasants would sweep into one area of a highway, piling up rocks and debris. While the military cleared that area, the peasants moved elsewhere, perpetually tying up troops in one section of the highway and maintaining the blockades in others. Like fleas, they caused the state to scratch in one place, leading only to itches all over.[67]

In September–October 2000, the neoliberal state was in a deep crisis, with tens of thousands of peasants having locked down much of the western half of the country. Since the Water-War of 2000 three serious social-movement organisations had proven their capacity to mobilise in different sectors and regions of Bolivian society, each with a prominent leadership figure: the *cocaleros* of the Chapare, with Evo Morales at their head; the CSUTCB in the *altiplano* and Northern valleys of La Paz, led by Felipe Quispe; and, finally, the Coordinadora rooted in the city of Cochabamba and the peripheral rural areas, led by Oscar Olivera. In September–October 2000, the three sectors and leaders had been at least tacitly working in tandem, but none alone was able to articulate a united alternative based on a social, political and economic project capable of embracing and moving forward forcefully the various social movements.[68]

However, by June–July 2001, a third wave of Aymara peasant-uprisings emerged. At this stage, the principal domains of struggle and mobilisation were contained in the La Paz provinces of Los Andes, Omasuyos, Manco Cápac, Camacho and Franz Tamayo. On 21 June, roadblocks were initiated in the highways at Huarina and Achacachi, followed shortly thereafter by state-repression. State-ammunition destroyed the lungs of indigenous-peasant

---

66. Hylton and Thomson 2005a, p. 50.
67. Mamani Ramírez 2004, p. 47.
68. García Linera 2002a, pp. 155–6; Patzi 2005a, pp. 223–4. In the end, sectoral negotiations between the state and the CSUTCB led to the 'Island of the Sun Accords', in which 'the government pledged to "address" peasant demands, including the repeal of neoliberal laws and ending forced eradication in the Yungas' (Hylton and Thomson 2005a, p. 50).

protester Severo Madani, and fatally wound Isabel Quispe, with a gunshot to her stomach.[69] Undoubtedly, the most important component of the days of June–July was the official consolidation of the General Headquarters of Qalachaka, conceived of as a militarised confederation of *ayllus* and other indigenous communities of the *altiplano*.[70] Over 20,000 indigenous activists gathered at Qalachaka, apparently armed with clubs, rocks, and old Mauser rifles from the Chaco War of the 1930s.[71] A photo, likely taken on one of the hills of Achacahi, circulated through the mainstream daily newspapers, showing a group of teenagers apparently 'armed' and sporting balaclavas in the style of the Zapatistas of the Lacandon jungle of southern Mexico.[72]

This series of revolts centred in the *altiplano* was racialised peasant class-struggle. The protesters sought to defend indigenous *usos y costumbres* in the communal management of water and land – under threat from privatisation-laws. They sought to assert Aymara indigenous pride in the face of racist state-repression that led to several civilian deaths. These were struggles for indigenous liberation. They were also anticapitalist, as peasants sought to defend communal customs against the blood and fire processes of capitalist expansion.

5.2.3 *Popular cultures of resistance and oppositional consciousness – Aymara radicalism*

In light of the dearth of grounded scholarly studies of the recent indigenous-peasant insurrections in the Aymara *altiplano*, one of the few available entry-points into their popular cultures of resistance and collective oppositional consciousness is through the political biography of their principal leader. There is no doubt that Felipe Quispe has been one of the most prominent and important leaders of indigenous struggle in the last two decades of Bolivian

---

69. García Linera, Chávez León, Costas Monje 2005, pp. 126–7.
70. García Linera 2002b, pp. 22–6.
71. García Linera, Chávez León, and Costas Monje 2005, p. 127.
72. It is not clear if the 'arms' were symbolic wooden rifles or old Mausers. What is important, as Aymara sociologist Mamani Ramírez has carefully pointed out, is that this photo, circulated through various media throughout the different departments of the country, became an image of a region in revolt, a self-conscious indigenous rebellion pitted against the state (Mamani Ramírez 2004, p. 53).

history.[73] During the mobilisations of the Aymara peasantry in 2000 and 2001, Quispe was the central focal point of popular struggle, more or less embodying and personifying the revolutionary sentiments of those blocking the roads and bringing the country to a standstill. Quispe articulated this collective voice audaciously and confrontationally in full view of the media and the Bolivian citizenry, and in the face of racist-neocolonial élites. For Aymara and other indigenous radicals, Quispe's public expressions provoked and inspired indigenous pride, and solidified a consciousness around the necessity of popular struggle. For the q'aras, or non-indigenous white and mestizo-élites, the same expressions from Quispe elicited reactions of fear, hatred and racism. His personal political trajectory sheds at least partial light on the collective history of indigenous movements over the last few decades in Bolivia, their ideological transitions, infrastructures of struggle, and their important contribution to the cycle of combined liberation across the country.

By all accounts, Quispe has led a seditious life. He was born in the community of Jisk'a Axariya, outside Achacachi.[74] After having been educated politically in revolutionary-Marxist organisations in the 1970s, he gravitated later in that decade to the small political party Movimiento Indio Tupaj Katari (Tupaj Katari Indian Movement, MITKA). MITKA was situated in the indianista wing of the broader katarista movement. MITKA was therefore distinct from the katarista currents closer to the CSUTCB of the time, and the Movimiento Revolucionario Tupaj Katari (de liberación) (Tupaj Katari Revolutionary Liberation-Movement, MRTK[L]). The latter currents maintained some residual peasantist, or campesinista, class-based ideological characteristics, alongside the elements of ethnic revindication common throughout katarismo.[75] Quispe was an important player in semi-clandestine indigenous-popular politics in the 1970s and early 1980s. But his real ascent probably began with the Extraordinary Congress of the CSUTCB in Potosí in 1988, where he was a representative

---

73. On a national scale, only Evo Morales has enjoyed a parallel status to Quispe in contemporary indigenous politics, as measured by the intensity of sentiments coming from various sectors of the population. Quispe was perhaps the figure most reviled and feared by the Bolivian ruling class in the early 2000s. By contrast, in the Aymara indigenous countryside of La Paz and Oruro, he received enthusiastic respect from the peasantry for his militant defence of indigenous self-determination and dignity in the face of racism and neoliberal capitalism.
74. Many of the basic biographical details of Quispe's life narrated here are drawn from Xavier Albo 2002.
75. Albó 2002b, p. 79; Quispe 2005a.

for a new militant-organisation, Ofensiva Roja de Ayllus Kataristas (Red Offensive of Katarista Ayllus, also known as Ayllus Rojos, Red Ayllus). The Ayllus Rojos were an eclectic amalgamation of Marxist-indigenous activists, bringing together *indígenista* Aymaras, miners, and urban Marxists (see Chapter 4).[76] As noted, in 1991–2 an armed wing of the Ayllus Rojos, the Ejército Guerrillero Tupaj Katari (Tupaj Katari Guerrilla-Army, EGTK), emerged and Quispe was a leading figure alongside Álvaro García Linera and Raquél Gutiérrez. Although EGTK never matured into a successful or large guerrilla-army, it did develop a popular base of sympathisers among the Aymara peasantry in Achacachi and the surrounding area, influenced some of the internal politics of the CSUTCB, and deposited ideological seeds of Aymara nationalism, the fruits of which were seen in the mobilisations of 2000 and 2001 in the *altiplano*.[77] In jail, Quispe gained popular credibility and respect among Aymara and other indigenous peasants for his guerrilla-past, and his fervent denunciations of the neocolonial nature of the Bolivian state.[78]

Already in the 1980s, Quispe had evoked the heroic collective memory of Tupaj Katari and the 1781 anticolonial rebellion he led. This was evident in Quispe's book, *Tupaj Katari vive y vuelve, carajo (Tupaj Katari Is Alive and Returning)*, published in that period. However, as a result of his devotion to political study in jail, when Quispe was released, his political oratory was now more markedly replete with historical references. Moreover, his credibility,

---

76. Quispe once remarked: 'When we speak about the indigenous, Aymara or Quechua, revindicating our ancestral culture, at the same time we are automatically embracing our brothers who work in the cities as workers or proletarians' (Quispe 2001, p. 189).

77. At the same time, Quispe is not prone to romanticising the historical impact of the EGTK: '...in the 1990s we had a revolutionary organization called Tupaj Katari Guerrilla-Army (EGTK). It was a political-military organisation that we thought would arrive in power through armed struggle and by being the vanguard of the people. It turns out that, with time, we saw that there wasn't support from the population. So, we ended up in jail for five years. I was captured on 19 August 1992 and remained in jail until 1997. When I left I returned to my community, like any other *comunario*, like any other peasant. From there the people chose me and told me that I had to be leader of the CSUTCB' (personal interview, 12 May 2005).

78. While incarcerated, Quispe read and studied, completing his high-school diploma. He was granted provisional freedom to attend classes in history at the Universidad Mayor de San Andres (UMSA) in La Paz, eventually completing his bachelor's degree.

gained through years of activism, guerrilla-struggle, and, now, incarceration, remained in tact, indeed strengthened.[79]

In the First Extraordinary Congress of the CSUTCB, between 26 and 28 November 1998, Quispe was elected Executive Secretary, essentially because he was seen as the consensus-candidate between the internally feuding factions of the CSUTCB aligned behind either Evo Morales or Alejo Véliz.[80] By this stage, Quispe had already become known in popular parlance by the moniker, 'el Mallku', 'leader' or 'Condor' in Aymara.[81] The CSUTCB developed a radical-indigenous politics once again under the leadership of Quispe. From 1998 to 2000, the organisational groundwork was laid for the 2000, 2001 uprisings. A process emerged through which the very state-institutions of the Bolivian republic were called into question for their failure to reflect the multinational character of Bolivian society and the basic oppression of the indigenous majority.[82]

Building on longstanding, historical collective memories of indigenous rebellion was a key facet of organising the capacity for mobilisation and the political consciousness of the movement's rank and file:

> So, we knew of the uprising of Manco II of 1536–1544. We knew of the uprising of Juan Santos Atahuallpa from 1742–1755. We also knew about the uprisings of Túpac Amaru, Túpac Katari of 1780–1783, and Zárate Willca in 1899...we see Katari as an example, as a model. He spent ten years preparing the Indian rebellion, and like that, successively, with other men, rose up against colonial power, and against the republic.[83]

Quispe's writings and interviews highlight both the role of a militant-layer of CSUTCB-organisers traveling to different rural communities, politicising, and raising the consciousness of the bases over months and years. At the same time, he emphasises the radicalisation of the grassroots themselves, their capacity to self-organise and mobilise, and ultimately to disobey the high command of the CSUTCB when it refused at times to sanction radical

---

79. Albó 2002b, p. 81.
80. García Linera, Chávez León, and Costas Monjes 2005, p. 121.
81. The name refers to a principal title of authority in traditional Aymara organisational structures (Albó 2002, p. 81).
82. Mamani Ramírez 2004, p. 24.
83. Quispe 2001, p. 165.

action against the state.[84] Quispe reflects in the interview on his own political and ideological trajectory away from isolated guerrilla-action and toward the power of mass-mobilisation as a basis for indigenous liberation. Originally, he put his faith in the possibility of forming a small vanguard of armed revolutionaries within the indigenous communities. 'But, you know what, it turned out that the mobilisations of April and September have clarified things for us', Quispe points out, 'in rebellion, I have learned that the true struggle has not been of a few people, but has been taken up by millions and millions of indigenous'.[85] He calls for an insurrection 'supported by our own resources from the communities and the unions', a rebellion of a 'communal and indigenous' character, which employs 'our own philosophical thought' and traditions.[86] Quispe points to the authentic protagonists of the uprisings in April and September:

> The true actors of the indigenous uprising have been the communities them-
> selves.... The cause was not only water, coca, territory, land. Rather, the
> cause already has sewn the seeds to takeover political power, to govern
> ourselves with a communitarian socialist system based in our *ayllus* and
> communities.[87]

The Aymara struggle for communitarian collective sovereignty and self-governance, on the one hand, was increasingly pitted against the capitalist, white-*mestizo* state, on the other.[88] In the regions of northern La Paz and central and southern *altiplano*, the *whiphala* – the multicoloured, chequered Aymara flag – is probably the most important political symbol of this struggle. It differentiates collective Aymara identity from the Bolivian identity promoted by the state and represented by the Bolivian flag. Further, the *wiphala* is understood today as a symbol of war and social struggle, as well as a commitment to communitarian social life and the *ayllus*.[89]

---

84. Quispe 2001, pp. 166–7.
85. Quispe 2001, p. 174.
86. Ibid.
87. Quispe 2001, p. 178.
88. Patzi 2005a, p. 217.
89. Mamani Ramírez 2004, p. 35. At the same time, it ought to be noted that the *wiphala* is a paradigmatic case of invented tradition (see Hobsbawm and Ranger 1983). The flag was not used by indigenous radicals in 1899, 1927, or 1946–7, for example. Thanks to Forrest Hylton for drawing my attention to this point.

The more radical sectors of the rebellions of 2000 and 2001 were ideologically oriented towards a fundamental, revolutionary challenge to the neoliberal-capitalist model in place since 1985. Large sections of the Aymara *altiplano*, aligned with Quispe in these contentious moments of confrontation with the state, were building the incipient ideological and organisational foundations for an alternative revolutionary and democratic state.[90] This alternative democracy envisioned by the indigenous activists on the road-blockades has been expressed intellectually by scholars working in the Bolivian context as *ayllu-* or *communal* democracy versus liberal-capitalist representative democracy.[91] Quispe, as we have seen, conceives of the rebellions as a communitarian-socialist challenge to the neocolonial-capitalist Bolivian state. He speaks of the reassertion of the communal system of the *ayllu*, adapted to the twenty-first century context, as a way of replacing the colonial institutions and practices inherited by the republicans at Bolivian independence in 1825.[92] In many respects, this notion of communitarian socialism in the countryside was the rural counterpart to the revolutionary, assemblyist forms of urban democracy experienced during the Water-War in Cochabamba through the creation of the Coordinadora and mass-meetings in the streets and plazas.

5.3 The 12–13 February 2003 *Impuestazo*

The epoch of left-indigenous insurrection begun in Cochabamba in 2000 surged forward dramatically in February 2003 with an historic insurrection by low-ranking police-officers in the city of La Paz, armed confrontation between the police and the military, and largely spontaneous revolts by the informal and formal sectors of the urban working classes and public-university and high-school students of La Paz and El Alto.[93] The police-insurrection and popular rebellion spread, albeit on a smaller scale, to the cities of Cochabamba, Santa Cruz, Trinidad, Oruro, and Sucre.[94] The armed assault on the protesting police-forces by the military protecting the presidential palace in the Plaza Murillo set off popular indignation throughout the urban

---

90. Patzi 2005a, p. 66.
91. Rivera Cusicanqui 1991, 2004, p. 20.
92. Quispe 2005b, pp. 71–5.
93. APDHB/ASOFAMD/CBDHDD/DIAKONIA/FUNSOLON/RED–ADA 2004, pp. 1–22.
94. García Mérida 2003a, b; Hylton 2003; Peredo 2003.

working classes of La Paz and El Alto and led to two days of revolt. The crisis of neoliberalism had reached a crescendo as the two wings of the state's coercive apparatus – the military and the police – disintegrated into internecine conflict. The workers in the streets were primarily indigenous, particularly so in the city of El Alto. Claudia Espinoza and Gozalo Gozálvez describe the masses in the streets as 'in the majority unemployed young men and women between 13 and 18 years of age, families congregated in protest, students, unemployed adults, self-employed informal workers, and to a lesser extent workers from the organised sectors...'.[95] The protests in February reignited the urban dimension of left-indigenous insurrection which had been eclipsed somewhat by the rural-Aymara indigenous insurrections and various *cocalero*-battles following the more urbanised Cochabamba Water-War. The anti-tax protests in El Alto and La Paz had a more spontaneous character than the Cochabamba Water-War and the Aymara peasant-insurrections. The importance of the existing urban infrastructure of class-struggle in building and leading the rebellion was less obvious. Various unions and social-movement organisations did play a part, but they tailed rather than led the February events. The organisations, grievances, demands, protest-repertoires, and geographical scope central to what unfolded in February are illustrated in Table 5.3, and the targets of protest in Table 5.4.

The class-struggle was waged in February 2003 against increases in taxation that targeted the formally-employed working class in particular. The spark of the police-mutiny was the 9 February announcement made by President Gonzalo Sánchez de Lozada (MNR) that there would be a new income-tax targeting salaried workers who made two-times or more the minimum-salary.[96] The tax was clearly a response to demands from the International Monetary Fund (IMF) that the Bolivian state shrink its ballooning deficit dramatically over the coming year.[97] A visiting delegation from the IMF demanded that the budget-deficit fall to 5.5 per cent of GDP in one year, meaning that the Bolivian government 'would have to come up with a combination of budget cuts and tax increases totaling more than $250 million', even as the devastating social consequences of years of neoliberal restructuring were still very

---

95. Espinoza and Gozalvez 2003.
96. Solón 2003, p. 16.
97. García Linera 2004a, p. 85.

Table 5.3   12–13 February, anti-tax revolt

Infrastructure/forces	Grievances	Demands	Protest-Repertoires	Geographical scope
argely spontaneous	Accumulated social consequences of neoliberalism	End to new regressive taxation	Street-clashes	*Centre*
informal/formal working classes		Resignation of President Gonzalo Sánchez de Lozada	Road-blocks	La Paz and El Alto
ES (Rank-and-File olice)	State-repression		Torching of state-property	
	Regressive taxation			*Periphery*
OR-El Alto	IMF intervention in Bolivian affairs	Resignation of Vice-President Carlos Mesa	Torching of neoliberal party-headquarters	Cochabamba, Santa Cruz, Trinidad, Oruro, Sucre
EJUVE-El Alto				
PEA Students	Illegitimacy of President Gonzalo Sánchez de Lozada	End to neoliberal development-model	Destruction of symbols of foreign and domestic capital	
MSA Students				
OB	Illegitimacy of traditional neoliberal political parties		Minor incidents of looting	
ovement Towards ocialism (MAS)				
ensioners				

much alive.[98] Underlying the immediate causes of the protests, however, was a deep substratum of issues: the prolonged exhaustion of the neoliberal-economic model; the increased organisational capacity of the overwhelmingly indigenous popular classes throughout the country constructed over time through the lived experiences of the string of insurrectionary rehearsals since 2000; and, finally, the corresponding crisis of the Bolivian neoliberal state as evinced in the declining legitimacy of the Sánchez de Lozada coalition government and the traditional neoliberal political parties more generally, the implosion of the coercive apparatuses of the state, and the escalation of profound fiscal contradictions of neoliberal capitalism in the Bolivian context. The February events have been described as 'perhaps the worst period of civil disorder the country has seen since its "popular revolution" of 1952'.[99] The protests targeted the headquarters of the central neoliberal political parties (MNR, MIR, ADN, and UCS), transnational corporations, international and domestic banks, neoliberal state-ministries, media companies (public and private), and other meaningful symbolic representations of neoliberal capitalism and state-repression (see Table 5.3). While relatively spontaneous, the protests showed

---

98. Schultz 2005, p. 18.
99. *The Economist* 2003.

at degree of politicisation and were consciously anti-neoliberal in character. The minimal looting and vandalism that occurred cannot realistically be portrayed as a central characteristic of the rebellion. The leitmotif of the February riots was urban working-class struggle from below against the neoliberal-capitalist order.

The uneven battles between the relatively poorly-armed police and the heavily-armed military – employing tear-gas, rubber-bullets, helicopters, tanks, snipers, and live ammunition –, and the repression of unarmed civilian-protesters, left a terrible wake of dead and injured in only two days.[100] Crowds gathered in the Plaza San Franciso, setting up makeshift barricades, and engaging in near-constant confrontations with the military. Protesters took over the Coca Cola and Pepsi bottling plants in El Alto.[101] The COB, teachers, and other unionised formal workers, the unemployed, students, and others, gathered to march in La Paz, demanding the resignation of Sánchez de Lozada.[102] The militarisation of La Paz and El Alto was extensive. Military tanks and assault-vehicles circled the Plaza Murillo. The scenes recalled an earlier era of military authoritarian rule in the country.[103] At an ideological level, we have seen that, already by the time of the Cochabamba Water-War, the ideological hegemony enjoyed by neoliberals within the Bolivian state was coming apart at the seams. In the words of La Paz-based activist Pablo Salón, 'The origins of February 12 and 13 come from much further back, and cannot be explained exclusively through the cause-effect relations of that conjuncture,

---

100. Employing documentation from an early inquiry conducted by the Bolivian National Institute of Forensic Investigation, a 2004 Amnesty International report states that 'hundreds of injuries and 33 deaths were reported among police officers, civilians and members of the military as a result of wounds caused by projectiles "fired by weapons of war..."' (Amnesty International 2004, p. 7). A 2005 report prepared by Jim Shultz under the auspices of the Cochabamba-based non-governmental organisation, Democracy Center, counts 34 dead and 182 seriously wounded (Schultz 2005, p. 29). The latter report includes a list of the names of the dead and wounded provided by the Bolivian Permanent Assembly of Human Rights. Amnesty International argues that, 'in light of the testimonies and reports gathered by the organization's delegation, press information, court documents and the high number of victims, the behaviour of the military forces in action on 12 and 13 February, would appear to have been neither "restrained" nor "proportional"' (Amnesty International 2004, p. 8).

101. Hylton 2003.

102. Espinoza and Gonzalvez 2003, pp. 31–2.

103. Salón 2003.

but rather through an explosive accumulation of seventeen years of applying the neoliberal model'.[104]

The ideological challenge to neoliberalism so vividly expressed in extra-parliamentary movements also expressed itself in the electoral arena in 2002, bringing to an end the viability of the 'pacted democracy' of the ADN, MIR, and MNR, and signaling the rise of two left-indigenous parties: the MAS and MIP.[105] Remarkably, Evo Morales won 21 per cent of the popular vote to Gonzalo Sánchez de Lozada's 22. This was a major gain for the most prominent left-indigenous party in the country.[106] The other stunning feature of the elections was the pronounced erosion of support for the MNR, MIR, and ADN. Together, these three parties had achieved more than 50 per cent of votes in every general election since 1985. In 2002, however, they took only 42 per cent of the popular vote.[107] Between 1997 and 2002, the number of indigenous legislators increased from 10 to 52 out of 130.[108] The February urban rebellions in La Paz and El Alto in 2003 cannot be understood in isolation from this large cycle of revolt and electoral change.[109] Instead, we need to consider the February revolt in light of the decomposition of the social forces backing neoliberalism in Bolivia and exercising control of the state, and the re-composition of left-indigenous social forces building on the experiences of insurrection since the 2000 Water-War. In other words, the February 2003 insurrection was a fundamental contribution to the ascendant insurrectionary cycle.

Conclusion

The power of the revolts of the Water-War can be traced to the strength of various infrastructures of class-struggle in rural and urban Cochabamba coming together under the umbrella of the Coordinadora and channelling an emergent popular-oppositional consciousness grounded in the combined politics of indigenous liberation and class-struggle against neoliberalism. The protests were intensified still further by the repressive responses from the

---

104. Solón 2003, p. 16.
105. Lazarte Rojas 2005, p. 391.
106. Albro 2005b; García Linera 2003.
107. Singer and Morrison 2004; Van Cott 2003b, c.
108. Albó 2002a, pp. 74–102.
109. Tapia 2002, pp. 29–30; Tapia 2004, pp. 151–2.

Table 5.4 Protest targets in La Paz and El Alto, February 12–13, 2003

Industrial and service capital	Neoliberal party-targets	State-ministries	Symbols of state-power	Financial capital	Media
National Brewery	MNR-Headquarters	Viceministry of Finance	Presidential Palace	Central Bank	State-media channel
Burger King	MIR-Headquarters	Ministry of Labour	Central Bank	ATMs	Red Bolivisión
Aguas del Ilimani	ADN-Headquarters	Ministry of Sustainable Development	Customs Office	Banco Sol	
Coca Cola Bottling Plant	UCS-Headquarters		Mayor's Office (El Alto)	Banco Mercantil	
Pepsi Bottling Plant	Car carrying son of leader of MIR	Offices of the Vice President	Ministry of Justice	Banco de Santa Cruz	
Supermarkets			District Supreme Court		
Electropaz			Military Court		
Pollos Copacabana			San Pedro Prison		
Café frequented by Bolivian economic and political élites.			Justicia Militar Regional de Bolivia		

Sources: La Prensa, 'Una turba incendio y destruyó 2 ministerios y Vicepresidencia', February 13, 2003; *The Economist,* 'What Will the IMF say now?' February 20, 2003; Forrest Hylton, 'Working Class Revolt in Bolivia: The Sudden Return of Dual Power', *Counterpunch,* February 15, 2003 (www.counterpunch.org); Forrest Hylton, 'Rumors of a Hard-Right Turn: Business as Usual in Bolivia?' *Counterpunch,* March 8, 2003 (www.counterpunch.org); Claudia Espinoza and Gonzalo Gozalvez (2003), 'Levantamiento popular del 12 y 13 de febrero en La Paz', *Observatorio Social de América Latina* 30, 10 (enero–abril): 29–36; Pablo Salón (2003), 'Radiografía de un febrero', *Observatorio Social de América Latina* 30, 10 (enero–abril): 15–27; Heinz Dieterich Steffan, 'Crónica de un levantamiento histórico: El Coraje del Pueblo', *El Juguete Rabioso,* febrero 16 de 2003: 4–5; and APDHB, ASOFAMD, CBDHDD, DIAKONIA, FUNSOLON, and RED-ADA (2003), 'Cronología de febrero de 2003', in *Para que no se olvide: 12–13 de febrero 2003* (La Paz: APDHB/ASOFAMD/CBDHDD/DIAKONIA/FUNSOLON/RED-ADA): 21–30.

state – leading ultimately to the death of a teenager, a serious blow to the legitimacy of the coercive measures taken to defend a hated status quo.

In the case of the Aymara peasant-insurrection, what stands out is the central importance of the dense existing infrastructure of indigenous-peasant class-struggle, rooted in agrarian unions, traditional communitarian *ayllus*, and, sometimes, combinations of the two. This layered infrastructure was able to find expression at higher geographical scales through the formal structures of the CSUTCB. Intricate networks facilitated the road-blockades, mass rural assemblies, destruction of state-offices, and protest-marches. They also helped to articulate the expression of an oppositional consciousness that combined the politics of indigenous resistance with peasant class-struggle. This consciousness drew, furthermore, from the distant precolonial past in its defense against market-encroachment upon communal management of land and water – *usos y costumbres* – at the same time as it adapted techniques and demands of the *katarista* resistance traditions to fit the new context of anti-neoliberal struggle. State-repression, leading to several deaths, contributed to the radicalisation of protest visions of change and methods of struggle by calling into question the moral legitimacy of existing state-power and the élite and racist interests it expressed.

The February anti-tax revolts were less determined by the existing infra-structures of class-struggle than the Water-War or the Aymara peasant-insurrections. Instead, they exhibited a more spontaneous, less structured character, with young people born around the time of DS21060 playing a distinguished role. Still, the radicalising role of state-repression was similar, leading even to calls for the resignation of the President and Vice-President at various points in the unfolding of the process. What is more, the February anti-tax rebellion brought the urban working classes of the capital-city and its adjacent shantytown – El Alto – into the centre of the growing left-indigenous insurrectionary cycle. The protesters of February added decisively to the anti-neoliberal component of the widening popular movements in the country and to the emergent oppositional consciousness of indigenous liberation and class-struggle. This became that much clearer during the Gas-War of October 2003, the subject to which we now turn.

Chapter Six

Red October: Gas-War, 2003

On an average day in the indigenous proletarian city of El Alto, *La Ceja* – the city's commercial heartland – bustles with thousands of women street-vendors dressed in traditional Aymara attire – bowler hats, boldy-coloured *polleras* (gathered skirts), and shawls to protect against the cold winds. Hundreds of mini-vans, with mainly young boys hanging out of sliding doors yelling destinations and fares to passers-by, clog the paved arteries that lead down to the neighbouring capital-city, La Paz. In September and October 2003, El Alto more closely resembled the revolutionary frontlines of a popular insurrection against a racist and repressive state and the depravities of neoliberal capitalism. Tires burned in the streets, the abundant stalls and fast-food chicken-outlets were shutdown, and dug-up roadways were made impassable, except by bicycle or on foot. El Alto earned its position as the vanguard of left-indigenous struggle in Bolivia, and as one of the most rebellious urban locales in contemporary Latin America. Bearing the overwhelming brunt of state-repression during the September and October events, *alteño* workers were essential to the overthrow of President Gonzalo Sánchez de Lozada.

The obstacles in the way of working-class collective action in the city were formidable: long work days; low rates of unionisation; heterogeneous work activity and small production-units that brought only small numbers of workers together; lack of social protection because of the proliferation of informal jobs; increasing numbers of women and youth in the labour-market who had little union-experience and knowledge of their rights and were therefore more intensely exploitable; and racist and sexist divisions both within the working class and between the working class and capital and the state. Scholars have pointed out that neoliberal restructuring in Latin America has caused segmentation and structural heterogeneity within the workforce of the region and the dispersion of workers away from concentrated production sites and stable jobs and into the informal economy. The expansion of the informal economy carries with it structural incentives for informal workers to attempt to solve their problems through individual initiatives rather than through collective action. All of these elements combined act as impediments to class-based collective action.[1] How, then, did El Alto's working classes overcome these structural barriers and take up the leadership of such an impressive series of insurrectionary protests?

The central argument of this chapter is that, during the October Gas-War, the largely informal indigenous working classes of El Alto utilised a dense infrastructure of class-struggle to facilitate their leading role in the events. A dialectical relationship emerged between the rank and file of neighbourhood-councils and the formal infrastructure and leadership of the Federación de Juntas Vecinales de El Alto (Federation of Neighbourhood-Councils of El Alto, FEJUVE-El Alto) and the Central Obrera Regional de El Alto (Regional Workers' Central of El Alto, COR-El Alto). Without the formal structures, the rank and file base would have been unable to co-ordinate their actions at a higher scale than their local neighbourhoods, while without the self-activity, self-organisation and radical push from the grassroots, the executive leadership of both El Alto organisations would have been more likely to engage in the normal processes of negotiation with the state, moderation of demands, and eventual fracturing and demobilisation of the rebellious movements. Meanwhile, the supportive role played by sectors of the working class with relatively stable jobs outside the informal economy was facilitated by the ideological and political orientation of social-movement unionism adopted by

---

1. Roberts 1998, pp. 59–67.

the two central organisations of the formal working class: the COB, and the FSTMB.

In addition to working through a complex network of working-class infrastructure – the grassroots neighbourhood-councils, FEJUVE-El Alto, COR-El Alto, the FSTMB, and the COB – the protests in El Alto drew on the rich popular cultures of resistance and opposition in Bolivian history: indigenous radicalism – associated with migrants from the Aymara *altiplano* – and revolutionary Marxism – associated with the migrants from the tin-mining zones. Both of these traditions had, over decades, left an indelible mark on the popular politics of resistance in the city. These traditions were markedly dense in El Alto, but also came to define the protests of September and October 2003 throughout the country more generally.

The working classes of El Alto constituted the most important social force in the insurrection, but depended on alliances with the indigenous peasantry – organised through its own infrastructure of rural class-struggle, the Confederación Sindical Única de Trabajadores Campesinos de Bolivia (Bolivian Peasant Trade-Union Confederation, CSUTCB), and the Federación Única Departamental de Trabajadores Campesinos de La Paz – Tupaj Katari (Departmental Federation of Peasant-Workers of La Paz, FUDTCLP-TK) –, the formal working class, and, to a lesser but important extent, sections of the middle class. Social-movement leaders effectively employed the call to nationalise gas as a collective action-frame that appealed broadly to peasants, workers, and parts of the middle class. The frame focused on the injustice of poverty in a resource-rich land, the foreign control of the gas-industry by multinational corporations, and the long history in Bolivia of colonial and neocolonial abuse related to the extraction of natural-resource wealth from the country.

Finally, state-repression at various intervals in September and October had the effect of radicalising the working-class and peasant-protests, provoking ruptures within the political élite, and drawing sections of the middle class into the popular movement for change. The Sánchez de Lozada government demonstrated early and sustained reticence for serious negotiation with the mobilised peasantry and urban working classes. Although fierce, the state's repression proved insufficiently strong to destroy the opposition, and thus only fuelled an intensified process of political, racial and class-based polarisation in the country. Repression effectively forged new solidarities within those sectors at the receiving end of the state's coercion.

All of these conditions together – a dense infrastructure of class-struggle and social-movement unionism, oppositional traditions of indigenous and working-class radicalism sustained by El Alto's migrant-population, alliances between the informal and formal sectors of the working class, the peasantry, and parts of the middle class, a collective-action frame of gas that appealed broadly to sentiments of the Bolivian populace, and fierce but insufficient levels of state-repression – ultimately explain the strength of the massive insurrectionary explosions that forced the resignation of President Sánchez de Lozada on 17 October 2003.

6.1　A portrait of El Alto

6.1.1　A city of migrant-labourers

In a celebrated passage of *The Communist Manifesto* Marx describes how the advance of industrial capitalism, 'replaces the isolation of the labourers, due to competition, by their revolutionary combination, due to association'. The bourgeoisie, through modern industry, produces its own grave-diggers, the proletarian class, which will eventually overthrow the bourgeois order.[2] In a parallel fashion, Bolivian neoliberalism in many ways is responsible for the creation of El Alto's urban-indigenous working-class movement, which subsequently mounted one of the most serious campaigns to bury the neoliberal model in Latin America in the opening years of the millennium. Neoliberalism in Bolivia, by helping to drive dispossessed miners and indigenous peasants into the cauldron of hyper-exploitation and insecurity that characterises the city, nurtured the breeding grounds of what became its most formidable enemy. In this new environment, the revolutionary-Marxist traditions of the ex-miners and the insurrectionary heritage of indigenous-rural rebellions coalesced in a potent and novel combination of left-indigenous struggle rooted in the complexities of urbanised racial oppression and class-exploitation.

Tenuously perched on the edge of the *altiplano*, at over 4,000 metres above sea level, El Alto's eastern edge breaks sharply down into the steep hillsides of the expansive basin containing La Paz. The northern neighbourhoods are

---

2. Marx and Engels 1985, pp. 93–4.

characterised by a greater concentration of Aymara residents, the result of rural-to-urban migration from the *altiplano*-departments of La Paz, and, to a lesser but still significant degree, Oruro and Potosí. The southern zone is more heterogeneous in sociocultural terms, including as it does important neighbourhoods with high concentrations of 'relocated' ex-miners who are predominantly Quechua. In 2001, 74 per cent of *alteños* over the age of 15 self-identified as Aymara, six per cent as Quechua, one per cent as of other indigenous or Afro-Bolivian heritage, and 19 per cent as non-indigenous.[3] The city functions as a critical thoroughfare connecting La Paz with the Chilean Pacific coast through the Panamerican highway that runs through the northern zone. In the southern zone, the Viacha and Oruro-Cochabamba highways carry people and commodities to the towns and rural zones of the *altiplano*, as well as destinations in other departments of the country, such as Oruro and Cochabamba.[4] Blocking roads is one popular repertoire of revolt that can effectively strangle the commerce of the western half of the country when carried out to its full potential, as it has been on several occasions in recent years.[5]

El Alto suffers from an acute lack of adequate housing and basic infrastructure. Simple adobe-houses, often constructed with family-labour, constitute 77 per cent of residential housing in the city. A mere 22 per cent of *alteños* can afford to live in brick-houses, and 37 per cent of households continue to go without access to toilets or latrines.[6] According to official data from the 2001 census, only 7 per cent of *alteño* households have all basic necessities satisfied. El Alto's water-utility was privatised in 1999 and handed over to Aguas del Illimani, a private consortium controlled by the French multinational Suez. Almost 200,000 residents do not have access to Illimani's water- and sewage-services because they live outside the 'served area' as defined by the contract between Illimani and the Bolivian state. Moreover, an additional 70,000 *alteños*

3. Albó 2006, p. 333.
4. Gill 2000, pp. 35–6.
5. If the formal working class enjoys greater opportunities than most informal workers to interrupt the process of capital-accumulation through disruption at the point of production – through strikes and other methods – informal workers are still able at times to break down accumulation in the sphere of circulation – particularly through roadblocks. Commodities can no longer reach their destinations in internal and external markets when key roads are shutdown.
6. Arbona and Kohl 2004, p. 261.

who live within the perimeters of the served area lack access because they cannot afford the US$445 connection-fees.[7] Unsurprisingly, in this context, social-movement struggles have often turned on themes of basic necessities such as access to water and sewage;[8] occasionally, these localised battles are linked to broader political objectives and demands for structural transformation of the state and economy as was the case in the Gas-War of 2003.

In 1950, when El Alto was still a part of La Paz, its population was 11,000.[9] Over the next half-century, El Alto grew at the relatively rapid rate of 8.2 per cent per annum, with an intense growth-spurt between 1976 and 1986.[10] In the 1980s, two critical shocks set off a spike in the number of migrants flooding the ranks of El Alto's neighbourhoods. The first was a series of El Niño related droughts between 1982 and 1983 that struck the rural hinterland of the *altiplano* with a vengeance, driving thousands of peasants off their land.[11] The second moment, of course, was the mass-firing and 'relocation' of tin-miners following the privatisation of the mines in 1985. By 1992, 405,492 people inhabited the city, increasing to 647,350 by 2001, and a projected 870,000 by 2007.[12] Apparently almost 1,000,000 will live there by 2010.

6.1.2   El Alto's working classes as historical formations

El Alto is a poor city. Official data indicates that, in 2001, 70 per cent of the population lived below the poverty-line.[13] The structure of the working class in neoliberal El Alto mirrors the broader trends of working-class Bolivian life since the mid-1980s, as described in detail in Chapter 4. Thus, 98 per cent of the approximately 5,045 production-units in industrial manufacturing in the city are small or micro-enterprises. The workers employed in such production-units constitute 59 per cent of workers employed in industrial manufacturing in the city.[14] These jobs are precarious, low-paying, and involve long workdays.

---

7. Spronk 2007b, p. 20.
8. Laurie and Crespo 2007.
9. Sandoval Z. and Sostres 1989, p. 22. El Alto became an independent municipality in 1988.
10. The accelerated urbanisation in Bolivia in the second half of the twentieth century largely followed wider trends in the Global South (Davis 2006).
11. Farthing et al. 2006.
12. Albó 2006, p. 332; Arbona & Kohl 2004, p. 258.
13. *La Razón* 2005c.
14. Rossell Arce and Rojas Callejas 2000, p. vi.

Moreover, they do not provide social-protection benefits to employees.[15] As Table 6.1 shows, industrial manufacturing constitutes the second most important area of employment for *alteños* and, in particular, *alteño* men. Commerce, restaurants and hotels employ the most *alteños*, with women predominating in this sector. Following these two, in declining order of importance, are social services, construction, and transportation and communications.[16] One consequence of neoliberal restructuring in the city has been, 'the expansion of a vast reserve army of unemployed or marginally employed people, also conceptualised as an "informal economy", from which a few emerge as incipient entrepreneurs but in which the vast majority experience new and old forms of oppression'.[17] If the shape and character of the world of work has changed in El Alto as a result of neoliberalism, the working class has not disappeared. In fact, the working classes – defined expansively as those who do not live off of the labour of others – have only grown in number.

Table 6.1   El Alto – Employment by Sector

Sector	Total	Men	Women
Total	276,777	159,389	117,388
Manufacturing Industry	69,799	43,360	26,439
Construction	27,345	26,892	453
Transport and Communications	27,169	26,716	453
Commerce, Restaurants and Hotels	90,522	26,036	64,486
Social and Community-Services	48,220	26,465	21,855
Other Sectors	13,724	26,465	21,755

Source: Rossell and Rojas 2006, p. 65.

---

15. Rossell Arce and Rojas Callejas 2000, p. vii.

16. Lesley Gill describes the 'heterogeneous mix of street vendors, petty merchants, and artisans', in the streets of El Alto (Gill 2000, p. 68). 'Women sell fruits, vegetables, and a variety of trinkets on the streets…frequently accompanied by small children', Gill observes, while, others commute to La Paz each morning as, 'domestic servants, gardeners, shoe-shine boys, and part-time handymen…' (Gill 2000, p. 1). Teenage daughters and elderly women are often tasked, meanwhile, with the unpaid reproductive work of carrying for younger siblings or grandchildren (Gill 2000, p. 41).

17. Gill 2000, p. 2.

As has been the case elsewhere in Bolivia and Latin America, the informal sector has been expanding over the last few decades in El Alto at the expense of the formal sector. In 1992, the city's informal sector – excluding the domestic segment – made up an already preponderant 64 per cent of the labour-market. This percentage increased to 69 per cent by 2000.[18] The few large industries that do exist in El Alto have scarcely been subjected to scholarly investigation.[19] What stands out, in any case, is the thinness of the web of large industries in the city. Of the thousands of small production-units that exist, activity is focused in textiles, acrylic and natural-wool weaving, leather-making, carpentry, metal-mechanics, machine-making and repairs, shoemaking, and plaster-work.[20] Unregulated clandestine tanneries, silver and goldsmithing jewel-artisans, machine-shops, low-end shoe-producers, natural and acrylic wool-weavers, and leather-jacket and sports clothing units, also proliferate in the *alteño* landscape, alongside street-vendors and transport- and construction-workers.[21] According to the most recent data, of the economically active population (EAP) in El Alto, 41 per cent are self-employed workers, 22 per cent are manual labourers, and 21 per cent are non-manual labourers. Add to these categories domestic servants and non-remunerated family-labourers, and one has the contemporary cartography of El Alto's working classes. Together, the working classes constitute 93 per cent of the city's EAP. Owners and bosses, together with independent professionals, constitute the remaining seven per cent.[22]

---

18. Rossell Arce and Rojas Callejas 2000, p. 29.

19. Perhaps the most extensive study contains information on five large enterprises: a Coca-Cola bottling plant, a tannery, a wooden-door factory, a weaving factory, and a plastics-factory (Rossell Arce and Rojas Callejas 2000).

20. PNUD/UNDP 2005, pp. 88–115; Rossell Arce and Rojas Callejas 2000, p. 14.

21. Agadjanian 2002; Rossell Arce and Rojas Callejas 2000, pp. 24–36. Many of the micro-shoemaking units work on a subcontracting basis for larger shoe-companies based elsewhere (Rossell Arce and Rojas Callejas 2000, p. 40). The textile-industry, for its part, further contracts piecemeal work out to individual workers – overwhelmingly female – who are based in their homes (ibid.). In recent years, trade in used clothing from the United States has also surged in El Alto, making its way to the massive market of 16 de Julio. As Lesley Gill reports, the trade has fostered an incipient process of bourgeois class-formation through the role of importers in amidst the generalised informal working-class milieu of the city (Gill 2000, p. 43).

22. Rossell Arce and Rojas Callejas 2000, pp. 24–36. Work in El Alto is incredibly precarious, one consequence of which is the frequent transition of individuals from one section of the economy to another: 'There is considerable movement from one work site to another: from factory work to part-time construction jobs, from domestic service to street vending to artisanry, and so forth. Long-term stable employment is

6.1.3 *Political cultures of resistance and opposition*

The rich traditions of indigenous radicalism in the rural Aymara *altiplano* and the revolutionary Marxism of the tin-miners have left an indelible mark on the popular politics of resistance in contemporary El Alto. Relocated miners and Aymara peasants were inserted into the insecure and exploitative social reality of the urban class-structure of the city described above. Migration from the mines or from the countryside is a recurring theme in most *alteños'* recollections of the last twenty years. Roberto de la Cruz, a leading figure in COR-El Alto in October 2003, for example, recalls: 'Miners migrated to El Alto, indigenous-peasants migrated to El Alto, all in search of work'. But the new arrivals to the shantytown often found their hopes for employment and a marginally better life dashed: 'Unfortunately, when they arrived they did not find work. As a consequence, since 1985 problems accumulated, necessities accumulated that have never been attended to by the government. At some point this situation had to blow up. That is what occurred when we saw an opportune moment for rebellion in October'.[23] Oppositional cultures of resistance competed with other political currents – including populism and neoliberalism – whose agents employed the often-effective tools of clientelism to win local elections throughout the 1980s and 1990s.[24] And yet, when economic and state-crisis shook Bolivia in the closing years of the 1990s, and left-indigenous struggles began to emerge in waves throughout various rural and urban parts of the country, El Alto's array of neighbourhood- and community-organisations moved away from populism. The period of the Gas-War witnessed a remarkable reversal of the depoliticisation and fragmentation of working-class and popular indigenous life under neoliberalism, in part through the recovery of historical memories of indigenous and revolutionary-Marxist political cultures of resistance and

---

virtually unkown' (Gill 2000, p. 35). While there are no reliable statistics available, a significant number of *alteños* maintain dual residence in the city and in rural communities in the department of La Paz as a way of combating the precariousness of eking out a livelihood in the city and maintaining ties to their communities (Albó 2006, p. 334). This is a common phenomenon of working-class families in the Andes (Striffler 2004). Some urban dwellers also own land in rural communities while others hope to inherit some from their families. Still others return regularly to their rural communities to fulfill obligations to their parents or community, or to participate in political assemblies and meetings (Albó 2006, p. 334).

23. de la Cruz 2005.
24. Lazar 2004; Mayorga 2002; Quisbert Quispe 2003; Sandoval Z. and Sostres 1989.

opposition, redefined in light of the new complexities of a radically altered sociopolitical and economic context.

Relocated miners were able to *recreate* and *refashion* their historical memory of the protests, organisation, and battles in the mining zones in a way that made them relevant to the challenges and stark realities of an impoverished, cosmopolitan shantytown. In other words, their political organising in El Alto did not rely on a romantic nostalgia or simplistic longing for the rehabilitation of a past already exhausted.[25] Historical divisions that had often separated mining activists from the rural indigenous peasantry had to be confronted as dispossessed peasants and relocated miners found themselves thrust into the informal working-class froth of El Alto.[26] Many ex-miners began, over time, to recognise and identify politically with their indigenous heritage in a way that was not emphasised in the mines. They began gradually to forge new ties of solidarity with radical indigenous-peasant groups in the neighouring *altiplano* and with ex-peasant Aymara indigenous migrants who had settled in the city.[27]

The life-story of Tomás Mamani exemplifies the impact of the miners' organising skills and ideological contribution to popular resistance in El Alto. Tomás worked as a miner in Colquiri between the ages of 12 and 41. In 2005, he had been living in El Alto for fifteen years and working as a driver of one of the thousands of *micros*, or mini-vans, which working-class Bolivians use to get around the major cities in the country. He lives in the neighbourhood of Santiago II in El Alto, where ex-miners tended to congregate over the years, coming to constitute a majority of the inhabitants. Adapting his political formation in the mines to his new life in the shantytown, Tomás played a leading role in the neighbourhood's revolt during October 2003, suffering a serious leg-injury as a result of clashes with the armed forces. Soon after the October Gas-War, he was elected president of the neighbourhood-council of Santiago II, and helped to organise the neighbourhood once again in the May–June 2005 uprisings against President Carlos Mesa.[28] Similarly, Alicia Claure, a member of the executive committee of FEJUVE-El Alto in 2005, recalled the way in which her political formation in the mining communities continued to affect

---

25. Cajías de la Vega 2004, p. 22.
26. Arbona 2008, p. 25; Choque 2005a.
27. Cajías de la Vega 2004, p. 22; Hylton and Thomson 2004, p. 18.
28. Mamani 2005d.

her sense of self, political identity, and her strength as a female activist in El Alto:

> I was formed politically in the mining centers. I was raised in a mining cen-
> tre where I saw poverty, injustice, and the exploitation of man. I witnessed
> all of this since I was a little girl. I've suffered a lot.... My experience in the
> mines made me a strong woman, with the will to be able to continue defend-
> ing [our rights] and the rights of our children.... We left the mining zone as
> part of those who were relocated in 1987.... Out of necessity, many women
> and men, with our children, left the mining zones following the little bait the
> government dangled in front of us in this period, a few meagre dollars that
> hardly lasted any time at all. We arrived in the city with our children. Many
> families arrived only to break up because of the economic situation and lack
> of work. There is quite of bit of delinquency with our children. Some of our
> husbands became drunks. All this rage. The government is to blame for the
> lack of jobs.[29]

Remarkably, in spite of the despair that migration to El Alto often engendered in the families of ex-miners, their traditions of working-class resistance facilitated the slow rearticulation of their political efficacy through a reconstituted infrastructure of class-struggle.

The political impact of rural-indigenous migration – and especially Aymara migration – to El Alto has been similar to that of the relocated miners in a number of respects. The most striking facet of the city is that 82 per cent of residents describe themselves as indigenous.[30] Politically, this collective indigenous self-identification has expressed itself through the use of the *wiphala* in every major march, demonstration and strike, and the visible use of *ponchos* by a significant minority of men in protests, as well as the much more prevalent – and daily – use of *polleras* by indigenous women. Remarkably, during the height of the October Gas-War, the use of the Aymara language took over the public space in many of the streets of El Alto during different periods of the confrontation: '...the people began to speak Aymara in El Alto.... They always speak Spanish, but during those days of uprising they began to speak in Aymara, to organise the resistance, the barricades, links between districts,

---

29. Claure 2005.
30. INE 2001.

all of this, in Aymara... it expressed a sentiment to speak Aymara: "We are this, we're emancipated, we're rebelling, and we're speaking Aymara. Power speaks Spanish" '.[31]

Like the ex-miners whose lives in El Alto were initially characterised by a deep sense of loss, rural-to-urban indigenous migrants also encountered a city which delivered far below their expectations: 'These indigenous sought better opportunities in the cities than they had in the countryside. The reality is that their dreams were not realized, their utopias and illusions about a better life in the city'.[32] Like the ex-miners, however, the new indigenous arrivals began to join in collective fights to gain basic services for the city, and eventually to challenge neoliberalism more widely. The indigenous migrants informed these struggles with their histories of rebellion in the rural *altiplano*. 'Rural communal syndicalism', Patricia Costas Monje points out, has been important in forging the social-movement structures and repertoires of contention in the urban context of El Alto, 'above all the [legacy of] the Aymara emergence in the 1970s. The *katarista* movement has left its mark on the forms of the new scenario of social movements today'.[33] The reformulation of rural communal-syndicalist patterns of organisation, community-governance and resistance in the setting of El Alto is captured vividly in the words of Benecio Quispe Gutiérrez, himself an Aymara rural-to-urban migrant living in El Alto. He stresses how the communitarian traditions of the indigenous countryside are antithetical to liberal capitalism and have informed the popular cultures of indigenous resistance and opposition in contemporary urban Bolivia:

> The most interesting thing about the city of El Alto is that the Aymaras and Quechuas who migrate to this city do not migrate solely as biological human beings; rather, they bring with them their entire cultural baggage...a politi-cal culture. The politics of the *ayllus* is unique. The Aymara political culture is the negation of the liberal political culture.... In liberalism generally the capacity of decision making is representative. A person or a group of people are delegated the capacity to decide. But one of the central characteristics of the Aymara political culture is that decision-making capacity is situated in the collectivity organised in an assembly.... Therefore it is the community

---

31. Gosálvez 2005.
32. Patzi 2005b.
33. Costas Monje 2005.

that is sovereign and not the leader. And when they migrated, obviously, they brought all of this political cultural baggage here to the city. This is why in many places – the neighbourhood councils, the school councils – this is still practiced, where the expression of decisions is that of the collectivity organised in assembly.[34]

Organisationally, the neighbourhood-councils of each block, *barrio* (neighbourhood), and zone of the city, ascending all the way up to the peak-organisation of FEJUVE-El Alto, mirror important features of the traditional rural-indigenous community-structure, the *ayllu*.[35] Little by little, suggests Aymara *alteño* sociologist Pablo Mamani Ramírez, the city of El Alto has become a pivotal urban reference-point for the indigenous population of the *altiplano* and Bolivia as a whole. It embodies the reality of urban-indigenous working-class social relations in a context of sharp racism, and the indigenous traditions of struggle that have been adapted from the countryside within that context.[36] For Mamani Ramírez, it is evident that the popular neighbourhoods of El Alto are places where the communitarian organisation and collective logics of reciprocity and resistance of the rural *ayllus* and mining zones have been revitalised within a distinct urban context.[37]

6.2 El Alto's infrastructure of class-struggle

El Alto's dense web of informal and formal associational networks help to explain how the oppositional political cultures of the ex-miners and rural-indigenous migrants were sustained beneath the surface throughout much of the 1980s and 1990s, and how collective capacities for indigenous-proletarian class-struggle were unleashed as left-indigenous protest began its ascent across the country beginning in 2000.[38] The historical memory of the miners and rural indigenous were maintained as 'living legacies of discussion and debate' and were rebuilt, refashioned, and strengthened through 'engagement in new struggles'.[39] Despite the decline in the rate of unionisa-

---

34. Quispe 2005.
35. Albó 2006, pp. 335–6.
36. Mamani Ramírez 2005, p. 52.
37. Mamani Ramírez 2005, p. 83.
38. Arbona 2005, p. 7; Arbona 2007, pp. 128–9.
39. Sears 2005, p. 33.

tion and the informalisation of the world of work, alternative associational fabric in the communities of El Alto provided space for the slow rearticulation and transformation of these historical memories. The dense infrastructure of class-struggle in El Alto was the most important factor behind the incredible strength and militancy of the October 2003 and May–June 2005 Gas-Wars. From the often invisible networks at the neighbourhood-level to the top functional and territorial associations of the working classes in the city – COR-El Alto and FEJUVE-El Alto – the urban infrastructure was able to mobilise, articulate, and sustain the militant-rebellion against class-exploitation, racial oppression, and imperialism. COR-El Alto and FEJUVE-El Alto managed to unite community class-struggle for basic services with the wide-reaching political demands of the indigenous working classes of the city. The protests were able to go as far as they did because COR-El Alto and FEJUVE-El Alto also built alliances with radicalised peasants of the *altiplano* and the peak-national organisation of the formal working class, the COB, and of the miners, the FSTMB.[40]

At the base-level, the most important formal community-infrastructures organised on a territorial basis are the hundreds of *juntas vecinales*, or neighbourhood-councils, which are then articulated vertically into the city-wide FEJUVE-El Alto.[41] On a functional basis, small-scale street-vendors and market-vendors are organised into associations of their own to protect their economic and political interests. Those workers that have been able to unionise their workplaces or maintain pre-existing unions, are affiliated to COR-El Alto at the federation-level in the city, and to the COB at the national level. These various associations and federations represent the formal infrastructure of class-struggle in El Alto. Within and around them exists a complex myriad of

---

40. In the bleaker scenario of the 1990s, when El Alto's popular movement had not yet emerged, civil-associational life in the city still played an important role in meeting the basic survival-needs of *alteños*. Lesley Gill partially credits the density of social networks in the city with the relatively low levels of violent crime compared to other Latin-American cities with similar structures of inequality, exploitation, and racism. Gill paints a portrait of an 'intricate network of grassroots associations' including 'mothers' clubs, neighborhood committees, civic associations, labor organizations, soccer leagues, and folkloric groups' and even, despite their often problematic nature, 'some NGOs and churches that struggle against considerable chaos and disarray to sustain a modicum of economic security, decency, and social solidarity' (Gill 2000, p. 31).

41. Lazar 2006, pp. 186–7.

dynamic and often invisible informal community and workplace social networks that reinforce the capacities of the formal infrastructure.

6.2.1 FEJUVE-El Alto

The structure of FEJUVE-El Alto today brings together representatives of all the districts of El Alto. An executive committee (EC), made up of 29 secretaries, is elected every two years during an ordinary congress of the federation. The results of the election must then be recognised by CONALJUVE.[42] The EC provides leadership to FEJUVE-El Alto; ultimately, however, its mandate derives from the ordinary congresses held every two years. These congresses define the strategic objectives of the federation. Four delegates from every neighbourhood-council in El Alto, elected through neighbourhood-assemblies, participate in the ordinary congresses.[43] Extraordinary congresses are more regular gatherings that are called by the EC to address specific agendas. *Ampliados*, or general meetings, in which the presidents of each neighbourhood-council must participate, are convened by the EC on a monthly basis in periods of relative political dormancy. In emergency-periods of intense political engagement, they can be held at any juncture to address issues that require urgent attention. Lastly, the EC itself meets at least every two weeks to co-ordinate the activities of the various secretaries.[44]

At the base-level, neighbourhood-assemblies are convened on a weekly or monthly basis, depending on the neighbourhood and the political period. At these gatherings, organised by the leadership of each neighbourhood-council, rank-and-file *alteños* express their immediate needs and desires, strategise on how best to address them, and voice their criticisms and/or support for the more general direction being taken by the EC of FEJUVE-El Alto.[45] Presidents of each neighbourhood-council are then meant to articulate the views of the rank and file to the EC of FEJUVE-El Alto and other neighbourhood-council presidents at the extraordinary congresses and *ampliados* in which they participate on a regular basis.

---

42. García Linera 2005e, p. 896.
43. García Linera 2005e, p. 598.
44. Ibid.
45. García Linera 2005e, p. 599.

Each neighbourhood-council, in order to be recognised by FEJUVE-El Alto, must represent various zones in the city that together contain more than 200 residents. These local-level councils have in some ways acted as alternative organising infrastructure for workers in El Alto who are unlikely to work in a unionised workplace through which they can effectively organise as workers given the obstacles that have been highlighted above. Membership in neighbourhood-councils is based on ownership or rental of a housing unit in an *alteño* neighbourhood. Each family or household sends one delegate to attend neighbourhood-assemblies as their representative; each household-representative shares the same duties and obligations at these assemblies.[46] The patriarchal gender-dynamics in the majority of homes in the city are such that men are over-represented at all levels in the process, from the neighbourhood-assemblies all the way to the EC of FEJUVE-El Alto. In the EC established in 2004, for example, only 10 of the 29 elected members were women. Each neighbourhood-council has its own executive committee with a number of secretaries. These committees co-ordinate the day-to-day activities of their councils, but receive their mandates from the neighbourhood-assemblies and are expected to reflect the wishes of the rank and file when they represent them at the extraordinary congresses and *ampliados*.[47]

6.2.2   COR-El Alto

While the depth and breadth of industrialisation in Bolivia was always limited, the bulk of industrial manufacturing that did exist in the department of La Paz became increasingly concentrated in the shantytown of El Alto beginning in the late 1960s and early 1970s. This industrial activity, in addition to expanding working-class formation in various other sectors of the growing shantytown's economy, allowed for the gradual emergence of a series of labour-federations created by workers to defend their immediate material interests as well as the interests of the Bolivian working classes more generally.

The Federación de Trabajadores, Gremiales, Artesanos y Comerciantes Minoristas (Federation of Organised Workers, Artisans, Small Traders and

---

46. García Linera, Chávez León, and Costas Monje 2005, pp. 599–600.
47. García Linera, Chávez León, and Costas Monje 2005, p. 595.

Food-Sellers of the city of El Alto, FTGACM) was established in 1970, for example. The Federación de Trabajadores de Carne (Federation of Butchers) and the Federación de Panificadores (Bakers' Federation) created the Confederación Única de Trabajadores de El Alto (Workers' Confederation of El Alto, CUTAL) in 1987.[48] In 1988, CUTAL became COR-El Alto and the latter was recognised in the same year by the COB at its Seventh Ordinary Congress. Today, COR-El Alto is a sectorally-based organisation that seeks to represent various components of El Alto's working classes. It includes under its umbrella the FTGACM, the Federation of Market-Traders, and a number of trade-unions.[49]

COR-El Alto's executive committee is structured similarly to FEJUVE-El Alto. There are 27 secretaries in the committee who are elected in a Congreso Orgánico (Organic Congress), in which representatives from all the affiliated federations, associations, and trade-unions participate. Among COR-El Alto's founding principles is the continuous struggle for the interests of El Alto's working class.[50] Because the workers' organisation conceives of those interests in an expansive manner, it was able to form alliances with the territorially-based FEJUVE-El Alto, and to participate in high-profile social movements for basic public welfare in the city. As a consequence, COR-El Alto was pivotal in cementing ties between community-based social movements and union-based struggle in El Alto during the left-indigenous struggle between 2000 and 2005.

6.2.3   Dialectics of popular power

Over the course of September and October 2003, and especially between 8 and 17 October, left-indigenous popular sectors of El Alto reinvented and extended the assemblyist and participatory forms of democratic power from below that we earlier witnessed in the Cochabamba War of 2000 and, in rural form, during the 2000 and 2001 Aymara peasant-insurrections. FEJUVE-El Alto and COR-El Alto became the peak-institutional expressions and ultimate co-ordinators of the popular rebellion and incipient manifestations of collective self-government of the oppressed and exploited in one city. The

---

48. García Linera 2005e, p. 594.
49. Lazar 2006, p. 187.
50. Montoya Villa and Rojas García 2004, pp. 50–1.

state was temporarily replaced in El Alto by the popular sovereignty of the indigenous informal proletarian residents, organised at the highest level in FEJUVE-El Alto and COR-El Alto, but also at the base through spontaneous committees of various sorts, neighbourhood-assemblies, and the long-established network of roughly 500 neighbourhood-councils. A complex dialectic between spontaneous mass-actions from below, led and organised by the rank and file, and the higher-scale, city-wide leadership and infrastructure of FEJUVE-El Alto and COR-El Alto, made possible the heroic challenge to neoliberal capitalism and racist oppression during the Gas-War.

Most activists and scholars agree that FEJUVE-El Alto and COR-El Alto were the most important formal social-movement organisations in the city during this period.[51] Yet it would be profoundly misleading to give the impression that the executive leaderships of these two social-movement organisations simply issued decrees to which the rank and file subsequently responded. Mamani Ramírez, having lived through the events of October 2003, has made some of the most penetrating observations about how rank-and-file activities in the neighbourhood-councils and other informal networks often overtook and outpaced the leadership of FEJUVE-El Alto and COR-El Alto.[52]

Every urban space that was occupied by the radicalised residents of the shantytown, was eventually governed through neighbourhood-councils and self-organised 'committees in defence of gas', 'strike-committees', and 'self-defence committees'.[53] Plazas, although they were often sites of state-repression and violence, also became open spaces of organising neighbourhood-resistance, deliberating, and deciding collectively on strategies, tactics, and visions of change. Emergency neighbourhood-assemblies were convened by the leaderships of neighbourhood-councils and committees in defence of gas to decide on immediate actions, such as blocking an avenue, or preparing for an imminent incursion by the military into the neighbourhood. Regular nightly assemblies in the plazas were more reflective spaces in which the indigenous informal working-class residents could review the events of the day, evaluate their strategies of resistance, and plan for future actions. As state-repression intensified, the leaders of neighbourhood-councils were often forced to operate

---

51. Cori 2005; de la Cruz 2005; Gómez 2004; Merida Gutiérrez 2005b; Pabón Chávez 2005a; Patana 2005.
52. Mamani Ramírez 2005, p. 69.
53. Mamani Ramírez 2005, p. 72.

in a clandestine fashion, therefore providing even greater space for the constant renewal of informal leaderships at the neighbourhood-level, and more important roles for the self-organised strike-committees and committees of other types.[54] These spontaneous grassroots-formations can be understood as the informal infrastructure of the rank and file. The very self-organisation and self-activity of the mass-base of rank-and-file indigenous proletarians of the city through pre-existing informal networks is what *strengthened* and *enabled* the dynamism of the formal structures of FEJUVE-El Alto and COR-El Alto and made the rebellion possible.[55]

Gonzalo Gozalvez, a journalist and activist with extensive experience inside the popular movements of El Alto speaks of the dialectic between the rank and file and the leadership and formal infrastructure of FEJUVE-El Alto and COR-El Alto:

> The neighbourhood-councils were permanently coordinating actions in El Alto. There was no spokesperson of the movement. There wasn't anyone that the government could turn to, to speak as the representative of the movement.... The neighbourhood-councils, through their leaders, articulated the grassroots. It was an impressive articulation of each block, each neighbourhood, each zone, of each district.... [At the height of the conflict] there were [frequent meetings] of FEJUVE. So, there was this sort of organisation. But, from my perspective, this was nothing more than the articulation the people's opinion.[56]

---

54. Mamani Ramírez 2005, pp. 82–83.
55. Chávez 2005a; Cori 2005. Mamani Ramírez calls these forms of territorial self-government that were established in October – the neighbourhood-councils and self-organised committees – *microgobiernos barriales*, or neighbourhood-microgovernments (Mamani Ramírez 2005, p. 72). Each microgovernment became a pivotal point for collective decision-making through assemblies, and as they spread from neighbourhood to neighbourhood and district to district, the web they spun effectively immobilised the shantytown. Barricades were built, roads were upturned, and trenches were dug. The indigenous working-class microgovernments were spaces in which the communitarian organisation and logics of the Andean *ayllu* and traditions of militant union-democracy from the mines were re-socialised and given new life in the novel community-setting of twenty-first century El Alto (Mamani Ramírez 2005, p. 83). With almost 500 neighbourhood-councils effectively self-governing and defending the city against the repressive forces of the state, El Alto became ungovernable territory, into which the state could only hope to enter sporadically, mete out repression, and then retreat (Mamani Ramírez 2005, p. 85).
56. Gozálvez 2005.

6.3 Infrastructure of the formal working class and social-movement unionism

What made the older organisational structures of the FSTMB and the COB critical allies in the struggle, despite the dramatic trends in the informalisation of the Bolivian world of work over the previous two decades, was their strategic orientation toward social-movement unionism. Most important, in this regard, was their perspective of reaching out to all of the oppressed, struggling for the working classes and the peasantry as a whole, rather than for the particular interests of the minority of the working classes who remained formally employed in the opening years of the twenty-first century.[57] A representative COB-document released on 30 September 2003, the day after the start of a general strike, asserted the organisation's commitment to building broad alliances with all sectors of the working classes, and celebrated the radical measures taken by many different movements:

> We express our satisfaction with the militant-support of the peasant-comrades who continue with the road-blockades, of the urban and rural teachers' unions who have integrated themselves into the struggle, of the street vendors... with their marches..., the miners who are preparing to radicalise their protests, the butchers who have announced that they are joining the people's struggle, the university-professors and students who are also adopting measures in support of the popular movement... the pensioners for their courage in struggling for their rights, and the factory-workers for their union-discipline in the days of protest.[58]

The FSTMB similarly embraced social-movement unionism. The miners had always stressed that their struggle was part of the struggle for all of the working classes and the oppressed rather than simply being about improving the material well-being of their own sector's membership. Such a politics is evident in a representative FSTMB-communiqué released immediately after the overthrow of Gonzalo Sánchez de Lozada on 17 October 2003. In it, the miners clarify what the objectives of the FSTMB had been during the Gas-War: the nationalisation of hydrocarbons; the re-nationalisation of all the state-owned enterprises privatised throughout the 1990s; the abrogation of

---

57. Cruz 2005; Solares Barrientos 2005.
58. COB 2003b.

the INRA-law because it subjected indigenous and peasant-land and territory to the laws of the market; the egalitarian redistribution of land and defence of the collective rights of indigenous communities to land and territory; the restitution of the social rights of Bolivian workers eroded over the years of neoliberal restructuring; rejection of Bolivian participation in the proposed Free-Trade Area of the Americas; and the refusal to grant impunity to those in government – the 'butchers of October' – who were behind the high levels of state-repression in September and October.[59]

The COB and the FSTMB helped to organise and co-ordinate the struggle at a larger scale than would have been possible if El Alto's infrastructure of class-struggle had remained in isolation. The COB was a vital public face for left-indigenous struggle in these months, gaining wide exposure in the media and articulating a series of revolutionary positions. The COB and FSTMB were able to mobilise large numbers of formal-sector workers during the Gas-War, and contributed to the militant-energy of the mass-demonstrations in which they participated. Finally, the miners carried with them into the cycle of protests their longstanding cultural association with the Bolivian revolutionary Left. Thus, even when they did not contribute the largest number of protesters, the symbolic impact of their participation was frequently enormous.

6.4 Narrative of the Gas-War: dialectics of state-repression and mass-radicalisation

This section provides an analytical narrative of the Gas-War, focusing on the dialectics of state-repression and mass-radicalisation. Table 6.2 highlights the key social forces involved at various stages in the Gas-War, key turning points in the months of September and October, and the escalation of protest demands over time, particularly following central moments of state-repression, the dates of which are highlighted in bold in the table.

At the outset of September 2003, the popularity of Gonzalo Sánchez de Lozada's administration was in steep decline. In an urban poll of residents of Cochabamba, El Alto, La Paz, and Santa Cruz, 70 per cent of respondents disapproved of the government's record during its first year in office. A

---

59. FSTMB 2003b.

remarkable 84 per cent of residents of El Alto held this view.[60] The future of natural-gas development in Bolivia had already deeply penetrated popular political discussions in the streets and countryside, and continued to be a contentious subject in the halls of Congress as well.[61] The state-owned natural-gas and oil-company, YPFB, was privatised in 1996. Under the administration of ex-dictator Hugo Bánzer (1997–2001), a deal was then initiated between the Bolivian state and the Spanish-British-US energy-consortium Pacific LNG and San Diego-based Sempra Energy. Under the proposed arrangement, natural gas would be exported through a Chilean port to markets in Mexico and the Californian coast of the United States. A year after the start of his second mandate as president in 2002, Sánchez de Lozada sought to close the gas-export deal, contributing a focal point and unifying issue to the left-indigenous social forces in insurrection during September and October 2003.[62]

The idea of using a Chilean port to export gas was provocative to Bolivian-nationalist sentiments across the political spectrum, which have long sustained an antipathy toward Chile, rooted in latter's annexation of Bolivia's coastline during the Pacific War of the late 1870s and early 1880s. However, much more important than basic resentment of Chile's nineteenth-century foreign relations was a profound sense that since natural gas had been privatised in 1996, the resource had been pillaged by transnational corporations with little to no benefit accruing to the Bolivian population. Re-establishing Bolivian social control over natural gas – and other natural resources – soon was understood by left-indigenous movements as the only way to avoid the cruel repetition of hundreds of years of exploitation of domestic natural resources – silver and tin historically – and of the labourers used by capital to extract them.

Table 6.2   Chronology of the September–October 2003 Gas-War

8 September 2003 – Between 3,000 and 10,000 peasants began a march from the community of Batalla toward El Alto. The march was organised under the auspices of the FSTCLP-TK, led by Rufo Calle, and the CSUTCB, led by Felipe Quispe. Demands included the following: (a) that the government fulfill obligations regarding 72 peasant demands articulated in the 2000 and 2001 Aymara peasant-rebellions and agreed to by the government in the Isla del Sol Accords; (b) that Edwin Huampu, wrongly imprisoned for murder, be released; and (c) that the proposed deal to export naturalgas through Chile be abandoned.

---

60. *Los Tiempos* 2003a.
61. *La Prensa* 2003f.
62. Hylton and Thomson 2004, p. 18; *Associated Press* 2003.

The Federación de Transportes Interprovincial (Federation of Inter-Provincial Truckers, FTI) initiated a strike to correspond with the peasant-actions.

A separate march of peasants occurred the same day, beginning in the community of Caracaollo, and set toward reaching El Alto. This march was led by one of the militant COR-El Alto leaders, Roberto de la Cruz, who had travelled earlier to Caracollo to help to organise the march with his peasant-comrades. Both peasant-marches converged on the city of El Alto on 8 September, a sea of *wiphalas* held high above marchers' heads. They were greated in the city by university-students from UPEA, activists with FEJUVE-El Alto, street-vendors, and others. All sectors agreed to reject the export of gas under neoliberal conditions, Bolivian participation in the proposed Free-Trade Area of the Americas (FTAA), and the Ley de Seguridad Ciudadana (Citizen-Security Law, LSC). The latter had been introduced in order to increase massively the punishment for participation in road-blockades. Activists found guilty under the provisions of this law could face between five and eight years in jail.

Also on this day, FEJUVE-El Alto and COR-El Alto convened a civic strike in the city of El Alto against the implementation of new municipal legislation, *maya y paya*, or 'first' and 'second' in Aymara. Analyses conducted by two popular organisations concluded that the new legislation was intended to provide the municipal government with the information necessary to increase taxes on building and home-construction in El Alto. The strike included the blockading of the principal streets in all nine districts of the city. While they were led by FEJUVE-El Alto and COR-El Alto, the protests were supported by the Federación de Mujeres Bartolina Sisa (Women's Federation – Bartolina Sisa), the student-federation of UPEA, the Federación de Mujeres de El Alto (Women's Federation of El Alto), street-vendors' associations, and the La Paz wing of the Movimiento Sin Tierra (Landless Movement, MST). Roberto de la Cruz and Felipe Quispe, two of the most visible leaders in the day's events, called publicly on Evo Morales to join the growing movement against the government.

10 September – CSUTCB and FSTCLP-TK militants initiated a hunger-strike in the auditorium of the Aymara-language radio-station in El Alto, Radio San Gabriel. Over 2,000 peasant-activists participated, including Felipe Quispe. Among the many demands, the most pressing and non-negotiable objective continued to be the release of Edwin Huampu. Among other organisations actively supporting the hunger-strike were the FTI, the rural teachers' unions of the *altiplano*, and the UPEA student-federation. Critically, the hunger-strike was also publicly supported by the COB, with the COB's leader Jaime Solares making appearances in the media linking the hunger-strike to a wider struggle for social justice and a critique of neoliberalism.

12 September – Troops from the National Police and the armed forces were deployed throughout the *altiplano*, with specific concentrations in the roadways connecting the capital-city to the Lake Titicaca region. That same day, *cocaleros* (coca-growers) and other groups in the semi-tropical Yungas region, in the northern part of the department of La Paz, announced that road-blockades would be established there in the coming days. The *cocaleros* mobilised around local anti-eradication demands, but at the same time added their voices to the wider claims emerging around natural-gas development and opposition to the penalisation of civil resistance by way of the LSC.

Also on September 12, the COB released its 'Programme of Struggle' from which the wider movement of the indigenous peasantry and working classes were able to draw.

Mid-September – A whole series of social movements announced their tactics and strategies of radicalisation to come into effect in the near future: a general blockade of roads in the Yungas, the continuation of the civic strike in El Alto and blocked roads in the *altiplano*, the deepening of the hunger-strike of the Aymara peasantry in an El Alto radio-station, further pressure by teachers' union mobilisations in La Paz, UPEA student-actions, and growing radicalism among the associations of pensioners in La Paz. In the face of these conflicts, the government once again emphasised that it would maintain order and the rule of law through the use of the armed forces if deemed necessary. The COB, in response, declared itself in a state of emergency and announced that it would organise wide-scale and immediate civil resistance if the government declared a state of siege.

15 September – FEJUVE-El Alto initiated the start of El Alto's second civic strike in September. It continued over the next three days. The peasant hunger-strike in El Alto led by Quispe entered its second week. Road-blockades in the northern part of La Paz were deepened, as were those in the *altiplano*.

18 September – A new march of Aymara peasants, numbering over 11,000, arrived in the community of Mullasa, just outside of La Paz.

19 September – Day of national protest in defence of natural gas was a great success. Over 50,000 people mobilised in La Paz and 20,000 in Cochabamba. The Coordinadora, led by Oscar Olivera, and the MAS, led by Evo Morales, were instrumental actors in the initial call for this day of protest. The COB, the Coordinadora, the MAS, and the Movimiento Indígena Pachakuti (Indigenous Pachakuti Movement, MIP), the political party led by Quispe, were essential to organising the large number of activists who took part in the day's events. An additional 10,000 marched and mobilised in the city of Oruro, as did militant miners in the Llallagua, Catavi, and Siglo XX mines. To the south of La Paz and Cochabamba, and southeast of Oruro, the colonial city of Sucre hosted to marches in solidarity with the day of protest. Potosí also witnessed substantive concentrations of protesters who gathered in defence of gas, while the roads in the *altiplano* and northern La Paz remained occupied by militant peasants.

20 September – Military troops sent to invade Warisata where they commence a slaughter of indigenous community-members. The massacre was the result of a 'humanitarian operation' led by Minister of Defence, Carlos Sánchez Berzaín, in which troops were mobilised to 'liberate' roughly 1,000 Bolivian and international tourists from the community of Sorata. They had been stranded by road-blockades, but were well cared for by the insurrectionary-indigenous communities. Sánchez Berzaín arrived on the scene in Warisata via helicopter, infuriating indigenous protesters who were already profoundly frustrated by the government's failure to respond to any of their demands. The police entered Warisata and began shooting tear-gas to disperse the population. The indigenous community-members responded by throwing rocks at police. In the face of this defensive resistance, first the military and then the police fired their weapons, according to the testimony of witnesses in Warisata. The police claimed to have responded only when attacked by the indigenous protesters. At the end of the day, on 20 September, five indigenous peasants and one soldier were dead, and over a dozen people were injured. Among the dead was an eight-year-old girl.

20–7 September – The COB called for an indefinite general strike to begin on 29 September, and a nation-wide campaign of road-blockades. The hunger-strike in El Alto continued. The *cocaleros* of the Chapare announced that they would be blocking the highway connecting Cochabamba to Santa Cruz. The MST called for land-takeovers. It is worthwhile noting the fact that neither Evo Morales personally nor the MAS as a political party were conduits of this mobilisation. Indeed, shortly after the Warisata massacre, Morales traveled to Libya for a conference on indigenous issues and did not return to the country until 27 September.

29 September – The COB-led strike started out slowly but gathered steam in following days.

30 September – the COB held an open assembly in the Plaza San Francisco and from there led a march through the streets of La Paz. Participants in the march included rural and urban teachers, UPEA-students, administrative workers of the public university of La Paz, the Universidad Mayor San Andrés (UMSA), and street-vendors and teachers from El Alto. Traffic was sporadically paralysed in the capital and the march divided into three streams and wound through the downtown-avenues.

Various social-movement actions were registered elsewhere in the country. Retired teachers in El Alto threatened further protests of solidarity with teachers of El Alto and La Paz. The Aymara peasantry of the *altiplano* sustained its road-blocks in the La Paz provinces of Manco Capac, Los Andes, Omasuyos, Larceja, Muñecas, Camacho, and Villarroel, as well as the hunger-strike in Radio San Gabriel in El Alto.

The dissident fraction of the CSUTCB, led by *masista* Román Loayza and in dispute with the larger faction led by Felipe Quispe, announced that it would initiate further road-blockades in the coming days as part of the call for a national blockade of roads. Traffic between the departments of La Paz, Oruro, Potosí and Cochabamba was irregular due to road-blocks. Inter-provincial truckers continued their strike – called initially on September 8.

The Asociación de Carcineros (Association of Butchers) and the Federación de Trabajadores en Carne de El Alto y La Paz (Federation of Meat-Workers of El Alto and La Paz, FUTECRA) announced that their slaughterhouses would close on 1 October in support of the COB's call for a general strike and in solidarity with the protests of the Aymara peasantry.

The *cocaleros* of the Chapare and the Yungas declared that further mobilisations and road-blocks by their sectors would begin on October 6. Miners observed the COB's strike-call, and in the mining zones of Huanuni, Totoral, Avicaya, and Colquiri – in the department of Oruro – they began blocking roads. The UPEA student-federation expressed again their commitment to daily marches and mobilisations. Also responding to the COB's strike were the street-vendors' associations of El Alto, rural and urban teachers' unions, and health-care workers in La Paz.

Also on 30 September, the Coordinadora en Defensa del Gas initiated a march of 100 to 300 people, led by Oscar Olivera, from Cochabamba to Warisata, in solidarity with the fallen martyrs of the community and the general struggle of the Aymara struggle in the *altiplano*.

2 October – The COB made its most important intervention in the September–October Gas-War. The workers' confederation convened an open assembly in the Plaza San Francisco with the largest turnout yet of any assembly during almost a month of growing rural and urban discontent. It was at this assembly that the demand for the resignation of Sánchez de Lozada became entrenched in the base of the popular left-indigenous struggle in the country, as the crowd chanted in unison for the collapse of the presidency, *Fuera Goni! Out With Goni!* The voices of resistance accumulated throughout the day. Román Loayza announced that by 6 October, the affiliates of his wing of the CSUTCB would unify with the general strike initiated by the COB. The *cocaleros* of the Chapare reiterated their intention of joining the national blockade of roads with greater intensity. *Cocaleros* in the Yungas scattered rocks and other debris on the highways leading in an out of South and North Yungas, making transit impossible.

Regular business-activity was shut down for the fourth consecutive day by a myriad of left-indigenous sectors in the city of Oruro. Meanwhile, in the conservative southern department of Tarija, the Regional Workers' Central (COR-Tarija) initiated a hunger-strike. The Departmental Workers' Central of Santa Cruz (COD-Santa Cruz) also announced a plan for marches in the coming days, while COD-Beni declared a 24-hour strike to begin the next day, on 3 October. Gas and the president's resignation were now the centripetal axes of revolt.

The most important activities of the day occurred in El Alto. FEJUVE-El Alto and COR-El Alto declared that their third civic strike would begin on 8 October – following the success of the first two on 8 and 15 September. Already, on the day of the announcement of the strike to come, the city was paralysed. Protesters in El Alto clashed with the police and military, responding to state-coercion with rocks, clubs, sticks, and dynamite. Dozens of protesters were injured or detained. With greater and greater adherence to the call for Goni's resignation amongst left-indigenous social forces, even the moderate leadership of the MAS began publicly to express its support for the call.

The government responded to the events of the day by militarising El Alto and La Paz. The perimeters of the Plaza Murillo were sealed with uniformed armed forces personnel, and military troops were stationed outside of all public government buildings in La Paz. The Minister of Services and Public Works, Carlos Morales, complained about the loss of millions of dollars because of the ongoing protests since the beginning of September. Meanwhile, the President attempted to convince international reporters at a press-conference that the protesters were confused about the issue of gas because the government had not actually decided on whether to export natural gas through a Chilean or Peruvian port. Addressing an international press-conference, Sánchez de Lozada explained why mobilisations persisted in spite of the reasonableness of his government: '[Bolivians] are like children who scream before you can explain something'.[63]

A final important highlight marking 2 October was the fact that the 'Aymara peasantry – with coca, alcohol, and *aptapi* (communal feasting) – began the celebration that marks the beginning of the preparation of the soil for sowing, and put protest on hold. The insurgent momentum now passed to the city of El Alto'.[64]

3–7 October– Marches and mobilisations continued daily in La Paz, El Alto, and Cochabamba, with protesters demanding the immediate resignation of Gonzalo Sánchez de Lozada. Also during this week, the idea of convening a participatory and revolutionary constituent assembly to refound the Bolivian state began to acquire new resonance amongst the popular sectors.

8 October – There was an explosion of grassroots-activity in El Alto as the third civic strike was kicked off. Two civilian protesters suffered bullet-wounds and many others were injured by rubber-bullets. Approximately 800 miners arrived outside of El Alto, having marched from Huanuni to join the forces led by the COB against the exportation of gas under current conditions and for the resignation of Sánchez de Lozada.

The blockade of roads in the *altiplano* of the department of La Paz persisted in density and scope. There were sporadic road-blocks in the department of Cochabamba. New social sectors announced that they would be mobilising in support of the COB. In the city of Cochabamba, there was a march of students and administrative staff of San Simón Univeristy (UMSS), and protests led by the Departmental Workers' Central (COD-Cochabamba), teachers, and *cocaleros*.

In Potosí, there was a mass-march led by staff and students from Tomás Frías University and the Civic Committee of Potosí. In Sucre, the mobilisations were smaller than elsewhere, but San Francisco Xavier University closed its doors, and the COD-

---

63. *La Patria* 2003d.
64. Hylton & Thomson 2007, p. 113.

Sucre called a 48-hour strike. Health-care workers and the rural and urban teachers' unions observed the strike-call. Even in Santa Cruz, a small number of students from Gabriel René Moreno University marched in solidarity with the mobilisations occurring elsewhere in the country.

Commemoration of the thirty-sixth anniversary of the death of Ché Guevara in Bolivia was deeply politicised throughout the country given the polarisation of the moment.

9 October – Early in the morning, another martyr was added to those who had fallen in defence of gas. A combined operation of police and military forces intercepted the miners in Ventilla before they could arrive in El Alto. After an extended battle between the miners and the state-troops, the partially destroyed body of José Luis Atahuichi, a 40-year-old miner, lay on the ground and 21 other miners were left injured. The miners claimed that Atahuichi was killed by a grenade lobbed by military forces, while government- and military officials asserted that he was killed when a stick of dynamite he was carrying blew up prematurely. The same day, military troops attempted to clear blockades throughout the southern zone of El Alto, and another civilian-protester was killed. Ramiro Vargas Astillo, 22, died shortly after being shot in the head by state-forces.

10 October – The third day of El Alto's strike, 10 October, brought to more civilian-deaths and a score of injuries, as tear-gas and bullets were used against protesters. Downtown Cochabamba was occupied again, as the women's *cocalero*-federation, university-students, truckers, and other groups, mounted demonstrations.

11 October – La Paz had virtually run dry of gasoline, natural gas, and diesel-fuel. The government instituted a state of emergency through presidential Supreme Decree 27209. Activists in El Alto had initiated 24-hour per day vigils and blockade of the Senkata petroleum-plant, located in the city, to prevent natural-gas supplies from getting down to La Paz. Government sent a caravan of tanks and military-transport trucks to Senkata. Confrontations erupted and the military shot indiscriminately into the crowd.

12–13 October – The carnage wrought over these two days surpassed in condensed time the collective brutalities of the state since the outset of September. An attempt to militarise El Alto completely – with the use of tanks, troops, and helicopters – was made on 12 October. This spawned wide-scale resistance. By some accounts, 26 people were killed that day.

On 13 October, over 100,000 people marched from El Alto to La Paz carrying *wiphalas* and Bolivian flags, adorned with small black plastic-bags commemorating the fallen martyrs. Massive levels of resistance persisted in El Alto. Banks, factories owned by transnational corporations, and businesses identified with figures in the government were bombarded with rocks. Electropaz and Aguas del Tunari, two foreign companies that sell electricity- and water-services in El Alto, had already been destroyed by protesters days earlier. As evening encroached on the Bolivian Andes, an additional 28 civilians were dead in La Paz and El Alto.

Also on 13 October, Vice-President Carlos Mesa appeared on television saying that his conscience would not allow him to support the repression, although he did not yet resign. Jorge Torres, Minister of Economic Development, did resign, and ex-ombudsperson, Ana María Romero, condemned government-violence. Other political élites, such as Juan del Granado, the mayor of La Paz, began calling for the resignation of Sánchez de Lozada.

That same evening, Sánchez de Lozada appeared defiantly on television denouncing the protesters as seditious enemies of democracy. The US-embassy in Bolivia, under the leadership of ambassador David Greenlee, issued a communiqué portraying the protests as 'an attack against democracy and the constitutional order'. Moreover, the embassy emphasised, 'sticks and rocks are not a form of peaceful protest'.[65]

The Assembly of Human Rights, the Catholic Church, and the Confederación de la Prensa de Bolivia (Bolivian Press-Confederation, CPB), sent a joint letter to President Gonzalo Sánchez de Lozada stating that no one could any longer speak truthfully about 'confrontations' between military forces and protesters. Citing the use of machine-guns against Bolivian civilians, the three institutions declared that what had occurred was an authentic massacre. The letter demanded that the government withdraw its military and police-forces from the city of El Alto immediately. It also accused the government of being unwilling to negotiate in good faith. The consequence, the letter concluded, was a hardening of positions on all sides.

Between 8 and 17 October, left-indigenous popular sectors of El Alto practiced novel forms of assemblyist and participatory democracy – reminiscent of the Cochabamba Water-War, but on a much larger scale. The state lost control of the city to these new forms of popular power, and was able only to make sporadic incursions to repress and retreat.

15 October – This was a relatively quiet day in the capital-city and El Alto. In La Paz, a large peaceful assembly gathered in the Plaza de los Héroes, adjacent to the Plaza San Francisco. *Cocaleros*, miners, teachers, unemployed workers, indigenous peasants, FEJUVE-El Alto activists, pensioners, and university-students and professors, among many others, gathered with the united purpose of bringing down Sánchez de Lozada. In El Alto, people gathered to bury the dead and to pledge that the martyrs of the Gas-War would not die in vain. Facing an elaborate network of peasant road-blockades and mass peaceful mobilisations and general strikes in three major cities – La Paz, El Alto and Cochabamba – and similar scenarii in several other secondary cities, President Sánchez de Lozada did not on this day deploy the military arsenal of the state.

By this day, there had been 67 civilian deaths and over 400 injuries since the beginning of September. Influential middle-class figures initiated a hunger-strike calling into question the moral legitimacy of the Sánchez de Lozada government in light of the high death-toll. The middle-class hunger-strike eventually spread throughout most of the rest of the country. A manifesto signed by various prominent intellectuals was released calling for the resignation of Sánchez de Lozada and a new transitional government.

16 October – Mass-demonstrations defined this day. The road-blocks and strike in El Alto were intensified. A massive march descended from El Alto to La Paz, led by FEJUVE-El Alto and COR-El Alto. Indigenous peasants from Potosí began a march toward La Paz, joining with others in Oruro along the way. In the eastern lowlands, indigenous activists of the Ayoreo, Guaraní, Chuquitano, Yucararé, and Mojeño peoples began a hunger-strike in solidarity with their Andean brothers and sisters. Evo Morales reiterated the position of the MAS in support of a constitutional exit to the crisis. Mesa appeared on television again distancing himself from the President, while retaining his position as Vice-President such that his constitutional ascension to the presidency could legally occur in the event that Sánchez de Lozada resigned. For his part, Sánchez de Lozada appeared on CNN that evening and stated that he enjoyed the support of two thirds of the Bolivian citizenry.

News reached the capital that a new march of miners from Huanuni to La Paz had been allowed to pass unimpeded by military troops along the route. Diplomats

---

65. Lindsay 2003.

from neighbouring Argentina and Brazil asked the Bolivian President to resign. The US-embassy and a tiny sector of the political élite were all that remained behind the President.

17 October – Mobilisations were massive, and their geographical scope no less impressive. Oruro and Cochabamba were alive again with street-protests and demonstrations. The critical points in the highways and road-crossing the Chapare were blocked by *cocaleros*. Over 800 people across the country had now joined the hunger-strikes. Marching *cocaleros* completed their two-day journey from the Yungas to La Paz, supporting the final push for the President's resignation. The miners from Huanuni, allowed to pass by military posts the day before, were greeted in El Alto as heroes before they joined the mass-demonstration down the hillsides of La Paz and into the Plaza San Francisco.

Mauricio Antezana, the government's spokesperson, resigned. Manfred Reyes Villa of NFR publicly took the position that the government must listen to the people and resign. Rumours began to fly through the capital that Sánchez de Lozada had already fled to Miami or Peru, and a festive atmosphere began to envelop La Paz and El Alto.

Over 400,000 people now occupied La Paz – mainly indigenous workers and peasants, with a lesser number of middle-class protesters. US-ambassador David Greenlee continued to support Sánchez de Lozada. Sánchez de Lozada and his family fled the country for exile in Miami. Various other important figures in the cabinet also fled to the United States or various Latin-American countries. There hope was to escape persecution for their role in the 67 deaths and 400 injuries.

Carlos Mesa officially took over as the new President of Bolivia at 10:30pm that evening.[66]

6.4.1 *Indigenous-peasant revolt and urban tremors in September*

The Aymara peasantry of the western *altiplano* were the first to act.[67] The initial 'insurrectionary energy' of the 2003 rebellions emerged from the overwhelmingly Aymara indigenous province of Omasuyos, next to Lake Titicaca, and close to the country's capital-city.[68] They mobilised initially around a list of demands including broad anti-neoliberal themes as well as more specific conjunctural issues relating both to their sector's economic interests and to defending their collective right to indigenous self-government. Under the

---

66. This table was compiled through a qualitative analysis of the following newspapers between 1 September 2003 and 20 October 2003: *Correo del Sur; El Diario; El Juguete Rabioso; El Pulso; La Patria; La Prensa; La Razón; Le Monde Diplomatique (edición boliviana); Los Tiempos; Opinión;* and *Vóz*. It also relies on primary archives in the offices of the COB and the FSTMB in La Paz. In the few instances in which the sequence of events from these primary sources is insufficiently documented, it relies on the following secondary sources: García Linera 2004b; Gómez 2004; Hylton and Thomson 2007; Mamani Ramírez 2004; and Patzi 2005.
67. García Linera 2005a.
68. Hylton and Thomson 2004, p. 16.

leadership of Felipe Quispe, the CSUTCB was central to articulating this peasant-mobilisation, as was the FUDTCLP-TK, led by Rufo Calle.[69]

A peasant-march of 8 September 2003, from the community of Batalla to El Alto, was the first mobilisation of the Gas-War and had as its principal aim the release of Edwin Huampu (see Table 6.2).[70] Coinciding with the Aymara peasant-convergence on El Alto was a civic strike in the city organised by FEJUVE-El Alto and COR-El Alto against new municipal legislation, *maya y paya*, that would have increased taxes on building and home-construction.[71] Two days later, on September 10, with no government-response to their demands forthcoming, CSUTCB and FUDTCLP-TK militants, with the help of *jilaqatas* and *mama t'allas* (traditional authorities) from the Aymara peasant-communities of the rural provinces of La Paz, initiated a hunger-strike in the auditorium of the Aymara-language radio-station in El Alto, Radio San Gabriel. The most pressing objective continued to be Huampu's release, but the strikers also opposed a number of neoliberal agricultural policies, the FTAA, and the export of natural gas through Chile.[72] The hunger-strike quickly garnered the support and solidarity of several other urban and rural popular organisations, including the COB, and plans to erect road-blocks in the *altiplano* were finalised. *Cocaleros* of the Yungas and the Chapare regions expressed their solidarity with peasant-actions developing in the *altiplano*.[73]

In a grim foreshadowing of the repression that was to follow shortly, President Sánchez de Lozada and Minister of Defence, Carlos Sánchez Berzaín, proclaimed that order would be restored and maintained in the country and that the armed forces were prepared to act.[74] Two days later, the National

---

69. FSTCLP–TK is affiliated to, but often acts autonomously from, the CSUTCB.

70. Huampu, a leader of Los Andes province in the department of La Paz, had been incarcerated in a La Paz prison for murdering two people. In fact, Huampu had simply carried out the sentence arrived at by the community of Cota Cota, in the province of Los Andes, to deal with two individuals who they had determined were cattle-hustlers. The death-sentence was an unusually harsh measure relative to normal practices of community-justice in the region, but the Aymara protesters asserted their right to administer communitarian justice in line with their *usos y costumbres* and rejected the criminal persecution by the state of one indigenous community member for executing what was effectively a collective decision (Patzi 2005, p. 251; Gómez 2004, pp. 20–1).

71. Hylton and Thomson 2007, p. 111; *La Prensa* 2003f; *La Razón* 2003a.

72. *La Prensa* 2003c.

73. *La Prensa* 2003d; *El Diario* 2003a, *La Prensa* 2003b, *La Razón* 2003i.

74. *La Patria* 2003b; *La Prensa* 2003l; *Los Tiempos* 2003c.

Police and armed forced were deployed at various points in the *altiplano*.[75] By mid-September, peasants, teachers, the working-class organisations of El Alto, university-students, the COB and others were radicalising and announcing protest-actions to come. In the face of these conflicts, the government once again emphasised that it would maintain order and the rule of law through the use of the armed forces.[76]

6.4.2 *The collective frame of gas*

By this stage, it had become clear that the future of natural-gas development was the overarching frame tying each movement to the others.[77] The so-called Estado Mayor del Pueblo (Peoples' High Command, EMP), played a role in articulating a more lucid position on this matter, from which the various social movements could draw.[78] The Coordinadora and the MAS were instrumental in calling for a national day of protest in defence of gas to be held on Friday, 19 September. COR-El Alto and FEJUVE-El Alto immediately responded to the call and announced that they would lead mass-marches on La Paz from El Alto on the national day of action.[79] The Aymara peasantry of the *altiplano* and the *cocaleros* of the Yungas also pledged that there would be co-ordinated marches in solidarity with the call for mobilisations in defence of gas.[80] The COB likewise promised to lead a march later on the same day

---

75. *La Prensa* 2003h.

76. *Opinión* 2003a. Sánchez de Lozada also began to offer consultations with the public, ostensibly to determine the popular will with regard to natural-gas development and export, but because these offers were made in the more general context of increasing militarisation, criminalisation of social-movement activity, and military alerts and threats, they were not taken seriously by social movements, nor for that matter by most of the rest of the population.

77. *La Patria* 2003a. One indication that the different social sectors were participating for reasons greater than their particular interests became evident when, late in September, both the *maya y paya* legislation was abrogated and Edwin Huampu released, but neither CSUTCB nor El Alto's social-movement organisations slowed their mobilising momentum.

78. The EMP had been an on-again off-again rocky alliance since its inception in early 2003 that encompassed the *cocaleros* of the Chapare and the Movimiento al Socialismo (Movement Towards Socialism, MAS), both led by Evo Morales, the COB, led by Jaime Solares, and the newly-formed Coordinadora de Defensa del Gas (Coordinator in Defence of Gas), led by Oscar Olivera, and other groups.

79. *El Deber* 2003a.

80. *La Razón* 2003d, m.

in La Paz.[81] Again, the government responded by reciting its mandate to maintain order and the rule of law. Operatives of the Grupo Especial de Seguridad (Special Security-Group, GES) and reinforcements of police-troops were deployed to Cochabamba.[82]

Roberto de La Cruz directed sharp words at the President: 'gas will be the mother of all battles, if the gringo government insists on selling off our hydrocarbons at the price of a dead chicken'.[83] Morales likewise told the press that, 'If Goni decides to give gas away to Chile this government will not last 24 hours. We are going to strike and blockade until we recover the gas'.[84] Here, we can begin to appreciate the call to nationalise gas as the fundamental collective-action frame during the insurrectional episodes of September and October. As Álvaro García Linera puts it, 'There is a sort of collective intuition that the debates over hydrocarbons [natural-gas and oil] are gambling with the destiny of this country, a country accustomed to having a lot of natural resources but always being poor, always seeing natural resources serve to enrich others'.[85] The 'injustice' of the frame is clearly delineated: being poor in a resource-rich land. The 'us' included the indigenous-popular classes struggling for a socially just development-model. The structural significance of natural gas to the political economy of Bolivia made the strategic frame materially plausible and accounted for its wide resonance throughout the country.[86] The 'them' identified included the transnational gas-corporations that formed part of the energy-consortium Pacific LNG (Repsol-YPF, British Gas, and Pan-American Engery), the neoliberal model personified in the presidency of Sánchez de Lozada, and American imperialism writ large. Finally, the pathways of change advocated by the frame to overcome the injustice it evoked eventually involved the ousting of the neoliberal president and the nationalisation of gas. 'All of a sudden', one of Bolivia's finest journalists observed, 'gas is on the lips of everyone. The unions, popular meetings, congresses, communities, blockades and spontaneous reunions like those in [Plaza] San Francisco' have developed their opposition to the sale of gas under the neoliberal

---

81. *Opinión* 2003d, *La Razón* 2003f.
82. *Los Tiempos* 2003b.
83. *Opinión* 2003d.
84. *Vóz* 2003.
85. García Linera 2005a.
86. Spronk and Webber 2007, pp. 33–8.

framework as a unifying cause.[87] In the event, the day of national protest in defence of gas was a major success (see Table 6.2).

6.4.3 State-massacre in Warisata and the radicalisation of left-indigenous struggle

The protests of 19 September demonstrated that, while the Aymara peasantry had started the cycle of insurrection known as the Gas-War of 2003, by late September El Alto had become the new fulcrum of popular mobilisation in the country.[88] FEJUVE-El Alto and COR-El Alto co-ordinated road-blocks of the principal routes connecting La Paz to El Alto. Schools were shut down, the streets of the city were completely barricaded, and stores and street-vendors ceased operations. Thousands of *alteño* marchers snaked their way down the La Paz hillsides to join the large concentrations of people in the Plaza San Francisco. The columns of protesters from El Alto were met in La Paz by teachers, factory-workers, peasants, truckers, street-vendors, health-care workers, and pensioners.[89] The COB let it be known that it would be holding an emergency National Assembly on 1 October in Huanuni, in the department of Oruro, where strategic discussion over a possible general strike and co-ordinated nation-wide campaign of road-blocks would occur.[90] The basis of an insurrectionary alliance led by the largely informal working classes of El Alto, and supported by the peasantry, the formal working class, and sections of the middle class, was beginning to emerge. New levels of state-coercion soon acted as the spark that consolidated these forces.

The first shock of state-repression since the *impuestazo* of February 2003 radicalised social movements. On 20 September, military troops invaded Warisata and began killing indigenous community-members (see Table 6.2).[91] Rather than suppress the movements of September, this moment of state-repression extended, deepened and radicalised left-indigenous struggle both within the rural Aymara zone where the killing took place, and, crucially, in El Alto over the next couple of weeks. By mid-October, protests, road-blockades, hunger-strikes, and militant-clashes with the military and police-forces rocked huge

---

87. Espinoza 2003a.
88. Espinoza 2003a.
89. *El Diario* 2003c, *La Prensa* 2003k, *La Razón* 2003g.
90. *La Razón* 2003h.
91. García Linera 2004b, p. 62.

swathes of the country and precipitated the resignation of Gonzalo Sánchez de Lozada. In the context of September and October 2003, the deaths caused by state-repression, 'evoked a feeling of unity, of solidarity, of identification with those abused by power'.[92]

The Comisión de Derechos Humanos de la Cámara de Diputados (Human-Rights Commission of the Chamber of Deputies, CDHCD), the Asamblea Permanente de Derechos Humanos de Bolivia (Permanent Assembly of Human Rights of Bolivia, APDHB), and the opposition-parties within Congress criticised the government for causing the violence against the activists on the road-blockades and for not privileging dialogue with the peasant-leadership. Evo Morales directly accused the Minister of Defence, Sánchez Berzaín, of being one of those principally responsible for the indiscriminate use of force.[93] In response, the government simply ratcheted up its rhetoric in defence of law and order. Sánchez de Lozada told the nation that his government would not accede to social pressures, and would proceed to take down immediately any blockade of highways, in any part of the country, erected under any pretext.[94]

Felipe Quispe of CSUTCB, still on hunger-strike in El Alto, offered an immediate and scathing condemnation of the military incursion in Warisata. He said that negotiations between CSUTCB and the Minister of Agriculture, Guido Áñez, and the Vice-Minister of Government, José Luis Harb, had been proceeding but now had to be abandoned because of the peasant-massacre.[95] 'The government extends one hand to us and with the other kills our brothers', said Quispe.[96] Almost immediately, the CSUTCB alerted Bolivians that the peasant-organisation was in a state of emergency, and blockades were erected in a series of provinces in the department of La Paz: Río Abajo, Ingavi, Muñecas, Inquisivi and Pacajes.[97] Rural Aymara-language radio-stations served the same purpose as the radical miners' stations had in an earlier era of Bolivian history. Four times daily, the Aymara-community radio-stations transmitted the resolutions of the different meetings occurring in different communities and the strategic and tactical positions being promoted by the

92. Suárez 2003b, p. 17.
93. Los Tiempos 2003e.
94. La Prensa 2003g.
95. Los Tiempos 2003e.
96. Los Tiempos 2003d.
97. García Linera 2004b, p. 62.

CSUTCB based on these rank-and-file community-assemblies. This was the principal means through which ordinary peasants learned of the twists and turns of the struggle as it developed in September.[98]

Recalling this period almost two years later, the October 2003 leaders of FEJUVE-El Alto and COR-El Alto remembered the Warisata massacre as a turning point in the radicalisation of the first Gas-War. Mauricio Cori, executive secretary of FEJUVE-El Alto at the time, told me that repression in the *altiplano* and the deaths in Warisata in particular enraged the residents of El Alto. In his view, the alliances forged between Felipe Quispe and CSUTCB and the social organisations of El Alto, such as FEJUVE-El Alto, were crucial in articulating an immediate popular response that demonstrated the popular sentiment of the time.[99] The leadership of COR-El Alto felt the same way. Roberto de la Cruz described how the popular-movement demands in this period evolved from the nationalisation of gas to the resignation of Sánchez de Lozada because of the intensification of repressive tactics on the part of the state: 'If Goni hadn't left there would have been civil war, because the people were calling for civil war'.[100] Finally, the archival research I conducted in the offices of the COB and FSTMB shows that both of these union-federations quickly expressed their solidarity with the peasantry in the wake of the Warisata deaths and took measures to condemn publicly and to mobilise against the state's repressive tactics.[101] Only four days after the events in Warisata, for example, the COB convened an emergency National Assembly in Huanuni. At the assembly, the COB condemned the repression of indigenous peasants in the *altiplano* by the armed forces and police. The workers who had assembled in Huanuni agreed to support, 'the struggle that peasant comrades are sustaining, and other sectors of the workforce in the country, against a political system that has lost popular support'.[102] In short, state-repression had only fuelled the fire.

---

98. Espinoza 2003b.
99. Cori 2005.
100. de la Cruz 2005.
101. COB 2003a, COBc, COBe; FSTMB 2003c, FSTMBd.
102. COB 2003e.

6.4.4 The formal working class steps in

Immediately after the Warisata killings, President Sánchez de Lozada's approval-rating fell to 9 per cent.[103] From this point forward, the largely informal working classes of El Alto became the indubitable vanguard of left-indigenous struggle in the country, articulated most forcefully through FEJUVE-El Alto and COR-El Alto. While secondary to the informal proletarians of El Alto, the formal working class played an essential supporting role in the insurrectionary alliance. It is important not to minimise, as many scholarly and journalistic accounts have, the strategic importance of the actions of the miners, organised in the FSTMB, and the only nation-wide confederation of workers, the COB.

Early in the conflict, on 12 September, the COB had already released a 'Programme of Struggle', from which the wider movement of the indigenous peasantry and informal working classes was able to draw.[104] The programme called for the abrogation of the existing Hydrocarbons-Law and the nationalisation and industrialisation of natural gas for the benefit of the Bolivian popular classes. It stressed how recovering natural gas from the transnationals had become a historical imperative in the current Bolivian conjuncture, and a central facet of restoring sovereignty and dignity for Bolivians. The document also demanded that Bolivia not participate in the proposed Free-Trade Area of the Americas. On the domestic front, it called for the restoration of job-stability and employment-creation and the end of labour-flexibilisation policies. It demanded increases in public spending on health and education, the strengthening of public universities, and the cessation of the privatisation of higher education. The workers' organisation defended UPEA's right to autonomy, a key demand of the university's student-federation. The programme also demanded that the state reinsert itself in the productive processes of the economy and in the mining sector in particular. The COB pledged to defend the existing social-security system and demanded further improvements in this area, along with better pensions.[105]

The COB's programme also defended the collective rights to land and territory of landless peasants and indigenous communities throughout Bolivia.

---

103. *La Patria* 2003c.
104. COB 2003d.
105. COB 2003d.

It rejected the politics of coca-eradication and defended the right to grow and sell the coca-leaf and derivative products, a vital issue for indigenous peasantries in the Chapare and Yungas regions. The COB rejected the commodification and private management of water. Instead, the workers' central, following the lead of the social movements behind the Cochabamba Water-War, called for the nationalisation of and social control over water-resources throughout the country. It also demanded the nationalisation of the mines, and all the strategic state-owned enterprises that had been privatised in the 1990s: YPFB, ENFE, ENTEL, COMIBOL, LAB, and others. Furthermore, the COB demanded jobs for the unemployed and rejected any tax-increases that targeted the working classes. Finally, the Programme of Struggle denounced the criminalisation of protest and defended direct action and popular mobilisation as a basic democratic right.[106]

In terms of concrete action, the COB called for an indefinite general strike and a nation-wide campaign of road-blockades to begin on 29 September.[107] On 2 October 2003 the workers' confederation made its most important intervention in the September–October Gas-War. It convened an open assembly in the Plaza San Francisco with the largest turnout yet of any gathering during almost a month of growing rural and urban discontent.[108] The crowds at the assembly unified around the call for the nationalisation of gas, but also for the first time consolidated the demand for the resignation of Sánchez de Lozada.[109] Gas and the president's resignation were now the centripetal axes of revolt.

6.5 ¡El Alto de pie! El Alto on its feet! Democratic insurgency, state-repression, and élite-fractures

The beginning of the second week of October 2003 witnessed the efflorescence of grassroots-insurgency in El Alto, vicious state-repression, and the first major fissures inside the ruling bloc. This period of wide-scale revolt began with the civic strike in El Alto on 8 October, the third such strike since the beginning of September. Streets were closed down. Public institutions and private businesses were shut down. There was virtually no circulation of

---

106. COB 2003d.
107. COB 2003e.
108. Gómez 2004, p. 68.
109. Hylton and Thomson 2007, p. 113.

traffic. Fierce clashes between the national police and armed forces and activists shook the shantytown with tear-gas, gun-fire (from state-forces), dynamite, rocks and clubs. At the end of the day, two civilian protesters had suffered bullet-wounds, and many others had been injured by rubber-bullets. The *autopista* highway connecting La Paz to El Alto was blockaded and full of people preventing traffic-flow in either direction.[110] When 800 miners arrived from Huanuni, they announced that they would convulse the cities of El Alto and La Paz the following day.[111] Elsewhere in the country, old mobilisations were sustained and new ones sprung to life. A miner and another protester were killed the next day, 9 October. The government's response to the conflicts of that day treaded familiar ground. A visibly angry Sánchez de Lozada addressed a press-conference in La Paz. He stressed that the social mobilisations in the country were entirely lacking in legitimacy, and that, moreover, they were being led by 'a minority who wants to divide Bolivia', and to destroy democracy in the country.[112]

El Alto's protests continued.[113] The city's avenues were so tightly locked down with the blockades and barricades by the third day of the strike that scarcely a bicycle could traverse through them. Basic foodstuffs and natural gas were becoming scarce in La Paz after more than three weeks of social protests across the country.[114] That Sánchez de Lozada had to go was clear to all the insurgent-groups. FEJUVE-El Alto, COR-El Alto, the COB, the FSTMB, and the CSUTCB, pledged publicly to refuse sector-by-sector negotiations with the government.[115] Felipe Quispe pointed out that Sánchez de Lozada 'is not only an American gringo, but a butcher', while Jaime Solares of the COB argued: 'It no longer makes sense to talk with someone who is rejected by the people. The workers want him to leave government'.[116]

On 11 October, following an attempt by a caravan of military troops to break the human barricade around the Senkata petroleum-plant in El Alto, the armed forces shot indiscriminately into the crowds and surrounding neighbourhoods, gunning down men, women, children and the elderly in the

110. *La Razón* 2003l.
111. FSTMB 2003a; *La Prensa* 2003i.
112. *La Prensa* 2003e; *Opinión* 2003b, c.
113. Suárez 2003a, p. 41.
114. *El Deber* 2003b.
115. *El Diario* 2003b, *La Razón* 2003c.
116. *El Diario* 2003b.

process. Chants of 'Goni, Assassin!' erupted in response.[117] But the violence merely intensified over the next two days (see Table 6.2). By some accounts, there were 26 deaths on 12 October, including one soldier.[118]

Salvaging the existing government had become an impossible task for the ruling class. The role of state-repression in undermining the legitimacy of the government was once again underlined. A series of cracks in the governing coalition were pried open, the levels of self-organisation, self-activity, and mass-mobilisation of the *alteño* working classes developed further, and, within a short period, sections of the middle class were drawn to the side of the popular struggle. From the perspective of the left-indigenous popular movements, the government was beyond redemption. As one journalist reported, 'The number of deaths grows. All the fears of previous days are transformed into rage'.[119] The state-violence exacted in El Alto, 'had opened an abyss between government and society annulling any possibility of negotiation', according to García Linera. 'It was no longer important what Sánchez de Lozada offered, he was no longer a morally valid interlocutor...'.[120]

Explosive state-violence and popular resistance persisted throughout the next day, 13 October. Bread and meat were scarce in La Paz, and downtown in the capital vehicular traffic was almost non-existent. As 100,000 marchers from El Alto descended through the working-class hillside neighbourhoods of La Paz large numbers of residents applauded, while others joined the march.[121] Protesters came within three blocks of the Plaza Murillo once they had reached the core of La Paz. They sang the national anthem in an effort to persuade the rank and file of the armed forces to join the struggle

117. García Linera 2004b, p. 7; Mamani Ramírez 2005, pp. 61–3.

118. Mamani Ramírez 2005, p. 68; Suárez 2003a, p. 45. It is important to note that the circumstances leading to the death of the soldier, Cigmar García, are disputed. The official version of García's death is that he was kidnapped, beaten, and then assassinated by protesters. The version offered by witnesses from the El Alto neighbourhood in which he died, Villa Ingenio, is quite different. They claim that the soldier refused to shoot on the civilian protesters and was consequently executed by a military captain (Gómez 2004, p. 97). The plausibility of the latter account is heightened by the fact that flowers appeared at the site of the soldier's death as well as a letter recording the events surrounding his death as told by the neighbourhood-witnesses. Given the political and social context of El Alto during these days, the neighbourhood-residents would have been in no mood to honour the death of just any soldier.

119. Suárez 2003a, p. 47.

120. García Linera 2004b, p. 63.

121. Gómez 2004, pp. 101–6; *La Prensa* 2003m.

against the state.[122] Ultimately, the protesters were convinced by soldiers not to attempt to enter the Plaza Murillo because the armed forces were under orders to use lethal force if such a an attempt were made.[123] Wide-scale civil resistance endured in El Alto in the face of another wave of state-crackdown. Juan Melendres, of COR-El Alto, and Mauricio Cori, of FEJUVE-El Alto, promised that *alteños* would continue their struggle until the régime of Sánchez de Lozada was ousted from power.[124]

The first visible signs of élite-rupture surfaced. Vice-President Carlos Mesa appeared on television saying that his conscience would not allow him to support the government as it implemented a policy of repression and death. Mesa did not resign from his position as vice-president, however. Jorge Torres, Minister of Economic Development, did resign, and the widely-respected ex-ombudsperson, Ana María Romero, strongly criticised the government for the violence it was perpetrating against civilians and demanded that the president leave office. José Luis Paredes – the mayor of El Alto and a prominent member of the Movimiento Izquierda Revolucionario (Revolutionary Left Movement, MIR), which was an integral part of Sánchez de Lozada's governing coalition – added his voice to those calling for the President's resignation.[125] In a derisive response to these splits in his government and the widening disgust with his policies within élite- and middle-class circles of public opinion, Sánchez de Lozada appeared on television on the evening of 13 October and denounced the protesters as seditious enemies of democracy. He vowed, in turn, to continue to protect democracy.[126] The US-embassy was the last pillar in Sánchez de Lozada's shrinking pool of allies. Richard Boucher, spokesperson for the State Department, stated, 'The international community and the United States will not tolerate any kind of interruption in the constitutional

---

122. *La Prensa* 2003m.
123. Gómez 2004, p. 111.
124. *La Prensa* 2003a.
125. Gómez 2004, p. 120. On 14 October, the fissures in the ruling class deepened. Juan del Granado, the Mayor of La Paz, began calling for the President's resignation, as did the millionaire businessperson and leading member of the MIR, Samuel Doria Medina. A number of members of the Nueva Fuerza Republicana (New Republican Force, NFR) also joined the opposition against Sánchez de Lozada. Finally, dozens of artists and intellectuals from La Paz united behind María Romero and demanded an end to the reign of Sánchez de Lozada.
126. Gómez 2004, p. 103; Suárez 2003a, p. 49.

order and will not recognise any régime that emerges as a result of anti-democratic procedures'.[127]

Meanwhile, the state had lost all control over El Alto. Beneath the waves of repression between 10 and 17 October, a collective sentiment of resistance radiated throughout the neighbourhoods of the city. Bonds of solidarity and coordination between adjacent neighbourhood-councils, districts, and zones of El Alto were created. Virtually every space in the city was occupied and controlled by neighbourhood-councils, in near-constant confrontation with the state.[128] A number of radio-stations and TV-channels assisted in mass-based co-ordination from below. These included the reporting and call-in programmes on Radio Televisión Popular (Popular Radio Television, RTP) and the radio-station Red Erbol and Radio San Gabriel.[129] As the strength of left-indigenous social forces grew and consolidated, the *alteño* working classes began to mirror a process Marx identified as 'revolutionary practice'.[130] In their struggle to satisfy their needs, the rank and file of the left-indigenous movements came increasingly to recognise their common interests and become conscious of their own social power; through their self-activity they came to see themselves as subjects capable of altering the structures of Bolivian society as well as changing themselves in the process through self-organisation and self-activity from below.

The events of the first two weeks of October events set the stage for the final mass-mobilisations that would topple Sánchez de Lozada's government on 17 October. The new strength of middle-class protest at this stage helped set the agenda of what would come after.

6.6 Middle-class moment: Goni's resignation

In stark contradistinction to the indigenous working-class and peasant-protagonists of the uprising in El Alto and the *altiplano*, the sections of the middle class that joined the opposition on 15 October were morally opposed to the repressive tactics of Sánchez de Lozada but desired nothing more than his resignation and a smooth constitutional succession of power to then

---

127. *La Razón* 2003b.
128. Mamani Ramírez 2005, p. 69.
129. Mamani Ramírez 2005, p. 71.
130. Lebowitz 2006, pp. 19–20; McNally 2006, p. 375.

Vice-President Carlos Mesa. This political line overlapped precisely with the position taken in preceding days and weeks by Evo Morales and the MAS. By 15 October, the time for negotiations had long since passed for those in opposition to the government. With 67 civilians dead and over 400 injured in September and October under his watch, Sánchez de Lozada had lost all moral legitimacy.[131] Influential middle-class figures, evoking the memory of mining women in the struggle for democracy against the dictatorship of Hugo Bánzer (1971–8), initiated a hunger-strike in La Paz in repudiation of state-violence.[132] The hunger-strike, organised in the Iglesia Las Carmelitas church, was led by Ana María Romero and brought together a range of well-known intellectuals, artists, religious figures, business-people, and human-rights activists.[133] The hunger-strikers organised their action under the framework of 'no more death' and called for peaceful actions by protesters, constitutional succession, and the restoration of the rule of law.[134]

Large demonstrations defined the next two days. A massive march on 16 October, led by FEJUVE-El Alto and COR-El Alto, descended once again from El Alto into La Paz, converging with the congregated masses in the Plaza San Francisco. Over 300,000 protesters gathered.[135] Evo Morales reiterated the position of the MAS in support of a constitutional exit. 'This is the moment to rescue Bolivia from the economic, political and social crises', he told the media. 'We are not going to negotiate as long as Gonzalo Sánchez de Lozada continues as President and we support the constitutional succession of Carlos Mesa'.[136] Mesa himself reappeared on television ratifying his decision to distance himself from the government without rescinding his position as vice-president of the country; thus his succession to the presidency in the event of Sánchez de Lozada's resignation was becoming a clearer possibility.[137] Mesa's

---

131. ASOFAC-DG 2007, p. 3.
132. *Opinión* 2003f.
133. Suárez 2003a, p. 53.
134. *Opinión* 2003f . A manifesto of various *paceño* (residents of La Paz) intellectuals released the same day asserted that, 'We cannot be indifferent before the deaths.... We express our solidarity with the city of El Alto and with the families of those who have been assassinated...' (Suárez 2003a, p. 51). The manifesto appealed to Sánchez de Lozada to step aside and for a transitional government to take his place in the interest of stemming all violence and deeper divisions within Bolivian society (Suárez 2003a, p. 53).
135. Hylton and Thomson 2007, p. 116.
136. *Opinión* 2003e.
137. *La Prensa* 2003j.

rhetoric appealed to the middle class. 'I am not with the philosophy that reasons of state justify death', he told the nation. 'But neither am I with the radical banners that the moment has arrived to destroy everything in order to construct a utopia that nobody wants or knows where it is going'.[138]

The position of the oppositional sectors of the middle class, the MAS, and Carlos Mesa gathered momentum and, with no clear political alternative to the left of this new coalition, Mesa, the MAS, and the oppositional middle class were able to establish sway over the popular movement.[139] Sánchez Berzaín appeared on television and, without irony, declared that there was no sense in being against the government because the protesters had lost the battle, 'they have no possibility of winning'.[140] Gonzalo Sánchez de Lozada appeared on CNN that evening and stated that he enjoyed the support of two thirds of Bolivians.[141] But, in the real world, the tide had turned decisively against the government.[142] The US-embassy and a fraction of the political élite were all that remained behind the President. García Linera argues that, from 16 October onward, there was no longer a government, in effect, and that therefore it was only a question of hours before Sánchez de Lozada resigned or the country erupted into civil war. The intervention of the middle classes had shifted the balance of social forces in favour of resignation and constitutional succession. The masses were united in their absolute resistance to the neoliberal state. They were able to paralyse that state, but had no alternative project with which to replace it. Thus the stage was cast for Mesa to take up the minimum-programme of the insurgent indigenous proletarians and

138. Rohter 2003.
139. With the benefit of hindsight, a number of activists I spoke to in 2005 saw October 2003 as a missed revolutionary opportunity. For them, what was missing was a revolutionary-socialist and indigenous-liberationist party to the left of the MAS. Such a party, with organic links to the left-indigenous popular-social movements, might have been able to bring together the disparate anticapitalist and indigenous-liberationist forces, to provide leadership, strategy, and ideological coherence. An articulated revolutionary project, and a revolutionary political organisation or party, on this view, might have had the wherewithal in 2003 to overthrow the existing capitalist state and rebuild a new sovereign power rooted in the self-governance and of the largely indigenous proletarian and indigenous majority. Addressing this important counterfactual question exceeds the scope of this book, but see Webber 2008a, 2008b, 2008c, and 2009a, Webber 2009b.
140. Suárez 2003a, p. 59
141. Sánchez de Lozada cited a poll published on the website of Radio Fides. It was revealed the next day by Radio Fides that their website had been hacked and that the results of the poll were precisely the inverse: 75 per cent of Bolivians were in favour of the president stepping down (Suárez 2003a, pp. 59–61).
142. Gómez 2004, p. 134.

peasants – resignation of Sánchez de Lozada, a constituent assembly, and a new hydrocarbons-law – without challenging the fundamental precepts of the neoliberal order.[143]

Roughly 400,000 protesters filled the streets of downtown La Paz on 17 October. The President left his residence in the afternoon and arrived at Military College in La Paz. From there he took a helicopter-flight to Santa Cruz and composed a letter of resignation which was faxed to Congress later that evening. From Viru Viru airport in Santa Cruz, Sánchez de Lozada fled to Miami, accompanied by his wife, Ximena Iturralde, six family-members – including his daughter, congressional deputy-member Alejandra Sánchez de Lozada –, Minister of Defence, Carlos Sánchez Berzaín, and Health-Minister, Javier Torres Goitia.[144] Carlos Mesa became president at 10:30pm according to constitutional procedures in the event of a president's resignation. All the political parties with representation in Congress supported the constitutional succession.[145]

Conclusion

This chapter has sought to provide a detailed portrait of the working classes of El Alto and how they were able to overcome structural barriers standing in the way of collective action through the use of the city's dense infrastructure of class-struggle and combined cultural traditions of revolutionary Marxism and indigenous liberation. Sectors of the formal working class were able to play a supporting role in the insurrections because of the orientation toward social-movement unionism adopted by the COB and the FSTMB. Similarly, the CSUTCB and the FUDTCLP-TK provided the radicalised Aymara peasantry with a rural infrastructure of class-struggle through which to kick off the September–October Gas-War with marches and hunger-strikes, and to support the insurrectionary process throughout the duration of the period with road-blockades and mass peasant-assemblies in the western *altiplano*. Congealing the alliance between the peasantry, the informal working classes,

---

143. García Linera 2004b, pp. 33–66.
144. *La Razón* 2003e . Also fleeing the country for fear of facing trial for their roles in the 67 deaths and 400 injured were Minister of Government, Yerko Kukoc (to Mexico), and Minister of the Presidency, José Guillermo Justiniano and Vice-Minister of Government, José Luis Harb (both to Argentina).
145. *La Razón* 2003j.

the formal working class, and, eventually, fractions of the middle class, was a collective-action frame around the call to nationalise natural gas, and the extensive but insufficient use of state-repression against civilians on the part of the government of Sánchez de Lozada. Ultimately, the dense infrastructure of class-struggle and social-movement unionism, oppositional traditions of indigenous and working-class radicalism, alliances between the peasants, workers, and the middle class, the collective gas-frame, and state-repression, came together to force the resignation of Sánchez de Lozada on 17 October 2003.

Carlos Mesa then assumed office. Son of two of Bolivia's most highly-regarded mainstream-historians, Mesa was a film-critic in the late 1970s and early 1980s, publishing *La aventura del cine boliviano* in 1985. Later, he became a radio-journalist, before turning to TV-journalism where he became well-known and well-respected in middle-class circles. Mesa also established credentials as a historian by co-writing with his parents a thick general history of Bolivia. Throughout the 1990s, his fame grew as a TV-journalist and political analyst on the programme, *De Cerca*, or *Up Close*.[146] Mesa had never been a member of the MNR, even after agreeing to run as Sánchez de Lozada's vice-presidential running mate in the 2000 elections. He utilised this stature as an independent intellectual without party-affiliation to distance himself from a régime in which he had in fact played a key role as vice-president.

Upon assuming the presidency, he pledged to piece together independent forces into the government and to restore the credibility of the political class in the eyes of the Bolivian population. In response to the popular October Agenda, for which left-indigenous forces had struggled, he promised a referendum on natural gas, a constituent assembly, and modification of the Hydrocarbons-Law. While the Constitution established that his mandate ought to last until 6 August 2007, Mesa argued that Congress could convene elections as soon as it deemed it reasonable to do so. Mesa requested a grace-period in which social movements would withdraw from mass-actions and let him study their demands and proceed with governing the country peacefully.[147] In the midst of the jubilation surrounding the fall of Sánchez de Lozada, Mesa was initially well received by the key-sectors that had mobilised in September and October. That would soon change.

---

146. *La Razón* 2003k.
147. *La Razón* 2003j.

Chapter Seven

Carlos Mesa and a Divided Country: Left-Indigenous and Eastern-Bourgeois Blocs in the Second Gas-War of May and June 2005

> I rebel so that my daughter will no longer be your domestic servant

> Felipe Quispe[1]

Between late May and early June 2005, mass-mobilisations re-enacted October 2003, bringing down the presidency of Carlos Mesa on 6 June 2005, and then preventing his replacement by two representatives of the far Right – Hormando Vaca Díez (MIR) and Mario Cossío (MNR).[2] The second Gas-War erupted out of a context of deep political polarisation in the country, with distinct racial, regional, and class-dimensions. These various politicised and interrelated antagonisms expressed themselves politically in the formation and consolidation of *left-indigenous* and *eastern-bourgeois* blocs that contended for power. The balancing act Mesa attempted between the two blocs ultimately proved untenable.

As in the past, when left-indigenous social forces mobilised, right-wing élites reacted out of class-fear

---

1. Quispe said this after being captured in 1992. Quoted in Cingolani 2005.
2. Vaca Díez and Cossío had been constitutionally entitled to assume the presidency in the event of Mesa's resignation as they were head of the Senate and Chamber of Deputies, respectively. In the event, the President of the Supreme Court, Rodríguez Veltzé, became the interim president, and general elections, originally scheduled originally for August 2007, were brought forward to December 2005.

and racial hatred. However, unlike in the past, Mesa as head of state refused to employ lethal state-coercion. The dynamics of state-repression were thus distinct in May–June 2005 when compared to the rebellious episodes of the first Gas-War. In the case of Gonzalo Sánchez de Lozada, fierce state-repression in September and October 2003 was nonetheless insufficient to crush the mass left-indigenous mobilisations, and thus helped rather to intensify and strengthen them as new social solidarities were created among the repressed population. Carlos Mesa, adapting to the post-Sánchez de Lozada setting, made opposition to state-repression a central facet of the legitimacy of his government from the outset, and was therefore highly constricted in his ability to employ the coercive apparatuses of the state when left-indigenous insurrection erupted. Because Mesa refrained from employing sufficient state-repression to quell rebellion, while at the same time refusing to concede to the demands of the social movements, the rising tide of revolt in late May and early June could not be restrained.

The indigenous informal working classes of El Alto, organised through FEJUVE-El Alto and COR-El Alto, were again the principal actors in the May – June Gas-War of 2005. Sectors of the formal working class played a dynamic supporting role, as they had in the first Gas-War. Again, the largely Aymara peasantry of the *altiplano* were important allies of the formal and informal sectors of the working class.[3] All of these sectors together constituted the most essential and radical actors of the 2005 Gas-War. They fought for the full nationalisation of hydrocarbons and a revolutionary constituent assembly.[4]

---

3. The CSUTCB continued to play a role in organising this group in May and June, although the peasant-federation was now divided into a majority-faction loyal to Quispe, and a minority-faction loyal to Roman Loayza. Loayza, in turn, was loyal to the MAS party, under the leadership of Evo Morales. Just as important, the Federación Única Departamental de Campesinos Trabajadores de La Paz, Tupaj Katari (Departmental Federation of Peasant-Workers of La Paz – Túpaj Katari, FUDCTLP–TK), led by Gualberto Choque, overtook to a certain degree the leadership role played by the national command of CSUTCB (Quispe), in terms of organising and mobilising the radical Aymara peasantry within the department of La Paz. The FUDCTLP–TK was a part of the CSUTCB (Quispe), but played a vitally independent organising and mobilising part in the May–June Gas-War; Choque emerged as one of the most dynamic and visible leaders of the peasantry, with a powerful and articulated revolutionary vision. In Cochabamba, the Coordinator of Gas, led by Óscar Olivera, continued as an umbrella-organisation in Cochabamba, but the heart of the mobilisations, protests, and strikes was firmly embedded in El Alto and La Paz.

4. Many leaders and rank-and-file activists in this array of social-movement and union-organisations sought revolutionary change of the structures of society, econ-

The role of the middle class in 2005 was different from in the 2003 Gas-War, however. Whereas, in October 2003, sections of the middle class had led a hunger-strike to protest against the brutal state-repression of Sánchez de Lozada, in 2005 they defended Mesa's régime against radical left-indigenous movements. Another key distinguishing feature of the second Gas-War was the intensified regionalisation of political struggle. Sensing the impossibility of re-conquering the state at the national level, the most powerful fractions of the Bolivian capitalist class began to entrench themselves politically in the eastern-lowland departments, a defensive measure to protect their interests as best they could against the ascending left-indigenous movements. This defensive move expressed itself in the eastern-bourgeois bloc.

Carried over and deepened in the events of May and June 2005 from the insurrections of 2003 was the strengthening collective consciousness of indigenous liberation and popular class-struggle from below within the radicalising proletarian and peasant-masses. One of the specific contributions of this chapter to the book is its attempt to convey a better sense of day-to-day dynamics in the development of this consciousness among activists in the midst of struggle. My presence during many of the marches, assemblies, and meetings throughout this period in La Paz and El Alto provided me with a unique window into these processes.

7.1 Carlos Mesa and a divided country: left-indigenous and eastern-bourgeois blocs

For the duration of Carlos Mesa's government (17 October 2003–6 June 2005), Bolivia was characterised by a deepening political polarisation along the axes of class, race and region. As illustrated in Table 7.1, two social blocs emerged. On the one hand, a left-indigenous bloc, rooted primarily in the most heavily indigenous departments of La Paz, Cochabamba, Oruro, Potosí, and Chuquisaca, was solidified on the basis of a similar alliance of popular classes and indigenous organisations as in the first Gas-War in 2003.

---

omy, and polity. They frequently invoked the constituent assembly as a body that would *replace* the existing legislative, executive, military, and judicial apparatuses. On this view, the assembly would be a process through which Bolivia would be fundamentally *refounded* by, and in the interests of, the poor indigenous urban and rural majority.

This bloc's demands were known as the October Agenda, because they were essentially carried over from the unfulfilled promise of the October 2003 Gas-War. Naming it the October Agenda, moreover, commemorated the martyrs and wounded of the earlier insurrection. The details of the October Agenda are outlined in Table 7.1. The principal collective-action frame of May and June 2005 was again the nationalisation of gas; however, the call to convene a constituent assembly was also central to the second Gas-War, and more important than it had been in the first. The principal social organisations of the left-indigenous forces, as depicted in Table 7.1, were FEJUVE-El Alto, COR-El Alto, the COB, FSTMB, rural and urban teachers, FUDTCLP-TK, Confederación Sindical Única de Trabajadores Campesinos de Bolivia (Quispe) (Bolivian Peasant Trade-Union Confederation, CSUTCB (Quispe)), and the Coordinator of Gas.

The other constellation of social forces to consolidate itself between October 2003 and June 2005 was an eastern-bourgeois bloc, led by the regional bourgeoisies of the hydrocarbons-rich departments of Tarija and Santa Cruz, as well as their allies in Beni and Pando (see Table 7.1). Collectively, these departments are known as the *media luna*.[5] Although led by bourgeois forces, and embracing a political project that protected the interests of dominant regional capitalists, the eastern-bourgeois bloc nonetheless enjoyed considerable support from the popular rural and urban classes of these departments. While the hegemony of neoliberal ideas had been crushed – at least temporarily – in the departments where the left-indigenous bloc was strongest, they continued to resonate in those of the *media luna*.[6]

The capitalist class of the eastern lowlands had enjoyed direct access to the highest reaches of the state between 1985 and 2003. They held important ministerial positions and dominated the traditional neoliberal parties – the MNR,

---

5. A reminder on the geography of the country may be useful at this stage. Bolivia is divided into nine departments, or states. In local parlance, they have been separated traditionally into those of the *altiplano*, or high plateau (La Paz, Oruro and Potosí), the valleys (Cochabamba, Chuquisaca and Tarija), and the eastern lowlands (Pando, Beni and Santa Cruz). In the contemporary period the term *media luna* (half moon) has gained political currency as a way of describing Pando, Beni, Santa Cruz and Tarija. The *media luna* departments are also frequently called the 'eastern lowlands' today despite Tarija's traditional positioning in the 'valley'-departments, and Pando's location in the northwest of the country.

6. This is not to say that neoliberal hegemony, even in Santa Cruz, Tarija, Beni, and Pando, was without contradiction or free from opposition.

Table 7.1   Political polarisation in 2005

Eastern-bourgeois bloc	Left-indigenous bloc	Oscillating actors
Social forces	*Social forces*	*Social forces*
CPSC	FEJUVE-El Alto	Carlos Mesa
Civic Committees – Tarija, Pando, Beni	COR-El Alto	MAS
	COB	Middle Class
FEPB-SC	FSTMB	CSUTCB (Loayza)
CAO	Rural and urban teachers	Cocaleros
Cattle-Ranchers' Federation	FSTCLP-TK	
Hydrocarbons-Chamber	CSUTCB (Quispe)	
CAINCO	Coordinator of Gas (Olivera)	
Finance, agro-industrial, petroleum-capital	Overwhelmingly indigenous working classes and peasantry	
January Agenda	*October Agenda*	*Mixed Agenda*
Departmental autonomy	Nationalisation of natural gas	*Carlos Mesa*
Regional control over natural resources	Revolutionary Constituent Assembly	Initial rhetorical support for October Agenda shifts to right-wing discourse against left-indigenous bloc by March 2007
Departmental control over most tax-revenue	Resignation of Carlos Mesa	
Departmental authority over all policies excluding defence, currency, tariffs, and foreign relations	Indigenous liberation from internally colonial race-relations	Continuous practical support for perpetuation of neoliberal development model
'Free-market' capitalism	Nationalisation and social/ workers' control over natural resources and strategic industries	*Middle Class*
Openness to foreign direct investment		Follow Mesa as he shifts right
Racism toward indigenous majority	Radical redistribution of wealth and land	*MAS*
State-repression against left-indigenous protesters		Support for Mesa government until March 2005
		Subsequent support for modest reformism
		Increase to 50 per cent royalties in hydrocarbons-tax régime (against nationalisation)
		Support for non-revolutionary constituent assembly

MIR, and ADN – that governed through a series of pacted coalitions over this period. The October 2003 insurrection, even if it did not fulfill the revolutionary objectives of many in the left-indigenous camp, did defeat Gonzalo Sánchez de Lozada and cut out in this way the direct and unmediated access to the state-apparatus enjoyed by bourgeois forces in the east. The fortunes of the three key neoliberal parties tumbled still further in the December 2004 municipal elections in which their performances were abysmal.

The eastern-bourgeois bloc thus sought strategically to entrench itself in the regions where it was able, knowing that establishing hegemony at the national level was not plausible in the short to medium term, given the balance of social forces in society at that juncture. This quintessentially defensive strategy expressed itself in the January Agenda of 2005, which was meant to counter the left-indigenous October Agenda of 2003. The January Agenda – so designated in the aftermath of a large mobilisation of over 300,000 supporters in the city of Santa Cruz in January 2005 – was based on an ideological commitment to 'free-market' capitalism, openness to foreign direct investment, and bitter racism toward the indigenous majority of the country (see Table 7.1). It was articulated more precisely through the demand for departmental autonomy for the four departments of the *media luna* within the Bolivian state. Autonomy, in this context, meant, '(1) regional control over natural resources (e.g., land, timber, gas, and oil), (2) the right to retain control over two-thirds of all tax revenues generated in the department, and (3) authority to set all policies other than defense, currency, tariffs, and foreign relations'.[7]

The various fractions of the *cruceño* capitalist class – finance, agro-industry, and petroleum – were able to close ranks under the banner of autonomy and forge the foundations of the eastern-bourgeois bloc. The Cámara Agropecuaria del Oriente (Eastern Agricultural Chamber, CAO), the Federación de Ganaderos (Cattle-Ranchers' Federation), the Cámara de Hidrocarburos (Hydrocarbons-Chamber), and the Cámara de Industria y Comercio (Chamber of Industry and Commerce, CAINCO), proved capable of working together effectively through their shared peak-organisation, the Federación de Empresarios Privados de Bolivia – Santa Cruz (Federation of Private Entrepreneurs of Bolivia – Santa Cruz, FEPB-SC). In 2004, the FEPB-SC broke ranks with the Bolivia-wide business-association, the ConFederación de Empresarios Priva-

---

7. Eaton 2007, p. 74.

dos de Bolivia (Confederation of Private Entrepreneurs of Bolivia, CEPB) to devote itself to the autonomist movement. This leant a certain popular credibility to its claims that the FEPB-SC represents the territorial interests of Santa Cruz, and in related ways to the whole *media luna*, rather than the core-interests of a small group of capitalists nation-wide. The autonomist movement as a whole has, in this way, effectively incorporated, and/or co-opted, various sections of non-élite civil-society organisations, trade-unions, and indigenous movements.[8] Together, the fractions of the capitalist class represented in the FEPB-SC financed and controlled the primary political tool in the autonomist struggle, the Pro Santa Cruz Committee (CPSC).

Carlos Mesa owed his presidency to the mass left-indigenous mobilisations of September and October 2003, and he took up variations on the key slogans of those mobilisations as his own.[9] He promised, for example, to reform the hydrocarbons-industry and to introduce a constituent assembly. But while Mesa was indebted to the popular forces that facilitated his ascent, he was clearly not *of* the left-indigenous social bloc.[10] Details of the President's mixed agenda are highlighted in Table 7.1. At the same time, Mesa was not enmeshed in the eastern-bourgeois bloc in the way that Sánchez de Lozada had been. Mesa was not a member of a political party, and thus stood outside the MNR, MIR, ADN triad to a certain degree.

Mesa attempted to mediate between two polarised social blocs.[11] He initially forged tenuous but important ties with popular left-indigenous movements by promising reform and adopting rhetoric of change. As president, he offered cosmetic changes at the fringes of the neoliberal-economic model, while fundamentally wedding his government to the perpetuation of the basic structure of the political, economic and social system introduced to the country in 1985.[12] Mesa defended the principal interests of the dominant economic classes, transnational capital operating in Bolivia, and the key international financial institutions, particularly the IMF. Yet, in rhetoric and practice, he was forced to take a softer approach to his advocacy of neoliberalism than had

---

8. Eaton 2007, pp. 86–9.
9. Chávez 2005b.
10. Remember that he had been Sánchez de Lozada's vice-president, and a high-profile public advocate of deep neoliberal restructuring in the late 1990s and early 2000s in his role as TV-journalist and political commentator.
11. Tapia 2005.
12. Cáceres 2005a; Hylton and Thomson 2007, p. 118; Lora 2005b.

Sánchez de Lozada.[13] The particular historical circumstances that allowed him to become president in the first place, and the latent mobilisation-capacity of the left-indigenous bloc, always just beneath the surface, could not have allowed him to do otherwise.

Mesa choreographed a sophisticated dance between the two social blocs until the beginning of 2005.[14] In the ensuing months, however, growing discontent with Mesa's insufficient concessions to the October Agenda, reignited popular mobilisations of left-indigenous movements. These, in turn, fostered counter-mobilisation by the autonomist movement of the *media luna*.[15] The back-and-forth spiral provided oxygen to the hardest currents of each side. By March 2005, Mesa, underestimating the strength of the left-indigenous bloc, opted for an open realignment with the eastern-bourgeois bloc, throwing the country into a pivotal face-off situation that eventually played itself out in Bolivia's Second Gas-War of May–June 2005.

As indicated in Table 7.1, it is also essential to understand that there were two other groups that effectively dangled between the two blocs in the country – sections of the urban middle classes, especially outside the departments of the *media luna*, and, the MAS party, under the leadership of Evo Morales. Their distinct actions at different intervals helped to reinforce one bloc or the other. Because Mesa was not a member of the MNR and because he had betrayed Sánchez de Lozada in the closing weeks of the October 2003 Gas-War, he did not have a predictable and loyal base of support in either the Chamber of Deputies or the Senate. The MAS, as the second largest party in Congress after the MNR, was consequently an important potential ally. From the perspective of the less radical elements within the MAS, tangible benefits would accrue to their own party as well through an alliance with Mesa. Hoping to deepen the reform in Mesa's soft neoliberal reformism, Evo Morales entered into an unofficial alliance with the executive power which lasted from October 2003 until March 2005, ensuring the political survival of the President. The alliance eventually fell apart during debate over the depth of reforms to be incorporated into the new hydrocarbons-law. In the wake of this breakdown, Mesa shifted markedly to the right, and the MAS – hesitatingly

---

13. Arze and Poveda 2004; Escobar de Pabón 2004; Espada 2004; Kruse 2004; Pérez Luna 2004; Rojas 2004; Villarroel and Huanca 2004.
14. Cáceres 2005a.
15. Chávez 2005d; Chávez and García Linera 2005; Lora 2005a.

and inconsistently – forged new alliances with the reignited, radical sectors of the left-indigenous bloc.[16]

The middle class – that second swing-group – played a different role from that in October 2003 (see Table 7.1). In the first Gas-War, the urban middle classes engaged in hunger-strikes in support of the left-indigenous overthrow of Sánchez de Lozada. They were responding in part to the brutal repression of civilians orchestrated by the régime. In March 2005, however, when Mesa shifted to the right, the middle classes went with him. Indeed, many went so far as to mobilise actively against the left-indigenous bloc from March until June 2005.

The country became increasingly polarised along race-, class- and regional lines throughout the Mesa presidency, but accelerating sharply in January 2005 with a Water-War against privatisation in El Alto and the emergence of the January Agenda of the autonomist movement in the *media-luna* departments of Santa Cruz, Tarija, Pando, and Beni.[17] The advancing social polarisation between January and March 2005 laid the basis for Mesa's ultimately unsuccessful attempt to align himself more closely with the eastern-bourgeois bloc, and Morales's efforts to build closer ties between his party and the more radical social movements of the left-indigenous bloc. Neither Mesa nor Morales were able to fully overcome the contradictions of their new allegiances by the end of March.

Thus, by early April 2005, the polarisation of left-indigenous and eastern-bourgeois blocs persisted, but in an altered form. Mesa's reunion with the eastern-lowland right-wing after his first 'resignation'-speech in March was short-lived.[18] He dangled once again between the blocs, but his position was dramatically more tenuous given the breakdown of his alliance with the MAS. The MAS had shifted to the left out of necessity, but it did not abandon its hopes for coming to office through elections in 2007, or earlier if elections were pushed forward. The party thus committed itself to extra-parliamentary activism to promote a modest change to the tax-régime on hydrocarbons

---

16. Chávez 2005c.

17. Spronk 2007a, Spronk 2007b; Spronk and Webber 2005, 2007.

18. Mesa threatened to resign in March 2005, but quickly retracted this threat when it seemed that a possible alliance with the eastern-bourgeois bloc could be constructed provided Mesa break all ties with the MAS. The MAS was thus expelled from the tacit government-coalition by Mesa in March, but the President's alliance with the far Right never took hold properly.

(as distinct from the call for full nationalisation coming form other social movements). There were, then, two hard blocs on the Left and Right, and between the two, a fluid, shifting middle ground. A lull in protests set in by the beginning of April 2005. The underlying contradictions, however, had not been resolved. They rose to the surface in mid-May with the approval of a new hydrocarbons-law that fell short of the MAS-proposal for 50 per cent royalties, and made a mockery of the more radical demand of nationalisation coming from the left-indigenous bloc. The result was the May–June 2005 Gas-War.

7.2 Nationalisation-frame, class-infrastructure, repertoirs of contention

7.2.1 The collective frame of gas-nationalisation

By early May, the shape of the second Gas-War was coming slowly into view. The social movements of the left-indigenous bloc had inventoried their resources and mobilising capacities and decided the time to act was upon them. The CSUTCB faction led by Felipe Quispe had made the nationalisation of gas an official priority in its convention of December 2003. FEJUVE-El Alto had approved the demand as a key objective at its General Congress of 2004, when a new executive committee was elected behind this mandate. The COB, the FUDTCLP-TK, the Coordinator of Gas, the FSTMB, and a myriad of other actors had also been on board since the October 2003 Gas-War made the nationalisation of hydrocarbons a popular priority.[19] The discovery of huge deposits of natural gas 'is by a long way the most important development in Bolivia's economic history in the last 80 years', as Álvaro García Linera points out.[20] The 'issue of the nationalisation of hydrocarbons', he rightly suggests, 'puts into play the possibility of a material and productive basis for an alternative economic model to neoliberalism'.[21] The significance of the historical moment, the burden of their responsibility to wrestle control of the country's natural resources away from private transnational companies and into the hands of workers and peasants, was not lost on the activists of the left-indigenous bloc. 'The demand of the city of El Alto is

---

19. García Linera 2005c, p. 57.
20. García Linera 2005c, p. 52.
21. García Linera 2005c, p. 55.

the recovery of our hydrocarbons', explained Rafael Mamani of FEJUVE-El Alto. 'In October 2003, we made an agenda and there were many dead and wounded.... Today...we are asking that the [Mesa] government respect that agenda'.[22] Indeed, the unparalleled importance of the battle to nationalise this industry is revealed in the fact that the issue was often intimately fused in the thoughts of activists with the question of revolutionary power and the fundamental transformation of Bolivian society:

> In 2003, the fundamental objective was to kick out Goni [Sánchez de Lozada], after 20 years of neoliberalism. He was the face of neoliberalism. It was he who imposed the privatization of hydrocarbons, and it was he who was the enemy. However, now, after all of this process that we have lived through, we have realized that it was not one man, it was the whole system. And now the masses are much more politicized.... [The events] of May and June are experiences that showed that the masses are more politicized, more ideological, more convinced that change is not replacing one man, but the system. Clearly and concretely, it is the dominant castes, the oligarchy, that are defending power. We have to overthrow them.... We believe that we have to have optimism, to arrive at the final objective of our struggles, which is the change of the political, economic and social system. This, undoubtedly, is going to mean major sacrifices, but with the security that this sacrifice is going to be for us, and for future generations.[23]

The above passage, from an interview with the FSTMB's executive secretary Miguel Zubieta on 23 June 2005, exemplifies the high stakes of the Gas-War as understood by social-movement leaders, and, just as importantly, their opponents.

Based on my participant-observation in many popular-movement assemblies and mobilisations in El Alto and La Paz, as well as interviews with leading activists during this period, it is clear to me that the unifying frame of the May–June insurrection was the nationalisation of hydrocarbons. A secondary, but nonetheless important theme, was the constituent assembly.[24]

---

22. Mamani 2005c.
23. Zubieta 2005b.
24. Iquiapaza 2005; Mamani 2005a; Martela 2005a; Solón 2005; Suárez 2005. It is important to repeat that underpinning these frames was a *consciousness of combined liberation* that sought fundamental transformation of class- and race-relations in the country. I examine this core set of issues in the following chapter.

7.2.2   *Infrastructure of class-struggle and the left-indigenous bloc*

Although there were occasionally discrepancies in the responses of interviewees as to the *weight* assigned to different social-movement sectors within
the left-indigenous bloc during May and June, there was surprising consis-
tency regarding *which* basic sectors constituted this bloc.[25] The same rural and
urban infrastructures of class-struggle that were instrumental to the strength
of rebellions in 2003 were at work again in 2005.

Analysis of these interviews, combined with an extensive qualitative study
of the major national newspapers over the relevant period of insurrection,
and my own observations in La Paz and El Alto, indicate a relatively trans-
parent panorama of the major players. At the forefront of the struggle were
FEJUVE-El Alto and COR-El Alto, as the principal community-infrastructures
of class-struggle available to the informal proletarians of the city. FEJUVE-El
Alto and COR-El Alto relied, in turn, on crucial alliances with the Aymara
peasantry of the *altiplano*, organised through CSUTCB (Quispe) and FUDT-
CLP-TK, and with sections of the formal working class organised at the
national level through the COB. Particularly important in terms of the formal
working class were the miners, channeled through the FSTMB, and the urban
and rural teachers. Health-care workers played a backing role in La Paz. The
Coordinator of Gas, led by Óscar Olivera, offered a Cochabamba flank to this
radical base of the May–June 2005 Gas-War.

Also mobilised in extra-parliamentary actions, but with a distinct agenda
rooted in modest reformism, was the MAS, under the leadership of Evo
Morales. Here, the major affiliated social sectors were the CSUTCB faction led
by Román Loayza, and the *cocaleros* of the Chapare and the Yungas.

7.2.3   *Repertoires of contention*

A principal method of struggle was the road-blockade, executed with stunning scope and intensity. At the height of the May–June insurrection, 90 per
cent of the highways in the country, spanning all nine departments, were
blocked. This ground to a halt the transit of almost all commodities, vehicles,

---

25. Chávez 2005a; Mamani 2005a; Mendoza Mamani 2005; Solares 2005b; Solón
2005; Zubieta 2005b.

and people along these routes.[26] The general strike in El Alto, accompanied by the territorial takeover of the city by activists operating within neighbourhood-councils and other elements of the community infrastructure of class-struggle, was another critical method. Close to 90 per cent of industrial activity in the city of El Alto was paralysed for weeks, beginning on May 23 when the general strike called by FEJUVE-El Alto and COR-El Alto began.[27] The combined effect of blockades, mobilisations and strikes on tourism was dramatic. Foreign embassies called on their citizens to vacate the country. Anecdotally, a representative of the Plaza Hotel in La Paz told one reporter that they were operating at 10 to 15 per cent capacity at best.[28] Third, there was a series of mass-mobilisations, marches, protests and clashes with the police and armed forces that surpassed in geographical range as well as absolute numbers of participants the ones of October 2003. A fourth and novel component was added to the repertoire of the left-indigenous bloc in May and June 2005 – the physical occupation by protesters of natural-gas fields, refineries, and petroleum- and natural-gas distribution-centres in various parts of the country.[29] This was yet another strand in a multi-pronged assault on the economy in an effort to assert social control over natural resources that had been commodified in the years of neoliberalism.

7.3 Narrative of the May–June Gas-War

7.3.1 Tension mounts in early May

At the beginning of May a congressional proposal for a new hydrocarbons-law, stipulating a new regulatory régime of 18 per cent royalties and 32 per cent taxes in the natural-gas and petroleum-sectors, was passed on to President Mesa for deliberation. It had taken Congress a year and a half after the October 2003 Gas-War to approve a new hydrocarbons-law, and a full nine months after it was first introduced for discussion in congressional sessions. Outside of the confines of parliamentary politics, social movements immediately expressed their discontent with the proposed law and began to organise

---

26. García Linera 2005c, pp. 58–9; García Linera 2005d; Ramírez and Stefanoni 2005b.
27. La Razón 2005k.
28. La Razón 2005l.
29. García Linera 2005c, p. 59.

a collective response.[30] As early as 11 May, an emergency general assembly of FEJUVE-El Alto was incredibly animated. Gerardo Bustamante, representing COR-El Alto, addressed those assembled in the meeting hall:

> Comrades, we're going to call a public meeting of all the organic social organisations of El Alto and organise…measures at the level of the city. We will declare El Alto as the capital…as the bastion of the workers' struggle.… The workers, the neighbours, and El Alto altogether, must be our organisation. Through the neighbourhood councils and the assemblies the people must take power. We are not going to hand over power once again to the white collar bourgeoisie. Comrades, during these days we have gained experience and we know how to lead ourselves. If we govern ourselves in this way, we will be able to govern at the national level of our country. Comrades, help me yell out: Long Live the Neighbourhood-councils! Long Live the Regional Workers' Central [COR-El Alto]! Long Live the Bolivian Workers' Central [COB]![31]

At the same meeting, Jaime Solares invited the activists of FEJUVE-El Alto, 'to finish what we started in October. Finishing what we began in October means that people must take power, close down the Congress'.[32] As the workers in El Alto prepared for revolution beneath the banner of natural-resource recovery, the IMF, transnational petroleum-enterprises, and various domestic business-groups offered a critique from the Right of the proposed law approved by Congress. They demanded that Mesa veto the law because if passed, they argued, it would dissuade future investment in the industry that was vital for the country's very economic survival.[33]

Pressure turned in on Mesa from all sides. With no social base left to speak of, Mesa clung to the hope that he might circumvent a headlong fall into the abyss. The consummate TV-journalist-president, he relied once again on a televised address to the nation.[34] He spoke of 'the most intense polarisation of the country since the crisis of October 2003. A polarisation in which ideo-

---

30. *La Prensa* 2005g; *La Razón* 2005p, *La Razón* 2005v; Chávez 2005c; *El Mundo* 2005; *La Razón* 2005u, *La Razón* 2005v.
31. Bustamante 2005b.
32. Solares 2005a.
33. *El Nuevo Día* 2005; *La Prensa* 2005j, x; *La Razón* 2005b, *La Razón* 2005e, *La Razón* 2005g, *La Razón* 2005aa, *La Razón* 2005dd.
34. Mesa Gisbert 2005a.

logical positions, conceptions of the future, visions of the country, regional positions, positions of organised groups', are leading the nation toward irreconcilable confrontation. According to Mesa, the situation had degenerated into 'an extremely worrying scenario', in which the integrity of the country was at stake. 'I believe, and I say this with all of my heart', Mesa warned the citizens, 'that the unity of Bolivia today is in serious risk'.[35] Mesa called for an Encuentro por al Unidad de Bolivia (Gathering for the Unity of Bolivia) to be held on Monday, 16 May, the day before he would be required to submit his verdict on the hydrocarbons-law.[36]

7.3.2 Élite-ruptures

The attempt to organise an *encuentro* delivered Mesa's latest injury in a long line of political punishments. The president could not secure a majority in Congress behind the gathering, and, therefore, the Supreme Court refused to participate as well. Multiple sectors from within the left-indigenous and eastern-bourgeois blocs who had been invited also refused to attend. Embarrassingly, Mesa was forced to cancel the initiative.[37] Ruptures in the always fragile élite-alliance with Mesa, first sealed in the aftermath of his threat to resign in March, began to widen into deep chasms.[38] Representatives of the MNR criticised Mesa for taking so long to deliberate on the law approved by Congress, arguing that this reversed all the advances made in the past nine months of congressional sessions.[39] Eloy Luján, leader of the NFR, chastised Mesa for evading his responsibility to govern and lead the country.[40] Óscar Eid of the MIR said that Mesa appeared to be intensely confused in his most recent address to the nation, and that his ambiguity and indecisiveness in dealing with the hydrocarbons-law was bringing the whole process back to square one.[41] Over the next week, the columns and reportage of the mainstream print-media and the news-programmes on television

---

35. Mesa Gisbert 2005a.
36. *La Razón* 2005y.
37. *El Alteño* 2005b, *La Prensa* 2005a, *La Prensa* 2005q, *La Prensa* 2005v, *La Razón* 2005h, *La Razón* 2005r.
38. *La Prensa* 2005l.
39. *La Razón* 2005t.
40. *La Razón* 2005t.
41. *La Razón* 2005t.

provided a near constant barrage of criticisms against the President.[42] Business-organisations began explicitly to insist that Mesa restore order to the country and apply the laws in the face of popular-movement mobilisation.[43]

7.3.3 Moderates and radicals

On the other side of the divide, preparations were developing for mass-protests on 16 May, the day before Mesa would have to make his decision on the hydrocarbons-law. Two wings of protest emerged that converged on some issues, but remained divided on the core-themes. The moderates, on the one hand, gathered behind the MAS for the March from Caracollo to La Paz. They continued to demand 50 per cent royalties on petroleum-profits, despite the fact that the frame of full nationalisation had quickly resonated much more deeply in the left-indigenous bloc. This march was also explicitly advertised by the MAS-leadership as an alternative to road-blockades rather than as an act of solidarity with blockades being planned elsewhere in the country by other sectors. However, as events proceeded, many of the rank and file participating in the march from Caracollo to La Paz would themselves become adherents of the nationalisation-wing of the protest-movement.

The latter wing, the radical core of the left-indigenous bloc, was led by FEJUVE-El Alto and COR-El Alto.[44] They were planning massive marches from El Alto into La Paz for 16 May, behind the demand of nationalisation, a revolutionary constituent assembly and – for the majority – the closure of Congress.[45] Taking their cue from FEJUVE-El Alto's and COR-El Alto's calls for action on May 16, an array of social-movement sectors announced their intentions to participate. Urban teachers at a national level, organised through the CMUB, said they would participate by initiating a nation-wide strike and road-blocks that day. In El Alto itself, the Federación Regional de Transporte 1 de Mayo (May 1st Regional Federation of Truckers, May 1-FRT), and the Federación de Trabajadores en Salud (Federation of Health-Care Workers,

---

42. *La Razón* 2005z.
43. *La Razón* 2005s, *La Razón* 2005bb.
44. Stefanoni 2005.
45. There were divisions within the executive committee and rank and file of FEJUVE–El Alto over the issue of closing down the Congress and physically occupying the Plaza Murillo. However, as the movement intensified, the organisation congealed behind the radicals calling for this action.

FTS), alongside many other groups, formally committed to participating in the march on La Paz. The leadership of the COB was attending the emergency-assemblies of FEJUVE-El Alto during this period, and they made a formal call on their affiliates across the country to be prepared to take action on 16 May. Elsewhere, the MST and the Confederación de Naciones Indígenas y Originarios (Confederation of Aboriginal and Indigenous Nations, CNIO) – also led by Roberto de la Cruz – announced that they would co-ordinate blockades of the highway between Oruro and La Paz in the community of Collana, to coincide with the mass-protests of El Alto and the capital.[46]

7.4 The Second Gas-War begins: the marches of 16 May

In the end, 16 May marked a turning of the tide, after which there was no way that the left-indigenous bloc, nor the more moderate wing of protesters led by the MAS, could accept any hydrocarbons-law that did not lead to nationalisation, or, at least, a radical reform of the industry. Jaime Solares encapsulated the general sentiments of the movement: 'We are tired of so much manipulation. What we are demanding is the immediate nationalisation of hydrocarbons because this will generate more jobs. We need a patriotic president and not one who defends the interests of transnational corporations'.[47] Roberto de la Cruz put it more succinctly: 'El Alto made Carlos Mesa Gisbert President, and we can also remove him'.[48]

At around 8:00am on that Monday morning, I arrived in El Alto. Massive crowds of mostly poor indigenous Bolivians gathered on the cusp of the mountainside that descends into the capital-city. Workers in the massive informal sector, ex-miners 'relocated' to the shantytown after privatisation of the mines in 1985, the unemployed, indigenous peasants, recent migrants from the countryside pushed from their former livelihoods through the devastation of the agricultural economy in the high plateau, pensioners, university-students, women in traditional indigenous dress with their unique bowler-hats, shoeshine boys, Trotskyist teachers, communists, socialists, *indigenistas*, neighbourhood-activists, populists, and many others milled around in a jovial

---

46. *El Alteño* 2005a, *El Alteño* 2005b, *La Prensa* 2005f, *La Prensa* 2005k, *La Prensa* 2005m, *La Prensa* 2005r, *La Razón* 2005d, *La Razón* 2005n, *La Razón* 2005q.
47. *El Diario* 2005.
48. *El Diario* 2005.

mood eating breakfast on the street, provided by women street-venders who erected their food-stands alongside the march for the country's natural gas.

The size of the demonstration was impressive, even if accurate figures were impossible to acquire. It took three hours to march the roughly 7 miles from the edge of El Alto to downtown La Paz. When we were close to the edge of downtown, one could look up the mountainside to the start of El Alto, and see steady and thick waves of protesters still just beginning their participation in the march. A young Aymara man in front of me carried a sign: 'Bolivia will neither be a colony of the Yankees nor of the transnationals!' Another placard read: 'Out With the Transnationals! Bread! Work! Education!' A long trail of trade-union and social-movement banners were carried down the hillsides, together with Bolivian flags and indigenous *wiphalas*. Along the way, the chants of protesters and casual conversations made clear the demands: nationalisation of gas, a constituent assembly, the shutdown of parliament, and the removal of Mesa. But, underlying all of this, was the more basic sentiment expressed by one worker marching next to me: 'The governments have been on the side of the transnationals, and the rich. We want a government on the side of the people'. As the waves of demonstrators seemingly had no end, participants in the march started speculating: 'Another October?'

Once we arrived in the centre of La Paz, excitement grew as the front lines of the mobilisation veered away from the road leading to the Plaza San Francisco (a frequent point of convergence for demonstrations), instead opting for the route leading to the Plaza Murillo which hosts the Presidential Palace. Two blocks away from the Plaza, the march encountered its first line of heavily armed police, decked out in riot-gear and grim faces. The marchers chanted and sung for the police to join them, pointing out that they had the option of uniting with the people or acting as the assassins of the state.

The march turned up a different street, opting out of confrontation at this point and circling around for an attempt to take the Plaza from another location. A few blocks later the march stopped short and the frontlines began jeering and yelling at the next police-barricade. In the tradition of the Bolivian tin-miners – the old vanguard of the Bolivian Left – dynamite was exploded, not with the intention of killing anyone, but making some noise and building up the energy of the protesters. This act, in conjunction with protesters on the frontlines physically removing one of the blockades that had been set up, sparked a police-response. They used their tear-gas canisters, and soon after, rubber-bullets. Also, for the first time, the state used one of its special anti-disturbance vehicles, the 'Neptuno', which looks like a cross between a tank and a banking security-truck. The Neptuno's special feature is a powerful water-gun that hoses people to the ground, inciting panic among escaping crowds in the narrow colonial streets of the capital. The stores on these streets were all closed and barricaded allowing no means of reprieve but to run from the state-reaction to mobilisation. This area of the city is heavily populated with kindergartens, and primary and secondary schools. Many youngsters suffered from the tear-gas that had everyone running and crying – and more than a few vomiting – blocks away from the actual confrontation. While in no sense a bloody replay of Sánchez de Lozada's massacre in October 2003, Monday nonetheless left the crowd notably stirred up and angered in comparison to the jovial breakfast reunion in El Alto.

The demonstrations on 16 May were much wider than my personal experience could possibly convey. In La Paz, traffic was halted everywhere in downtown for most of the day. Tear-gas, anti-disturbance vehicles, and rubber-bullets from the coercive wings of the state were met with clubs and bottles from protesters.[49] At least four were injured by rubber-bullets, including a peasant-activist, an UPEA student, and a 14 year-old boy. A fourth unidentified man was hit in the foot with a rubber-bullet. One witness reported that a man had been seriously injured next to his eye, while a leader of the teachers' union claimed another had been hit squarely in the chest with yet another rubber-bullet.[50] Elsewhere in the country, road-blocks were erected. For example, highway-traffic was halted between Oruro and Cochabamba.[51] Meanwhile, in the rural parts of La Paz, the FSTCLP-TK publicised the fact that dense road-blockades in all twenty provinces of the department would be erected the next day, on 17 May.[52]

7.4.1   The absence of lethal state-repression and further élite-ruptures

Mesa, unlike Sánchez de Lozada, did not respond to the protests with lethal repression, to the growing dismay of the eastern-bourgeois bloc. The latter

---

49. *La Razón* 2005o, *La Razón* 2005w.
50. *La Prensa* 2005n; *La Razón* 2005a.
51. *La Razón* 2005o.
52. *La Prensa* 2005d.

began to shift its support toward the resignation of Carlos Mesa, demanding that it be followed immediately by a constitutional succession. Hormando Vaca Díez (MIR) from Santa Cruz, and Mario Cossío (MNR) from Tarija, were essentially acting as the congressional face of the eastern-bourgeois bloc by this point, and they were in line to succeed Mesa. Congress-people from the MNR, MIR, and NFR made public comments that the President had been critically weakened and that there may have to be a constitutional succession. One congressional deputy of the MNR, Luis Eduardo Siles, said, for example, that his party would support a constitutional succession, 'and if the idea is succession, the President of the Senate, Hormando Vaca Díez is the one who has to assume responsibility'.[53] Mesa's Director of Conflict-Prevention, Gregorio Lanza, accused sections of the MNR, that had been and integral part of Sánchez de Lozada's administration, of seeking to destabilise the Mesa government.[54]

7.5 The new hydrocarbons-law

Carlos Mesa waited until the last possible minute to return the hydrocarbons-law to Congress. In a surprising move, the President refused both his right to veto or promulgate the law, and, instead, simply returned it to Congress without any specific suggestions for amendment. This obliged the President of the Senate, Vaca Díez, to assume responsibility for promulgating the law, which he did in Congress on the afternoon of 17 May. That evening, Mesa's government purchased airtime on all the leading television-channels. Interrupting the regular after-dinner programming, he delivered an hour-long speech declaring the issue of hydrocarbons a matter that could now be set aside, as a new and definitive law had been passed.[55] In an attempt to avert the country's eyes to something new, Mesa introduced the details of a social and economic plan for the nation, which he said combined productivity and solidarity.[56] Rather than calming the political environs, however, Mesa's

---

53. *La Prensa* 2005p.
54. *La Prensa* 2005i.
55. Mesa Gisbert 2005b.
56. *La Prensa* 2005e, *La Prensa* 2005h, *La Prensa* 2005t, *La Prensa* 2005w; *La Razón* 2005f, *La Razón* 2005x.

strategy merely stoked the smoldering tinder strewn all about him. Over the next three weeks, he would be engulfed entirely in flames.

It was immediately clear, for example, that the President had lost any and all support from the traditional neoliberal parties within Congress. In an animated and angry speech in Congress, before promulgating the new law, Vaca Díez positioned himself to succeed Mesa as president. He denounced Mesa for his destructive indecisiveness as leader of the country. The response was extended applause from all parties save the MAS. Political analysts of all stripes asserted that the President had exhausted what little had remained of his political capital, and that his social base within the citizenry had dissipated irreversibly.[57]

7.5.1 Left-indigenous bloc responds to new hydrocarbons-law

The social forces of the left-indigenous bloc, meanwhile, perceived limitations of the new law as an affront to the memory of the fallen martyrs of October 2003. The MAS, too, despite its malleable notions of what would constitute nationalisation, and the party's general moderate reformism, found this pill too bitter to swallow. The following four days witnessed a series of demonstrations in La Paz against the new law.[58] Attending the long and dynamic emergency assembly of FEJUVE-El Alto that evening, I recorded the executive committee's summary of the decisions made after extended debate and deliberation involving representatives from all the districts of the city. They resolved to move forward with a new wave of mobilisations, assemblies, and marches, while continuously returning to their grassroots rank and file for purposes of organising, educating, and allowing for mass democratic participation as the process unfolded. The miners pledged to continue pressure-tactics and mobilisations.[59] In an interview on 23 June 2005, Miguel Zubieta recounted how the FSTMB had spent all of 2004 pushing for social movements across the country to set aside their particular demands and unite behind the singular frame of nationalisation. In the protests of May and June, miners contributed activists and organisational skill to the national blockade of roads throughout the mining zones of the western *altiplano*, particularly

---

57. *La Prensa* 2005s, *La Prensa* 2005w.
58. Cáceres 2005b.
59. *La Prensa* 2005o.

in Oruro and Potosí. They engaged in street-battles with police and military forces in La Paz, and ultimately led the battle in Sucre to prevent Vaca Díez from coming to power after Mesa resigned on 6 June.[60]

In the wake of the passage of the new law on 17 May, the COB called for the shutting down of Congress and Mesa's resignation. The FUDTCLP-TK executed their road-blocking plans in the rural provinces of La Paz. The National Roads-Service confirmed that road-blockades had been extended to the four principal highways, including the international connections to Chile and Peru in the western part of the country. Health-care workers in La Paz announced an upcoming 48-hour strike. COD-La Paz, an affiliate of the COB, decided in an assembly to continue with further mobilisations and a march in favour of nationalisation. Salustiano Laura, one of the organisation's executives, said, 'We are not going to drop our arms until we've achieved nationalisation. We are not going to forget the fallen of October; and we are going to demand that the traitors resign from their positions'.[61] Juan Carlos Valencia, of COR-El Alto, agreed, declaring that 'for us, nationalisation is everything'. He said that Congress must be shut down, and that Mesa must resign: 'Now more than ever the only instrument of struggle is to go out into the streets...'.[62] A 48-hour general strike was announced in the city of Potosí, where workers rejected the new hydrocarbons-law and called for nationalisation.[63]

Over the next several days, clashes between protesters and the armed forces of the state occurred in various parts of the country, but were particularly volatile in the capital. The miners of the FSTMB were a militant-presence in La Paz over these days, interrupting traffic and setting off dynamite-explosions close to the military and police-barricades surrounding the Plaza Murillo.[64] The capital was rocked with a series of mobilisations denouncing the new law and demanding nationalisation. COR-El Alto and FEJUVE-El Alto decided to hold a general strike beginning on Monday, 23 May, the same day that the MAS-led marchers from Caracollo would arrive in La Paz.

Between 18 and 21 May there were violent clashes between protesters and the armed forces throughout the country, although they resulted in no

---

60. Zubieta 2005b.
61. *La Prensa* 2005o.
62. *La Prensa* 2005o.
63. *La Prensa* 2005o.
64. *La Prensa* 2005b.

reported deaths. FEJUVE-El Alto, COR-El Alto, the COB, and the FSTMB led actions in and around El Alto and La Paz. The rural teachers, who finished a 72-hour strike on 18 May, immediately declared their support for moves toward a general strike of various sectors for the following day. As all of this was transpiring, CONAMAQ initiated a hunger-strike in La Paz in support of a constituent assembly and were immediately supported by the Coordinadora de Pueblos Étnicos de Santa Cruz (Coordinator of Ethnic Peoples of Santa Cruz, CPESC), on the other side of the country. In Oruro and Potosí, as well, a number of different social movements demonstrated in support of the constituent assembly demand. Joining the growing wave of militancy, professors and students from La Paz's public university, UMSA, marched together for the nationalisation of hydrocarbons and a constituent assembly. In Oruro, 50 peasants from the Oruro branch of the MST occupied a large landholding. Cochabamba was also a centre of revolt. Peasants, workers affiliated with the COD-Cochabamba, members of the Coordinator of Gas, university-students, truckers, and neighbourhood-councils from the impoverished southern zone of the city, together surrounded the Gualberto Villarroel natural-gas refinery and protested agaisnt the new hydrocarbons-law.

7.5.2 *Revolutionary consciousness grows within left-indigenous bloc*

Interviews conducted on 20 May with two activists from FEJUVE-El Alto, Jorge Mendoza Mamani and Luciano Suárez, are revealing in the sense that they convey the heightening intensity and pace of mobilisations, rising expectations, and deepening visions of profound change ahead. I spoke to them after a neighbourhood-council meeting in Santiago II, a neighbourhood of mostly relocated ex-miners in El Alto. 'We are rising up in yet another insurrection to such an extent that many leaders are now calling for revolution', Mendoza Mamani explained. 'Therefore, there is going to be complete change. I know there is going to be complete transformation. Whether it be peacefully or through force, there is going to be total change'.[65] Suárez, likewise set out a radical strategy, focusing on the complete shut down of Congress:

---

65. Mendoza Mamani 2005.

May and June is a continuation of October. We committed a grave error in October 2003. We did not shut down Congress, which is full of corrupt leaders. The only thing [the Mesa government] has done is approve a law that favour petroleum-companies, not the people. Therefore, the mobilisation that is occurring now is a continuation of the mobilisations of October. Our demands repeat the theme of gas and the theme of a constituent assembly. In other words, the October Agenda must be fulfilled.[66]

7.5.3 *Divisions between moderates and radicals deepen*

On 23 May, *alteño* protesters greeted the MAS-led march from Caracollo in a spirit of solidarity as the marchers entered their city en route to La Paz. At the same time, many held placards reminding the MAS-leadership that the demand of the left-indigenous bloc was full nationalisation, not 50 per cent royalties.[67] As the march from Caracollo descended into La Paz, it was reinforced by the various *alteño* social-movement and union-organisations. Once downtown, miners and street-vendors clashed with police in the vicinity of the Plaza San Francisco, but no serious injuries were reported.[68] Tear-gas and anti-disturbance vehicles were used against the crowds. Traffic was suspended throughout much of La Paz and the city's bus-terminal was closed down. Protests and strike-activity in El Alto led American Airlines to cancel all its flights to the capital, while domestic airlines continued to fly, but with a substantially reduced number of flights.[69] Tens of thousands of demonstrators gathered in the downtown-streets of La Paz. While Mesa remained reluctant to use lethal force against civilians, the Minister of Government, Saúl Lara declared that in order to guarantee order and to avoid incidents of violence in the streets because of social protests, the armed forces and police were now officially in a state of emergency.[70]

The main event of the day, however, was an open assembly in the Plaza San Francisco, organised by the MAS to coincide with the arrival of the march from Caracollo. Thirty thousand people filled the Plaza and listened to a range of speakers representing all the principal sectors of the left-indigenous

---

66. Suárez 2005.
67. *La Razón* 2005j.
68. *La Prensa* 2005c.
69. *La Razón* 2005m.
70. *El Alteño* 2005c.

bloc. Looking out over the crowd was like peering into a sea of 'chequered rainbows'.[71] Over their heads, the crowd held up thousands of multi-coloured *wiphalas* in an impressive display of indigenous liberation. However, divisions between the MAS-leadership and some of its rank and file, on the one hand, and the rest of the demonstrators, on the other, were apparent in the speeches and the crowd's responses. Of the sixteen key speakers, Morales was the only one who did not hold a position in favour of the full nationalisation of hydro-carbons.[72] I positioned myself in the midst of the large and growing assembly to listen and observe. As Morales was speaking, miners and other affiliates of the COB, as well as some other sections of the crowd, attempted to drown him out with chants of 'Nationalisation!' and 'Close down Congress!' Gualberto Choque of the FUDTCLP-TK rose to speak at the assembly as well, calling for the nationalisation of hydrocarbons, the resignation of Mesa, and the full national recovery and assertion of social control over all natural resources in the country.[73]

Fractures in the popular movement between radicals and moderates were also evident concerning the issue of closing down Congress, as well as in the different ways various sectors understood the demand for a constituent assembly. Morales, for example, stressed that the MAS was calling for an assembly, but insisted that this could not be convened by the movements themselves, but rather had to proceed through the existing channels of the state. Morales emphasised that, 'we are not calling for the closure of the Congress of the Republic, because it is the symbol of democracy'. Consider that statement against a passage from the speech delivered by Jaime Solares at the same gathering: 'Congress must be shut down for having sold out the people. Carlos Mesa must also resign'.[74] 'Not for the first time, Morales functions as a dam against a popular flood onto the nation's highways, into its streets and perhaps even the presidential palace', Forrest Hylton reported from La Paz later that week. According to Hylton, 'Morales has a vested interest in maintaining a dynamic of limited mobilisation. Currently the only effective break on popular insurrection, Morales poses as the defender of democracy in hopes of winning over the middle class'. As Hylton correctly points out,

---

71. Hylton and Thomson 2005a.
72. *La Razón* 2005i.
73. *La Prensa* 2005u.
74. *La Razón* 2005aa.

neither Morales, 'nor the MAS want to see the constitutional order unravel, as both have had their sights set on the 2007 elections since 2002, when Morales nearly won the presidential race'.[75]

One of the most extraordinary speeches of this period was delivered at an emergency-assembly in FEJUVE-El Alto on 27 May. It helps to draw out the distinctions between the type of demand for a constituent assembly coming from the MAS and the conceptualisation of what such an assembly would entail for many of the social forces within the left-indigenous bloc. Gualberto Choque, leader of the FSTCLP-TK, began his salutations to FEJUVE-allies in Aymara before quickly passing into Spanish. He explained that the struggle of indigenous peasants of which he was apart was 'not against the government' alone, but also 'against the system' that has been ruling over the indigenous majority for centuries.[76] The distinction between the radical visions of revolutionary transformation within the left-indigenous bloc, and those of the MAS who continued to believe in the possibility of reforming liberal capitalism by operating within its institutions of formal electoral democracy, were made clear in Choque's description of the constituent assembly that he envisioned:

> Where is this constituent assembly going to come from? There is no longer going to be a congress. There is no longer going to be a government.... We will organise ourselves in a constituent assembly where there will be workers, peasants, carpenters, shoe-shiners, women, and men.... We will need to define what kind of country we want, what kind of economy we want.... We are going to do these things...after a *pachakuti* as the Aymaras and Quechuas say, after a grand revolution, as socialists and Marxists say. In our federation we've said that if one has an old shoe, what should one do, save it or throw it out? Obviously, throw it out brothers. This system is an old shoe, rotten and full of corruption. We have to destroy it once and for all, so that a new system can be born in its place.... If in the end we are going to struggle for this revolution, to follow through with this, we are only going to be able to do it through social movements. It will be the insurgency of the Bolivian people.[77]

---

75. Hylton 2005a.
76. Choque 2005b.
77. Choque 2005b.

From 23 May onward, the left-indigenous bloc escalated its mobilisations throughout much of the country, with La Paz and El Alto again acting as the epicentre of revolt. The forms of assemblyist popular democracy through neighbourhood-councils and other parts of the infrastructure of class-struggle that had first appeared in El Alto in October 2003 were reignited. The councils acted as a machinery of mobilisation and the main fora for collectively deliberating on the best way forward. The councils co-ordinated soup-kitchens to keep people fed. They organised the controlled and limited opening of food-stalls at certain intervals during the strike so that *alteños* could gather supplies. They also utilised their ties to the countryside of the *altiplano* to bring in foodstuffs from the peasantry to sustain the strikers.[78] As one conservative journalist noted, El Alto was slowly suffocating La Paz.[79]

On the afternoon of 24 May, an emergency-assembly was held at the headquarters of FEJUVE-El Alto. The press was locked out while the first two hours of intense discussion and debate took place. Entering the assembly-hall when they called in the press, I was hit by the intense heat of over 500 bodies cramped into a room with a normal standing capacity of maybe 300. The temperature in the room reflected well the sentiments of those gathered there. The memory of the dead and injured of October 2003 was palpable in the speeches of each of the representatives of the nine districts of the city as they took the stage to communicate to the press and the assembly more generally the final resolutions of the meeting. They demanded the radicalisation of mobilisations and the strike; marches to La Paz; the nationalisation of hydrocarbons; a constituent assembly; a human-rights trial of Sánchez de Lozada and his co-conspirators; the resignation of Carlos Mesa; and the closure of Congress. Invoking the memory of the October martyrs, Carlos Barrerra, president of District Eight, proclaimed, 'We have an enormous responsibility. On our backs we carry the thousands and thousands of the poor. We need to proceed as in October. All the movements in the streets need to unite for the one hundred per cent recuperation of our natural resources!'

---

78. Ramírez and Stefanoni 2005a.
79. Molina 2005.

7.5.4 *Revolutionary visions of left-indigenous bloc*

By the end of May, the Bolivian capital was being positively shaken by the 'largest, most radical protest marches since October 2003'.[80] The question of revolutionary power was everywhere in the air. Assemblies at the neighbourhood-level throughout El Alto were asking *¿y ahora qué?*, now what? There was massive support for ending the presidency of Carlos Mesa, and for preventing Vaca Díez or Cossío from taking his place. Likewise, the idea for shutting down Congress entirely was widely supported. But the answer to what alternative popular power would take the place of the old state was far from clear. As one FEJUVE-El activist commented, 'we talk a lot about how to paralyze the city, but not about a method of power'.[81]

Outside the communities of El Alto, these questions were also being fervently debated. The FSTMB, for example, was firmly in support of revolutionary transformation, although it too could not explain how to arrive at this end without a revolutionary party. 'In reality, Congress sold out the Bolivian people', Juan Cardozo Pacheco, the FSTMB's General Secretary, told me on 31 May. 'We don't want to be governed by people who defend transnationals, by people who are against the Bolivian people, against our natural resources', he explained. 'That is why it is important the Congress be shut down, so that the people can take power'.[82] Speaking at an assembly hosted by students at the UMSA-campus in La Paz, Miguel Zubieta talked about the necessity of constructing an Indigenous Popular National Assembly 'that could replace the power which oppresses us, not only in Congress but in the executive'. Both of these institutions, for Zubieta, 'only function to obey the orders of their transnational bosses, the International Monetary Fund, and the World Bank'. He called on the FEJUVE-El Alto, COR-El Alto, FUDTCLP-TK, the FSTMB and other popular organisations to help build such a counter-power to the existing state, with each sending delegates to this popular assembly. 'Democracy is not practiced through the ballot box in the conditions under which we live, comrades', Zubieta declared. 'The only way of structuring an authentic and real democracy is by building, enriching, and constructing our indigenous, popular, and national assemblies'.[83]

---

80. Hylton 2005a.
81. Ramírez and Stefanoni 2005a.
82. Cardozo Pacheco 2005.
83. Zubieta 2005a.

Later, speaking at the same UMSA-assembly as Zubieta, Choque denounced the ruling-class and mainstream-media's racist condemnation of the social movements struggling for revolutionary power:

> They accuse our social movements, and especially the peasant-movements, of being irrational. They describe us as so many terrorist Indian brutes.... The grand intellectuals formulate these opinions in the highest spheres of the media...but we respond to them by demanding the recovery of all natural resources. We are providing a political line for people, that this is the road we must follow to be free...free from capitalism, free from this garbage called imperialism.... This is a political, ideological position that was born in the minds of the brothers of the countryside, from the minds of those who some say are poor Indian brutes. But this is the line we are bringing forward, and we hope, brothers from the cities, that you will ascribe to this objective and that finally we can drive forward an authentic liberation, an authentic democracy.[84]

The first week of June drove from the capital the few tourists who remained, as foreign embassies advised their citizens to flee the country. Rumours of military coups permeated daily conversations on the streets. Inflationary prices and dwindling supplies stoked runs on the supermarkets, pushing prices up still further. Natural gas and gasoline were quickly being exhausted in La Paz. In Santa Cruz, violent right-wing youth from the Unión Juvenil Cruceñista (Cruceño Youth Union, UJC) attacked indigenous peasants who had been expressing their solidarity with the rebels in the Andean west. Mesa continued to avoid the use of lethal force, but barricaded the Plaza Murillo with the police and the military, as dynamite, tear-gas, and rubber-bullets were exchanged in the surrounding avenues and downtown-corridors. On 6 June, Mesa finally announced his permanent and irrevocable resignation as President of Republic. That morning, between 400,000 and 500,000 protesters had occupied the capital in a gigantic display of mobilisation, unprecedented in Bolivian history. Standing on the edge of the Plaza San Francisco in the middle of downtown, I turned full circle for a visual panorama and saw no end to the masses of indigenous peasants and workers in all directions.

The battle had not ended, however. Between 7 and 9 June, a major struggle ensued between the left-indigenous bloc, the MAS, and sections of the

---

84. Choque 2005c.

middle class, on one side, and the eastern-bourgeois bloc on the other, over the attempt by Vaca Díez and then Cossío to take Mesa's place as President. After this heroic last stand of the May–June Gas-War by the left-indigenous bloc, neither Vaca Díez nor Cossío were able to assume office. Late on the evening of 9 June, Vaca Díez and Cossío told the public that neither would be taking over the presidency, therefore freeing the way for Rodríguez Veltzé, President of the Supreme Court, to do so. Veltzé became the interim-president of Bolivia, with the singular mandate of overseeing new general elections in December 2005. The left-indigenous insurrectionary cycle begun in 2000 drew to a close, as mobilisations across the country subsided, and the logic of the forthcoming electoral contest replaced the logic of mass extra-parliamentary mobilisation.

Conclusion

Carlos Mesa's legitimacy as president was always contingent on his opposition to lethal state-repression against civilians. This allowed him to succeed Sánchez de Lozada and delicately govern between the polarised left-indigenous and eastern-bourgeois blocs with relative success between October 2003 and March 2005. However, the contradictions of a president acting ultimately in the interests of transnational and allied domestic capital while refusing to repress a dynamic and growing movement of workers and peasants were destined to become unsustainable. When he did not repress the growing wave of mobilisations in May and June, and simultaneously maintained his intransigent position against the nationalisation of hydrocarbons, Mesa ended up fueling the left-indigenous mobilisations on the one hand, while losing the support of the eastern-bourgeois bloc, on the other.

The insurrections of May and June 2005 were led by the informal indigenous working classes of El Alto, with the determining support of important peasant-allies from the *altiplano* and sectors of the formal working class. The key components of the latter were miners and teachers, and, to a lesser extent, health-care workers. Behind these key social forces, an enormous and heterogeneous array of sections of the rural and urban popular classes participated in the monumental mobilisations of hundreds of thousands that ultimately pulled Mesa down and prevented Vaca Díez and Cossío from succeeding him.

The middle class, meanwhile, was an important pillar of support for the Mesa régime. Unlike in October 2003, when sections of the middle class outside the *media luna* supported the left-indigenous insurrections in the face of indiscriminate state-violence being perpetrated by the state, in May and June 2005 the same urban middle class tended to support Mesa. They joined the left-indigenous mobilisations in a limited and supportive role only after Mesa had resigned and the potential for a turn to the far Right – and more ugly repression – reared its head under the guise of Vaca Díez. The collective-action frame of gas-nationalisation continued to be the principal factor binding together the disparate insurrectionary groups. The additional call for a constituent assembly, however, was more important in May and June 2005 than it had been in September and October 2003. Also novel in May and June was the intensified regionalisation of racial and class-struggle, expressing itself most fully in the formation and consolidation of the eastern-bourgeois bloc in the departments of the *media luna*.

Divisions between moderates and radicals were more evident in the extra-parliamentary mobilisations than they were in the first Gas-War. The divisions were expressed mainly between the various social forces constituting what I have called the left-indigenous bloc and those social forces aligned with the MAS. The MAS, under the leadership of Evo Morales, played an important role in the political dynamics that unfolded over these two historic months. Having been severed from the governing coalition by Mesa in March 2005, the MAS returned somewhat to extra-parliamentary activism. However, it did so under a set of reformist goals that distinguished the party from the radical sectors of the left-indigenous bloc. The MAS never lost sight of its objective of winning office through elections. To do so, its strategy since 2002 had been to present an increasingly moderate face to the urban middle class. Winning the 2007 general elections was a long-term objective, and, when elections were rescheduled for December 2005, the immediacy of this project took precedence over all else. Thus, the MAS played a part in the mass-mobilisations of May and June, but ultimately acted as a dam,[85] helping to prevent a potentially revolutionary flood from washing away the reigning power-structures of Bolivian society.

---

85. Hylton 2005a.

Chapter Eight

Combined-Oppositional Consciousness

In Chapter One, it was argued that social class structures the totality of social relations, but that this
totality cannot be reduced to class. Societies are also
constituted by other social relations such as race,
gender, sexuality, and nationality. Therefore, an
analytical framework of class-formation and class-
consciousness must take into account the interpenetration of different social relations in the real world.
Class-consciousness is most straightforwardly
understood as the way in which the experiences
of being thrust through birth or other involuntary
means into a class-situation, 'are handled in cultural
terms: embodied in traditions, value-systems, ideas,
and institutional forms'.[1] To be more explicit about
the unique overlapping of indigenous identity and
class-consciousness in the Bolivian context, Chapter
One introduced the more precise concept of *combined-oppositional consciousness*. This is a collective
consciousness in which the politics of class-struggle
and indigenous liberation are tightly interwoven.

One of the most dynamic ways in which the combination of class and indigenous consciousness in
El Alto expressed itself during the Gas-Wars of 2003
and 2005 was through the notion of *vecino*. Literally

---

1. Camfield 2004, p. 437.

translated, *vecino* means *neighbour*. Yet, in the context of Latin-American shantytowns, *vecino* often 'implies important bonds of community, characterised by common experiences, values, and reciprocal ties of solidarity'.[2] In the context of El Alto, the *vecino*-identity has 'multiple gradations, some more worker, others more indigenous, peasant, or more commercial....There was no single actor when they mobilised themselves, or no single identity that mobilised itself in El Alto', during the recent rebellions, according to Álvaro García Linera.[3] While the use of *vecino* to valorise the mixed character of racial and class-consciousness was most prevalent in El Alto, a similar combined consciousness prevailed outside of the *alteño* context. Activist workers of the formal working class, particularly in the FSTMB and the COB, tended to emphasise their class-identities over their indigenous ones, but this did not mean the total negation of the latter. Radicalised Aymara peasants tended to emphasise their indigenous identities over class, but like their working-class counterparts, this did not preclude their conscious participation in peasant class-struggle, and worker-peasant alliances.

Another component of combined-oppositional consciousness is the profound interpenetration of Bolivia's two longest-standing popular cultures of resistance and opposition in contemporary El Alto, and to some degree in neighbouring La Paz. Revolutionary Marxism and indigenous-liberationist traditions became inextricably intertwined in the ideologies and everyday practices of popular struggle. Revolutionary memories of historic indigenous insurrections and their heroes, as well as past conquests and rebellions of the revolutionary Left, were referred to in explicit terms by the activists I interviewed. They drew inspiration from these figures and revolutionary moments. The ritualised remembering that went on linked twenty-first-century struggles with the distant past, rooting and fortifying recent left-indigenous practice in centuries of insurrectionary tradition. One important way that these memories have been sustained is through 'family-traditions of resistance'.[4]

Anti-imperialist critique of various transnational structures of domination and exploitation was also an important feature of the combined-oppositional consciousness forged in the period of the Gas-Wars. Anti-imperialism was

---

2. Oxhorn 1995, p. 113.
3. García Linera 2005a.
4. Kampwirth 2002, p. 10.

often tied in the narratives of the activists I spoke with to analyses and denunciations of capitalism as a system of exploitation and racial domination as a system of oppression. Bringing together revolutionary-Marxist and indigenous-liberationist popular cultures of resistance, as well as the multifaceted critique of imperialism, was the more specific oppositional focus in many activists' stories on the privatisation of natural resources – specifically, hydrocarbons (natural gas and oil) and water.

A final piece of the combined-oppositional consciousness this chapter analyses is constituted by the explicitly forward-looking, the 'freedom-dreams' of activists.[5] Most important in this regard are the ways in which the principal protagonists of the Gas-Wars envisioned a better society along four principal lines: (i) equality, the end of poverty, and the abolition of social classes; (ii) a future free of racism; (iii) dignity, social justice, and basic necessities; and (iv) socialist and indigenous-liberationist democracy.

My arguments are rooted in the perceptions, beliefs, and values of the activists I interviewed. They were members of the most important social-movement and trade-union organisations in El Alto and La Paz – the infrastructure of class-struggle – that brought together the popular movements of the two Gas-Wars and gave them their political expression. These organisations represented the peak-articulations of vast sedimentary layers of rank-and-file activism beneath. The interviewees were some of the leading 'organic intellectuals' of indigenous liberation and working-class struggle in early twenty-first century Bolivia. Lengthy, in-depth interviews – sometimes lasting three hours – were the only conceivable way of drawing out the richness, complexity, and contradiction of combined-oppositional consciousness.[6]

---

5. Kelley 2002.
6. See Gramsci 1971, pp. 5–23 on organic intellectuals. Ultimately, in my view, there is no substitute for direct, concrete, and face-to-face participation and observation in the base-level activities of periods of swelling activism. The multidimensionality of how actors experience and understand these events are impossible to capture in general survey-questions. So, whatever the limitations of sources that constitute this chapter, I was privileged to have been present in La Paz and El Alto during this extraordinary epoch of popular ferment.

8.1 *Lo vecinal, vecino,* and the oppositional consciousness of race and class

Rather than a single collective identity or consciousness, the concept of *vecino* might be thought of as a moving and dynamic combination of different elements of race and class: 'In some cases "indigenous" becomes the identity in discourse, in symbols, and in other cases it's "worker", and in other cases "*vecino*", and in other cases small business people. These become the mobilised identities'.[7] According to García Linera, 'El Alto is an interesting mix between a type of indigenous-migrant identity of the first generation, with a worker-indigenous identity – both of which are not contradictory. There is an indigenised-worker identity and an identity closer to worker-*mestizo*. There are distinct variations, depending to which zone of the city you go to'.[8]

The journalist and activist Gonzalo Gosálvez, elaborated on this notion of *vecino* more fully, concluding that, in fact, it might best be understood as the concept most frequently employed in the everyday language of *alteños* to express the political combination of race and class, and the impossibility of separating these two sets of social relations in the actual material world. For Gosálvez, indigenous resurgence and class-struggle complement each other in the shantytown and are often combined through collective action around basic services:

> [There] was [an] Aymara indigenous nationalist content of October. There were also workers, the workers' neighbourhoods that organised themselves… reviving their combativeness, their organisation, and perhaps with less of this [Aymara] identity. But [the miner's identity] wasn't in conflict with the Aymara resurgence; rather it expressed its brotherhood with that other idea, of the Aymara indigenous. And in addition there was that simple idea of *lo vecinal*, neighbouhood identity, that, in addition to indigenous identity and union organisation, is about working to recover the basics, of water and employment….It's difficult to believe but there is a real affective connection, a relationship between human beings, who recognise each other, respect each other, and collaborate with each other….*Lo vecinal*, neighbouhood identity, comes out of struggling for water, for lights, for

---

7. García Linera 2005a.
8. García Linera 2005a.

paved roads, because all the conditions are terrible in El Alto. Everyone has to count on everyone to work for everyone. So, I believe that this is a third element which is very important. Perhaps it has been what has articulated the others, it has condensed the indigenous and the miner. Out of the neighbourhood form has grown this political, ideological, cultural content of the neighbourhood-councils.[9]

Activists in the shantytown also used the idea of the power of *los vecinos* in El Alto's social movements to depict rank-and-file popular control, self-organisation, and self-activity. *Vecino*, in this sense, resembles what scholars in another context refer to as 'a model of heroism and possibility', whose task it is to 'transform the nature of power through popular insurgency and organisational forms of control from below'.[10] Keeping the specificities of El Alto's context in mind, this popular insurgency is inevitably informed by struggles against racial oppression and class-exploitation.

This passage from an interview with Abel Mamani, president of FEJUVE-El Alto in 2005, describing the October Gas-War, is representative of many others in terms of its emphasis on rank-and-file activism and its portrayal of the popular power of *los vecinos* in the shantytown's social movements:

In October 2003 the movements rose up. More than anything the social grassroots emerged, the people themselves. At first mobilisations in El alto were not that big, but they grew day by day and consolidated themselves....Everything that happened came from the grassroots. It was the rank-and-file who mobilised, the *vecinos*: women, men, the elderly, children. Everyone collaborated to block the streets.[11]

Or in the words of Gerardo Bustamante as he addressed a general assembly of FEJUVE-El Alto:

The workers, the *vecinos*, and El Alto in its entirety, is our organisation. Through the neighbourhood-councils and the assemblies the people must take power. We are not going to hand over power once again to the white collar bourgeoisie. Comrades during these days [in May and June 2005] we have gained experience and we know how to lead ourselves; and if we

---

9. Gosálvez 2005.
10. Roman and Velasco Arregui 2007, p. 263.
11. Mamani 2005a.

govern ourselves in this way, we will be able to govern at the national level in our country.[12]

The nuances of *vecino* in El Alto – of indigenous consciousness, workers' consciousness, and popular power of the rank and file from below – expressed in these few passages are emblematic of my experiences in dozens of interviews and participatory observation in the main social-movement, trade-union, and indigenous organisations in El Alto. These complexities impinge on the ways in which indigenous, worker-, and *vecino*-consciousness expressed itself politically in the recent uprisings.

Different individual activists in El Alto – often active within the same social-movement organisations – may emphasise class-struggle over indigenous resistance, or vice versa, but, when one observes the concrete reality of the popular movements on the ground, it seems that drawing tight distinctions between the two issues would be to construct an artificial dichotomy of the most unhelpful kind. Pablo Solón, a social activist and the future Special Ambassador for Trade and Integration in the Evo Morales government, explained the situation clearly when I asked him to describe the relationship between indigenous resistance and class-struggle in the contemporary urban social movements in Bolivia:

> There is a mix. Here we can't make much of a difference between social-movement and indigenous movement. The social movements here have a strong indigenous identity. If one listens to the discourses of the principal exponents of El Alto, all of them make reference to their Aymara roots, for example. So, they are not two distinct things. Rather, I would say that more than ever they are bound together. Some place more emphasis on one aspect, and others on another aspect, but they complement one another.[13]

The flexibility and interchangeability of the subjective understandings of class-struggle and indigenous liberation elicited in my conversation with Remigio Condori – a leading activist in COR-El Alto – are demonstrative of wider trends among activists in the city. Early in our conversation he suggested that, 'Our principal political position [in COR-El Alto]...is to defend the working class of the Bolivian people, of the *alteño* people'. And yet, in

---

12. Bustamante 2005a.
13. Solón 2005.

the same conversation, he explained to me that, 'The struggle has changed in the twenty-first century. Now it is the urban-indigenous struggle. Now the struggle is in the hands of urban-indigenous peoples'.[14] Rather than a contradiction, however, the multiple interviews I conducted in conjunction with extensive participatory observation over ten months in El Alto, suggest to me that 'urban-indigenous peoples' referred to by Condori, are one and the same as the 'working class of the *alteño* people'. At times, certain sides of this consciousness are emphasised, but, in the collective struggle as a whole in El Alto, indigenous-liberation politics and class-struggle are almost invariably occurring at the same time.

As a consequence, Gerardo Bustamante of COR-El Alto, addressing a general assembly of FEJUVE-El Alto in the days immediately prior to the three-week general strike that eventually forced president Carlos Mesa to resign, can refer to El Alto as 'the bastion of the workers' struggle' to unrestrained applause.[15] At the same time, Samuel Mamani Heredia, a recognised activist in FEJUVE-El Alto, emphasised to me in an interview that, 'The grassroots [of the social movements in El Alto] are indigenous. We are from the countryside. We came to El Alto, to La Paz, to the city, in search of a better life. Unfortunately, we didn't find a better life....Our people, as indigenous peoples, and the *alteño* city have never been more united'.[16] Without consciously invoking Fausto Reinaga's[17] concept of 'two Bolivias' composed of the indigenous majority on one side and the white-*mestizo* élite on the other, Samuel suggested that, 'Currently two Bolivias exist. Therefore the indigenous people and the *alteño* people are never going to share ideas and interests with the current rulers'.[18] On the surface, Gerardo's and Samuel's political understanding of the origins and direction of the popular struggle seem quite different, but throughout the different layers of the social movements in El Alto these differences in inflection and tone – towards indigenous liberation or class-struggle – are negotiated fluidly and smoothly, without hard disjunctures and disagreements. Rather, the struggles for both emancipatory projects are ultimately perceived as one common objective.

---

14. Condori 2005.
15. Bustamante 2005b.
16. Mamani Heredia 2005.
17. Fausto Reinaga was a radical intellectual of indigenous-liberation theory.
18. Mamani Heredia 2005.

The narrative of Henry Merida Gutiérrez, raised in the mining camp of Caracoles in the western *altiplano* and Secretary of Human Rights in COR-El Alto, speaks to this commonality of resistance: 'The class-struggle is joined together with indigenous resistance. It is the same indigenous people who are in the mines, who are everywhere. The class-struggle is a constant struggle as long as there is hunger and misery. While there is an upper class gentleman who eats a $US10 breakfast, and another who doesn't eat breakfast at all. [In this situation] there will always be class-struggle'.[19] Henry's emphasis is on class-struggle, but class-struggle understood as inextricably intertwined with the struggle of the indigenous majority who he rightly sees as constituting the vast majority of the rural and urban working classes and peasantry. My conversations with Carlos Barrera of FEJUVE-El Alto evoked a similar response. On the one hand he told me that, 'real politics is how to recognise the class-struggle, the opposing poles: the bourgeoisie and the proletariat, the antagonism between rich and poor, in permanent struggle'. And yet, he also recognised that, 'The problem here in this country is obviously not only a social problem [of class]....[In Bolivia] alongside the social problem there exists racial discrimination, the exclusion of one group....In October these tendencies existed, but they combined within the social struggles, the social problem, and the problem of exclusion, the racial problem'.[20]

Thus, when the urban Aymara Elizabeth Cuellar, an activist in FEJUVE-El Alto, stresses class in her depiction of the central issues at stake in El Alto, one should not leap to the conclusion that she counterposes class-struggle to indigenous liberation: 'The class-struggle continues. The class-struggle is the struggle of the proletarian class, the class with necessities, the class without work. The struggle of the *alteño* people, of the Bolivian people is that'.[21] The same logic in reverse applies to the FEJUVE-El Alto activist Cipriana Apaza Mamani's emphasis on Aymara resistance and two Bolivias. Her focus on Aymara resistance should not be read as precluding class-struggle: 'Aymara resistance is the people's resistance....We have to keep in mind... there are something like two worlds [in Bolivia], one world where there is everything

---

19. Merida Gutiérrez 2005a.
20. Barrera 2005.
21. Cuellar 2005.

and another world, where we are. We see this quite clearly. We are completely unrecognised [by the dominant culture]. This is what we suffer'.[22]

8.2 Popular cultures of resistance and opposition: revolutionary memories

Just as there is no sense in building strict dichotomies between *indigenous* and *proletarian* in El Alto, it becomes clear that a meaningful understanding of the ideologies at play in the streets during October 2003 and May–June 2005 will have to come to grips with the interpenetration of revolutionary-Marxist and indigenous-liberationist traditions in the multilayered social world of El Alto. The intricacies are perhaps nowhere better unravelled than in the following passage from an interview with Aymara activist Benecio Quispe, in which he explained to me the social content of the October 2003 rebellions:

> I think that it's very difficult to differentiate whether [the political ideologies in the streets during the mobilisations in October] were truly Marxist, or truly *indianista*. What is clear is that here in Santiago Segundo [a neighbourhood in El Alto], there are many relocated ex-miners. But these ex-miners have also not lost all of their cultural roots. That is to say, the miner, the proletariat, here has an indigenous colour. There is no white proletariat. There is therefore something in common in that sense, so that the miner is also Aymara or Quechua. They experience a double exploitation, as much for their ethnic origin as for their position in the labour-market.[23]

In the urgent words of FEJUVE-El Alto activist Brígida Gutiérrez de Medina, the same blending and complexity is made clear: 'In the streets it was a total mix. There were Marxists and there were indigenous, too. There was everyone together because the people's blood was boiling'.[24]

Vidal Choque captures some of this vitality in his descriptions of the spontaneously-formed assemblies of 20 to 30 people in the neighbourhoods of El Alto during the October Gas-War, as the state intensified its repressive response to the popular insurgency:

---

22. Apaza Mamani 2005.
23. Quispe 2005.
24. Gutiérrez de Medina 2005.

There were many small assemblies during the struggle.... They would make decisions on how best to proceed. I participated...and listened to people talk about reviving the memory of *katarismo*; that memory came alive again. Tupaj Katari rose up against the system in [an earlier] historical period because he didn't want to be a part of Bolivia, because this Bolivia is unjust. The *kataristas* [in the 1970s] began to talk about two Bolivias, using the theory of [Fausto] Reinaga.... Today there is so much inequality, in which the poor live one life, and the rich live a different life. The rich have luxury-cars, live in luxurious neighbourhoods. And so we talked a little bit about Marxism or socialism, because this provides a view of a life where there aren't people so well off, but where everything is equal.... We need a social revolt, a government of the people, a government of the Aymara people. They say we need a social revolt, an insurrection.... We began to talk about all of Marxism, indigenism, a little bit of everything.[25]

Choque's narrative elucidates the ways in which the period of intensified mass-mobilisation in El Alto heightened the politicisation of rich ideas around borrowing from past struggles of Tupaj Katari in the late eighteenth century and the *katarista*-indigenous movement of the 1970s, and melding them with the Marxist and socialist theories of the twentieth and twenty-first centuries in the unique social milieu of urban El Alto.

As historian Brooke Larson writes, 'stories of [the Aymara indigenous hero] Tupac Catari's six-month 1781 siege of La Paz still haunt the nightmares of its upper-class inhabitants'.[26] She might have added that, on the other side of the racialised class-divide, these same stories have inspired contemporary indigenous radicals in their urban repertoires of insurrection and rural road-blockading for much of the current decade. Before Katari was drawn and quartered for his role in the 1781 revolt, he warned the colonialists that he would 'return as millions', and the protagonists of recent rebellions see themselves as the embodiment of this return.

My interviews in El Alto and La Paz provide additional evidence to reinforce claims made previously by scholars that indigenous traditions and memories of struggle dating back to the eighteenth century continue to reverberate in the contemporary struggles in El Alto and the rural countryside of the

---

25. Choque 2005d.
26. Larson 2004, p. 204.

altiplano.[27] The names of Tupaj Katari and Bartolina Sisa are invoked regularly in the social-movement bases of Bolivian radicalism today, linking the emancipatory objectives of current battles with those of the distant past. Mercedes Condori Quispe of FEJUVE-El Alto explained to me:

> These struggles have continued for 500 years, with different names and in different forms, because our people resisted, survived. They wanted to exterminate us, but they couldn't do it. Still today we realise that we out number them. That is to say, there are few who have enough to eat, and we are many who are dying of hunger. Those without enough to eat have resisted for years and years....On the day Tupaj Katari was drawn and quartered he said I will die but millions are going to return behind me, and they returned. Now, we are millions. We have kicked out a government [Sánchez de Lozada in October 2003]. We have returned and we are well organised.[28]

What comes to the fore in this passage is the deep interpenetration of race and class, even when the collective memory being used is explicitly associated with anticolonial-indigenous heroes and rebellions. Mercedes clearly considers the indigenous majority, which has survived and resisted against all odds for five hundred years, as equivalent to those who do not have enough to eat. The opponents of indigenous liberation are not simply white-*mestizo* oppressors of the indigenous population on the basis of race, but are also the ruling-class antagonists 'who have enough to eat'.

A second relevant passage in this regard is a section of a presentation by Gualberto Choque – Executive Secretary of the Federación Única Departmental de Trabajadores Campesinos de La Paz – Tupaj Katari (Departmental Federation of Peasant-Workers of La Paz – Tupaj Katari, FUDTCLP-TK) – at a public forum of social movements in downtown La Paz following the forced resignation of president Carlos Mesa in June 2005. Here is a sample of what I recorded:

> We obey the mandate of... our ancestor, the great man Tupaj Katari, and his consort Bartolina Sisa, who also provides us with a vision, a political and ideological line. Katari said [before he was killed by the Spanish colonialists] why are you crying because they are going to kill me? You must not cry

---

27. Hylton and Thomson 2007; Thomson 2002, 2003; Webber 2007.
28. Condori Quispe 2005.

for me. They are only going to kill me, and after me millions and millions are going to return. And where are those millions? Brothers and sisters, we are those millions and it is our responsibility to execute the political line that Tupaj Katari provided to us, so that finally in this country there will exist a true democracy, true justice, and development which will serve our children.[29]

Evidence of the transmission of these collective indigenous memories of resistance in the key sectors of social-movement protagonism – both rural and urban – is abundant in the early twenty-first century.

The interviews suggest that we need to pay more attention to the ways in which the historical memories of the revolutionary Left and the Marxism of the tin-miners, and other militant trade-union struggles of the twentieth century, continue to inform and enrich the collective consciousness of contemporary urban Bolivian movements, often in combination with longstanding indigenous traditions of liberation-politics. Alongside these indigenous traditions, the re-adapted traditions of ex-miners and the revolutionary Left stand out most clearly in the interviews I conducted.

The experiences of Félix Choque are one example of this collective memory of the miners which comes continually into play in the popular movements of the contemporary Bolivian period. 'As the combative mining sector we have always been and always will be in every struggle', he told me. During the period of neoliberalism, Félix said, 'We know that they tried to destroy us, the miners, but we are continuing to struggle once again. I think that, in reality, we are struggling with even greater strength; in spite of all these handicaps that we have acquired, we continue on our feet'. I asked Félix what his personal experience was during the October 2003 Gas-War:

> We are children of mining workers. We were born in the mines. I think that maybe it [October] was like reliving this experience once again, because we were living in 1965 when Barrientos likewise massacred us in the mines. ...October was another experience like this for us. We saw that still today the miners continue on their feet. We are not going to surrender as easily as they thought. October was one more experience in my life. I have

---

29. Choque 2005c.

always been in this constant struggle for better days, for better salaries, and above all for the mining sector.[30]

It should be emphasised, moreover, that the legacies of the revolutionary Left in the political circles of contemporary Bolivian radicalism are not restricted in their influence to the organised trade-union movement. They have also left an indelible imprint on many of the leading individuals in the indigenous movements and the collective consciousness of indigenous organisations in contemporary Bolivia. This finding corresponds closely to historian Greg Grandin's interpretation of twentieth-century history in Guatemala and elsewhere in Latin America. Grandin points out that many scholars, in celebrating the focus of 'new social movements' on 'culture, community, sexual, and gender identities and interests and for moving away from class-analysis', sometimes lose perspective both on the continuing relevance of class and the continuities between 'old' movements of the left and 'new' identity-based movements. 'Despite their inability to incorporate culture and race into their analyses and visions of progress', Grandin contends, 'left political parties and labor organizations in Bolivia, El Salvador, Guatemala, Chile, and Peru, for some examples, drew significant support from rural, often indigenous communities'.[31] And in the current context of many of these same countries, 'movements led by native Americans are the most forceful agents of the kind of democratic socialism that was advanced by the old left'.[32]

We have seen in an earlier chapter that key figures in the re-emergence of indigenous radicalism – such as Felipe Quispe – were intimately informed by revolutionary-Marxist ideas and influenced through their contact with organised Marxist revolutionaries and political groupings. Rather than an isolated case, Quispe's story is reflective of a common experience. To clarify this point further we can pause to reflect on the political trajectory of Félix Patzi, recognised by many as a leading theorist of indigenous liberation and an activist-intellectual in the political circles of El Alto:

30. Choque 2005a.
31. Grandin 2005, pp. 192–3.
32. Grandin 2005, p. 193. Grandin points out, for example, that in Guatemala the contemporary Maya movement is populated with leaders who began their politicisation in the guerrilla-organisations of the 1960s and 1970s. He argues that, 'more than just a direct connection, many of the identities that drive today's social movements were shaped in the crucible of old left politics' (Grandin 2005, p. 193).

I became politically active at the end of high school in a left-wing movement here in Bolivia....We called ourselves the Movimiento de Unión Popular Socialista [Movement of Popular Socialist Unity, MUPS]. It was more of a movement dedicated fundamentally to reflecting theoretically about Marxism and beginning analysis than it was a party. I was educated in this way. However, since that time I have moved a long way [from those views] even though I have not become an *indigenista* or *indianista* either; rather, I took all of the elements of the economic and political structure of the aboriginal peoples [in Bolivia] in order to propose a [new] social model, starting with [the bases of] that society, without denying modernity. That, briefly, characterises my political formation.[33]

8.3 Revolutionary memory and family-traditions of resistance

A final point to make in our reflections on the role of revolutionary memories in forging combined-oppositional consciousness is the way in which Bolivian families sometimes acted as conduits for the transmission of radical ideologies and practices over generations. In her study of women's participation in guerrilla-movements in Nicaragua, El Salvador, Chiapas and Cuba, Karen Kampwirth called this phenomenon, 'family-traditions of resistance'.[34] Kampwirth explains how,

[s]ome women were set on the path toward revolutionary activism by an early childhood experience of resistance to authority. Those experiences ranged from a mother's activism in a union, or a father's membership in an opposition political party, or an uncle's visiting in the middle of the night and talking about the guerrillas when the children were thought to be asleep. That resistance to authority was sometimes as immediate as a girl's battle with her parents for the right to attend school. All those experiences, which I call family-traditions of resistance, planted seeds that would germinate many years later, when the structural, ideological, and political conditions were right.[35]

---

33. Patzi 2005b.
34. Kampwirth 2002, p. 10.
35. Kampwirth 2002, p. 11.

Both the secondary literature on Bolivian popular movements and my own interviews suggest that, while we should be careful always to understand family-traditions of resistance within the larger context of wider political-oppositional traditions of the miners and indigenous radicalism, they nonetheless appear to have had a prominent and independent role of their own in shaping many individuals' self-understanding and political formation. Brief glances at the life-histories of Gonzalo Gozálvez and Vidal Choque help to unveil some of the common ways in which these family-traditions of resistance function.

In a conversation lasting several hours, the journalist and activist Gonzalo Gozálvez charted for me his own biography and the role of his family in inculcating traditions of resistance within him. For Gonzalo, it was clear that this was a very common form of political and ideological transmission in Bolivia. He told me that his grandfather, on his father's side, had been a textile factory-worker in La Paz and played an important role in organising rank-and-file workers during the armed insurrectionary period of the 1952 National Revolution. He helped lead a group of armed workers that took over the military air-base in El Alto during three days of intense conflict. Gonzalo related to me that his grandfather had earlier participated in the Chaco War, and while he 'was not a military person' he nonetheless garnered valuable military experience from that war which he later used in the popular revolt of 1952. Gonzalo's grandparents on his mother's side were rural teachers in the mining zones, and thus his mother was raised in those zones. As a consequence she witnessed multiple massacres of miners and their families when the military intervened to crush strikes and other forms of resistance during the post-1964 era of dictatorships. All of these experiences were transmitted to Gonzalo through family-stories during his childhood: 'With this history in my childhood, [combined with the] poverty and difficult conditions [in which my family lived], I acquired a certain type of sentiment, of self-respect, a pride in who I was'.[36]

This general family-experience provided a political basis for a deeper understanding of political events when he later personally experienced a series of military coups and cycles of repression in the late 1970s and early 1980s, along

---

36. Gozálvez 2005.

with the other families in the *barrios marginales* 'peripheral poor neighbour-hoods' of La Paz: 'I believe this is where one learns how to respect who one is, to respect human life', Gonzalo told me. He managed to get into university where he became politically active in various left-wing groupings, writing and editing for journals and magazines on the Left. From this foundation, he helped form Bolivia Indymedia, and participated in various alternative radio-, internet-, and print-media that played a vital role in keeping activists informed during the height of the uprisings in October 2003.

A similar conversation with Vidal Choque underlines the ways in which family-traditions of resistance help to translate wider political cultures of resistance and opposition into tangible changes in consciousness in the politi-cal formation of individuals. In Choque's case, his father conveyed to him the history of Marxism and *indigenista* traditions of resistance in the Bolivian context. Vidal was born and raised in the Aymara countryside of the western *altiplano*, before moving to El Alto with his family when he was ten. His father was an important figure in the short-lived guerrilla-army, the Ejército Guerril-lero Túpaj Katari (Túpaj Katari Guerrilla-Army, EGTK), in the 1980s and early 1990s. Vidal's father was captured and imprisoned without trial for five years beginning in 1992, along with well-known figures such as Bolivia's current Vice-President Álvaro García Linera, and indigenist radical Felipe Quispe. His father's imprisonment was extremely hard on the family, as Vidal and his six siblings were left to live without a father and only the meagre income of his mother to pull them through. Vidal described this period as a difficult and sad one for himself and his family.

At the same time, it was a period in which Vidal experienced a dramatic personal transformation rooted in political maturation and radicalisation, pri-marily through extended visits to his father in San Pedro, a prison in La Paz. He told me about his long conversations with his father on politics, Marxism, armed struggle, and the history of indigenous ideologies, cultures and reli-gions in the Bolivian setting, as well as elsewhere in Latin America. Vidal's father provided him with books on Marxism and indigenism which proved to have a profound impact on his political formation:

> It was a beautiful thing to begin to read those things.... I began to enjoy this time in the prison with my father. I was reading books on Marxism, indi-genism, Fausto Reinaga, and [Eduardo Galeano's] *The Open Veins of Latin America*. I was beginning to understand more fully what the real problem

was, through books on agrarian reform. I was gaining consciousness. I was saying to myself that I am sitting here with an ex-guerrilla, and I was asking my father questions....I began to make decisions [and become politically involved]....So, when October 2003 arrived I already had a developed ideology. And with a group of youth in October, we began to organise ourselves to go zone to zone in El Alto during the first days of struggle to raise awareness.[37]

Vidal went on to explain to me that, in the opening days of the October Gas-War, his neighbours in El Alto came knocking on his door suggesting that he had a unique responsibility and capacity, as the son of a former guerrilla-leader, to help to organise the *barrios* of El Alto and participate in a leading way in the popular left-indigenous struggles of that period. Vidal's modesty and initial fear led him initially to resist the urging of his neighbours. Eventually, though, he succumbed to their prodding and became extremely involved. His family-led politicisation, based mainly on reading books and story-telling, became much more powerful in the process, as he personally witnessed some of the most brutal massacres of unarmed civilians in El Alto. This was the sort of 'practical, deeply experiential learning' that occurs through participation in massive social upheavals.[38] The experience of participating in the developing forms of popular power from below reinforced his political vision of the necessity of transformative change in Bolivia through mass-based struggle and resistance. At the time of our interview in 2005, Vidal, at twenty years old, was the author of a widely circulated pamphlet on the history and future of Aymara popular struggle in western Bolivia. He was deeply respected as an important component of the youth-contingent of activist-leaders in the movement.

8.4 Anti-imperialism: structures of domination and exploitation

In the popular movements of El Alto and La Paz combined-oppositional consciousness included a multifaceted anti-imperialism. The critique of imperialism was wide-ranging, and identified transnational corporations, the US-state, and international financial institutions such as the World Bank

---

37. Choque 2005d.
38. McNally 2006, p. 376.

and International Monetary Fund (IMF) as the key protagonists of the imperial assault on Bolivia during the neoliberal period. Some interviewees, and,
in particular, current and former miners, linked their analysis of imperialism with a critique of capitalism as a system, identifying conflict between
the domestic bourgeoisie, transnational capital, and imperialism, on the
one hand, and the largely indigenous popular classes, on the other, as the
key fulcrum of contention in contemporary Bolivian society. Other activists linked their anti-imperialism more decisively to racial domination. Some
specifically identified the way in which capitalism is racialised in Bolivia,
rooting itself in the exploitation of the indigenous majority. Ricardo Yujra
Flores, a member of the executive committee of the Federación Sindical de
Trabajadores Mineros de Bolivia (Trade-Union Federation of Bolivian Mine-
Workers, FSTMB), began his reflections on neoliberalism in a typical fashion:
'In 1985, with Supreme Decree 21060, a massive number of workers were fired
in this country....Everything was given away to the transnationals, all the
state-enterprises of this country'.[39] Miguel Zubieta, general secretary of the
FSTMB, perceived the years of neoliberal restructuring as devastating for
the popular economy, initiating as it did the privatisation of natural resources.
Zubieta goes further, however, identifying how the neoliberal project was, in
many respects, an expression of an intentional ruling-class strategy to fragment and weaken the popular-sector infrastructures of class-struggle:

> In 1985 a politics designed by imperialists began... the famous decree 21060
> initiated a politics of depredation. Our natural resources were transferred
> from state-owned enterprises to private transnational corporations. How-
> ever, it didn't stop there. It also initiated a wave of anti-union, anti-working-
> class actions that led to the weakening of union-organisations, and, princi-
> pally, the COB and its spinal column, the FSTMB....Roughly 30,000 miners
> were fired and relocated in the cities, mainly in El Alto, and thousands more
> had to take shelter in the cooperative mining sector....This fact signified
> a great depoliticisation inside the masses and inside the workers' move-
> ment, a decline in ideology which allowed, in the long term, the passage of
> 20 years in which completely predatory policies were imposed.[40]

---

39. Yujra Flores 2005.
40. Zubieta 2005a.

Responding to my question regarding the motivations for the popular struggle to recover natural-resource control from private hands in Bolivia, Mercedes Condori Quispe, of FEJUVE-El Alto, pointed out what seemed to her self-evident and intolerable: 'We saw that it was the transnationals who were governing us'.[41] Many objected to the nefarious networks linking the power of transnational corporations, the US-state, and the Bolivian governments during the neoliberal era. For example, Edgar Ramos, an indigenous journalist and activist based in El Alto explained: 'In Bolivia large transnational business conglomerates have created a network of economic alliances with political sectors and subsidiary companies. These are the sectors that have supported various governments politically and economically....October 2003 was a rejection of managing the state in this way, through foreign oligopolies that have their representatives in this country'.[42] The FEJUVE-El Alto activist Juan Antonio Martela described the consequences of the sort of network that Ramos describes: 'The Bolivian people are tired of our leaders allying with the United States...they provide instructions from there. Some of our rulers pretend to be patriots but...if they were patriots they would defend Bolivia rather than defending transnational corporations'.[43]

A central component of the anti-imperialist politics in question was driven by opposition to transnational-corporate control over natural resources in Bolivian territory, and, in many cases, territory seen as specifically indigenous. Gualberto Choque of FUDTCLP-TK described to a public forum in La Paz how the indigenous peasants of the *altiplano* in the department of La Paz view the situation:

> We understand that we cannot have development in the countryside, we cannot have good education – or any education at all – so long as a few are robbing our money; and these few are transnational corporations who obey foreign capital and, more appropriately, imperialism....We have demanded the recovery of our strategic natural resources that are fundamental to the development of our country.[44]

---

41. Condori Quispe 2005.
42. Ramos 2005.
43. Martela 2005a.
44. Choque 2005c.

Jaime Solares of the COB saw the machinations of imperialism in Bolivia as being part of a larger dynamic of capitalism on a world-scale, during a historical period in which the US exercises massively asymmetrical power over other nations:

> Capital needs to make capital, and to continue with this objective the unipolar imperialist world has the thinking that, first, it has to consolidate itself as the military police force of the world, threatening intervention everywhere. As always, imperialism has expressed itself through the American policy of imposing puppet governments that favour the empire and large corporations that run the financial world. This is a problem. The World Bank and the International Monetary Fund are financial institutional appendices of this international situation. We are fighting against all of this.[45]

The ways in which combined-oppositional consciousness identified structures of domination and exploitation often moved through imperialism to arrive at a critique of capitalism itself. This was particularly common with ex-miners, current mining activists involved in the FSTMB, and within FEJUVE-El Alto. Miguel Zubieta put it most clearly when I asked him to describe the political project of the FSTMB in today's context:

> The project today is the same one that we have been striving for over decades, because it has been decades that the same enemy, capitalism, has been exploiting us. Before it was liberalism, now its neoliberalism, later it will be post-neoliberalism. Whatever nickname you give it, it's the same capitalism. It means to extract the riches of countries, to concentrate power in the hands of a few, and to exploit the worker, providing the lowest minimum-wage possible, without conditions of industrial or social security. This has been the same for decades.[46]

Julio Pabón Chávez, secretary of economic development in FEJUVE-El Alto and a former factory-worker in La Paz who migrated to El Alto, also conveyed a distinctly Marxist analysis of the permanent class-struggle between the proletariat and the bourgeoisie within Bolivian capitalism:

---

45. Solares 2005b.
46. Zubieta 2005b.

We no longer want to submit ourselves to the levels of abuse that we have suffered. The bourgeoisie has always dominated the impoverished classes; those who have nothing are those who have been most abused. We have had to sacrifice ourselves in order to survive. On the other hand, those who have so much, the large capitalists, they constantly suck more out of us, make us work, make us bend over backwards just to survive; and then they take the profits.[47]

The words of Social-Security Secretary of the COB, Jorge Solares Barrientos, are perhaps the most eloquent summary of the multifaceted anti-imperialism I have been describing. Here is how Solares Barrientos encapsulates the systemic critique:

Since 1985, a politics of neoliberalism, of the free market, was established. The state shrunk in terms of its share in the economy, and in relation to the share of private corporations, maybe with the idea that these private corporations were going to provide solutions for workers and human beings. It was going to generate jobs, development, industries, etc. But it didn't turn out like that. Just the opposite, neoliberal policies failed in our country because since 1985 we gave away our strategic enterprises to private corporations. There is more unemployment, hunger, poverty, prostitution, delinquency and many of the Bolivian industries have been shut down.... The politics of neoliberalism is the giving away of our natural resources, our highways, our communications [sector], our mining industry, our oil, etc. in a way that favoured, and continues to favour, transnationals rather than Bolivians. This government and the governments in the past followed this politics through instructions from international organisations, and ... American imperialism. But the model failed, not only in Bolivia but in Latin America as a whole. We see social organisations in Ecuador, Argentina, and Venzuela have been resisting as well, fighting to improve their living conditions.[48]

---

47. Pabón Chávez 2005a.
48. Solares Barrientos 2005.

8.5 Natural resources are not private property

A common thematic running throughout the interviews was a critique of the privatisation of natural resources, and hydrocarbons and water in particular. This critique seems to have synthesised various elements of combined-oppositional consciousness – indigenous and class-awareness, popular cultures of resistance, revolutionary memories of past struggles, and anti-imperialism – into a coherent focus. Álvaro García Linera nicely articulates the centrality of decommodifying water in forging left-indigenous movements in the early twenty-first century. He begins his recollection with a description of processes of privatisation within the general ideological and political context of the neoliberal period:

> The theme of water has been a detonating theme of social mobilisation. In the 1980s and 1990s Bolivia suffered [through] processes of privatisation of public resources. [These processes unfolded] in the middle of a crisis of left thought, the cooptation of indigenous leaders by the state, and a hunger for modernisation, privatisation and the way of the free-market.... There was a cultural and ideological hegemony in Bolivia, of liberalisation and modernisation.[49]

For García Linera, fissures started to appear in the neoliberal edifice as it became clearer to the bulk of the population just how few of the many grand promises made by various governments since 1985 had come to fruition. He describes the slow proliferation of ill-will toward the neoliberal model during the late 1990s. The move to privatise water in Cochabamba proved to be the spark that ignited this general discontent into a prolonged cycle of left-indigenous revolt:

> ... the detonator of the mobilisation that would convert this malaise into collective action was when the state wanted to begin privatising non-state public resources such as water. Water in the Bolivian countryside is a non-state public resource, with systems of traditional administration going back 700, 800, 900 years. The water from the rivers, lakes, and summits, are regulated by very complicated communal systems.... In 1999, the intent [of the state

---

49. García Linera 2005a.

and the World Bank] was to privatise [these communal systems] through the granting of private concessions.[50]

In addition to rural areas, non-state communal governance of water is also practiced in various poor-urban communities.[51] In the countryside and poor-urban neighbourhoods alike, these communal systems of administration are central material facets in the reproduction of these communities. Inextricably tied to this material basis of reproduction are the cultural traditions of indigenous communities and the innumerable ways in which water, like land and territory, lends meaning to the past and present:

> Land and water are basic, fundamental elements of the reproduction of peasant-communities. There is a memory of their [community-] histories, their dead, and their future [connected to the communal self-governance of water and land]. When [water] started to be privatised it produced some of the articulations of social mobilisation that caused the Water-War in Cochabamba in 2000.[52]

García Linera's narrative also reflects clearly the way in which race and class were conjoined in popular struggles rooted in the sinews of everyday necessities. The defence of the communal nature of water, and everyone's basic human right to it, facilitated the construction of alliances between various sectors of the rural and urban working classes and oppressed indigenous majority:

> Water played a role in articulating indigenous and peasant rural forces, and forces from the urban periphery – and also the urban centre in the case of Cochabamba.... [The process of struggle] to defend this resource became a unifying, mobilising, and politicising factor in local structures of daily life... extending the political horizons of society to indigenous, popular, and urban [social forces].[53]

The mobilisations against the privatisation of water in Cochabamba were repeated on a smaller scale in January 2005 in the city of El Alto. The latter conflict saw the urban-indigenous working classes confront the private

---

50. García Linera 2005a.
51. Spronk 2007b, p. 17.
52. García Linera 2005a.
53. García Linera 2005a.

consortium Aguas del Illimani – controlled by the French company Suez – which won a private concession to administer the local water-supply in 1997. A basic grievance animating the protest was the fact that over 200,000 *alteños* did not have access to potable-water or sewage-systems because, while living in El Alto, they lived outside the 'service-area' that Aguas del Illimani was willing to administer. Moreover, an additional 70,000 residents who lived within the parameters of the service-area could not afford the connection-fees and therefore were also prohibited from accessing the available services.[54]

The collective fight for this basic service was soon informed by a politics which challenged not simply the notion of access to water-services, but the entire idea that water could ever be justly commodified, could function as a means for profit-making, just another good to be bought and sold. Activists in El Alto emphasised how water is integral to life itself. The movement against its privatisation was linked again to indigenous traditions of communal governance of water, to the struggle to reassert social control over all natural resources in Bolivia, and, finally, to the more generalised demand to end the domination by transnational corporations of more and more basic elements of social life through processes of accelerated commodification under neoliberal capitalism.

Activists repeatedly reminded me of the importance of water as a basic human right, and its centrality to the wider range of left-indigenous mobilisation in 2005.[55] Henry Merida Gutiérrez, Secretary of Human Rights of the Central Obrera Regional de El Alto (Regional Workers' Central of El Alto, COR-El Alto), described the fight to reverse the commodification of water and other natural resources as a 'national priority'.[56] Samuel Mamani Heredia, on the executive committee of FEJUVE-El Alto, stressed the ways in which the popular mobilisation for access to potable-water and sewage-systems in El Alto was connected to resistance against the exploitation of Bolivian natural resources by transnational corporations.[57] His sentiments were echoed by another FEJUVE-El Alto activist Cipriana Apaza Mamani: 'How long must we suffer, must we be dominated by transnationals?'[58] Likewise, the vice-

---

54. Pabón Chávez 2005a; Spronk 2007b, pp. 18–20.
55. Martela 2005b.
56. Merida Gutiérrez 2005b.
57. Mamani Heredia 2005.
58. Apaza Mamani 2005.

president of one of El Alto's neighbourhood-councils, Alfredo Yujra Fernández, pointed out that underlying the popular indignation of the movement against privatised water in El Alto was the essential and lamentable fact that 'transnationals continue to exploit our natural resources' while so many Bolivians are left without the essential services necessary for a dignified life.[59]

Some interviewees also argued that the battle for social control of water in El Alto was emblematic of indigenous relations with all natural resources. Benecio Quispe Gutiérrez, an Aymara intellectual and activist living in El Alto, explained:

> In the Aymara culture water is life; it cannot enter our minds that one could use it commercially.... The collective use of water is pitted against the project to privatise water. Water is life and cannot be privatised. They cannot privatise water, llamas, sheep, cows, and trees. We need them all.[60]

Journalist and activist Luis A. Gómez complements this view when he discusses the way in which the many indigenous-peasant activists he has interviewed in the rural provinces of La Paz understand the *pachamama*, or mother-earth, and by extension the way in which natural resources ought to be treated:

> The *pachamama* is the mother from which we come [they say]. It's what sustains us and everything around us. It is not a thing that we pour water on and then things grow out of; we work with her, and she gives back to us; that is the notion. The cosmo-vision of the universe begins from there. They say that it's clear that the *pachamama* is beneath what we see, and everything that is above us; that is, everything that exists in our habitat. We don't live separately [from all of this]....[The *pachamama*] is the mother who gives to us, and you can't exploit her. The *pachamama* punishes such exploitation.[61]

Informed both by urban and rural indigenous and working-class traditions of communal self-governance of water-systems, the struggle against the commodification of water in El Alto was an essential component of a rising consciousness among the popular classes and oppressed indigenous peoples of the way in which capitalism dispossesses them of their collective rights and

---

59. Yujra Fernández 2005.
60. Quispe Gutiérrez 2005.
61. Gómez 2005.

social wealth. Through their organised resistance they began to imagine what it would be like to reassert communal control over natural resources:

> I think that since the Water-War [in 2000] a change occurred, a change that was later consolidated in the October Gas-War [in 2003]. A feeling emerged that we are the owners of something. Capitalism exists as a system in places where the people don't feel like they are the owners of anything, and above all that they are the owners of the general social wealth.... This changed in October. The people began to feel like they were owners of a few things: their dignity and the relationships between people; and they even began dreaming of being owners of the natural resources.[62]

If the celebrated inauguration of Bolvia's most recent insurrectionary cycle was the Cochabamba Water-War, the Gas-Wars of October 2003 and May–June 2005 were its apogee. The latter episodes of contention saw the collective struggles against the commodification of natural resources extend from water into a much wider framework, at the heart of which was the demand to re-nationalise hydrocarbons (natural gas and oil) and to assume social, democratic control of the industry. The nationalisation-demand was informed by a number of different threads of collective memories of popular struggle in Bolivian history and of visions for a better future based on the just development of the country's natural resources.

One dominant motif in the narratives of activists around the question of recovering popular control of natural gas was their collective understanding of the stark injustice thrown up by the paradox of Bolivia's tremendous resource-wealth juxtaposed with the impoverishment of the majority of its population. For most of the interviewees, this paradox can be explained by the systematic exploitation of Bolivia's natural resources and its indigenous labourers by centuries of colonial and imperial domination by outside powers. Ending this brutal cycle was therefore a principal basis for the centrality of natural gas in activist understandings of the popular struggle. Pablo Solón's explanation reflected the common views of many:

> Bolivia is a country that was very rich in natural resources and yet was always in the end left very poor. Potosí was long ago a splendorous city of gold. Today, however, it is an extremely poor city. This also happened

---

62. Gosálvez 2005.

with silver. Then came the tin era, and the results were the same. There were Bolivians like Patino, who was one of the 10 richest men in the world, and at the same time Bolivia was very far from getting out of poverty. So [behind the October 2003 revolt] was the vision of the people to recover and nationalise hydrocarbons, natural gas; to recover the possibility of using this resource for the benefit of the nation. It was an action to avoid what occurred before.[63]

Moreover, Solón suggests, the activists drew on historical examples that illustrated that nationalisation had been possible in the past and could work again in the current setting:

In Bolivian history there were two nationalisations of hydrocarbons. One in 1936 after the Chaco War, and the other in 1969. So it was not only in the imaginations of the people, in a negative sense that what happened before must not occur again. There was also this experience of what opportunities were made possible when these resources were nationalised in the past. Therefore, this discourse and this demand gripped people very rapidly because it was rooted very profoundly in history.[64]

'What happened in our mine, Cerro Rico in Potosí', FEJUVE-El Alto activist Jorge Mendoza Mamani asked me rhetorically, 'where we had so much wealth, mostly silver?' For Jorge and others the answer was self-evident: 'Bolivia would not be so poor if the Spanish and other foreign powers like the United States had not looted' the country.[65]

Luciano Suárez, an ex-miner and president of the neighbourhood-council of District 8 in El Alto, echoed the sentiments of Jorge. For Luciano, the uprisings in 2003 and 2005 were a unique opportunity to change the trajectory of the country which had been exploited and abused by the Spanish, British, and American imperialists over several centuries:

We cannot let happen what happened with tin and with silver. At this moment in Oruro and Potosí we have mountains that have been opened up and drilled, leaving behind various mines. But where did all that money go that the deposits of these mines produced? It went outside the country. We

---

63. Solón 2005.
64. Solón 2005.
65. Mendoza Mamani 2005.

remember that our history began with the arrival of the Spanish who took the riches that we had, and finished with the British and then the Americans doing the same. We haven't gained anything. We don't want this to occur with gas. We want gas … to improve conditions in health, education, and the infrastructure of the country.[66]

Others, such as Benecio Quispe, shared this overarching critique, but added emphasis to the particular exploitation of indigenous people in this process of colonial extraction of natural resources, and how indigenous reawakening in the form of contemporary mass-movements was rooted in a collective understanding of this history:

Bolivia has been one of the countries with the most natural resources, above all with mining in the *altiplano*. But it hasn't benefited in any respect from these natural riches; natural resources have benefited other countries, other people, corporations … not Bolivia, and even less the indigenous population. In this context the Aymara, Quechua, and Guaraní peoples have become conscious of the central importance of their natural resources, and above all of natural gas. Many, perhaps, have also exaggerated its potential, pinning their hopes on it as though it is going to be a grand solution; clearly it won't be. But it will mean an improvement in the revenues of the state. So, it played an important role in bringing together different people together, in creating a consciousness of what is ours.[67]

Another historical component to the struggle for social control over natural gas came to light in the way in which several activists understood the privatisation of hydrocarbons in the late 1990s as a comprehensive betrayal of the memory of the mostly indigenous martyrs of Bolivia's Chaco War against Paraguay between 1932 and 1935. So, for example, according to FEJUVE-El Alto activist Mercedes Condori Quispe, in October 2003, 'when the people saw that their brothers were asking for something that had been asked for many years ago, by our grandparents during the Chaco War, to protect our hydrocarbons, the people once again responded to this demand'.[68] García Linera helps to situate this collective memory in more detail:

---

66. Suárez 2005.
67. Quispe 2005.
68. Condori Quispe 2005.

[The movement for the recovery of] hydrocarbons articulated... the historical memory...of the Indians who died in the Chaco War defending the petroleum that was supposedly in [the department of] Tarija. 50,000 people died in this war; and at that time we had a country of about 1.5 or 2 million people. 50,000 is a lot of people! A lot! And the majority of the dead were Indians....They died for petroleum – that turned out not to be there – but they went to die. And there's not a peasant family in El Alto or the *altiplano* that doesn't have a dead or mutilated grandfather, or a survivor of the Chaco War. This is important, very important. One starts to see the stories of contemporary adolescents who weren't in the Chaco War but who remember that their father went, that their grandfather went.[69]

The battles around natural gas and other natural resources in the uprisings based in El Alto and La Paz, then, were intimately connected to the historical memories of colonial exploitation of Bolivia's natural resources and the collective memories of the indigenous martyrs of the Chaco War. On these foundations, the left-indigenous movements in the Gas-Wars began to articulate a critique of the privatisation of natural gas as part of the more general neoliberal politico-economic model, and started to formulate a collective notion that these natural resources were the common property of Bolivia's popular classes and indigenous majority, rather than the private property of transnational corporations. Finally, the left-indigenous movements grounded these critiques in conceptualisations of how natural-gas endowments might contribute to building a socioeconomic system rooted in justice and fairness, rather than exploitation, poverty, and inequality.

Julio Pabón Chávez, Secretary of Economic Development of FEJUVE-El Alto, expressed the anger of many at the privatisation of the state-owned natural-gas and oil-enterprise, YPFB, for what they saw as next-to-nothing: 'FEJUVE's proposal is the nationalisation of all natural resources, the few that remain, because the most precious of our natural resources have been looted from our country for the price of a dead chicken. Natural gas is the last resource that remains'.[70] Elizabeth Cuellar agreed with Julio, and articulated the widely held view that the natural resources of Bolivia – and, in particular,

---

69. García Linera 2005a.
70. Pabón Chávez 2005b.

natural gas – are the collective common property of Bolivians, rather than commodities to be exploited for profit by foreign transnationals:

> Everyone knows that our country has this wealth, and is giving away our natural resources to foreigners.... This is why we have to rise up, to reclaim our gas. It is the last resource that we have, because they have exploited almost everything. Mining has been entirely exploited. Our last resource is natural gas, and so we have had to rise up.[71]

Emblematic of many people's expectations relating to the nationalisation of natural gas, Remigio Condori, an activist in COR-El Alto, argued that the increases in state-revenue could be reinvested in social areas like education and health to the collective benefit of all: 'Nationalise gas so that the revenue can be used to help the sectors of society most in need, with education and health; so that the revenue can be reinvested to boost the economy'.[72] Battles for the decommodification of these resources helped to congeal working-class and indigenous identities in common fronts with shared objectives and visions of change.

8.6   Freedom-dreams

Taking seriously the notion that the best social movements can 'enable us to imagine a new society', I asked activists in the popular movements of the Bolivian indigenous Left what kind of future they were struggling for, what kind of Bolivia they hoped to construct through their mass-mobilisations.[73] What their responses made clear to me was that at the height of popular contention in 2003 and 2005 left-indigenous emancipatory visions increasingly acquired a revolutionary character. These freedom-dreams constitute the last element of combined-oppositional consciousness. In my view, the passages below point to a widely-held collective imagination of a future of socialism and indigenous liberation. In their freedom-dreams, activists tended to think of these broad projects with reference to different elements of emancipation, from the reigning social relations of domination, oppression, and exploitation.

---

71. Cuellar 2005.
72. Condori 2005.
73. Kelley 2002, p. 9.

One way to conceptualise their responses is to categorise them along four thematic axes that arose most frequently in the interviews.

8.6.1 *A future of equality without social classes*

What was most striking in the freedom-dreams of activists was their common emphasis on the necessity of building a more egalitarian society, free of poverty and class-exploitation. 'Definitely what we want is equality in our country', FEJUVE-El Alto activist Rafael Mamani explained to me: 'In the current situation what happens is that the rich get richer while the poor get poorer each year. Poverty increases in our country and the rich double and triple their wealth every year'.[74] Similarly, this is how Carlos Rojas, another FEJUVE activist, imagined liberation:

> The people must be liberated from so much oppression that has existed for so long.... Liberation will be when in some manner there is no more social discrimination, and when there is not a situation where a few have wealth and others have nothing. I believe that equality, an equal distribution of wealth can solve this fundamental problem.[75]

Rodolfo Mancilla, sitting under a picture of Ché, also spoke to me of the issue of equality when he was describing the vision of the popular struggle in El Alto:

> Ché sought equality between classes, that everyone should have food, and today we as leaders see that there needs to be this kind of equality between classes, and that everyone can eat, have the right to a place to live. None of these things exist in this country. The poorest do not have any rights.[76]

The Secretary of Housing for FSTMB, Félix Choque, also an ex-miner and twenty-year resident of El Alto, was representative of the great majority of interviewees when he described the injustice of inequality based on social class in the current Bolivian context:

> There should be equality, equality of social classes. There shouldn't be some who have more and others who have less, because everyone has capacity. As the poor we have always been marginalised, and I believe that through

---

74. Mamani 2005c.
75. Rojas 2005.
76. Mancilla 2005.

struggle we are going to continue forward. I think that in the not too distant future the mine-workers, the factory-workers, the popular sectors, we are going to arrive in government.[77]

Choque explained that the left-indigenous movements quite simply, 'want a better Bolivia, a Bolivia with equality, where there is no discrimination, no poverty'.[78]

8.6.2   *Indigenous liberation: a future free of racism*

When I asked Elizabeth Cuellar, an activist in FEJUVE-El Alto, what sort of Bolivia she was fighting for, she began her multidimensional response with an emphasis on eliminating discrimination of the indigenous majority, and then tied that issue to the imperial domination of transnational corporations and the necessity of popular sovereignty for Bolivia:

> For a better Bolivia, obviously. A Bolivia that is free of discrimination, free of these huge abusive transnationals that come here only to squeeze out Bolivian blood. A sovereign and free Bolivia; a Bolivia free of corruption for our children, so that we leave behind a better future for our children and grandchildren.[79]

One of the most powerful expressions of revolutionary-indigenous vision came from Gualberto Choque, the principal leader of the mostly-Aymara peasants of the department of La Paz in 2005. In his address to a public forum of social activists and trade-unionists gathered at the public university in downtown La Paz in early July 2005, he stressed that indigenous liberation could only come through revolution, and that, moreover, this revolution would have to based on unity with all the oppressed and exploited and extend regionally throughout Latin America, and, perhaps, even the world:

> In the countryside we understand that change is going to come, change understood as a revolution. We have waited for many years for change to come from the city to the countryside. But the only things from the city that have come to the countryside are coup d'états, deceit, lies, falsities, drink, alcoholism, and immorality. But it's not the fault of you here, it's the system's

---

77. Choque 2005a.
78. Choque 2005a.
79. Cuellar 2005.

fault. It is the guilty party.... Revolution is now coming from the country-side to the city.... We are talking about what we call Latin America, and why not the whole world? Brothers and sisters, we must be united. We are speaking of a politics of unity, not one of hate and revanchism. We are not talking about settling things for ourselves, and forgetting about everyone else. No, brothers and sisters, to finish, and excuse me if I'm getting emotional, I want to say that we have a responsibility to build the revolution...so that we can govern ourselves free of opportunists, Yankee imperialism, and imperialism that comes from wherever it might come.[80]

Benecio Quispe's thoughts on indigenous emancipation nicely complement Gualberto's. Benecio related to me the centrality of the *ayllu* traditional-communitarian structure in the countryside as a basis for extending communitarian anticapitalism and indigenous liberation throughout the country. Further, for Benecio, authentic indigenous liberation is explicitly opposed to the simplistic and hollow idea of simply filling liberal structures with indigenous individuals to replace the white-*mestizo* élite of today:

> We have to build a non-liberal, non-capitalist society in which racism can disappear. From the structures of the *ayllu* we have built an economic and social model.... In political terms I think it's also possible to apply the communal model of the *ayllu*, where the collectivity decides and the representative is restricted to obeying, coordinating, channeling, and executing the decision of the collectivity organised in assembly. This is how the *ayllu* functions today in Bolivia.... We would be breaking with racism, so that people have to value themselves as people.... I want to make one thing clearer. We are not talking about a system in which the Indians replace the *q'aras* [the white-*mestizo* élite]. Now there are exclusively *q'aras* as presidents, ministers, military leaders. We are not talking about replacing these with Indians, simply putting the Indians on top.... To substitute the *q'aras* with Indians would...not change anything. The framework would continue, as we would have only changed its colour. What we are talking about replacing is the liberal capitalist model with another model that refuses that social structure.[81]

---

80. Choque 2005c.
81. Quispe 2005.

Quispe's thinking on these matters best reflects the ways in which many of the freedom-dreams encapsulated in the consciousness of combined liberation were rooted in examples of actually existing social struggles and rival centres of incipient popular power set up in opposition to the capitalist state in the countryside and cities of Bolivia. In Quispe's case, the indigenous *ayllus* of the rural *altiplano*, and the neighbourhood-councils of El Alto, are seen as prefigurative, concrete foundations for a free society of the future.

8.6.3 *Dignity, social justice, and basic necessities*

'We are also human beings', German Mamani told me, 'We want to live with dignity'.[82] Part of that dignity, that so many interviewees demanded, was access to basic social services, essential human rights that all human beings deserve: 'We have to have our basic services: potable water and sewage systems'.[83] Others included the right to employment, 'so that in the future our children will have employment, so that they don't have to beg'.[84] In the offices of FEJUVE in central El Alto, Juan Anotnio Martela encouraged me to travel through the various neighbourhoods of El Alto, and particularly into the poorest most marginal sectors of the shantytown's periphery: 'You can go and see how there is no water, no electricity, no transportation. For these reasons the people continue to mobilise'.[85] Nestor Salinas, an activist whose brother was killed by state-forces in the October 2003 uprising, said that in Bolivia the movements are struggling so that, 'at a minimum [people] will have bread to eat each day, water to drink; at a minimum, they will have electricity....We have to help these people grow so that these people will have what they need. That is the social power I am talking about'.[86]

Alicia Claure of FEJUVE-El Alto articulated most clearly the multiple aspects of dignity, social justice, and basic necessities that so many *alteños* stressed to me were at the centre of popular struggle and their visions of a better future:

---

82. Mamani 2005b.
83. Mamani 2005b.
84. Martela 2005b.
85. Martela 2005b.
86. Salinas 2005.

> We are struggling for change, a just life, with work, sources of employment, health-care, education, housing; where we will be able to lead a calm life; where we will have some income. It will not be something miraculous. At a minimum, we want to limit the hunger of our children, so that we will no longer be able to see hunger, no beggars in the street. We want, at a minimum, a life with dignity, because the Political Constitution of the State says we have the right to one, no? The right to education and housing. But they are not fulfilling these rights.... We want a calm and dignified life with work, where our children can study, where they will be able to work, and be able to live with dignity.[87]

What most infuriated activists like Rafael Mamani was the crassness of right-wing politicians and the mainstream-newspapers when they repeatedly referred to protesters as irrational. For Rafael, it was dumbfounding that élites could fail to recognise the obvious absence of basic services for the poor in Bolivia and the right of the poor to collectively demand those basic necessities and a dignified life:

> ... many people say that we're supposedly crazy, that we have been possessed, that we must be getting paid [to protest]. We're not crazy or possessed, it's simply that poor people have needs. A deputy [in the Congress] does not have needs. His family is made up of business-people...but poor people who are in the streets live by the day and sometimes don't have bread to bring home. Some have only 5 or 10 bolivianos [daily]. Imagine that people are trying to live off this. It's extremely painful, we feel it in our hearts, the way these wealthy men (señores) have taken advantage of our country and our people.[88]

Carlos Rojas shared Rafael's disbelief in the face of a society that treats animals better than the indigenous majority. In light of this, Rojas argued, there is a need for 'a Bolivia where, at least, there is bread, employment, where everyone has a roof over their heads. We want to build this Bolivia. We don't want a Bolivia where a few in the oligarchy live well, eat well, enjoy

---

87. Claure 2005.
88. Mamani 2005c.

life, have mansions... so that even their dogs...eat better than us. We don't want that Bolivia'.[89]

8.6.4 Socialist and indigenous-liberationist democracy

'In October the people called for the funeral of imperialism, the burial of the capitalist system', Remigio Condori suggested to me: 'The people of El Alto want to govern themselves. What does self-government look like?....Our leaders will be our worker- and indigenous brothers....[Together we will] take power'.[90] Remigio's interpretation of the scope and vision of October were widely shared among social-movement and trade-union activists, as will be evidenced in part from passages below. At a very basic level, liberal-capitalist democracy was perceived to have profoundly underperformed in the Bolivian context. The activists tended to think of democracy in a much more profound sense, which included the elimination of class-exploitation and inequality and involved popular democratic control of workers, peasants, and the indigenous majority over all aspects of their lives through collective co-operation and deliberation.

Jorge Mendoza Mamani, a FEJUVE-El Alto activist, said: 'We want Bolivia to be free and democratic...there won't be rich and poor, with the poor becoming poorer. What we want is equality, because we all want to live in peace, in a democratic country with equality. This is what we are searching for'.[91] Edgar Patana, COR-El Alto's executive secretary, explained what was wrong with democracy as it was conceived by the neoliberal governments in power since the mid-1980s:

> Bolivia is a poor country, and as a poor country we simply ask that our government expresses solidarity with the Bolivian population. Under dictatorial governments of the past in the first instance we demanded democracy. Unfortunately, this democracy has not benefited in any way the Bolivian people. Now we are living with this corrupt democracy, in which a few families...continue in power....There is super-exploitation of work-hours and terrible poverty here in the city of El Alto. We sincerely are not able to

---

89. Rojas 2005.
90. Condori 2005.
91. Mendoza Mamani 2005.

see how we are supposed to be able to survive here. We want better health-care. There are no medical centres, only a third-rate hospital. In the city of El Alto there is nothing. Therefore we want better salaries, health-care, and education.[92]

On this view, health-care, education, equality, and living salaries are not separate from democracy, but rather integral to its authenticity.

For many of the activists I spoke to, authentic democracy and indigenous liberation were seen as incompatible with capitalism. This is evident in the following passage from Miguel Zubieta, for example, in which he argues that there will never be social peace and stability until the poor govern directly. Necessarily, for Zubieta, that will require the overthrow of capitalism:

[We are fighting for] a system in which the poor govern our country.... We don't want to see our children dying in the countryside because of the absence of medical attention; not attending schools because they have no money; fainting in classes because they haven't had sufficient food.... We want another system in which the majority is attended to with the riches that are ours. We want that, because if, to the contrary, that does not exist there will never be peace. The very Bible says that peace is the fruit of justice, and if there is no social justice there is not going to be peace. This is the objective. I believe that Christ also struggled for that; and I don't know if Christ was a communist, but he also talked of these things. That is what we want, because capitalism is very wicked, perverse, bloodthirsty, inhuman, and terrorist.[93]

For Juan Cardoso Pacheco, general secretary of the FSTMB, what is required is, 'a socialism where there is justice and equality so that all Bolivians feel that they are owners of their own destiny'.[94] Socialism, as Jorge Solares Barrientos, Secretary of Social Security in the COB, explains, is a system without oppressors and oppressed:

The people are seeking a country that is governed by the poor, in which the wealth that is created by the working people is redistributed for the improvement of living conditions for the workers and their families... that there is social justice. The position of the COB and its unions, which includes

---

92. Patana 2005.
93. Zubieta 2005a.
94. Cardozo Pacheco 2005.

taking into account the aboriginal indigenous peoples of Bolivia, is that we must arrive at socialism in this country, a system, naturally, which is not managed by oppressors. There would be no oppressors, no oppressed. This is what the Bolivian Workers Central is seeking.[95]

The idea that socialism was the only possible way out of the morass of injustices extended, in some cases, well into mainstream-institutions of El Alto, such as the office of the human-rights ombudsman. One high-ranking employee told me the following:

> I think the hope has always been for better living conditions: that there would be work; that my child can go to school and won't have to shine shoes in the morning or at night. The people live full of hopes. They want a different life, they want bread, work. The only way of resolving the situation is to organise a revolutionary party.... The majority of people work more than 14 hours a day.... This causes conflict within families. The lack of sufficient food, the insecurity of families, the general insecurity felt by everyone, that there is no bread, no work, and no food. So we are seeking a better system.... I believe that if there was leadership and clear ideas, I believe that we could build a Marxist social model, a socialist society. This would solve the problems of the majority of the population. And it is possible to do. October [2003] has shown us this. It's one of the other lessons of October.[96]

Socialist democracy for many meant participatory forms of collective popular organisation from below and the establishment of power directly in the hands of the oppressed and exploited themselves: '... the proletarian class, the peasantry, and the miners...these sectors will be those who govern in parliament'.[97] Vidal Choque came to the same conclusion based on his experiences growing up in the *altiplano* and El Alto:

> I learned to see...that the country could be free and satisfy the needs of the oppressed people....I saw so much poverty, unemployment. I see families who live on one piece of bread for the day, or three pieces of bread shared between a family of ten. So, I saw this reality and it led to the idea that this

---

95. Solares Barrientos 2005.
96. Anonymous 2005.
97. Calcina 2005.

country must be governed by the workers, by the indigenous, by the impoverished class, so that the basic necessities of these people will be met.[98]

According to Félix Patzi, the experiments in direct-assemblyist democracy and collective self-governance during the popular rebellions in El Alto can be read, in some ways, as prefigurative formations of how an alternative society based on multifaceted liberation might be structured:

> The most fundamental aspect of the movement in October was that it began to design a project of an alternative society, not a society exclusively for the indigenous, not a social protest exclusively of the indigenous, but rather a project for society in its entirety.... They practiced it [in October], they didn't simply talk about it, in the decisions to blockade, and in the decisions to negotiate. The leaders did not play an important role. It was the grassroots who began to decide on the actions, form information-groups and assemblies. From one district a representative would go by bicycle to another to inform them and read out the resolutions of the assembly. This was how decisions were made in a collective manner. The struggle itself showed clearly a little bit of how a political communitarian system would work.[99]

What stands out through all the narratives of social activists living and struggling in El Alto and La Paz, is the multi-pronged nature of their freedom-dreams. They dream of socialist emancipation, and are inspired by struggles elsewhere in Latin America. They dream of equality, the abolishment of poverty, and the construction of a society free from class-exploitation. Inextricably bound up with their visions rooted in class-struggle, are their dreams of a society without racism, without the brutal racist oppression of the indigenous-proletarian and peasant-majority. The freedom-dreams at the root of the recent struggles sought elementary dignity and social justice. To achieve these ends, they rooted their dreams in concepts of socialist and indigenous-liberationist democracy. More than simply dreams, as Patzi's observations suggest, the consciousness of combined liberation grew out of the actually existing social struggles of Bolivia's left-indigenous insurrectionary epoch, and the experiences of popular democratic power that arose as an essential part of each explosive, rebellious episode.

---

98. Choque 2005d.
99. Patzi 2005b.

Conclusion

The combined-oppositional consciousness that this chapter has sought to analyse is best conceived as the sum of five interrelated components. First, the activists of the principal social-movement organisations and trade-unions – the infrastructure of class-struggle – in El Alto and La Paz showed a remarkably mixed consciousness regarding indigenous and class-identities. In El Alto, particularly, this combination expressed itself in the notion of *vecino*, a fundamental melding of worker- and urban-indigenous consciousness. Linked to this notion, too, was the central importance of popular power as expressed through the rank-and-file activists of El Alto during the Gas-War, the popular power of *los vecinos*. Throughout El Alto, La Paz, and the countryside of the western *altiplano*, depicting race and class as social relations hermetically sealed off from one another would be profoundly misleading. In the daily activities of social life, and in the most intense moments of popular mobilisation, indigenous and worker-realities are inextricably tied to one another.

Second, the popular cultures of resistance and opposition evident in the Gas-Wars of 2003 and 2005 exhibit the profound interpenetration of revolutionary-Marxist and indigenous-liberationist traditions adapted and renovated to fit the novel contexts of the twenty-first century. Activists rely on the revolutionary memories of past rebellions, heroes, and traditions of insurrection, and frequently retain these memories through family-traditions of resistance.

Third, combined-oppositional consciousness contains within it a multifaceted critique of imperialism. This opposition to structures of domination and resistance is frequently incorporated into resistance against capitalism as a system of exploitation, and racism as a system of oppression.

Fourth, a nuanced and forceful opposition to the privatisation of hydrocarbons and water provided a focus within combined-oppositional consciousness for the expression of its other related elements.

Fifth, and finally, combined-oppositional consciousness was expressed in a forward-looking dimension through the elaborate freedom-dreams of activists. These tended to turn on the thematic lines of equality, the end of poverty, and the abolition of social classes; a future free of racism; dignity, social justice, and basic necessities; and socialist and indigenous-liberationist democracy.

Chapter Nine

Conclusion: Bolivia, Venezuela, and the Latin-American Left

The central thesis of this book is that the specific combination of elaborate infrastructures of class-struggle and social-movement unionism, historical traditions of indigenous and working-class radicalism, combined-oppositional consciousness, and fierce but insufficient state-repression, explain the depth, breadth, and radical character of recent left-indigenous mobilisations in Bolivia. This argument runs against the main presuppositions of the prevailing liberal-institutionalist understanding of contemporary indigenous social movements and political parties in Latin America, and stresses the importance of social class, political economy and history in a way that calls into question some of the central concerns of 'New Social-Movement (NSM)', strategy-oriented, and neo-Marxist frameworks in social-movement studies. The purpose of this concluding chapter is to revisit the limitations of extant social-movement theories and liberal institutionalism, and to reexamine the core-theoretical concepts that inform the alternative Marxist and indigenous-liberationist analytical approach offered in the book, bringing to bear key aspects of the empirical evidence developed in Chapters 2 to 8. From here, the chapter turns outward, situating developments in Bolivia in the context of the broader left turn in

Latin-American politics over the last decade and the global-economic crisis that began in 2007. Particular attention in this wider panorama of regional political economy is paid to the ongoing Bolivarian process in Venezuela and social and political changes in the Bolivian setting since Evo Morales assumed office in early 2006.

9.1 Social-movement theory

Social-movement theory in the advanced capitalist countries was principally divided in the 1970s and 1980s between European identity-oriented (NSM) and American strategy-oriented traditions of research and analysis. The perspective of NSM-theorists portrays Marxism as class-reductionist and tends to emphasise culture, the social construction of meanings, new collective identities, the centrality of civil society against the state, and discontinuity between what are seen as 'new' as opposed to 'old' collective actors. NSM-analysts see social movements around sexuality, ecology, ethnicity, the environment, and gender, as expressive collective action rather than instrumental struggle. Strategy-oriented theorists working in the United States in this period, on the other hand, highlighted the political character of social movements, conceptualising them as strategic and instrumental conflicts over goods in the political market. Thinkers in this school do not see such an abrupt discontinuity between so-called new and old collective actors, and theorise social movements as simultaneously occupying the spheres of both the state and civil society. More recent developments in the strategy-school place new emphasis on the multiple variables that constitute political-opportunity structures in society. Over the course of the 1980s and 1990s, Latin-American social-movement studies was most heavily influenced by the NSM-school, although as the transition from bureaucratic authoritarian to limited electoral régimes began to appear more secure in the mid-1990s across much of the region, the concept of 'political-opportunity', central to the strategy-theory, began to resonate more widely in social-movement literature.

Neo-Marxism also continued to be an important influence in some social-movement theorising about Latin America. This approach brings important attention to bear on the way changing economic relationships affect the emergence and shape of collective action in Latin America. In neo-Marxism, as in the case of more classical Marxism, the emphasis is on history, political economy, social structure, and conflict. At the same time, neo-Marxists have purged their analyses of any commitment to revolutionary socialism and increasingly conceptualise social class and the state in Weberian terms.

Despite their different strengths, each of these schools of thought suffers from important weaknesses. NSM-theory, in an exaggerated dismissal of Marxism and 'totalising' approaches more generally, tends to neglect social class, political economy, and history. In celebrating social movements' embrace of identities other than those rooted in class, NSM-scholars sometimes neglect the ongoing relevance of class, and see major chasms everywhere between old class-based movements and new identity-based movements, whereas in reality the picture is far muddier – for both historical and current cases of collective action. The historical record in Latin America shows that many old class-struggles for socialism were supported by the various non-class-identity groups celebrated by NSM-theorists – indigenous peoples, women, and others –, while at the same time, today's identity-groups are often at the centre of popular class-struggles against neoliberalism, as has been emphasised repeatedly in this book with regard to indigenous proletarians and peasants in modern Bolivia.

For its part, the strategy-school of social-movement studies tends to leave by the wayside issues of gender and other identities. The socially constructed and contested nature of political-opportunity structures themselves is also frequently left unexamined. Political change, such as democratisation, and institutional processes, such as changes in the form and character of the apparatuses of the state, are relatively privileged in comparison to the school's very limited treatment of foundational changes in political economy and their effects on collective action. When they are addressed at all, issues of class-formation and class-struggle are woefully underdeveloped in the strategy-oriented social-movement literature. Neo-Marxism fills several of the gaps in NSM- and strategy-analyses, but because it has abandoned any commitment to revolutionary anticapitalism, and, indeed, is often ideologically opposed to revolutionary movements, the school frequently exaggerates the reformist character of Latin-American social struggle, and consistently underestimates revolutionary opportunities, as well as revolutionary characteristics within many actually-existing movements and oppositional ideologies. Further, neo-Marxism has unpersuasively argued for the superiority of Weberian structural class-analysis – which sees class merely as a position in a stratified social

hierarchy – over the Marxist conceptualisation of social classes as social relationships and historical processes, the perspective advanced in this book.

My Bolivian study seeks to bring back political economy and history to
the centre of social-movement analysis. It contends that social class and
class-struggle must be taken far more seriously than they have been if we
are to fruitfully analyse the left-indigenous insurrectionary cycle of the early
twenty-first century. NSM-theorists are likely to counter that this is a crude
relapse into class-reductionism. But the class-perspective developed here consciously incorporates other social relations – most emphatically indigenous-
liberation struggles – into its analytical frame, and explicitly points to the
ways in which historical materialism as a tradition has not always been class-
reductionist, and need not always be so in the future. In an effort to overcome
the overaccumulation of variables symptomatic of the most recent strategy-
oriented theorising on political-opportunity structures – with its all-encompassing sponge-effect discussed in Chapter 1 – I focus specifically on a small
set of concepts crucial to my framework: working classes as historical formations, infrastructures of class-struggle, social-movement unionism, popular
cultures of resistance and opposition, state-repression, and combined-oppositional consciousness.

9.2   Liberal institutionalism and Latin-American indigenous struggles

As part of the 'third-wave' democratisation-literature, a central normative
and political motif of liberal-institutionalist studies of identity-politics in
Latin America in the 1990s was the concern that the exclusion of indigenous communities from formal political life could intensify ethnic conflict
and threaten the consolidation of fragile liberal democracies in the region.
This approach assumes that liberal-democratic political institutions, together
with an underlying capitalist economy, can be at least potentially favourable
to the emancipatory aims of indigenous peoples. Constitutional reforms in
several Latin-American countries in the 1980s and 1990s included recognition
by states of their societies' multiethnic and pluricultural characters. Liberal
institutionalists see this cultural recognition by states as a major advance for
indigenous rights, even though the reforms coincided with ongoing neoliberal
economic restructuring that typically had adverse impacts on the material

well-being of the same indigenous populations that were supposedly experiencing an advance in rights.[1]

Analytically, liberal institutionalists describe contemporary indigenous movements and parties in Latin America as primarily ethnic phenemona, occurring largely in rural settings, in response to changes in citizenship-régimes, party-systems, and political-opportunity structures.[2] There is a tendency in this literature to emphasise the novel contribution of recent indigenous movements to the region's politics – a new politicisation of ethnicity. The movements are then situated analytically as part of a wave of allegedly non-class-based identity-movements that are said to have proliferated in Latin America since roughly the late 1960s.

In my study of Bolivia, I found that, notwithstanding the framework's capacity to explain certain important changes in the institutional structures of the state as they relate to indigenous populations, liberal institutionalism suffers from a number of serious problems. While there are certainly new components to the indigenous struggles of the late-twentieth and early-twenty-first centuries in Bolivia when compared to earlier movements, it is fundamentally important that the deep historical trajectory of indigenous resistance, starting at least with the great anticolonial rebellions against the Spanish *conquistadores* in the eighteenth century, be taken fully into account in any theoretical approach. The emphasis on the novel politicisation of ethnicity in liberal institutionalism means that the adherents of this school really cannot come fully to grips with this historical backdrop. Further, my study reveals that depictions of indigenous movements in Bolivia as principally non-class, ethnic phenomena are deeply flawed. Recent popular struggles in Bolivia have been characterised by the deep interpenetration of race and class. Their strongest manifestations, moreover, have been urban and working-class rather than rural and peasant, although both rural and urban movements have been important. The most powerful insurrections were rooted in El Alto, an informal proletarian and indigenous city. Movements there responded to the social costs of neoliberal-economic restructuring, and tied together the

---

1. For the liberal-institutionalist perspective, see Albó 2002a; Assies, van der Haar, and Hoekema 1998; Cojtí Cuxil 2002; Davis 2002; de la Peña 2002; Laurie, Andolina, and Radcliffe 2002; Plant 2002; Sieder 2002; Van Cott 2000. For a discussion of some of the contradictions of neoliberal multiculturalism, see Hale 2002, 2004, 2006.

2. Van Cott 2005; Yashar 2005.

aims of indigenous liberation from racial oppression and socialist emancipation from class-exploitation and imperialism. Such movements are best understood as the foundation of a reconstituted indigenous Left that takes the politics of indigenous liberation seriously while not abandoning questions of class. It is a misleading simplification at best to suggest that the politics of the Left in Bolivia has been replaced by a politics of ethnic conflict and strife. The mass-movements of the early twenty-first century described in this book were left-indigenous in character and profoundly rooted in longstanding traditions of indigenous and working-class radicalism.

Liberal institutionalism also naturalises the existence of capitalism and the market, as if they were 'universal and inevitable laws of nature' and therefore assumes their essential uncontestability.[3] This is in part a reflection of the wider retreat of left intellectuals and the descent into deep pessimism following the collapse of Communism: 'Left intellectuals, if not embracing capitalism as the best of all possible worlds, hope for little more than a space in its interstices and look forward to only the most local and particular resistances. At the very moment when a critical understanding of the capitalist system is urgently needed, large sections of the intellectual left, instead of developing, enriching and refining the required conceptual instruments, show every sign of discarding them altogether'.[4] How the contradictions of capitalist social relations impinge on complex and multifaceted indigenous reality in Latin America is consequently left largely unexamined.

Liberal institutionalists do explore theories of citizenship, but they consistently underestimate the way in which capitalism, in uniquely separating the political sphere from the economic, tightly circumscribes the possibilities of meaningful citizenship within that system.[5] In separating indigenous political struggle from the sphere of capitalist social relations within which, and often against which, these struggles occur, has caused liberal institutionalists to reach political conclusions very distant from the movements they purport to study. I have tried to expose this problem most fully in my exploration of combined-oppositional consciousness, drawing attention to the often explicit

---

3. Wood 1995, p. 1.
4. Ibid.
5. For a representative discussion of citizenship from a liberal-institutionalist position, see Yashar 2005, pp. 31–53. On the separation of the political and economic spheres under capitalism, see Wood 1995, pp. 19–48.

anticapitalist character of indigenous-left struggle in Bolivia. My conclusions, in this regard, correspond closely with the recent findings of William I. Robinson who argues that throughout Latin America 'Transnational capital seeks to integrate indigenous into the global market as dependent workers and consumers, to convert their lands into private property, and to make the natural resources in their territories available for transnational corporate exploitation'.[6] Threatened in this fashion by the implications of global capitalism indigenous populations have often responded in kind: 'Indigenous struggles spearhead popular class demands; these are *struggles against (transnational) capital* and for a transformation of property relations. Ethnicity and class have fused in the new round of indigenous resistance, which has become a – perhaps *the* – leading edge of popular class mobilisation'.[7]

Noting the limitations of liberal institutionalism, I seek to develop a novel theoretical entry-point into the world of extra-parliamentary revolts in Bolivia between 2000 and 2005 that is also capable of taking into account the deep historical backdrop that preceded them. I am indebted in this undertaking to a growing Latin-American literature that approaches indigenous struggles through the lens of Marxism and/or critical-race theory, taking seriously the intersections between indigenous resistance and class-struggle in particular.[8]

Thus, while the dominant liberal-institutionalist literature has, in the main, neglected the interrelations between the politics of class-struggle and indigenous resistance, it is important to point out that excellent recent studies from other theoretical traditions have broached the subject in fruitful ways. It is notable, however, that even when the interaction between race and class has been addressed explicitly, the focus of analysis has mostly been tightly confined to the countryside.[9] Henry Veltmeyer's study of the Chiapas uprising in Mexico in 1994, and Jasmin Hristov's examination of smallholding indigenous-peasant resistance in Cauca, Colombia since the 1970s, are two exemplary cases of erudite historical and materialist treatments of indigenous movements set in a broader context of class-struggle and the dynamics of

---

6. Robinson 2008, pp. 303–4.
7. Robinson 2008, p. 303, emphasis in the original.
8. Escárzaga and Gutiérrez 2005; García Linera 2005b; Gould 1990, 1998; Grandin 2005; Gutiérrez and Escárzaga 2006; Hale 1996, 2006; Harvey 1998; Hristov 2005; Hylton 2006; Hylton and Thomson 2007; Rivera Cusicanqui 2003 [1984]; Sawyer 2004; Stephen 1996, 2002; Veltmeyer 1997.
9. Otero 2004; Otero and Jugenitz 2003.

capitalism.[10] While such studies have much to teach us about the politics of culture and class in rural settings, this theoretical approach of non-dogmatic Marxism has not been sufficiently developed in relation to its urban dimension – the processes of urban class-formation and indigenous struggle, as well as the rural-urban dynamics of indigenous resistance and class-politics in Latin America today. I therefore try both to respond to the weaknesses of liberal institutionalism and to build on existing historical-materialist analyses of indigenous and class-politics through inclusion of the urban dimension. In order to do so, it is necessary to focus upon and to elaborate a set of core theoretical concepts: working classes as historical formations; infrastructure of class-struggle; social-movement unionism; popular cultures of resistance and opposition; neoliberalism; the state; and combined-oppositional consciousness.

9.3 Working classes as historical formations

In approaching the theoretical complexities of social class, I draw mainly on the formulations of E.P. Thompson, Ellen Meiksins Wood, and David Camfield.[11] In particular, I use Camfield's concept of *working classes as historical formations*, an approach that sees class 'as a structured social process and relationship that takes place in historical time and specific cultural contexts'. An analytics of class, on this view, 'must consciously incorporate social relations other than class, such as gender and race'.[12] Class-formations emerge from the historical relations people experience with the relations of production and other antagonistic social classes.[13] While class 'is ultimately anchored and sustained' at the point of production, 'class relations pervade all aspects of social life', including households and communities.[14] For Thompson, 'The class experience is largely determined by the productive relations into which men [*sic.*] are born – or enter into involuntarily'.[15] Yet, 'class consciousness', Thompson points out, 'is the way in which these experiences', the experiences

---

10. Veltmeyer 1997; Hristov 2005.
11. Thompson 1963; Wood 1995; Camfield 2004, 2007.
12. Camfield 2004, p. 421.
13. Camfield 2004, p. 424.
14. Ibid.
15. Thompson 1963, p. 9.

of being thrust through birth or an alternative form of involuntary entry into a class-situation, 'are handled in cultural terms: embodied in traditions, value-systems, ideas, and institutional forms'.[16] In *The Making of the English Working Class*, Thompson argues that 'The working class did not rise like the sun at an appointed time', but rather 'was present at its own making'.[17] The importance of this observation is its insistence on human agency in the class-struggle, even though this agency is limited by the class-situations that people enter into involuntarily.

In this spirit, when I discuss the working classes of El Alto, I begin with a detailed examination of the city's class-structure – the class-situations into which *alteños* were thrust involuntarily – and the stumbling blocks this structure posed for working-class collective action at the beginning of this century. Workers in El Alto have long work-days and low rates of unionisation. The class-structure is characterised by heterogeneous work-activity and small production-units in which only small numbers of workers are brought together. Workers generally lack social protection because the majority works at informal jobs. Increasing numbers of women and youth participate in the labour-market and have little union-experience and minimal knowledge of their basic rights. Racist and sexist divisions in workplaces are common and promoted by management. Given these structural characteristics, the possibilities of collective action by these workers seemed dim.[18] The puzzle, then, is to explain how El Alto's working classes overcame these structural barriers and took up a vanguard-position in a series of mass-insurrections in the early twenty-first century.

Part of the answer is rooted in the longstanding popular traditions of indigenous and worker-radicalism described in Chapters Two and Three. Analysing working classes as historical formations means sharing Gramsci's preoccupation with the social origins of new classes, the role of history in the process of class-formation.[19] Rather than being cut abstractly out of theoretical structures, working classes are formed 'out of pre-existing social groups whose particular traditions, aspirations and cultural practices' have been

---

16. Thompson 1963, p. 10.
17. Thompson 1963, p. 9.
18. Roberts 1998, 2002.
19. Camfield 2004, p. 431.

'modified by the devastating experience of proletarianisation'.[20] I show how the protests in El Alto drew on the rich popular cultures of resistance and opposition in Bolivian history – indigenous radicalism, which is sustained by migrants from the Aymara *altiplano*, and revolutionary Marxism, sustained by the migrants from tin-mining communities.

Furthermore, I conclude that, during the September–October 2003 and May–June 2005 Gas-Wars, El Alto's informal indigenous proletarians utilised a dense infrastructure of class-structure to facilitate their leading role in events, and were able to develop a remarkably rich combined-oppositional consciousness. Finally, these moments of revolt in 2003 and 2005 drew their power from alliances between the informal working class, the radical Aymara peasantry, and sections of the formal working class. The formal workers in this alliance – principally organised through the COB and the FSTMB – adopted an orientation toward social-movement unionism, and this proved critical to their successful solidarity with informal workers. I revisit the concepts of infrastructure of class-struggle, social-movement unionism, and combined-oppositional consciousness below.

9.4 Infrastructure of class-struggle

The concept of infrastructure of class-struggle draws on sociologist Alan Sears's notion of infrastructure of dissent.[21] A developed infrastructure of dissent, for Sears, allows for the growth of individual and collective capacities of the oppressed and exploited such that they are better positioned to fight against hierarchical power-structures responsible for their oppression and exploitation. In Sears's conceptualisation of this term, a whole array of formal and informal networks are embraced – networks in workplaces, unions, communities and political organisations, alternative media, and informal gathering sites of radicals and dissidents of different stripes. When these networks are rich and dense, they help to sustain and strengthen popular collective memories of past struggles and develop sophisticated theoretical debates

---

20. Ibid.
21. Sears 2005, 2007.

among radicals regarding immediate political challenges and longer-term strategic decisions around building an effective socialist politics.[22]

The term is useful, with some modification, for discussing racialised class-struggle in the Bolivian context. Infrastructure of class-struggle, in my usage, refers to all those formal and informal networks – in the workplace, community, household, land, and territory – that orient, organise, politicise, and mobilise the class-struggles of the largely-indigenous proletarian and peasant-majority. The infrastructure of class-struggle, in this sense, acts as the incubator of the common experience through which working-class formation and oppositional consciousness is developed.

In the Water-War of 2000, I show how different rural and urban infrastructures of class-struggle came together under the umbrella-organisation of the Coordinadora, which was led by factory-worker Oscar Olivera. In the Gas-Wars of 2003 and 2005, the infrastructures of informal proletarian class-struggle – the Federación de Juntas Vecinales de El Alto (Federation of Neighbourhood-Councils of El Alto, FEJUVE-El Alto) and the Central Obrera Regional de El Alto (Regional Workers' Central of El Alto, COR-El Alto) – led the charge. The strength of these protests was reinforced, however, by the participation of radical Aymara peasants organised in their own rural infrastructures of class-struggle – the Confederación Sindical Única de Trabajadores Campesinos de Bolivia (Trade-Union Confederation of Bolivian Peasant-Workers, CSUTCB) and the Federación Única Departamental de Trabajadores Campesinos de La Paz – Tupaj Katari (Departmental Federation of Peasant-Workers of La Paz – Tupaj Katari, FUDTCLP-TK), and formal workers organised in their principal infrastructures of class-struggle – the Central Obrera Boliviana (Bolivian Workers' Central, COB) and the Federación Sindical de Trabajadores Mineros de Bolivia (Trade-Union Federation of Bolivian Mine-Workers, FSTMB).

9.5 Social-movement unionism

It is also clear, however, that the participation of the COB and FSTMB in the Gas-Wars would have been far less effective had they not adopted an orientation toward social-movement unionism. By this, we mean a militant and

---

22. Sears 2007.

deeply democratic unionism devoted to increasing the power and organisation of workers inside and outside of the workplace – a unionism of the workplaces, households, and communities of the entire working class, broadly conceived. As Kim Moody argues, social-movement unionism struggles to build workers' power in the workplace while at the same time attempting to amplify 'its political and social power by reaching out to other sectors of the class, be they other unions, neighbourhood-based organisations, or other social movements. It fights for all the oppressed and enhances its own power by doing so'.[23] Because the COB and the FSTMB embraced this form of militant unionism, they were able to forge effective alliances with the non-traditional infrastructures of class-struggle through which the bulk of informal workers in El Alto were organised – FEJUVE-El Alto and COR-El Alto.

9.6   Popular cultures of resistance and opposition

A population's perceptions of available and plausible options open to them are key components of revolutionary potential in any society.[24] Social classes and groups, and also individuals, rely on the existing 'repository of knowledge' in society in order to draw conclusions regarding the parameters of the possible and imaginable. Revolutionary processes are more likely to take sail and generate wide-scale support in societies where revolution is considered viable given traditions of celebrating past rebellions and movements in folklore and popular culture, or where revolutionary leaders make a point of publicly re-imagining and celebrating forgotten revolutionary heroes, movements, and revolts of the past, and draw on these to explain the possibilities and hopes of the present.[25]

In Bolivia, a major facet of fully explaining the strength and radical character of left-indigenous insurrections in the early twenty-first century, then, is through exploration of the country's longstanding traditions of popular resistance and opposition, and mapping of the routes through which they connect with, and are made anew by, movements in the present day. The intertwined histories of capitalist development, state-formation, and racialised class-struggle

---

23. Moody 1997, p. 5.
24. Selbin 2008, p. 135.
25. Ibid.

in Bolivia fuelled rich popular cultures of opposition and resistance between the late-eighteenth-century anticolonial insurrections led by Tupaj Katari and the left-indigenous insurrectionary cycle that unfolded between 2000 and 2005. Resilient features of Bolivian politics over much of this time-span were independent indigenous resistance and militant working-class activity sustained by myriad workers' organisations and left ideologies. Two traditions of struggle – indigenous resistance and worker-radicalism – left an indelible print on the popular cultures of opposition in the country, and were reinterpreted and refashioned by organic intellectuals within the infrastructures of class-struggle to respond to the novel community- and workplace-settings of the twenty-first century.

9.7 Neoliberalism

Together with the longer-term, structural and historical developments associated with the rise of capitalism, state-formation, cycles of class-struggle, and the formation of popular cultures of resistance and opposition, one must come to terms with the important changes to Bolivia's social formation wrought by neoliberal restructuring between 1985 and 2000 if a proper understanding of the 2000–5 cycle of revolt is the aim. It is imperative to understand that, on a world-scale, neoliberalism arose as a political project of the ruling classes in the advanced capitalist countries – led by the US – in response to the decline in profitability and stagflation of the early 1970s and the parallel rise of various leftist political threats to capital throughout the globe. The embedded liberalism of the postwar global economy was in crisis and neoliberalism was the strategy to restore capitalist class-power in all corners of the world.[26] Representing much more than the ten commandments of the Washington Consensus, neoliberalism is a class-based ideology that asserts increased exposure to the free market will resolve endemic problems of economic, social, political, and ecological life.[27]

The Bolivian experience of neoliberalism beginning in 1985 was deeply influenced by changes in global capitalism and the imperialist pressures of core-states – especially the United States – and the principal international

---

26. Albo 2007; Gowan 1999; Harvey 2003, 2005; Saad–Filho 2005.
27. Marois 2005, pp. 102–3.

financial institutions. However, the specificities of the domestic experience – the speed, depth, and breadth of neoliberal restructuring – were heavily determined by the shifting domestic balance of racialised class-forces in a period of extreme economic and institutional crisis following the hyperinflationary implosion of the Unidad Democrática Popular (Democratic-Popular Unity, UDP) government. The balance of class-forces moved away from the rural and urban indigenous popular classes and toward an increasingly coherent white-*mestizo* capitalist class, led by the internationally-oriented fractions allied with transnational capital. The new rulers employed a political and economic strategy of systematically dismantling the infrastructures of popular class-struggle, beginning with the powerful tin-mining unions. The implementation of neoliberalism in the country involved varied doses of coercion and consent. Polyarchic institutions were used to develop and deploy neoliberal policies, but there were parallel trends toward open authoritarianism and repression of popular actors at various junctures. Massive transformations of the class-structure and the world of work were one consequence of the reforms, and left-indigenous forces unaccustomed to the new environment suffered fifteen years of retreat in the face of right-wing advance. The fulcrum of class-struggle shifted from the miners to the *cocaleros* (coca-growers), but the *cocaleros* never enjoyed the same sort of power as the miners had at the height of their leadership of the Bolivian Left earlier in the twentieth century.

However, after years of uneven and modest economic growth in the early-to mid-1990s, the country was struck by recession in 1999, and the contradictions of neoliberal capitalist development helped bring about new shifts in the balance of racialised class-forces. As we know, the period between 2000 and 2005 witnessed a remarkable resurgence of popular class-mobilisation through new left-indigenous forces. Karl Marx once argued that the advance of industrial capitalism brings workers together, out of isolation, and into revolutionary combination through association, creating in the process the future grave-diggers of the bourgeois order.[28] In the case of El Alto in Bolivia – that leading locale of the left-indigenous insurrectionary cycle – I show that neoliberalism created its own worst enemy in a parallel fashion. Radical miners and peasants were dispossessed and driven into the shantytown – into revolutionary combination. Revolutionary-Marxist traditions

---

28. Marx and Engels 1985, pp. 93–4.

of the miners and indigenous-liberation traditions of the Aymara peasants commingled in emergent infrastructures of class-struggle to lay the basis for one of the strongest attempts to overthrow neoliberalism in recent memory.

9.8 The state and repression

Because of the social contradictions and political crises generated by capitalism the stability of the social order is routinely challenged. Capitalists, however, depend on some reasonable level of social stability in order to continue in their role. In the history of capitalism, maintenance or restoration of stability in the face of ongoing contradictions and crises has been a principal function of the state. Through legal and institutional channels, as well as through coercive force, the state sustains the property-relations that undergird capitalism.[29] In this book, the state has been understood theoretically as the political expression of dynamic racialised class-struggle occurring in historical time. The state, for our purposes, is understood to '[assume] a specific form that expresses politically the contradictory nature of capitalist social relations, just as the production-process expresses the relations economically'.[30] Under neoliberalism, the central state and administrative apparatus tends to become more authoritarian and even more distant from popular-democratic control.[31] The Bolivian state under neoliberalism was no exception.[32]

Against these more general characteristics of the state in theory, I have been particularly interested in this book to ascertain the dynamics of state-repression and popular movement responses at moments of crisis. It has been noted that governments that unwaveringly reject all claims made by popular movements and enforce those decisions by force end up either eliminating oppositional challengers if their repression is effective or sparking potentially revolutionary polarisation where it is not.[33]

Exploring this theoretical proposition in the case of the September–October 2003 Gas-War, I found that state-repression at different intervals over these two months radicalised working-class and peasant-protests, catalysed

---

29. Wood 2003, pp. 16–17.
30. Gordon 2006b, p. 31.
31. Albo 2007, p. 359.
32. Gill 2000.
33. Tarrow 1998, p. 149.

ruptures within the ruling élite, and drew sections of the middle class over to the side of the popular movements. Then-president Gonzalo Sánchez de Loazada consistently refused serious negotiation with the popular movements and rejected virtually all their demands. While he gave the green light to fierce state-repression – leaving 67 dead and over 400 injured – the level of repression was nonetheless insufficient to destroy the resistance, and consequently fuelled processes of polarisation in the country. Repression had the effect, in this case, of forging and consolidating new social solidarities within and between those sectors of the population at the receiving end of state-coercion.

The dynamics of state-repression and movement-response were distinct in the second Gas-War of May–June 2005. Then-President Carlos Mesa was forced to adapt to a situation in which he came to office through constitutional succession rather than popular election and followed directly on the heels of the extremely unpopular presidency of Sánchez de Lozada, a man for whom he had acted as vice-president. Mesa thus made opposition to state-repression a central feature of his claim to legitimacy and a measure of the political and moral distance he had travelled from the former president. He was consequently constrained in his ability to employ coercion against protesters from the outset of his administration. While, in the quiet early months of Mesa's reign, this proved unproblematic, by May and June 2005, the winds of revolt had returned to Bolivia and hundreds of thousands returned to the streets. In this case, a detailed analysis of the sequence of events showed that, because Mesa refrained from employing sufficient state-repression to suppress insurrection, while, at the same time, refusing to accommodate seriously any of the demands of the popular movements, the waves of rebellion continued to grow until they could not be restrained and the President was forced to resign.

My conclusions regarding state-repression during the first Gas-War, as well as during other rebellious moments in Bolivian history over the last several centuries, is theoretically significant in another sense because it calls into question the basic premise of the traditional political-opportunity thesis in social-movement studies. State-repression, because it shuts down opportunity, ought to have led to diminishing protests, according to the traditional thesis.[34] In the history of Bolivian struggles, more often than not, this was not the way

---

34. McAdam, McArthy, and Zald 1996b.

history unfolded. State-repression, because it was insufficiently powerful to wipe out opposition, repeatedly led to the radicalisation of popular protests. The relationship between social protest and state-response – repression, concession, or some combination of the two – is, I contend, frequently more dynamic and dialectical than is commonly understood in social-movement studies. State-élites and oppositional groups react and adjust to each other in dynamic and evolving ways in the course of rebellion. Transhistorical models of political opportunities and threats are unhelpful in unpacking this dialectical relationship. It is simply not the case in much of Bolivian history that collective action formulaically increased when opportunities opened and closed when opportunities contracted. The dual between state-action and reaction – repression/concession – and popular-movement action and reaction – radicalisation/retreat – has been much more complex. As others have suggested, the rich and varied empirical record around the world, and in different historical epochs, of failed revolutions, successful revolutions, modest protest-activity, and mass-mobilisation, exemplify this complexity and the ultimate futility of transhistorical modelling.[35]

9.9 Combined-oppositional consciousness

Drawing inspiration from Janes Mansbridge's concept of 'oppositional consciousness', David Camfield's notion of working classes as historical formations, and Robin D.G. Kelley's theoretical and historical work on 'freedom-dreams' and 'poetics of struggle and lived experience', I offer the final, and in some ways most important, theoretical and empirical contribution of this book – combined-oppositional consciousness.[36] In this book, combined-oppositional consciousness refers specifically to a collective consciousness that arose at the apogee of the Gas-Wars in which the politics of class-struggle and indigenous liberation came together in powerful unison. The conclusions I draw regarding this consciousness are based directly on the perceptions, beliefs, and values of the activists I interviewed in the leading social-movement and trade-union organisations of El Alto and La Paz. As this combined-oppositional consciousness was raised, it transformed individuals

---

35. Goldstone and Tilly 2001, pp. 180–92.
36. Mansbridge 2001a, b; Camfield 2004; Kelley 2002.

and collectivities in these two cities, by taking 'free-floating frustration and direct[ing] it into anger', by turning, 'strangers into brothers and sisters', and by building 'on ideas and facts to generate hope'.[37]

One way in which this combined consciousness revealed itself in El Alto – and to a lesser degree elsewhere in the country – was through the notion of *vecino*. Literally translated as neighbour, in the *alteño* context, *vecino* is a means of understanding and expressing the mixed character of class- and indigenous consciousness. A second component of the collective consciousness I describe is the profound integration of Bolivia's two longstanding popular cultures of resistance and opposition – indigenous and worker-radicalism. This expressed itself in the revolutionary memories of interviewees who talked repeatedly about past indigenous insurrections and their heroes, as well as historic conquests and revolts of the revolutionary Left. This 'repository of knowledge' helped make the left-indigenous insurrectionary cycle possible. Important mechanisms through which these memories have been sustained include family-experience and storytelling, what Karen Kampwirth calls 'family-traditions of resistance'.[38]

The third aspect of combined-oppositional consciousness that stood out in the narratives of activists was anti-imperialist critique. This anti-imperialism was more often than not connected to analysis and denunciation of capitalism as a system of class-exploitation and racial domination as a system of oppression. Again, interviewees connected the threads of revolutionary Marxism and indigenous radicalism in their analysis of imperialism and their determination to resist. This component of the narratives often focused eventually on more specific targets of opposition, particularly resistance to the privatisation and commodification of natural resources. Hydrocarbons (natural gas and oil) and water were the focal points in this regard. The fourth, and final, element of combined-oppositional consciousness relates directly to Kelley's forward-looking 'freedom-dreams'. This part of the narrative was usually elicited from activists through questions concerning the sort of future for which they were fighting. Interviewees typically envisioned roughly four pillars of this future society. They demanded equality, the end of poverty, and the abolition of social classes. They called for a future free of racism. They wanted dignity,

---

37. Mansbridge 2001b, p. 5.
38. Selbin 2008; Kampwirth 2002, p. 10.

social justice, and their basic necessities to be met. They fought for socialism and indigenous-liberationist democracy.

9.10 Bolivia and the left turn in Latin-American politics

The Bolivian revolutionary epoch of 2000 to 2005 did not develop in isolation. Left-indigenous struggles in the country represented merely the leading edge of wider anti-neoliberal resistance in Latin America, the region of the world which has most fervently contested the reigning power-structures of global capitalism since the late 1990s.[39] The correlation of forces in Latin America has long depended on the positions 'won, threatened, or lost' by the different social constellations of local capitalist classes, the oppressed of the countryside and the cities, and the various geopolitical and economic tentacles of imperialism.[40] In the early 1990s, the balance of forces weighed heavily against any socialist revival. Brutal authoritarian régimes had physically annihilated large sections of the Left in the 1960s and 1970s in countries such as Argentina, Chile, Brazil, and Uruguay. Mass guerrilla-insurgencies were crushed with sometimes genocidal ferocity in Central America in the 1980s. The debt crisis of the same decade ushered in twenty years of neoliberal restructuring throughout the region, with labour-unions, peasant-movements, and other infrastructures of popular power entering stark decline. Political blows to left prospects accumulated further with the Sandinista electoral loss in Nicaragua in 1990, and the isolation of Cuba following the collapse of the Soviet Union. Advocates of revolutionary socialism were easily dismissed as romantic utopians, and social movements and the political Left turned inward, focusing principally on local community-projects and losing sight of the objective of conquering power at the national stage. The parameters of politics were caught in the vice-grip of the Washington Consensus.

The tide began to turn, however, by the late 1990s. Profound contradictions of neoliberalism stoked a wave of political and economic crises. Popular

---

39. It is therefore bizarre how some otherwise insightful Marxist contributions to contemporary theories of imperialism and the contours of the global economy neglect serious discussion of the region's contested trajectory and what the eventual outcomes of these struggles might signify for possible reconfigurations of global structures of power and domination. See, for example, Callinicos 2009.

40. Katz 2009, 2007.

revolts responded to collapsing neoliberal legitimacy by the early years of the twenty-first century, bringing down heads of state in Argentina, Bolivia, Ecuador, and elsewhere. Rural and urban radicalisation and mobilisation began to mitigate the impunity with which the ruling classes and imperialism had set the economic and political agenda.[41] Contests for the trajectory of the region expressed themselves electorally as well, with self-described centre-left and left governments assuming office in large swathes of South and Central America, beginning, of course, with Hugo Chávez in Venezuela in 1998. It is fairly clear, though, that, while many of these new governments pose fierce rhetorical challenges to neoliberalism, in practice they tend to enact only 'mild redistributive programmes respectful of prevailing property relations'. Centre-leftists such as Lula in Brazil, Bachelet in Chile, or Kirchner in Argentina, have, in fact, proved capable of 'pushing forward a new wave of capitalist globalisation with greater credibility than their orthodox neoliberal predecessors'.[42] In these mildly reformist cases, there has been no meaningful redistribution of income or wealth, much less a challenge to capitalist social-property relations.

Sometimes situated alongside Cuba, Bolivia, and Ecuador, most Latin-American observers see Venezuela under Chávez as the most radical expression of the Latin America's left shift. The outcomes of Venezuela's contradictory Bolivarian path will without doubt set parameters for the scope of what is possible for socialist advance in Bolivia and elsewhere in the region in the medium term. Thus the following section proposes a brief assessment.[43]

9.11 Hugo Chávez and the Bolivarian process in Venezuela

Mainstream-punditry in North America and Europe associates Venezuela with the *bad* Left in contemporary Latin America. This Left is 'nationalist, strident, and close-minded', 'depends on giving away money', and has 'no real domestic agenda'. For the bad Left, 'the fact of power is more important than its responsible exercise', and for its leaders, 'economic performance, democratic values, programmatic achievements, and good relations with the

---

41. Katz 2007, p. 29.
42. Robinson 2008, p. 292.
43. The following paragraphs draw on Webber 2010a.

United States are not imperatives but bothersome constraints that miss the real point'.[44] George W. Bush's national-security strategy-documents claimed that Hugo Chávez was a 'demagogue awash in oil money', seeking to 'undermine democracy' and 'destabilise the region'. Donald Rumsfeld compared Chávez to Adolf Hitler, reminding us that Hitler, too, had been elected.[45] Not much has changed since Barack Obama took over the world's most powerful presidency. The White House message continues to be that Chávez runs a dangerously authoritarian régime in desperate need of 'democratisation'.[46]

Chávez has been a leading opponent of free trade deals between Latin-American countries and the United States, instead invoking the memory of independence-hero Simón Bolívar with his vision of a united South America to promote a series of trade-deals based on principles of solidarity.[47] Chávez is openly inspired by the Cuban Revolution and has a warm friendship with Fidel Castro, while stressing Venezuela's independent path towards a less state-centered and more pluaralistic twenty-first-century socialism. Chávez emphasises the need to forge stronger South-South connections against the imperialism of the core-capitalist states of the world-system. This explicitly anti-imperialist stance helps to explain the United States' support for reactionary forces in Venezuela, even in the relative absence of direct threats to American corporate interests.

The Bolivarian Alternative for the Americas (ALBA), first imagined by the Venezuelan government in 2001 as a counter to the North-American-led Free-Trade Area of the Americas (FTAA), is the most important expression of Venezuelan-led regional integration. Formally established in 2004 by Venezuela and Cuba, it expanded to include Bolivia, Nicaragua, Dominican Republic, Honduras, Ecuador, St. Vincent and the Grenadines, Antigua and Barbuda, and Paraguay.[48] Moreover, soon after Evo Morales's election in Bolivia in December 2005, Cuba, Venezuela, and Bolivia signed what they called a Peoples' Trade Agreement.

---

44. Castañeda 2006.
45. Grandin 2006. On US-imperialism in Venezuela over the course of the Bush presidency, see Golinger 2006, 2007.
46. For exemplary commentary from Secretary of State Hilary Clinton, see Henao 2009 and Suggett 2009.
47. Chávez 2003, Katz 2009, Kellogg 2007.
48. Hart-Landsberg 2009.

Chávez is revered by many on the Left across the globe, since few leaders of the Global South today openly and regularly denounce the crimes of American imperialism from a left-wing perspective.[49] Along with its record of poverty-reduction and anti-neoliberalism, pursued with popular support in the face of domestic right-wing and imperialist assaults, Venezuela helps to revive the idea of socialism as a viable political choice. This is an important development following the Soviet bloc's collapse and the discrediting of socialism in the wake of Stalinist policies, and explains why Venezuela has inspired so much attention and debate.

From the right, Chávez has sometimes been crudely lumped in with recent 'neopopulist' presidents elsewhere in the region, such as Alberto Fujimori in Peru, and Carlos Menem in Argentina.[50] Chávez's neopopulism, on this view, includes a feverishly authoritarian bent, where 'political competition' means '[o]pponents must be crushed', and where Chávez employs 'hate speech' that sounds 'more dictatorial than democratic'.[51] More serious discussion is occurring on the Left. There are those who think Chávez is a moderate social democrat and celebrate this stance as a reasonable and realistic response to the current hostile context of neoliberalism and imperialism.[52] Some social democrats, however, celebrate the perceived social gains of the Bolivarian process, but fear a 'regressive evolution' in the 'sphere of politics' in which they perceive a 'closing of the space for participation and democratic decision-making'.[53] Other leftists, while remaining critical of different components of the government's approach, contend that Chávez represents something more radical than social democracy, something even potentially revolutionary and transformative. They tend to stress the social and economic achievements of the régime thus far in the face of daunting odds.[54] Then there are those, myself among them, who orient themselves toward struggling within and for the socialist advance of the Bolivarian process, but who emphasise the contra-

---

49. Iran's Mahmoud Ahmadinejad is an example of a reactionary government opposed to US power. Chávez's unconditional support for Ahmadinejad's régime as it ferociously repressed mass-demonstrations in the streets of Tehran and elsewhere in June and July 2009 was a travesty that revealed the deeply flawed understandings of socialist internationalism within his government.
50. Weyland 2001.
51. Corrales 2009, p. 81.
52. Ali 2006.
53. López Maya 2007, p. 175.
54. Wilpert 2007; Lebowitz 2006; Ellner 2008; Robinson 2007.

dictions, obstacles, delays, setbacks, and bureaucratisation that have thus far stood in the way of genuine socialist transition from below; these obstacles, for the latter set of thinkers, represent the clear and present danger to the possibilities for emancipation of the popular classes from the exploitation of capital and the oppression of imperialism.[55]

The social advances of the radicalising Bolivarian process in Venezuela are important. According to the latest figures from the United Nations Economic Commission for Latin America and the Caribbean, Venezuela reduced its poverty- and extreme poverty-rates from 48.6 and 22.2 per cent of the population respectively in 2002, to 28.5 and 8.5 per cent by 2007.[56] The proportion of people living in poverty fell from 48.6 per cent in 2002, to 30.2 per cent in 2006, down to 28.5 per cent in 2007. In 2006 alone, as a consequence of sharp surges in social spending, the poverty-rate fell from 37.1 per cent to 30.2 per cent.[57]

Yet, these trends are typical of advances of centre-left régimes elsewhere in the region over the same period, a consequence of the conjunctural primary-commodity boom in Latin America between 2003 and 2007. For example, the urban areas of Argentina under the Nestor Kirchner's government registered a decline in poverty and extreme poverty from 45.4 and 20.9 per cent respectively in 2002, to 21 and 7.2 per cent in 2006. In 2000, Chile had a poverty-rate of 20.2 per cent, while the extreme poverty-level was 5.6 per cent. By 2006, those figures had fallen to 13.7 and 3.2 per cent respectively. What is more, Venezuela's poverty-rate of 28.5 per cent in 2007 continues to compare poorly to Chile's 13.7 (2006), Costa Rica's 18.6 (2007), and Uruguay's 18.1 (2007).[58]

Nonetheless, the Venezuelan figures, because they only measure income-poverty, substantially underestimate the Chávez administration's advances in poverty-reduction more broadly through large-scale improvements in the social wage of the working class, i.e., social services. Various mission-programmes, that bypass bureaucratic and unco-operative state-structures, are the principal means of delivering these social services. Barrio Adentro provides free health-care to the poor through the assistance of tens of thousands of Cuban doctors and the establishment of new community-clinics; Mercal is a state-distributor of food at subsidised prices; Robinson 1 and 2 are

55. See, especially, the Venezuelan magazine *Marea Socialista*.
56. CEPAL 2008, p. 16.
57. CEPAL 2007, p. 18.
58. CEPAL 2008, p. 16.

missions focusing on literacy and primary education for adults; Ribas and Sucre target secondary and university-education for individuals who never had the opportunity to attend or those who dropped out; and Vuelvan Caras provides state-funded training for employment and the creation of workers' co-operatives.[59]

Some results are impressive. In 2005, for example, UNESCO declared that Venezuela was 'a territory freed from illiteracy'.[60] The figures on health-care are also remarkable:

> In 1998 there were 1, 628 primary care physicians for a population of 23.4 million. Today, there are 19,571 for a population of 27 million. In 1998 there were 417 emergency rooms, 74 rehab centers and 1,628 primary care centers compared to 721 emergency rooms, 445 rehab centers, and 8,621 primary care centers (including the 6,500 'check-up points', usually in poor neighbour-hoods, and that are in the process of being expanded to more comprehensive care centers) today. Since 2004, 399,662 people have had antiretroviral treat-ment from the government, compared to 18,538 in 2006.[61]

This spending is contingent on massive oil-rents unique to Venezuela in the Latin-American and Caribbean context. From the first quarter of 2003, following the end of the oil-lockout, to the second quarter of 2008, Gross Domestic Product (GDP) grew 94.7 per cent, an incredible annual rate of 13.5 per cent.[62]

Social-democratic commentators emphasise that 'in spite of the expansion of government during the Chávez years, the private sector has grown faster than the public sector', with finance and insurance at the leading edge.[63] Absolute figures for social spending have been very high, but public social spending as a percentage of gross national product has not been impressive relative to the rest of Latin America. In the year 2004–5, for example, Argentina, Bolivia, Brazil, Chile, Colombia, Costa Rica, and Cuba, all showed higher rates of public social spending as a per centage of gross national product than Venezuela.[64]

---

59. López Maya 2007, p. 165.
60. Esteban 2008.
61. Weisbrot and Sandoval 2007, p. 9.
62. Weisbrot, Ray, and Sandoval 2009, p. 6.
63. Weisbrot, Ray, and Sandoval 2009, p. 7.
64. CEPAL 2007, p. 132.

From the time the *Chavistas* came to power until 2002, the share of national income going to the richest 10 per cent of the population fell minimally, while the share going to the bottom 40 per cent decreased marginally. In 1999, the richest 10 per cent of the population received 31.4 per cent of national income and in 2002, 31.3 per cent. Meanwhile, the poorest 40 per cent received only 14.5 per cent of the national income in 1999 and by 2002, just 14.3 per cent.

This situation has since improved, but there has hardly been a revolutionary wealth-transfer. Income-inequality as measured by the Gini index fell from 46.96 to 40.99 between 1999 and 2008. As a comparison, between 1980 and 2005 the United States experienced an accelerated concentration of wealth upwards, from 40.3 to 46.9 as measured by the Gini index.[65] Between 2002 and 2007 the share of income going to the bottom 40 per cent of households rose to 18.4 from 14.3 per cent, and the share going to the top 10 per cent of households fell from 31.3 to 25.7.[66] In 2007, across Latin-American countries, the poorest 40 per cent of households on average received 15 per cent of total income, and only in Uruguay did they receive more than 20 per cent.[67] Venezuela is now better than average in Latin America, but this is a region with the worst income-inequality in the world.

Huge concentrations of personal wealth and privilege remain untouched by the Bolivarian process. Almost 30 per cent of the population lives in poverty by ECLAC's measurements, which tend to underestimate poverty. As one analyst suggests, 'Any serious attempt to make Venezuelan society more egalitarian – let alone socialist – would begin with a radically progressive tax system aimed at redistributing wealth'.[68] How this might be done, in Venezuela and elsewhere, has become radically more complex in a ravaged global economy.

9.12 The global economic crisis and the future of the Latin-American Left

By April 2008, the International Monetary Fund (IMF) suggested that we were witnessing the largest financial crisis in the United States since the Great

---

65. Weisbrot, Ray, and Sandoval 2009, 10.
66. CEPAL 2008, p. 231.
67. CEPAL 2008, p. 75.
68. Sustar 2007, p. 24.

Depression. However, as David McNally has observed, this underestimated the scale of the crisis. First, while originating in the United States, the crisis is global. Second, the crisis is no longer narrowly financial, but is having a deep impact on the 'real economy'. 'Having started in the construction-, auto- and electronics-sectors', he observes, 'the slump is now sweeping through all manufacturing industries and spilling across the service-sector'.[69] Bankruptcies, factory-closures and layoffs are a response to overaccumulation – over 250,000 jobs have been lost in the North-American automobile-industry alone. Waves of downsizing in non-financial corporations feed the underconsumption-dynamic of this crisis. 'As world-demand and world-sales dive', McNally points out, 'the effects of overcapacity (factories, machines, buildings that cannot be profitably utilised), which have been masked by credit-creation over the past decade, will kick in with a vengeance'.[70] Typically for the world-capitalist system, we are increasingly witnessing the 'geographical displacement of crisis: attempting to offload the worst impacts onto those outside the core'.[71]

From the vantage-point of early 2010, the suggestion of Luiz Inácio Lula da Silva, President of Brazil, that the crisis would not seriously affect Latin America appears deeply naïve.[72] The slowdown of the 2003–7 commodity-driven boom deepened in Latin America over the first two quarters of 2008, sharpening severely since. Most economists now predict that 'Latin America will be the region hardest hit in the developing world, with the exception of Central and Eastern Europe, both in terms of reductions in per capita GDP and slower growth vis-à-vis the boom years'.[73] The significant accumulation of foreign-exchange reserves and reduction of dollar-denominated public debt during the boom years provided a temporary cushioning of the global crisis in Latin America, but this situation is unlikely to matter if the world-recession turns into a prolonged slump. 'The budget surpluses are temporary stopgaps to finance some stimulus packages', James Petras notes, 'but they are totally insufficient to reverse the fall in all export sectors, the drying up of private credit and the drying up of new local/foreign investment. In fact

---

69. McNally 2009, p. 36.
70. McNally 2009, p. 37.
71. Hanieh 2009, p. 61.
72. Cárdenas 2008.
73. Ocampo 2009, p. 705.

the first sign and substance of growing recessionary tendencies is the large outflows of capital by investors anticipating the crisis'.[74]

The drop in world-trade had already made itself felt by mid-2008; and then commodity-prices simply collapsed after September of the same year. Export-revenues for the region contracted at an annualised rate of 30 per cent in the final quarter of 2008, having a severe impact on GDP-growth.[75] The effects of collapsing remittance-flows have been uneven across different Latin-American countries, but are likely to inflict increasing pain on the popular classes over time as right-wing fuelled xenophobia, 'draconian restrictions on the movement of migrant-labour', and 'tighter control and regulation of the movement of labour' in the countries of the Global North deepen and expand.[76]

In Venezuela, the plunge in energy-prices has been the most important element of the crisis. Oil accounts for 90 per cent of the country's exports and more than half of government-revenues.[77] In July 2008, crude had reached the remarkable world-market price of $US147 per barrel. By December that year it collapsed to just $US32.40. In 2009 it slowly rose back to $US73 in early June amidst mainstream-economist optimism regarding so-called 'green shoots' in the world-economy, and Chinese strategic stockpiling. As stunningly bad US job-figures came out later that month, however, the green shoots wilted, and oil-prices fell to $US66.[78] The immediate fall in revenues for the Venezuelan government potentially threatens many social programmes domestically, as well as those anti-poverty, healthcare, and food-subsidy programmes elsewhere in the region that depend on financing from Venezuelan oil-rents.

Yet, this is an opportune moment for the Venezuelan process to reconcile its most profound internal contradictions, pushed by organised socialists in the labour-movement, radical social movements of the urban poor, and radical currents within the United Socialist Party of Venezuela (PSUV) itself. Up until now, oil-rents have lubricated a system of moderate redistribution to the popular classes without serious attack on the concentrated assets of a tiny élite and the ongoing expansion of the private sector. To defend and expand social programmes, and to move forward with a multifaceted transition to

---

74. Petras 2009.
75. Ocampo 2009, p. 708.
76. McNally 2009, p. 78; Hanieh 2009, p. 73.
77. *The Economist* 2008; Mander 2008.
78. McCarthy 2009.

socialism, a radical new wave of class-struggle from below will be required. This struggle will face opposition from the Right, which will use the crisis to seek to destabilise the Chávez régime, with the assistance of imperialist powers. Within *Chavismo*, bureaucratic conservative layers will defend a state-capitalist response to exiting the crisis, rather than deepening shifts toward a transition to socialism.

The Venezuelan internal struggles will have repercussions for the Latin-American Left. The bold revitalisation of ALBA, as a means of deepening South-South links throughout Latin America will require Venezuela's lead. Whether projects like Banco del Sur (Bank of the South) take on *socialist* forms, such as providing funds to finance land-reform and improvements in the lives of the popular classes region-wide, or whether reforms will subsidise the survival of local ruling-classes to improve their chances of competing with international rivals, will ultimately depend on the trajectory of class-struggle, not least in Venezuela.[79]

9.13   From pink to red?

Neoliberal ideology suffered great setbacks in Latin America during the last major regional recession (1998–2002), and during the uptick in radical popular movements between 2000 and 2005.[80] With the rise of different centre-left governments in much of the region, social movements have subsequently subsided, with some having been co-opted into the state-machinery. At the same time, the extreme Right has assumed or retained power in countries like Colombia, Mexico, Peru, Panama, and, most recently, Honduras and Chile.

Still, the Latin-American Left has the most potential of any region in the world to seize the moment of the global-economic crisis, given the expansion and consolidation of anti-neoliberal and anti-imperialist consciousness among much of the population over the last decade. A subjective shift from anti-neoliberalism and anti-imperialism toward revolutionary socialism from below is the urgent necessity of the day.[81] 'The current gap between favourable objective economic condition', Petras suggests, 'and the under-development

---

79. Katz 2009b.
80. See, among many others, Robinson 2008.
81. Katz 2007.

of (subjective) revolutionary socialist consciousness is probably a temporary phenomena: The "lag" can be overcome by the direct intervention of conscious socialist political formations deeply inserted in everyday struggles capable of linking economic conditions to political action'.[82]

The ultimate trajectory of the pink tide depends on the capacities of the Left to counter belligerent right-wing oppositions and ongoing imperialist meddling in the sovereign affairs of Latin-American nations; just as crucial, though, will be the course of the battle between different currents within the Left seeking to gain hegemony over the anti-neoliberal bloc. Latin America 'has moved into an historic conjuncture in which the struggle among social and political forces could push the new resistance politics into mildly social democratic and populist outcomes', William I. Robinson points out, 'or into more fundamental, potentially revolutionary ones'. Results 'will depend considerably on the configuration of class and social forces in each country and the extent to which regional and global configurations of these forces open up new space and push such governments in distinct directions'.[83]

Nowhere have the obstacles to transformation been more visible than in Bolivia. Despite its impressive capacity to mobilise, and despite its far-reaching anticapitalist and indigenous-liberationist objectives, the left-indigenous bloc of 2000–5 lacked a revolutionary party through which the necessary leadership, strategy, and ideological coherence might have been provided to overthrow the existing capitalist state and rebuild a new sovereign power rooted in the self-governance of the overwhelmingly indigenous proletarian and peasant-majority. Partially as a consequence, the fallout of the extraordinary mobilisations and profound crisis of state witnessed during September–October 2003 and May–June 2005 was not revolutionary transformation, but rather a shift in popular politics from the extraparliamentary terrains of the streets and countryside back toward the electoral arena, as elections were moved up to 18 December 2005.

This shift to the domain of electoral politics and the victory of the MAS in the December elections dampened the immediate prospects for socialist and indigenous-liberationist revolution growing out of the revolutionary epoch of 2000–5. This is the case because of the modestly reformist nature of the

---

82. Petras 2009.
83. Robinson 2007, p. 148.

MAS party, the relative decline in the self-organisation and self-activity of the popular classes in the wake of Morales' victory – a President who seemed to represent their interests –, and the common phenomenon of social movements draining themselves of their transformative energies, organisation, and capacity to build popular power from below in workplaces and communities when they adopt a pre-eminently electoral focus. Given the performance of the MAS during the Mesa interregnum, it should have been no surprise when the Morales régime continued to exhibit, over its first years in office, major continuities with the neoliberal model of political economy it inherited from antecedent governments.[84]

Reforms in the hydrocarbons- (natural-gas and oil-) sector have generated important new revenues for the Bolivian state, and the Morales government has built important ties with Venezuela, Cuba, Ecuador, and other countries which favour moves toward more Latin-American and Caribbean independence from US-imperial control. There have also been clashes between the Morales administration and the International Monetary Fund (IMF), and Morales threw out the US-ambassador during his first term for interfering in the sovereign affairs of the country. Morales is also an extremely important symbolic figure for indigenous movements through the Americas, and simply by becoming president struck a blow against white-*mestizo* informal apartheid rule in Bolivia.

However, Morales's first four years in office also witnessed the hollowing out of the left-indigenous demand for a revolutionary constituent assembly – the assembly introduced by the MAS government in 2006 purged the process of all revolutionary and participatory potential by seeking to appease the eastern-lowland bourgeoisie concerning its rules of conduct and content. The combined liberation-struggle for indigenous liberation and socialist transformation of 2000 to 2005 has been altered into a struggle of distinct stages. The MAS emphasises indigenous liberation today, with socialist transformation only a remote possibility, 50 to 100 years in the future. In terms of neoliberal-capitalist continuities, the Morales administration has, among other things, maintained central-bank independence, guaranteed private-property rights, and pledged commitment to fiscal austerity and low inflationary caps. Bolivian and foreign capital have been guaranteed continuing labour-market

---

84. See Webber 2008a, 2008b, 2008c, 2010b, and 2010c.

'flexibility', and land-reform has gone virtually nowhere, in spite of sustained rhetoric to the contrary.[85] Poverty-data, which does not go past 2007, shows almost no change in the rate since 2005 in spite of soaring natural-gas prices generating unprecedented rents for the state. Indeed, between 2005 and 2007 poverty *increased* from 59.9 to 60.1 per cent, and extreme poverty stayed steady at 37.7 per cent. Inequality, as measured by the Gini-coefficient, declined very modestly from 60.2 to 56.3 between 2005 and 2007. Even keeping in mind that these figures do 'not take into account any increase in access to government services such as health-care or education, and [do] not include the impact of the expansion of the [social programmes introduced]...in 2008', they do not correspond with largely uncritical left commentary on the Morales government.[86]

The economic and social policies of the Morales government, then, appear to exhibit important continuities with the inherited neoliberal model. There seems also to be little change in the overall strategy of political economy guiding the MAS-government as it begins its second term in office in early 2010. Advancing the project of indigenous liberation and socialist emancipation – so vividly articulated by popular forces between 2000 and 2005 – will therefore require renewed self-activity, self-organisation and strategic mobilisation of left-indigenous movements autonomous from the MAS-government.

For the international anticapitalist Left, the insurrectionary cycle in Bolivia in the first five years of the current century constitutes a rich source for inspiration and reflection. The assemblyist formations of revolutionary democracy in the streets and countryside were extraordinary expressions of popular power from below that ought to inform, in different ways, our strategies for revolution around the world. They are models of heroism and possibility.

---

85. See Webber 2008a, 2008b, 2008c. On labour-markets, see Escóbar de Pabón 2009a, 2009b. On the failures of agrarian reform, see Ormachea Saavedra 2009.

86. For poverty- and inequality-figures, see Weisbrot, Ray and Johnston 2009, pp. 16–19.

Appendix A

Formal Interviewees

On average interviews lasted between 30 and 45 minutes. A few reached four hours in duration, and a few others were as brief as 15 to 20 minutes.

1. Achacollo, Nemecia. Executive Secretary of the Federación Nacional de Mujeres Campesinas de Bolivia 'Bartolina Sisa' (National Federation of Peasant-Women of Bolivia 'Bartolina Sisa', FNMCB-BS). El Alto, 6 April 2005.
2. Alanoca Mamani, Jaime. General Secretary, Federación Única de Desocupados del Departamento de La Paz (Federation of Unemployed Workers of the Department of La Paz). La Paz, 31 May 2005.
3. Alegre Colque, Florentina. Leading activist in anarchist-feminist group, Mujeres Creando (Women Creating). La Paz, 29 June 2005.
4. Amantegui, Dr. Jorge A. Legal Advisor, Pro Santa Cruz Committee. Santa Cruz, 8 July 2005.
5. Anonymous Employee. Offices of the Human-Rights Ombudsperson of El Alto. La Paz, 12 May 2005.
6. Barrera, Carlos. Ex-Vice-President, FEJUVE-El Alto. El Alto, 11 May 2005.
7. Calcina, Fortunato. Secretary of Popular Participation, FEJUVE-El Alto. El Alto, 30 March 2005.
8. Canqui, Winston. Advisor to municipal councillor and M-17 activist Roberto de la Cruz, activist in El Alto. El Alto, 29 June 2005.
9. Cardozo Pacheco, Juan. General Secretary, FSTMB. La Paz, 31 May 2005.
10. Choque, Félix. Secretary of Housing, FSTMB. La Paz, 3 May 2005.
11. Choque, Gualberto. Executive Secretary, FUDTCLP-TK. El Alto, 27 May 2005.

12. Choque, Vidal. Journalist and university-student activist based in El Alto. La Paz, 14 March 2005.

13. Chura, Jorge. General Secretary, FEJUVE-El Alto. El Alto, 24 May 2005.

14. Churata, Placido. Secretary of Finance, Federation of Health-Care Workers (FENSEGURAL), important federation within COB. La Paz, 5 April 2005.

15. Claure, Alicia. Secretary of the Commission for Neighbourhood Defence, District 8, El Alto, FEJUVE-El Alto. El Alto, 30 March 2005.

16. Condori, Remijio. Secretary of Relations, COR-El Alto. El Alto, 1 April 2005.

17. Condori Cruz, Edilberto. Neighbourhood-council activist, FEJUVE-El Alto. El Alto, 4 April 2005.

18. Condori Quispe, Mercedes. Secretary of Finance, FEJUVE-El Alto. El Alto, 4 April 2005.

19. Cori, Mauricio. Ex-Executive Secretary, FEJUVE-El Alto. El Alto, 4 May 2005.

20. Cruz, Pedro. Permanent Secretary, COB. La Paz, 4 May 2005.

21. Cuellar, Elizabeth. Generational Secretary, FEJUVE-El Alto. El Alto, 30 March 2005.

22. De la Cruz, Roberto. Ex-General Secretary, COR-El Alto, municipal councillor in El Alto, founder of and activist in radical anticapitalist and indigenous-liberationist group in El Alto, M-17. El Alto, 12 May and 29 June 2005.

23. Dias V., Teófanes. General Co-ordinator, Comité de Defensa del Patrimonio Nacional de la Soberania y Dignidad (Committee for the Defence of Dignity, Sovereignty, and National Patrimony). La Paz, 31 May 2005.

24. Espinoza, Ernesto. Secretary of Conflicts, COR-El Alto. El Alto, 24 May 2005.

25. Fernández, Omar. Vice-President, Coordinadora, President, Federación Departamental de Regantes (Departmental Federation of Peasant-Irrigators of Cochabamba, FEDECOR). Cochabamba. 28 July 2005.

26. Ferreira, Javo. Leading member of Liga Obrera Revolucionario (Revolutionary Workers' League, LOR), a small revolutionary-socialist party, editor of newspaper *Palabra Obrera*. El Alto, 24 May 2005.

27. García Linera, Álvaro. Sociologist, left-wing intellectual, ex-guerrilla in the EGTK, social activist, prominent television-commentator, Vice-President under Evo Morales government. La Paz, 10 April 2005.

28. Gómez, Luis A. Journalist and activist based in La Paz. La Paz, 11 March 2005.

29. Gosálvez, Gonzalo. Journalist, intellectual, and activist, based in La Paz, founder of Bolivia Indymedia. La Paz, 9 April 2005.

30. Gutiérrez, Rafael. Director of UPEA. La Paz, 31 May, 2005.

31. Gutiérrez de Medina, Baígida Saida. Neighbourhood-council activist, District 1. El Alto, 4 April 2005.

32. Iquiapaza, Eliodoro. Vice-President, FEJUVE-El Alto. El Alto, 17 May 2005.

33. Kempff Suárez, Julio Enrique. General Manager, Federación de Empresarios Privados de Santa Cruz (Federation of Private Entrepreneurs of Santa Cruz, FPESC). Santa Cruz, 14 July 2005.

34. Lucana, Alberto. Secretary of Citizen Security, FEJUVE-El Alto. El Alto, 4 April 2005.

35. Madani, Leonicio. Secretary of Finance, FSTMB. La Paz, 3 May 2005.

36. Mamani Angulo, German. Secretary of Organisation, District 8, FEJUVE-El Alto. El Alto, 4 April 2005.

37. Mamani, Abel. Executive Secretary, FEJUVE-El Alto. El Alto, 5 May and 28 June 2005.

38. Mamani, Rafael. Secretary of Human Rights, FEJUVE-El Alto. El Alto, 20 May and 23 June 2005.

39. Mamani Heredia, Samuel. Member of executive committee of FEJUVE-El Alto. El Alto, 1 April 2005.

40. Mamani Ramírez, Pablo. Sociologist at UPEA and UMSA, activist in El Alto, author and indigenous-liberationist intellectual. El Alto, 15 April 2005.

41. Mamani Salamanca, Tomás. President of Neighbourhood-Councils of Santiago II. El Alto, 6 May 2005.

42. Mancilla, Rodolfo. Secretary General, Federación de Trabajadores, Gremiales, Artesanos y Comerciantes Minoristas (Federation of Organised Workers, Artisans, Small Traders and Food-Sellers of the city of El Alto, FTGACM), 31 March 2005.

43. Martela, Juan Antonio. Secretary of Organisation, FEJUVE-El Alto. El Alto, 31 March and 23 June 2005.

44. Mendoza Mamani, Jorge. Neighbouhood-council activist, District 2, El Alto. El Alto, 20 May 2005.
45. Merida Gutiérrez, Henry. Secretary of Human Rights, COR-El Alto. El Alto, 1 April 2005.
46. Miranda, Damaso. Secretary of Internal Relations, Federación de Traba-jadores, Gremiales, Artesanos y Comerciantes Minoristas (Federation of Organised Workers, Artisans, Small Traders and Food-Sellers of the City of El Alto, FTGACM). El Alto, 10 May 2005.
47. Núñez Tancara, Dionisio. Congressperson and Secretary of the Commit-tee for the Fight Against Narcotrafficking, MAS. La Paz, 19 May 2005.
48. Ojeda Marguay, Julieta. Leading activist in anarchist-feminist group, Mujeres Creando (Women Creating). La Paz, 29 June 2005.
49. Olivera, Oscar. President, Coordinadora, President, Federación de Fab-riles de Cochabamba (Federation of Factory-Workers of Cochabamba). Cochabamba, 22 July 2005.
50. Ortíz Antelo, Oscar M. General Manager, CAINCO. Santa Cruz, 11 July 2005.
51. Osinaga Rosado, Edilberto. General Manager, Cámara Agropecuaria del Oriente (Eastern Agricultural Chamber, CAO). Santa Cruz, 15 July 2005.
52. Pabón Chávez, Julio. Secretary of Economic Development, FEJUVE-El Alto. El Alto, 30 March 2005.
53. Patana, Edgar. Executive Secretary, COR-El Alto. El Alto, 10 and 17 May 2005.
54. Patz, Félix. Sociologist, professor at UMSA, indigenous-liberationist intel-lectual and activist. La Paz, 13 May 2005.
55. Pérez Morales, Miriam. Auxiliary Nurse, Secretary of Conflicts, Fed-eration of Health-Care Workers (FENSEGURAL), important federation within COB. La Paz, 5 April 2005.
56. Poñez, Sonia. Secretary of Health, CPESC. Santa Cruz, 18 July 2005.
57. Puma Morales, Adolfo. Secretary of Conflicts, FEJUVE-El Alto. El Alto, 4 April 2005.
58. Quisbert Quispe, Máximo. Sociologist, author of influential book on clientelism in FEJUVE-El Alto, La Paz, 4 March 2005.
59. Quispe, Felipe. Executive Secretary, CSUTCB, ex-guerrilla in EGTK, indigenous-liberationist author and intellectual. La Paz, 12 May 2005.

60. Quispe Gutiérrez, Benecio. Sociologist, professor at UPEA, ex-liberation-theologian, ex-member of Centro de Estudios Alternativos (Centre for Alternative Studies, CEA), a group of indigenous-liberationist activists and intellectuals, activist in El Alto and western *altiplano*. El Alto, 5 May 2005.

61. Ramos, Edgar. Journalist and activist based in El Alto. La Paz, 10 March 2005.

62. Ramos, Rafael. Secretary of Conflicts, Federación de Trabajadores, Gremiales, Artesanos y Comerciantes Minoristas (Federation of Organised Workers, Artisans, Small Traders and Food-Sellers of the City of El Alto, FTGACM). El Alto, 10 May 2005.

63. Rojas, Carlos. Secretary of Popular Participation, FEJUVE-El Alto. El Alto, 20 May 2005.

64. Salgueido Valda, Teddy. Secretary of International Relations, Federation of Health-Care Workers (FENSEGURAL), important federation within COB. La Paz, 5 April 2005.

65. Salinas, Nestor. Founder and leader of Familiares de los Fallecidos de Octubre, a group dedicated to bringing to justice those government-officials responsible for the deaths and injuries of civilians during the September–October 2003 Gas-War. El Alto, 1 April 2005.

66. Solares, Jaime. Executive Secretary, COB. La Paz, 3 May 2005.

67. Solares Barrientos, Jorge. Secretary of Social Security, COB. La Paz, 5 April 2005.

68. Solón, Pablo. Founder of Fundación Solón, a Bolivian NGO that campaigns against privatisation and neoliberal trade-agreements and for women's rights. La Paz, 27 June 2005.

69. Suárez, Luciano. President of Neighbourhood-Councils, District 8, El Alto. El Alto, 20 May 2005.

70. Terceras, Elva. Researcher, CEJIS. Santa Cruz, 11 July 2005.

71. Vilela, Jaime. Leading member of Movimiento Socialista de los Trabajadores (Socialist Workers' Movement), a small Trotskyist party. La Paz, 9 and 10 March 2005.

72. Yubanore A., Jaime. Secretary of Land and Territory, Acting Vice-President at time of interview, CIDOB. Santa Cruz, 13 July 2005.

73. Yujra, Alfredo. Vice-President of Neighbourhood-Council, Río Seco, FEJUVE-El Alto. El Alto, 4 April 2005.

74. Yujra Flores, Ricardo. Secretary of Relations, FSTMB. La Paz, 2 April 2005.

75. Zarco, Tomás. General Secretary, Student-Federation of UPEA (FUL-UPEA). El Alto, 24 May 2005.

76. Zubieta, Miguel. Executive Secretary, FSTMB. La Paz, 23 June 2005.

Appendix B
Methodology

This study draws selectively from the methodology of comparative-historical sociology. My analysis shares with this school a 'commitment to offering historically grounded explanations of large-scale and substantively important outcomes', as well as the contention that these 'fundamental processes could not – and cannot – be analyzed without recognising the importance of temporal sequences and the unfolding of events over time'.[1] The narrative mode common to comparative-historical sociology is employed throughout the book. This method best captures the ways in which social phenomena are sequential, temporally ordered, open-ended processes full of contingent and conjunctural episodes, occurring at the same time within broader longer-term structures that place limits on those contingencies.[2] In Marx's famous lines from *The Eighteenth Brumaire of Louis Bonaparte*, 'Human beings make their own history, but they do not make it just as they please; they do not make it under circumstances chosen by themselves, but under circumstances directly encountered, given and transmitted from the past. The tradition of all the dead generations weighs like a nightmare on the brain of the living'.[3]

The research for this book included the collection of data from a range of sources. The historical sections are based on a novel synthesis of different streams of historical writing on working-class and indigenous history, and the development of capitalism and state-formation in Bolivia. The chapters on left-indigenous popular movements and contemporary politics since 2000 are grounded in 10 months of field-research carried out between January and September 2005, and April and May 2006. During this time, I was based

---

1. Mahoney and Rueschemeyer 2003, p. 4.
2. Griffin 1993; Mahoney 2000, p. 510; Silver 2003, p. 30.
3. Marx 1981 [1852], p. 15. I have altered the gendered language of 'men' in the original to 'human beings'.

principally in La Paz, where I was able to make trips to neighbouring El Alto several times per week. During some weeks, I was in El Alto every day. While in La Paz, I was a visiting scholar at the Centro Boliviano de Estudios Multidisciplinarios (Bolivian Centre of Multidisciplinary Studies, CEBEM). I had a desk and computer and access to the centre's library. Over this ten-month period I also conducted research-trips to the cities of Santa Cruz and Cochabamba.

The bulk of my research entailed semi-structured formal interviews with popular-movement activists in El Alto and La Paz. In total, I conducted 81 formal interviews (see Appendix A). Because I was living in La Paz when the second Gas-War of May and June 2005 occurred, I was also privileged to observe and/or take part in numerous social-movement assemblies, meetings (large and small), public lectures and debates, strikes, protests, marches, clashes with the police and military, and the eventual overthrow of President Carlos Mesa in the beginning of June 2005, as over 500,000 people occupied downtown La Paz. Simply being a part of this general milieu led to countless informal conversations with activists of various kinds and levels of commitment to the popular movement, all of which greatly enhanced my comprehension of the dynamics of left-indigenous struggle in contemporary Bolivia.

In addition to interviews and tape-recording and transcription of the lectures and popular assemblies I attended, I was also permitted access to the archives of the FSTMB and the COB. These archives are held in their offices in La Paz, and contain all the relevant assembly resolutions and political communiqués from the 2003 and 2005 Gas-Wars. I also did extensive qualitative research in the leading national newspapers, *La Razón* and *La Prensa*, and additional archival work in smaller national newspapers and regional and local dailies. I did this through print-editions while in Bolivia, and through on-line archives while in Canada and the Netherlands. I also read every issue I was able to acquire of the numerous different national weekly and monthly magazines for the period between 2000 and 2005. Most important were *Barataria*, *Alerta Laboral*, *El Juguete Rabioso*, *Pulso* and the Bolivian edition of *Le Monde Diplomatique*.

As Javier Auyero demonstrates in his penetrating study of two Argentine women's experiences during two protest-episodes in that country, narrative and story-telling are indispensable, 'not only in creating the possibilities for collective action...but also in constructing the experiential meanings of events during and after the fact and thus the self-understandings of those who, on either side, participate in them'.[4] For Auyero, 'the stories that actors tell after the event not only speak about the ongoing political construction of the uprising (the 'social construction of protest') but also speak to the protesters' hopes, expectations, emotions, and beliefs at the time'.[5] However 'rusty, bent, and unpredictable... they are', these stories remain among the 'few keys' we have that can 'help us to understand the ways in which people make sense of collective struggle'.[6] In-depth stories of activist biographies and experiences during and immediately after periods of struggle are also one of the best ways of getting a grip on the transformative imaginations of activists during these periods, their visions of the new society they are seeking to establish. The extended quotations from activists that I employ throughout the last half of this book are the 'poetics of struggle and lived experience', the 'utterances of ordinary folk', and the 'cultural products of social movements' that provide us with 'the many different cognitive maps of the future of the world not yet born'.[7]

Ethnographic researchers of social movements have tended to convey a healthy scepticism with regard to transhistorical generalisations and categories purporting to explain various modes of collective action across geographies, space and time. Ethnographers, by portraying the messier and more complex character of social movements when viewed from a closer angle, 'have often provided compelling, fine-grained accounts of collective action', whereas 'they have been less consistent when it comes to developing dynamic analyses of either the larger political contexts in which mobilisations occur or the preexisting militant traditions and the organising processes that constitute movements' proximate and remote roots'.[8] Methodologically, I draw from ethnographic traditions in order to gain the 'privileged access' they provide 'to the lived experience of activists and nonactivists, as well as a window onto the "submerged" organising, informal networks, protest activities, ideological differences, public claim-making, fear and repression, and internal tensions,

---

4. Auyero 2003, p. 11.
5. Ibid.
6. Auyero 2003, p. 12.
7. Kelley 2002, pp. 9–10.
8. Edelman 2001, p. 309.

which are almost everywhere features of social movements'.[9] At the same time, I attempt to overcome the ahistoricism and parochialism characteristic of some ethnographic work on modern social movements, by linking the insights gathered from interviews and participant-observation with systematic historical contextualisation and detailed accounts of relevant structural change in the political economy at the national and international levels.

---

9. Edelman 2001, pp. 309–10.

References

Agadjanian, Victor 2002, 'Competition and Cooperation among Working Women in the Context of Structural Adjustment: The Case of Street-vendors in La Paz-El Alto, Bolivia', *Journal of Development Studies*, 18, 2–3: 259–85.

Albo, Gregory 2007, 'Neoliberalism and the Discontented', in *Socialist Register 2008: Global Flashpoints, Reactions to Imperialism and Neoliberalism*, edited by Leo Panitch, and Colin Leys, New York: Monthly Review Press.

Albó, Xavier 1987, 'From MNRistas to Kataristas to Katari', in *Resistance, Rebellion, and Consciousness in the Andean Peasant World, 18th to 20th Centuries*, edited by Steve J. Stern, Wisconsin: The University of Wisconsin Press.

——— 1995, 'And from Kataristas to MNRistas? The Surprising and Bold Alliance Between Aymaras and Neoliberals in Bolivia', in *Indigenous Peoples and Democracy in Latin America*, edited by Donna Lee Van Cott, New York: St. Martin's Press.

——— 1996, 'Bolivia: Making the Leap from Local Mobilisation to National Politcs', *NACLA Report on the Americas*, 29, 5: 15–20.

——— 2002a, 'Bolivia: From Indian and Campesino Leaders to Councillors and Parliamentary Deputies', in *Multiculturalism in Latin America: Indigenous Rights, Diversity and Democracy*, edited by Rachel Sieder, New York: Palgrave Macmillan.

——— 2002b, *Pueblos indios en la política*, La Paz: Plural editores.

——— 2006, 'El Alto, La Vorágine de Una Ciudad Única', *Journal of Latin-American Anthropology*, 11, 2: 329–50.

Albro, Robert 2005a, 'The Indigenous in the Plural in Bolivian Oppositional Politics', *Bulletin of Latin-American Research*, 24, 4: 433–53.

——— 2005b, 'The Waters is Ours, Carajo!: Deep Citizenship in Bolivia's Water-War', in *Social Movements: A Reader*, edited by June C. Nash, Hoboken: Basic Blackwell.

Alexander, Robert J. 1973, *Trotskyism in Latin America*, Stanford: Hoover Institution Press, Stanford University.

Ali, Tariq 2006, *Pirates of the Caribbean: Axis of Hope*, London: Verso.

Alto, FEJUVE-EL 2005, Resolutions of FEJUVE-El Alto Emergency Assembly – 17 May.

Álvarez, Sonia E., Evelina Dagnino, and Arturo Escobar 1998, 'Introduction: The Cultural and the Political in Latin-American Social Movements', in *Cultures of Politics/ Politics of Cultures: Re-Visioning Latin-American Social Movements*, edited by Sonia E. Álvarez, Evelina Dagnino, and Arturo Escobar, Boulder: Westview Press.

Anderson, Perry 1980, *Arguments Within English Marxism*, London: New Left Books.

Andreas, Peter 1995, 'Free-Market Reform and Drug Market Prohibition: US Politics at Cross-Purposes in Latin America', *Third World Quarterly*, 16, 1: 75–87.

Anonymous. 2005. Personal Interview, High-ranking employee, Office of the Human Rights Ombudsman, El Alto, 12 May.

Antezana, Luis H. 1983, 'Sistema y proceso ideológicos en Bolivia (1937–1979)', in *Bolivia, Hoy*, edited by René Zavaleta Mercado, Mexico: Siglo veintiuno editores.

Apaza Mamani, Cipriana 2005, Personal Interview, El Alto.

APDHB/ASOFAMD/CBDHDD/DIAKONIA/FUNSOLON/RED-ADA 2004, *12–13 de Febrero 2003: Para que no se olvide*, La Paz: Plural editores.

Arbona, Juan, and Benjamin Kohl 2004, 'La Paz – El Alto: City Profile', *Cities*, 21, 3: 255–65.

Arbona, Juan Manuel 2005, 'Los límites de los márgenes: organizaciones políticas locales y las Jornadas de Octubre de 2003', *Nueva Sociedad* 197: 6–15.

—— 2007, 'Neo-Liberal Ruptures: Local Political Entities and Neighbourhood Networks in El Alto, Bolivia', *Geoforum*, 38: 127–37.

—— 2008, '"Sangre de minero, semilla de guerrillero": Histories and Memories in the Organisation and Struggles of the Santiago II Neighbourhood of El Alto, Bolivia', *Bulletin of Latin-American Research*, 27, 1: 24–42.

Arellano-López, Sonia, and James Petras 1994, 'Non-Governmental Organisations and Poverty Alleviation in Bolivia', *Development and Change*, 25, 3: 555–68.

Arze Aguierre, René Danilo 1987, *Guerra y conflictos sociales: El caso rural boliviano durante la campaña del Chaco*, Cochabamba: CERES.

Arze, Carlos, and Tom Kruse 2004, 'The Consequences of Neoliberal Reform', *NACLA Report on the Americas*, 38, 3: 23–8.

Arze, Carlos, and Pablo Poveda 2004, 'Política de hidrocarburos: el cerco de las transnacionales', in *Economía y sociedad boliviana después de octubre de 2003: Análisis de un año de gobierno de Carlos Mesa*, edited by CEDLA, La Paz: CEDLA.

Arze Vargas, Carlos 2000, *Crisis del sindicalismo boliviano: Consideraciones sobre sus determinantes materiales y su ideología*, La Paz: CEDLA.

ASOFAC-DG 2007, *Avances, riesgos y retos del juicio de responsabilidades a Gonzalo Sánchez de Loazada y sus colaboradores*, La Paz: Asociación de Familiares Caídos por la Defensa del Gas (ASOFAC-DG), Defensor del Pueblo, Comunidad de Derechos Humanos.

Assies, Willem 1998, 'Indigenous Peoples and Reform of the State in Latin America', in *The Challenge of Diversity: Indigenous Peoples and Reform of the State in Latin America*, edited by Willem Assies, Gemma van der Haar, and André J. Hoekema, Amsterdam: Thela Thesis.

—— 2003, 'Davis versus Goliath in Cochabamba: Water Rights, Neoliberalism, and the Revival of Social Protest in Bolivia', *Latin American Perspectives*, 30, 3: 14–36.

Assies, Willem, Gemma van der Haar, and André J. Hoekema 1998, 'Diversity as a Challenge: A Note on the Dilemmas of Diversity', in *The Challenge of Diversity: Indigenous Peoples and Reform of the State in Latin America*, edited by Willem Assies, Gemma van der Haar, and André J. Hoekema, Amsterdam: Thela Thesis.

Associated Press 2003, 'Chronology of Events Leading to the Bolivian President's Resignation', *Associated Press*, 18 October.

Auyero, Javier 2003, *Contentious Lives: Two Argentine Women, Two Protests, and the Quest for Recognition*, Durham, NC.: Duke University Press.

Bannerji, Himani 2000, *The Dark Side of the Nation: Essays on Multiculturalism, Nationalism and Gender*, Toronto: Canadian Scholars Press.

Barrera, Carlos 2005, Personal Interview, El Alto, 11 May.

Becker, Marc 1993, *Mariátegui and Latin American Marxist Theory*, Athens, OH.: Ohio University Monographs in International Studies.

—— 2006, 'Mariátegui, the Comintern, and the Indigenous Question in Latin America', *Science and Society*, 70, 4: 450–79.

Benjamin, Thomas 1989, *A Rich Land, A Poor People: Politics and Society in Modern Chiapas*, Albuquerque: University of New Mexico Press.

Bergquist, Charles 1986, *Labor in Latin America: Comparative Essays on Chile, Argentina, Venezuela and Colombia*, Stanford: Stanford University Press.

Birner, Jóhanna Kristín, and Donna Lee Van Cott 2007, 'Disunity in Diversity: Party System Fragmentation and the Dynamic Effect of Ethnic Heterogeneity on Latin-American Legislatures', *Latin American Research Review*, 42, 1: 99–125.

Bouvard, Marguerite Guzman 1994, *Revolutionizing Motherhood: The Mothers of the Plaza de Mayo*, Wilmington: Scholarly Resources, Inc.

Brass, Tom 2002a, 'Introduction: Latin American Peasants – New Paradigms for Old?', *Journal of Peasant Studies*, 9, 3–4: 1–40.

—— 2002b, 'On Which Side of What Barricade? Subaltern Resistance in Latin America and Elsewhere', *Journal of Peasant Studies*, 29, 3–4: 336–99.

Brenner, Johanna 2000, *Women and the Politics of Class*, New York: Monthly Review Press.

Brockett, Charles D. 1991, 'The Structure of Political Opportunities and Peasant Mobilisation in Central America', *Comparative Politics*, 23, 3: 253–74.
—— 2005, *Political Movements and Violence in Central America*, Cambridge: Cambridge University Press.
Bulmer-Thomas, Victor 1996, *The New Economic Model in Latin America and Its Impact on Income Distribution and Poverty*, New York: St. Martin's Press.
Bustamante, Gerardo 2005, Personal Interview, El Alto.
Cáceres, Sergio 2005a, 'El Discurseador: Carlos Mesa', *El Juguete Rabioso*, 23 June.
—— 2005b, 'La nacionalización: los movimientos sociales se radicalizan y exigen', *El Juguete Rabioso*, 29 May.
Cajías de la Vega, Magdalena 2004, 'El poder de la memoria: Articulaciones ideológico-culturales en los movimientos sociales bolivianos', *Barataria*, 1, 1: 18–28.
Calcina, Fortunato 2005, Personal Interview, El Alto, 30 March.
Callinicos, Alex 2009, *Imperialism and Global Political Economy*, Cambridge: Polity Press.
Camaroff, John 1987, 'Of Totemism and Ethnicity: Consciousness, Practice and the Signs of Inequality', *Ethnos*, 52: 301–23.
Camfield, David 2004, 'Re-Orienting Class Analysis: Working Classes as Historical Formations', *Science and Society*, 68, 4: 421–46.
—— 2007, 'The Multitude and the Kangaroo: A Critique of Hardt and Negri's Theory of Immaterial Labour', *Historical Materialism*, 15, 2: 21–52.
Canel, Eduardo 1997, 'New Social-movement Theory and Resource-Mobilisation Theory: The Need for Integration', in *Community Power and Grassroots Democracy: The Transformation of Social Life*, edited by Michael Kaufman and Haroldo Dilla Alfonso, London: Zed.
Canessa, Andrew 2000, 'Contesting Hybridity: *Evangelistas* and *Kataristas* in Highland Bolivia', *Journal of Latin-American Studies*, 32, 1: 115–44.
Cárdenas, Mauricio 2008, *Global Financial Crisis: Is Brazil a Bystander?* Washington: The Brookings Institution, Latin America Initiative, 15 October.
Cardozo Pacheco, Juan. 2005, Personal Interview, El Alto, 31 May.
Castañeda, Jorge G. 2006 'Latin America's Left Turn', *Foreign Affairs*, May–June, available online at: <http://www.foreignaffairs.org/20060501faessay85302/jorge-g-castaneda/latin-america-s-left-turn.html>.
Centeno, Miguel A. and Patricio Silva (eds.) 1998, *The Politics of Expertise in Latin America*, New York: St. Martin's Press.
CEPAL 2007, *Social Panorama of Latin America 2007*, Santiago: Comisión Económica para América Latina y el Caribe.
—— 2008, *Panorama Social de América Latina*, Santiago: Comisión Económica para América Latina y el Caribe.
Chávez, Hugo 2003, *Discursos fundamentales: Ideología y acción política*, Caracas: Foro Bolivariano de Nuestra América.
Chávez, Marxa 2005a, Public Lecture, La Paz: La Comuna.
Chávez, Walter 2005b, 'El ex presidente Carlos Mesa: "Le pido perdón a la patria"', *El Juguete Rabioso*, 12 June.
—— 2005c, 'El otro indeciso: Evo Morales', *El Juguete Rabioso*, 29 May.
—— 2005d, 'Un recorrido histórico: Las luchas por la autonomía cruceña', *Barataria*, 1, 3: 60–5.
Chávez, Walter and Álvaro García Linera 2005, 'Rebelión Camba: Del dieselazo a la lucha por la autonomía', *El Juguete Rabioso*, 23 January.
Chávez, Walter and Miguel Lora 2005, 'La disputa por la renta petrolera', *Le Monde Diplomatique*, Bolivian edition, April.
Chomsky, Noam 1986, *Turning the Tide: U.S. Intervention in Central America*, Cambridge, MA.: South End Press.
—— 1983, *Towards a New Cold War: Essays on the Current Crisis and How We Got There*, New York, Pantheon.
Choque Canqui, Roberto and Esteban Alejo Ticona 1996, *Sublevación y masacre de 1921*, *Jesús de Machaqa*, La Paz: CIPCA-CEDOIN.

Choque, Félix 2005a, Personal Interview, La Paz, 3 May.
Choque, Gualberto 2005b, Personal Interview, El Alto, 27 May.
—— 2005c, Public Lecture, La Paz, UMSA.
Choque, Vidal 2005d, Personal Interview, La Paz, 14 March.
Cingolani, Pablo 2005, 'Civilización y barbarie, versión siglo XXI: la ciudad cercada', *El Juguete Rabioso*, 12 June.
Claure, Alicia 2005, Personal Interview, El Alto, 30 March.
COB 2003a, Comité Ejecutivo de la Central Obrera Boliviana – Gobierno desarrolla campaña de amedrentamiento y amenazas, Communique, La Paz.
—— 2003b, Comité Ejecutivo de la Central Obrera Boliviana – Protesta obrera se fortalece, Communique, La Paz.
—— 2003c, Instructivo, Comité Ejecutivo de la Central Obrera Boliviana, Communique, La Paz.
—— 2003d, Programa de lucha de la COB, Communique, La Paz.
—— 2003e, Resoluciones del ampliado extraordinario de la COB, Communique, La Paz.
Cohen, G.A. 1978, *Karl Marx's Theory of History: A Defence*, Princeton: Princeton University Press.
Cohen, Jean L. 1985, 'Strategy or Identity: New Theoretical Paradigms and Contemporary Social movements', *Social Research*, 52, 4: 663–717.
Cojtí Cuxil, Demetrio 2002, 'Educational Reform in Guatemala: Lessons from Negotiations between Indigenous Civil Society and the State', in *Multiculturalism in Latin America: Indigenous Rights, Diversity and Democracy*, edited by Rachel Sieder, New York: Palgrave Macmillan.
Conaghan, Catherine M. 1994, 'Reconsidering Jeffrey Sachs and the Bolivian Economic Experiment', in *Money Doctors, Foreign Debts, and Economic Reforms in Latin America from the 1890s to the Present*, edited by Paul W. Drake, Wilmington: Scholarly Resources Inc.
Conaghan, Catherine M., James M. Malloy and Luis A. Abugattas 1990, 'Business and the 'Boys': The Politics of Neoliberalism in the Central Andes', *Latin American Research Review*, 25, 2: 3–30.
Condarco Morales, Ramiro 1965, *Zárate, el 'Temible' Willca*, La Paz: Talleres Gráficos.
Condori Quispe, Mercedes 2005, Personal Interview, El Alto, 4 March.
Condori, Remigio 2005, Personal Interview, El Alto, 1 April.
Cook, María Lorena 2007, *The Politics of Labor Reform in Latin America: Between Flexibility and Rights*, University Park: Pennsylvania State University Press.
Cori, Mauricio 2005, Personal Interview, El Alto, 4 May.
Corrales, Javier 2009, 'For Chávez, Still More Discontent', *Current History*, 108, 715: 77–82.
Costas Monje, Patricia 2005, Public Lecture, La Paz: Comuna.
Crabtree, John 2005, *Patterns of Protest: Politics and Social Movements in Bolivia*, London: Latin America Bureau.
Crabtree, John, Gavan Duffy and Jenny Pearce 1987, *The Great Tin Crash: Bolivia and the World Tin Market*, London: Latin America Bureau.
Crespo Flores, Carlos 2000, 'Continuidad y ruptura: la "Guerra del Agua" y los movimientos sociales en Bolivia', *Obervatorio Social de America Latina* September: 21–8.
Cruz, Pedro 2005, Personal Interview, La Paz, 4 May.
Cuellar, Elizabeth 2005, Personal Interview, El Alto, 30 March.
Dandler, Jorge and Juan Torrico A. 1987, 'From the National Indigenous Congress to the Ayopaya Rebellion: Bolivia, 1945–1947', in *Resistance, Rebellion, and Consciousness in the Andean Peasant World, 18th to 20th Centuries*, edited by Steve J. Stern, Wisconsin: The University of Wisconsin Press.
Davis, Diane E. 1999, 'The Power of Distance: Re-Theorising Social Movements in Latin America', *Theory and Society*, 28, 4: 585–638.
Davis, Mike 2006, *Planet of Slums*, London: Verso.

Davis, Shelton H. 2002, 'Indigenous Peoples, Poverty and Participatory Develop- ment: The Experience of the World Bank in Latin America', in *Multiculturalism in Latin America: Indigenous Rights, Diversity and Democracy*, edited by Rachel Sieder, New York: Palgrave Macmillan.

de Chungara, Domitila Barrios 1978, *Let Me Speak! Testimony of Domitila, A Woman of the Bolivian Mines*, New York: Monthly Review Press.

de Franco, Mario and Ricardo Godoy 1992, 'The Economic Consequences of Cocaine Production in Bolivia: Historical, Local, and Marcoeconomic Perspectives', *Journal of Latin American Studies*, 24, 2: 375–406.

de la Cruz, Roberto 2005, Personal Interviews, El Alto, 12 May and 30 June.

de la Peña, Guillermo 2002, 'Social Citizenship, Ethnic Minority Demands, Human Rights and Neoliberal Paradoxes: A Case Study in Western Mexico', in *Multicultur- alism in Latin America: Indigenous Rights, Diversity and Democracy*, edited by Rachel Sieder, New York: Palgrave Macmillan.

de Mesa, José, Teresa Gisbert and Carlos D. Mesa Gisbert 2003, *Historia de Bolivia*, Fifth edition, La Paz: Editorial Gisbert-CIA S.A.

Díaz Machicao, Porfirio 1955. *Historia de Bolivia: Salamanca, la guerra del Chaco, Tejada Sorzano, 1931–1936*, La Paz: Gisbert.

Dore, Elizabeth 2006, *Myths of Modernity: Peonage and Patriarchy in Nicaragua*, Durham, NC.: Duke University Press.

Dunkerley, James 1984, *Rebellion in the Veins: Political Struggle in Bolivia, 1952–1982*, London: Verso.

—— 1992, 'Political Transition and Economic Stabilisation: Bolivia, 1982–1989', in *Polit- ical Suicide in Latin America: And Other Essays*, edited by James Dunkerley, London: Verso.

—— 1993, 'The Crisis of Bolivian Radicalism', in *The Latin American Left: From the Fall of Allende to Perestroika*, edited by Barry Carr and Steve Ellner, London: Latin America Bureau.

—— 2003, 'The Origins of the Bolivian Revolution in the Twentieth Century: Some Reflections', in *Proclaiming Revolution: Bolivia in Comparative Perspective*, edited by Merilee S. Grindle and Pilar Domingo, London and Cambridge, MA.: Institute of Latin-American Studies, University of London and David Rockefeller Center for Latin American Studies, Harvard University.

—— 2003 [1987], *Orígenes del poder militar: Bolivia 1878–1935*, Second Edition, La Paz: Plural editores.

Eaton, Kent 2007, 'Backlash in Bolivia: Regional Autonomy as a Reaction against Indig- enous Mobilisation', *Politics and Society*, 35, 1: 71–102.

Eckstein, Susan 1983, 'Transformation of a "Revolution from Below": Bolivia and International Capital', *Comparative Studies in Society and History*, 25, 1: 105–35.

—— 1989, 'Power and Popular Protest in Latin America', in *Power and Popular Protest: Latin American Social Movements*, edited by Susan Eckstein, Berkeley: University of California Press.

Eckstein, Susan and Frances Hagopian 1983, 'The Limits of Industrialisation in the Less Developed World: Bolivia', *Economic Development and Cultural Change*, 32, 1: 63–95.

Edelman, Marc 2001, 'Social Movements: Changing Paradigms and Forms of Politics', *Annual Review of Anthropology*, 30: 285–317.

EIU 2006, *Bolivia: Country Profile 2006*, London: Economist Intelligence Unit.

El Alteño 2005a, 'Fejuve marchará el lunes 16 de mayo', *El Alteño*, 12 May.

—— 2005b, 'Organizaciones alteñas ratifican movilizaciones', *El Alteño*, 12 May.

—— 2005c, 'Policía y FFAA en emergencia', *El Alteño*, 24 May.

El Deber 2003a, 'El Alto levanta el paro, en Caranavi hay bloqueos', *El Deber*, 17 Sep- tember.

—— 2003b, 'Protestas se intensifican, cocaleros a los bloqueos', *El Deber*, 11 October.

El Diario 2003a, 'Bloqueo de caminos en el norte de La Paz', *El Diario*, 13 September.

—— 2003b, 'COB y CSUTCB acordaron no negociar por separado', *El Diario*, 11 October.

—— 2003c, 'Multitudinaria marcha paralizó el centro paceño al mediodía', *El Diario*, 20 September.

—— 2005, 'Policía impidió que marchistas sitien el Parlamento Nacional', *El Diario*, 17 May.

Ellner, Steve 2008, *Rethinking Venezuelan Politics: Class, Conflict, and the Chávez Phenomenon*, Boulder: Lynne Rienner.

El Mundo 2005, 'La Sede de Gobierno puede quedar aislada si se confirman los bloqueos', *El Mundo*, 7 May.

El Nuevo Día 2005, 'Mesa decide el futuro de la ley del gas presionado por varios frentes', *El Nuevo Día*, 10 May.

Escárzaga, Fabiola and Raquel Gutiérrez (eds.) 2005, *Movimiento indígena en América Latina: resistencia y proyecto alternativo: Volumen I*, Puebla: Benemérita Universidad Autónoma de Puebla.

Escobar, Arturo and Sonia E. Álvarez (eds.) 1992, *The Making of Social Movements in Latin America: Identity, Strategy, and Democracy*, Boulder: Westview Press.

Escóbar de Pabón, Silvia 2004, 'Medidas paliativas para enfrentar el desempleo galopante', in *Economía y sociedad boliviana después de octubre de 2003: Análisis de un año de gobierno de Carlos Mesa*, edited by CEDLA, La Paz: CEDLA.

—— 2009a, *Situación de los ingresos laborales en tiempos de cambio*, La Paz: CEDLA.

—— 2009b, *Situación del Empleo en tiempos de cambio*, La Paz: CEDLA.

Espada, Juan Luis 2004, 'La vieja sujeción de la política fiscal', in *Economía y sociedad boliviana después de octubre de 2003*, edited by CEDLA, La Paz: CEDLA.

Espinoza, Claudia 2003a, '19 de Septiembre ¿Comienza otro ciclo?', *Pulso*, 19 September.

—— 2003b, ' "Plan Añutaya": la respuesta comunal', *Pulso*, 26 September.

Espinoza, Claudia and Gonzalo Gosálvez 2003, 'Bolivia arrinconada en la azotea de su historia: Levantamiento popular del 12 y 13 de febrero en La Paz', *Observatorio Social de América Latina*, 4, 10: 29–36.

Esteban, Fernando 2008, 'The Bolivarian Revolution at the Crossroads', *International Viewpoint*, 403, available online at: <http://www.internationalviewpoint.org/spip .php?article1504>.

Farcau, Bruce W. 1996, *The Chaco War: Bolivia and Paraguay, 1931–1935*, New York: Praeger.

Farthing, Linda 1995, 'Bolivia', in *Free Trade and Economic Restructuring in Latin America*, edited by Fred Rosen and Deidre McFadyen, New York: Monthly Review Press.

Farthing, Linda, Benjamin Kohl and Juan Arbona 2006, 'The Cities that Neoliberalism Built: Exploring Urbanisation in La Paz-El Alto, Bolivia', *Harvard International Review* 4 June, available online at: <http://www.harvard.org/articles/1433/>.

Fernández, Omar 2005, Personal Interview, Cochabamba, 28 July.

Fernández Terán, Roberto 2003, *FMI, Banco Mundial y Estado neocolonial: poder supranacional en Bolivia*, La Paz: Plural editores.

Finnegan, William 2002, 'Leasing the Rain', *The New Yorker*, 8 April.

Foran, John 1997, 'Discourses and Social Forces: The Role of Culture and Cultural Studies in Understanding Revolutions', in *Theorizing Revolutions*, edited by John Foran, London: Routledge.

Foweraker, Joe 1995, *Theorizing Social Movements*, London: Pluto.

FSTMB 2003a, Comunicado a la opinión pública, La Paz.

—— 2003b, Comunicado a los trabajadores y al pueblo boliviano, La Paz.

—— 2003c, Comunicado de la Federación de Mineros, La Paz.

—— 2003d, 'Muera la represión militar del gonismo', Communique, La Paz.

Gamarra, Eduardo 1994, 'Crafting Political Support for Stabilisation: Political Pacts and the New Economic Policy in Bolivia', in *Democracy, Markets, and Structural Reform in Latin America: Argentina, Bolivia, Brazil, Chile, and Mexico*, edited by William C. Smith, Carlos H. Acuña and Eduardo Gamarra, Miami: North-South Center Press.

—— 1996, 'Bolivia: Managing Democracy in the 1990s', in *Constructing Democratic Governance: South America in the 1990s*, edited by Jorge I. Domínguez and Abraham F. Lowenthal, Baltimore: The John Hopkins University Press.

García Linera, Álvaro 2002a, 'El ocaso de un ciclo estatal', in *Democratizaciones plebeyas*, edited by Raquel Gutiérrez, Álvaro García Linera, Raúl Prada and Luis Tapia, La Paz: Muela del Diablo.

—— 2002b, 'La formación de la identidad en el movimiento indígena-campesino aymara', *Fe y pueblo*, 2, 4.

—— 2003, 'Radiografía de las nuevas izquierdas: Potencialidades y límites', *Le Monde Diplomatique*, Bolivian edition, October.

—— 2004a, 'Crisis estatal y muchedumbres en acción', in *Para que no se olvide: 12–13 de febrero 2003*, La Paz: APDHB/ASOFAMD/CBDHDD/DIAKONIA/FUNSOLON/RED-ADA.

—— 2004b, 'La crisis de estado y las sublevaciones indígeno-plebeyas', in *Memorias de Octubre*, edited by Álvaro García Linera, Raúl Prada and Luis Tapia, La Paz: Muela del Diablo.

—— 2004c, 'The "Multitude"', in *¡Cochabamba! Water-War in Bolivia*, edited by Oscar Olivera and Tom Lewis, Cambridge, MA.: South End Press.

—— 2005a, Personal Interview, La Paz, 10 April.

—— 2005b, 'Indianismo y marxismo: El desencuentro de dos razones revolucionarias', *Barataria*, 1, 2: 4–14.

—— 2005c, 'La lucha por el poder en Bolivia', in *Horizontes y límites del estado y el poder*, edited by Álvaro García Linera, Luis Tapia and Raúl Prada, La Paz: Muela del Diablo.

—— 2005d, 'La segunda batalla por la nacionalización del gas', *El Juguete Rabioso*, 12 June.

—— 2005e, 'Los movimientos indígenas en Bolivia', in *Movimiento indígena en América Latina: resistencia y proyecto alternativo*, edited by Fabiola Escárzaga and Raquel Gutiérrez, Puebla: Benemérita Universidad Autónoma de Puebla.

García Linera, Álvaro, Marxa Chávez León and Patricia Costas Monje 2005, *Sociología de los movimientos sociales en Bolivia: Estructuras de movilización, repertorios culturales y acción política*, Second Edition, La Paz: Oxfam and Diakonia.

García Mérida, Wilson 2003a, 'Democracia boliviana: Bajo la bota militar', *El Juguete Rabioso*, 16 February.

—— 2003b, 'Una corriente policial de reforma ética e intelectual', *El Juguete Rabioso*, 16 February.

Gill, Lesley 1987a, 'Frontier Expansion and Settlement in Lowland Bolivia', *Journal of Peasant Studies*, 14, 3: 380–98.

—— 1987b, *Peasants, Entrepreneurs and Social Change: Frontier Development and Lowland Bolivia*, Boulder: Westview Press.

—— 1997, 'Relocating Class: Ex-Miners and Neoliberalism in Bolivia', *Critique of Anthropology*, 17, 3: 293–312.

—— 2000, *Teetering on the Rim: Global Restructuring, Daily Life, and the Armed Retreat of the Bolivian State*, New York: Columbia University Press.

—— 2004, *The School of the Americas: Military Training and Political Violence in the Americas*, Durham, NC.: Duke University Press.

Goldstone, Jack A. and Charles Tilly 2001, 'Threat (and Opportunity): Popular Action and State-response in the Dynamics of Contentious Action', in *Silence and Voice in the Study of Contentious Politics*, edited by Ronald R. Aminzade, Jack A. Goldstone, Doug McAdam, Elizabeth J. Perry, William H. Sewell Jr., Sidney Tarroy and Charles Tilly, Cambridge: Cambridge University Press.

Golinger, Eva 2006, *The Chávez: Cracking US Intervention in Venezuela*, New York: Monthly Review Press.

—— 2007, *Bush Versus Chávez: Washington's War on Venezuela*, New York: Monthly Review Press.

Gómez, Luis A. 2004 *El Alto de pie: Una insurrección aymara en Bolivia*, La Paz: HdP, La Comuna, Indymedia Qollasuyu Ivi Iyambae Bolivia.

—— 2005, Personal Interview, La Paz, 11 March.

Gosálvez, Gonzalo 2005, Personal Interview, La Paz, 9 April.

Gordon, Todd 2006a, 'Canada, Empire and Indigenous People in the Americas', *Socialist Studies*, 2, 1: 47–75.
—— 2006b, *Cops, Crime and Capitalism: The Law-and-Order Agenda in Canada*, Halifax: Fernwood Publishing.
—— 2007, 'Towards an Anti-Racist Marxist State Theory: A Canadian Case Study', *Capital and Class*, 91: 1–29.
Gotkowitz, Laura 2003, 'Revisiting the Rural Roots of the Revolution', in *Proclaiming Revolution: Bolivia in Comparative Perspective*, edited by Merilee S. Grindle and Pilar Domingo, London and Cambridge, MA.: Institute of Latin-American Studies, University of London and David Rockefeller Center for Latin-American Studies, Harvard University.
Gould, Jeffrey L. 1990, *To Lead as Equals: Rural Protest and Political Consciousness in Chinandega, Nicaragua, 1912–1979*, Chapel Hill: University of North Carolina Press.
—— 1998, *To Die in This Way: Nicaraguan Indians and the Myth of Mestizaje, 1880–1965*, Durham, NC.: Duke University Press.
Gowan, Peter 1999, *The Global Gamble: Washington's Faustian Bid for World Dominance*, London: Verso.
Gramsci, Antonio 1971, *Selections from the Prison Notebooks*, New York: International Publishers.
Grandin, Greg 2005, *The Last Colonial Massacre: Latin America in the Cold War*, Chicago: University of Chicago Press.
—— 2006, 'The Rebel and Mr. Danger: Is Bush's Nightmare Venezuela's Salvation?' *Boston Review*, May–June, available onlilne at: <http://www.bostonreview.net/BR31.3/grandin.html>.
Gray Molina, George and Gonzalo Chávez 2005, 'The Political Economy of the Crisis in the Andean Region: the Case of Bolivia', in *Political Crises, Social Conflict, and Economic Development: The Political Economy of the Andean Region*, edited by Andrés Solimano, Northampton: Edward Elgar.
Grebe López, Horst 1983, 'El excedente sin acumulación: La génesis de la crisis económica actual', in *Bolivia, Hoy*, edited by René Zavaleta Mercado, Mexico: Siglo veintiuno editores.
Green, Duncan 1999, 'A Trip to the Market: The Impact of Neoliberalism in Latin America', in *Developments in Latin American Political Economy: States, Markets, and Actors*, edited by Julia Buxton and Nicola Phillips, Manchester: Manchester University Press.
—— 2003, *Silent Revolution: The Rise and Crisis of Market Economics in Latin America*, Second Edition, New York: Monthly Review Press.
Grieshaber, Erwin P. 1980, 'Survival of Indian Communities in Nineteenth-Century Bolivia: A Regional Comparison', *Journal of Latin-American Studies*, 12, 2: 223–69.
Griffin, Larry J. 1993, 'Narrative, Event-Structure, and Causal Interpretation in Historical Sociology', *American Journal of Sociology*, 98: 1094–133.
Grindle, Merilee S 2000, *Audacious Reforms: Institutional Innovation and Democracy in Latin America*, Baltimore: John Hopkins University Press.
—— 2003, 'Shadowing the Past? Policy Reform in Bolivia, 1985–2002', in *Proclaiming Revolution: Bolivia in Comparative Perspective*, edited by Merilee S. Grindle and Pilar Domingo, London and Cambridge, MA.: Institute of Latin-American Studies, University of London and David Rockefeller Center for Latin-American Studies, Harvard University.
Guachalla, Luis Fernando 1978, *Jayucubas: comentarios y cronicas de la Guerra del Chaco*, La Paz: Los Amigos del Libro.
Gustafson, Bret 2002, 'Paradoxes of Liberal Indigenism: Indigenous Movements, State Processes, and Intercultural Reform in Bolivia', in *The Politics of Ethnicity: Indigenous Peoples in Latin-American States*, edited by David Maybury-Lewis, Cambridge, MA.: Harvard University Press and The David Rockefeller Center for Latin-American Studies.
Gutiérrez Aguilar, Raquel 2001, 'La Coordinadora de Defensa del Agua y de la Vida: Un año de la guerra del agua', in *Tiempos de rebelión*, edited by Álvaro García Linera,

Raquel Gutiérrez Aguilar, Raúl Prada, Felipe Quispe and Luis Tapia Mealla, La Paz: Muela del Diablo.

—— 2008, *Los ritmos del Pachakuti: Movilización y levantamiento indígena-popular en Bolivia (2000–2005)*, La Paz: textos rebeldes.

Gutiérrez de Medina, Brígida. 2005, Personal Interview, El Alto, 4 April.

Gutiérrez, Raquel and Fabiola Escárzaga (eds.) 2006, *Movimiento indígena en América Latina: resistencia y proyecto alternativo: Volumen II*, Puebla: Benemérita Universidad Autónoma de Puebla.

Gutiérrez, Raquel and Álvaro García Linera 2002, 'El ciclo estatal neoliberal y sus crisis', in *Democratizaciones plebeyas*, edited by Raquel Gutiérrez, Álvaro García Linera, Raúl Prada and Luis Tapia, La Paz: Muela del Diablo.

Haber, Paul Lawrence 1996, 'Identity and Political-Process: Recent Trends in the Study of Latin American Social Movements', *Latin American Research Review*, 31, 1: 171–88.

Habermas, Jurgen 1981, 'New Social Movements', *Telos*, 49: 33–47.

Hale, Charles R. 1996, *Resistance and Contradiction: Miskitu Indians and the Nicaraguan State, 1894–1987*, Stanford: Stanford University Press.

—— 2002, 'Does Multiculturalism Menace? Governance, Cultural Rights and the Politics of Identity in Guatemala', *Journal of Latin American Studies* 34: 485–524.

—— 2004, 'Rethinking Indigenous Politics in the Era of the "Indio Permitido"', *NACLA Report on the Americas*, 38, 2: 16–21.

—— 2006, *Más Que un Indio (More Than an Indian): Racial Ambivalence and Neoliberal Multiculturlism in Guatemala*, Santa Fe: SAR Press.

Hanieh, Adam 2009, 'Hierarchies of a Global Market: The South and the Economic Crisis', *Studies in Political Economy*, 83: 61–84.

Harris, Olivia and Javier Albó, 1986 [1974], *Monteras y Guardatojos: campesinos y mineros en el norte de Potosí*, La Paz: CIPCA.

Hart-Landsberg, Martin 2009, 'Learning from ALBA and the Bank of the South: Challenges and Possibilities', *Monthly Review*, 61, 4: 1–18.

Harvey, David 2003, *The New Imperialism*, Oxford: Oxford University Press.

—— 2005, *A Brief History of Neoliberalism*, Oxford: Oxford University Press.

Harvey, Neil 1998, *The Chiapas Rebellion: The Struggle for Land and Democracy*, Durham, NC.: Duke University Press.

Healy, Kevin 1991, 'Political Ascent of Bolivia's Peasant Coca Leaf Producers', *Journal of Interamerican Studies and World Affairs*, 33, 1: 87–121.

—— 1998, 'Coca, the State, and the Peasantry in Bolivia, 1982–1988', *Journal of Interamerican Studies and World Affairs*, 30, 2–3: 105–26.

Healy, Kevin and Susan Paulson 2000, 'Political Economies of Identity in Bolivia, 1952–1998', *Journal of Latin-American Anthropology*, 5, 2: 2–29.

Henao, Luis Andres 2009, 'Venezuelan TV Officials: Hillary Clinton Backs Us', *The Miami Herald*, 9 July.

Hertzler, Douglas 2005, 'Campesinos and Originarios! Class and Ethnicity in Rural Movements in the Bolivian Lowlands', *Journal of Latin-American Anthropology*, 10, 1: 45–71.

Hindery, Derrick 2004, 'Social and Environmental Impacts of World Bank/IMF-Funded Economic Restructuring in Bolivia: An Analysis of Enron and Shell's Hydrocarbon Projects', *Singapore Journal of Tropical Geography* 25, 3: 281–303.

Hipsher, Patricia L. 1998, 'Democratic Transitions as Protest Cycles: Social-movement Dynamics in Democratising Latin America', in *The Social Movement Society: Contentious Politics for a New Century*, edited by David S. Meyer and Sidney Tarrow, Lanham: Rowman and Littlefield.

Hobsbawm, Eric and Terence Ranger (eds.) 1983, *The Invention of Tradition*, Cambridge: Cambridge University Press.

Hristov, Jasmin 2005, 'Indigenous Struggles for Land and Culture in Cauca, Colombia', *Journal of Peasant Studies*, 32, 1: 88–117.

Huber, Evelyn, Dieterich Rueschemeyer and John D. Stephens 1997, 'The Pardoxes of Contemporary Democracy: Formal, Participatory, and Social', *Comparative Politics*, 29, 3: 323–42.

Huntington, Samuel P. 1991, *The Third Wave: Democratisation in the Late Twentieth Century*, Norman: University of Oklahoma Press.

Hylton. Forrest 2005a, 'Bolivia: The Agony of Stalemate, A Radical Democracy Movement Mobilises', *Counterpunch*, 2 June.

—— 2003, 'Working Class Revolt in Bolivia: The Sudden Return of Dual Power', *Counterpunch*, 15 February.

—— 2004, 'El federalismo insurgente: una aproximación a Juan Lero, los comunarios y la Guerra Federal', *Tinkazos*, 7, 16: 99–118.

—— 2005b, 'Tierra Común: Caciques, Artesanos e intelectuales radicales y la rebelión de Chayanta (1927)', in *Ya es otro tiempo el presente: Cuatro momentos de insurgencia indígena*, edited by Forrest Hylton, Felix Patzi, Sergio Serulnikov, and Sinclair Thomson, La Paz: Muela del Diablo.

—— 2006, *Evil Hour in Colombia*, London: Verso.

Hylton, Forrest and Sinclair Thomson 2004, 'The Roots of Rebellion: Insurgent Bolivia', *NACLA Report on the Americas*, 38, 3: 15–19.

—— 2005a, 'The Chequered Rainbow', *New Left Review*, II, 35: 40–64.

—— 2005b, 'Ya es otro tiempo el presente: Cuatro momentos de insurgencia indígena', in *Ya es otro tiempo el present: Cuatro momentos de insurgencia indígena*, edited by Forrest Hylton, Felix Patzi, Sergio Serulnikov, and Sinclair Thomson, La Paz: Muela del Diablo.

—— 2007, *Revolutionary Horizons: Past and Present in Bolivian Politics*, London: Verso.

Ibáñez Rojo, Enrique 2000, 'The UDP Government and the Crisis of the Bolivian Left (1982–1985)', *Journal of Latin-American Studies*, 32, 1: 175–205.

INE 2001, *Anuario estadístico*, La Paz: Instituto Nacional de Estatística.

Iquiapaza, Eliodoro 2005, Personal Interview, El Alto, 17 May.

Iriarte, Gregorio 1983, *Los mineros: Sus luchas, frustraciones y esperanzas*, La Paz: Puerta del Sol.

Irurozqui, Marta 1999, 'Las paradojas de la tributación: Ciudadanía y política estatal indígena en Bolivia, 1825–1900', *Revista de Indias*, 219: 705–40.

—— 2000, 'The Sound of Pututos: Politicisation and Indigenous Rebellions in Bolivia, 1826–1921', *Journal of Latin American Studies*, 32: 85–114.

Isbester, Katherine 2001, *Still Fighting: The Nicaraguan Women's Movement, 1977–2000*, Pittsburgh: Pittsburgh University Press.

Jaquette, Jane S. (ed.) 1989, *The Women's Movement in Latin America: Feminism and the Transition to Democracy*, Boston: Unwin Hyman.

Jenkins, J. Craig 1981, 'Sociopolitical Movements', *Handbook of Political Behavior*, 4: 81–153.

—— 1982, 'The Transformation of a Constituency into a Movement: Farm-Worker Organising in California', in *Social Movements of the Sixties and Seventies*, edited by Jo Freeman, White Plains: Longman.

—— 1983, 'Resource-Mobilisation Theory and the Study of Social Movements', *Annual Review of Sociology*, 9: 527–53.

Kampwirth, Karen 2002, *Women and Guerrilla Movements: Nicaragua, El Salvador, Chiapas, Cuba*, University Park: The Pennsylvania State University Press.

—— 2004, *Feminism and the Legacy of Revolution: Nicaragua, El Salvador, Chiapas*, Athens, OH.: Ohio University Press.

Karl, Terry Lynn 2000, 'Economic Inequality and Democratic Instability', *Journal of Democracy*, 11, 1: 149–56.

Katz, Claudio 2007, 'Socialist Strategies in Latin America', *Monthly Review* 59, 4: 25–41.

—— 2009a, *Las disyuntivas de la izquierda en América Latina*, Buenos Aires: Ediciones Luxemberg.

—— 2009b, 'América Latina frente a la crisis global', available online at: <http://katz.lahaine.org/>.

Kelley, Robin D.G. 2002, *Freedom Dreams: The Black Radical Imagination*, New York: Beacon Press.

Kellogg, Paul 2007, 'Regional Integration in Latin America: Dawn of an Alternative to Neo-Liberalism?' *New Political Science*, 29, 2: 187–210.

Klein, Herbert S. 1969, *Parties and Political Change in Bolivia, 1880–1952*, Cambridge: Cambridge University Press.

—— 2003, *A Concise History of Bolivia*, Cambridge: Cambridge University Press.

Knight, Alan 2003, 'The Domestic Dynamics of the Mexican and Bolivian Revolutions Compared', in *Proclaiming Revolution: Bolivia in Comparative Perspective*, edited by Merilee S. Grindle, and Pilar Domingo, London and Cambridge, MA.: Institute of Latin-American Studies, University of London and David Rockefeller Center for Latin-American Studies, Harvard University.

Kohl, Benjamin 2002, 'Stabilising Neoliberalism in Bolivia: Popular Participation and Privatisation', *Political Geography*, 21, 4: 449–72.

—— 2003, 'Restructuring Citizenship in Bolivia: *El Plan de Todos'*, *International Journal of Urban and Regional Research*, 27, 2: 337–51.

—— 2004, 'Privatisation Bolivian Style: A Cautionary Tale', *International Journal of Urban and Regional Research*, 28, 4: 893–908.

—— 2006, 'Challenges to Neoliberal Hegemony in Bolivia', *Antipode*, 38, 2: 303–26.

Kohl, Benjamin and Linda Farthing 2006, *Impasse in Bolivia: Neoliberal Hegemony and Popular Resistance*, London: Zed.

Korzeniewicz, Robert and William C. Smith 2000, 'Poverty, Inequality, and Growth in Latin America: Searching for the High Road to Globalisation', *Latin American Research Review*, 35, 3: 7–54.

Kruse, Thomas 2002, 'Transición política y recomposición sindical: Reflexiones desde Bolivia', in *Ciudadanía, cultura política y reforma del Estado en América Latina*, edited by Marco Antonio Calderón Mólgora, Willem Assies, and Ton Salmon, Michoacán: El Colegio de Michoacán and IFE.

Kruse, Tom 2004, 'Políticas comerciales: en pos del TLC andino', in *Economía y sociedad boliviana después de octubre de 2003: Análisis de un año de gobierno de Carlos Mesa*, edited by CEDLA, La Paz: CEDLA.

Laclau, Ernesto 1981, 'The Impossibility of Society', *Canadian Journal of Political and Social Theory*, 7, 1–2.

—— 1983, 'Transformations of Advanced Industrial Societies and the Theory of the Subject', in *Rethinking Ideology: A Marxist Debate*, edited by Sakari Hanninen and Leena Paldan, New York: International General/IMMRC.

Laclau, Ernesto and Chantal Mouffe 1985, *Hegemony and Socialist Strategy: Towards a Radical Democratic Politics*, London: Verso.

Langer, Erick D. 1989, *Economic Change and Rural Resistance in Southern Bolivia, 1880–1930*, Stanford: Stanford University Press.

—— 1990, 'Andean Rituals of Revolt: The Chayanta Rebellion of 1927', *Ethnohistory*, 37, 3: 227–53.

La Patria 2003a, 'Bloqueos preceden una "protesta nacional" contra la venta del gas', *La Patria*, 16 September.

—— 2003b, 'Campesinos en huelga de hambre instruyen el bloqueo de caminos', *La Patria*, 12 September.

—— 2003c, 'Humillación a campesinos aumenta rechazo al Presidente más impopular', *La Patria*, 24 September 24.

La Prensa 2003a, 'Alistan sus armas para que Goni renuncie', *La Prensa*, 14 October.

—— 2003b, 'Bloqueo de Yungas inicia la guerra del gas', *La Prensa*, 15 September.

—— 2003c, 'Dos mil campesinos ayunan, hoy se decide si hay bloqueo', *La Prensa*, 11 September.

—— 2003d, 'El Mallku prepara bloqueo y anuncia una "guerra civil"', *La Prensa*, 12 September.

—— 2003e, 'El Presidente deslegitima las protestas que crecen', *La Prensa*, 10 October.

—— 2003f, 'Exportación de gas detona el descontento', *La Prensa*, 9 September.

—— 2003g, 'Goni: No hay diálogo con bloqueos', *La Prensa*, 22 September.

—— 2003h, 'La Policía y las FFAA toman las carreteras en el altiplano', *La Prensa*, 13 September.

—— 2003i, 'Los mineros llegan a La Paz; advierten de una convulsión', *La Prensa*, 9 October.

—— 2003j, 'Mesa apuesta a ser neutral en conflicto social en curso', *La Prensa*, 17 October.

—— 2003k, 'Multitudinaria marcha la paralizó anoche La Paz', *La Prensa*, 20 September.

—— 2003l, 'Presidente instruye imponer orden ante la ola de protestas', *La Prensa*, 12 September.

—— 2003m, 'Vecinos piden la dimisión de Goni', *La Prensa*, 14 October.

—— 2005a, 'Declinación del Legislativo y Suprema arriesgan el Encuentro por la Unidad', *La Prensa*, 13 May.

—— 2005b, 'Desbloquean las carreteras pero las amenazas persisten', *La Prensa*, 19 May.

—— 2005c, 'El centro paceño colapsa por las marchas de diez sectores', *La Prensa*, 24 May.

—— 2005d, 'El conflicto se radicaliza con el bloqueo de carreteras', *La Prensa*, 17 May.

—— 2005e, 'El Gobierno compró los espacios estelares de TV', *La Prensa*, 18 May.

—— 2005f, 'El MAS marcha y no bloquea', *La Prensa*, 13 May.

—— 2005g, 'El MAS y 'antioligárquicos' llaman a movilizarse contra la nueva norma', *La Prensa*, 6 May.

—— 2005h, 'El plan de Mesa se ejecutará sin dividendos de ley del gas', *La Prensa*, 18 May.

—— 2005i, 'Gobierno acusa a sectores gonistas', *La Prensa*, 17 May.

—— 2005j, 'La incierta Ley de Hidrocarburos pone en riesgo el plan económico', *La Prensa*, 10 May.

—— 2005k, 'Las protestas comienzan con los sectores sociales divididos', *La Prensa*, 16 May.

—— 2005l, 'Los partidos quieren apurar la promulgación de ley petrolera', *La Prensa*, 15 May.

—— 2005m, 'Magisterio alista huelga', *La Prensa*, 13 May.

—— 2005n, 'Marchas cercan el centro paceño', *La Prensa*, 17 May.

—— 2005o, 'Marchas y bloqueos siguen, insisten en la nacionalización', *La Prensa*, 18 May.

—— 2005p, 'Mesa enfrenta al Congreso más debilitado que antes', *La Prensa*, 17 May.

—— 2005q, 'Mesa observa la ley petrolera y llama a una cita por la unidad', *La Prensa*, 11 May.

—— 2005r, 'Movilización de El Alto', *La Prensa*, 13 May.

—— 2005s, 'Partidos: Presidente cometió un error que le resta apoyo', *La Prensa*, 18 May.

—— 2005t, 'Políticos, empresarios y COB rechazan el plan económico', *La Prensa*, 18 May.

—— 2005u, 'Solares y Morales terminan peleados', *La Prensa*, 24 May.

—— 2005v, 'Vaca Díez deslinda responsabilidad ante fracaso del diálogo', *La Prensa*, 15 May.

—— 2005w, 'Vaca Díez firma una ley sujeta a cambios', *La Prensa*, 18 May.

—— 2005x, Varias presiones cercan a Mesa', *La Prensa*, 10 May.

La Razón 2003a, 'Dos marchas y un paro cívico bloquearon El Alto y parte de La Paz', *La Razón*, 9 September.

—— 2003b, 'EEUU apoya a Goni y dice que no reconocerá otro gobierno', *La Razón*, 14 October.

—— 2003c, 'El Alto rechaza el diálogo y evita la circulación hasta de bicicletas', *La Razón*, 11 October.

—— 2003d, 'El diálago en Yungas se rompió y los bloqueos cobran más fuerza', *La Razón*, 19 September.

—— 2003e, 'El ex Presidente está en Miami', *La Razón*, 18 October.

—— 2003f, 'El MAS y al meno diez sectores marcharán contra la venta del gas', *La Razón*, 19 September.

—— 2003g, 'El temor a los saqueos paralizó por completo a la urbe alteña' *La Razón*, 20 September.

—— 2003h, 'La COB apuesta al paro general', *La Razón*, 20 September.

—— 2003i, 'Los colonizadores inician hoy bloqueos en Yungas' *La Razón*, 15 September.

—— 2003j, 'Mesa gobernará sin políticos y hará referéndum y Constituyente', *La Razón*, 18 October.

—— 2003k, 'Mesa pasa de la pantalla a la silla presidencial en una carrera fugaz', *La Razón*, 18 October.

—— 2003l, 'Una jornada de violencia en El Alto provocó una veintena de heridos', *La Razón*, 9 October.

—— 2003m, 'Varios sectores unirán mañana sus protestas en torno al gas', *La Razón*, 18 September.

—— 2005a, 'Carlos Mesa define el futuro de la ley del gas', *La Razon*, 17 May.

—— 2005b, 'Diputados sancionan la ley del gas resistida por inversores y sectores', *La Razón*, 6 May.

—— 2005c, 'El 66,9% de los habitantes vive an la pobreza', *La Razón*, 6 March.

—— 2005d, 'El Alto prevé bajar por 4 caminos hasta el Congreso', *La Razón*, 16 May.

—— 2005e, 'El FMI dice que la nueva ley del gas es poco viable', *La Razón*, 31 May.

—— 2005f, 'El Gobierno cerró la página sobre los hidrocarburos', *La Razón*, 18 May.

—— 2005g, 'El gobierno prometió al FMI una ley del gas que sea equilibrada', *La Razón*, 10 May.

—— 2005h, 'El Legislativo y el Judicial le dan la espalda al encuentro de Mesa', *La Razón*, 12 May.

—— 2005i, 'El MAS le pone plazo al Congreso y sus bases piden nacionalización', *La Razón*, 24 May.

—— 2005j, 'El paro indefinido de El Alto redujo a medias las actividades', *La Razón*, 24 May.

—— 2005k, 'El sector industrial alteño está paralizada en un 90%', *La Razón*, 31 May.

—— 2005l, 'Gente de El Alto y de La Paz se perjudica con el bloqueo', *La Razón*, 31 May.

—— 2005m, 'La anormalidad caracterizó la jornada de movilizaciones', *La Razón*, 24 May.

—— 2005n, 'La movilización de mañana pretende la toma de La Paz', *La Razón*, 15 May.

—— 2005o, 'La Paz estuvo paralizada y la plaza Murillo fue cercada', *La Razón*, 17 May.

—— 2005p, 'Las organizaciones anuncian movilizaciones en todo el país', *La Razón*, 6 May.

—— 2005q, 'Las protestas apuntan a Mesa y al congreso por Constituyente y gas', *La Razón*, 16 May.

—— 2005r, 'Los actores que deciden no irán al diálogo propuesta por Mesa', *La Razón*, 12 May.

—— 2005s, 'Los empresarios le exigen a Mesa imponer el orden', *La Razón*, 15 May.

—— 2005t, 'Los políticos optan por la cuatela ante la convocatoria al diálogo', *La Razón*, 11 May.

—— 2005u, 'Los sectores anuncian movilizaciones', *La Razón*, 8 May.

—— 2005v, 'Los sectores piden el veto a la ley', *La Razón*, 7 May.

—— 2005w, 'Marchistas y bloqueadores se unen en dos carreteras', *La Razón*, 17 May.

—— 2005x, 'Mesa dejó que el Congreso asuma la paternidad de la nueva ley del gas', *La Razón*, 18 May.

—— 2005y, 'Mesa observa la ley del gas y pide una cumbre por la unidad del país', *La Razón*, 11 May.

—— 2005z, 'Mesa recibe las críticas de columnistas y políticos' *La Razón*, 17 May.

—— 2005aa, 'Morales y Solares hablan en sentidos contrarios' *La Razón*, 4 May.

—— 2005bb, 'Partidos y movimientos sociales le exigen a Mesa que se decide', *La Razón*, 15 May.

—— 2005cc, Petroleras frenarán sus inversiones por la nueva ley del gas', *La Razón*, 8 May.

—— 2005dd, 'Un acuerdo con el FMI complica la promulgación de la ley del gas', *La Razón*, 9 May.

Larson, Brooke 1998, *Cochabamba, 1550–1900: Colonialism and Agrarian Transformation in Bolivia*, Second Edition, Durham, NC.: Duke University Press.

—— 2004, *Trials of Nation Making: Liberalism, Race, and Ethnicity in the Andes, 1810–1910*, Cambridge: Cambridge University Press.

—— 2005, 'Redeemed Indians, Barbarised Cholos: Crafting Neocolonial Modernity in Liberal Bolivia, 1900–1910', in *Political Cultures in the Andes, 1750–1950*, edited by Nils Jacobsen, and Cristóbal Aljovín de Losada, Durham, NC.: Duke University Press.

Larson, Brooke, Olivia Harris, and Enrique Tandeter (eds.) 1995, *Ethnicity, Markets, and Migration in the Andes: At the Crossroads of History and Anthropology*, Durham, NC.: Duke University Press.

Laserna, Roberto 2000, 'Cochabamba: La Guerra contra el Agua', *Observatorio Social de América Latina*, 2: 15–20.

Laurie, Nina, Robert Andolina, and Sarah Radcliffe 2002, 'The Excluded "Indigenous"? The Implications of Multi-Ethnic Policies for Water Reform in Bolivia', in *Multiculturalism in Latin America: Indigenous Rights, Diversity and Democracy*, edited by Rachel Sieder, New York: Palgrave Macmillan.

Laurie, Nina and Carlos Crespo, 2007, 'Deconstructing the Best Case Scenario: Lessons from Water Politics in La Paz-El Alto, Bolivia', *Geoforum*, 38: 841–54.

Lazar, Sian 2004, 'Personalist Politics, Clientelism and Citizenship: Local Elections in El Alto, Bolivia', *Bulletin of Latin American Research*, 23, 2: 229–43.

—— 2006, 'El Alto, Ciudad Rebelde: Organisational Bases for Revolt', *Bulletin of Latin American Research*, 25, 2: 183–99.

Lazarte Rojas, Jorge 2005, *Entre los espectros del pasado y las incertidumbres del futuro: Política y democracia en Bolivia a principios del siglo XXI*, La Paz: Plural editores.

Lebowitz, Michael A. 2006, *Build It Now: Socialism for the Twenty-First Century*, New York: Monthly Review Press.

Lehm A., Zulema and Silvia Rivera Cusicanqui 1988, *Los artesanos libertarios y la ética del trabajo*, La Paz: THOA.

Léons, Madeline Barbara and Harry Sanabria 1997, 'Coca and Cocaine in Bolivia: Reality and Policy Illusion', in *Coca, Cocaine, and the Bolivian Reality*, edited by Madeline Barbara Léons, and Harry Sanabria, Albany: State University of New York Press.

López Maya, Margarita 2007, 'Venezuela Today: A "Participative and Protagonistic" Democracy?' In *Socialist Register 2008: Global Flashpoints, Reactions to Imperialism and Neoliberalism*, edited by Leo Panitch and Colin Leys, New York: Monthly Review Press.

Lora, Guillermo 1977, *A History of the Bolivian Labour Movement, 1848–1971*, Cambridge: Cambridge University Press.

—— 1983, 'La clase obrera después de 1952', in *Bolivia, Hoy*, edited by René Zavaleta Mercado, Mexico: Siglo vientiuno editores.

Lora, Miguel 2005a, 'Hacendados armados en el norte de Santa Cruz', *El Juguete Rabioso*, 15 May.

—— 2005b, 'Y ahora... ¿Quién podrá ayudarle?' *El Juguete Rabioso*, 9 June.

—— 2006, 'El plan tierra del gobierno respetará el latifundio productivo', *El Juguete Rabioso*, 14 May.

Los Tiempos 2003a, 'El 70% de la población de 4 ciudades no cree en Goni', *Los Tiempos*, 8 September.

—— 2003b, 'El Gobierno libra la primera batalla del gas', *Los Tiempos*, 19 September.

—— 2003c, 'El Gobierno prepara a las FFAA para evitar bloqueos', *Los Tiempos*, 12 September.

—— 2003d. 'Matanza de Warisata extiende los bloqueos y sube la tensión', *Los Tiempos*, 22 September.

—— 2003e, 'Vuelve el luto al país: operativo de rescate deja seis muertos', *Los Tiempos*, 21 September.

Lowrey, Kathleen 2006, '*Bolivia Multiétnico y Pluricultural*, Ten Years Later: White Separatism in the Bolivian Lowlands', *Latin American and Caribbean Ethnic Studies*, 1, 1: 63–84.

Löwy, Michael 1998, 'Marxism and Romanticism in the Work of José Carlos Mariátegui', *Latin American Perspectives*, 25, 4: 76–88.

Magdoff, Fred 2006, 'The Explosion of Debt and Speculation', *Monthly Review*, 58, 6: 1–23.

Mahoney, James 2000, 'Path Dependence in Historical Sociology', *Theory and Society*, 29: 507–48.

Mahoney, James and Dietrich Rueschemeyer 2003, 'Comparative Historical Analysis', in *Comparative Historical Analysis in the Social Sciences*, edited by James Mahoney, and Dietrich Rueschemeyer, Cambridge: Cambridge University Press.

Mallon, Florencia E. 1992, 'Indian Communities, Political Cultures and the State in Latin America, 1780–1990', *Journal of Latin American Studies*, 24: 35–53.

Malloy, James M. 1970, *Bolivia: The Uncompleted Revolution*, Pittsburgh: University of Pittsburgh Press.

—— 1991, 'Democracy, Economic Crisis and The Problem of Governance: The Case of Bolivia', *Studies in Comparative International Development*, 26, 2: 37–57.

Malloy, James M. and Eduardo Gamarra 1987, 'The Transition to Democracy in Bolivia', in *Authoritarians and Democrats: Régime Transition in Latin America*, edited by James M. Malloy, and Mitchell A. Seligson, Pittsburgh: University of Pittsburgh Press.

—— 1988, *Revolution and Reaction: Bolivia, 1964–1985*, New Brunswick: Transaction Books.

Mamani, Abel 2005a, Personal Interviews, El Alto, 5 May and 28 June.

Mamani, German 2005b, Personal Interview, El Alto, 4 April.

Mamani Heredia, Samuel 2005, Personal Interview, El Alto, 1 April.

Mamani, Rafael. 2005c, Personal Interviews, El Alto, 20 May and 23 June.

Mamani Ramírez, Pablo 2004, *El rugir de las multitudes: La fuerza de los levantamientos indígenas en Bolivia/Qullasuyu*, La Paz: Aruwiyiri.

—— 2005, *Microgobiernos barriales: Levantamiento de la ciudad de El Alto (octubre 2003)*, La Paz: Centro Andino de Estudios Estratégicos.

Mamani, Tomás 2005d, Personal Interview, El Alto, 6 May.

Mancilla, Rodolfo 2005, Personal Interview, El Alto, 31 March.

Mander, Benedict 2008, 'Venezuela: Chávez Vulnerable', *Financial Times*, 22 October.

Mann, Arthur and Manuel Pastor Jr. 1989, 'Orthodox and Heterodox Stabilisation Policies in Bolivia and Peru: 1985–1988', *Journal of Interamerican Studies and World Affairs*, 31, 4: 163–92.

Mansbridge, Jane 2001a, 'Complicating Oppositional Consciousness', in *Oppositional Consciousness: The Subjective Roots of Social Protest*, edited by Jane Mansbridge, and Aldon Morris, Chicago: Chicago University Press.

—— 2001b, 'The Making of Oppositional Consciousness', in *Oppositional Consciousness: The Subjective Roots of Social Protest*, edited by Jane Mansbridge, and Aldon Morris, Chicago: University of Chicago Press.

Mariátegui, José Carlos 1971, *Seven Interpretive Essays on Peruvian Reality*, Austin: University of Texas Press.

Marois, Thomas 2005, 'From Economic Crisis to a "State" of Crisis?: The Emergence of Neoliberalism in Costa Rica', *Historical Materialism*, 13, 3: 101–34.

Martela, Juan Antonio 2005, Personal Interviews, El Alto, 31 March and 23 June.

Marx, Karl 1981 [1852], *The Eighteenth Brumaire of Louis Bonaparte*, New York: International Publishers.

Marx, Karl and Friedrich Engels 1985, *The Communist Manifesto*, New York: Penguin Books.

Mayorga, Fernando 2002, *Neopopulismo y democracia: Compadres y padrinos en la política boliviana (1988–1999)*, La Paz: Plural Editores.

Mayorga, René Antonio 1978, 'National-Popular State, State Capitalism and Military Dictatorship in Bolivia: 1952–1975', *Latin American Perspectives*, 5, 2: 89–119.

McAdam, Doug 1996, 'Conceptual Origins, Current Problems, Future Directions', in *Comparative Perspectives on Social Movements: Political Opportunities, Mobilizing Structures, and Cultural Framings*, edited by Doug McAdam, John D. McCarthy, and Mayer N. Zald, Cambridge: Cambridge University Press.

McAdam, Doug, John D. McArthy, and Mayer N. Zald (eds.) 1996a, *Comparative Perspectives on Social Movements: Political Opportunities, and Cultural Framings*, Cambridge: Cambridge University Press.
—— 1988, 'Social Movements', in *Handbook of Sociology*, edited by Neil Smelser, New York: Sage Publications.
McAdam, Doug, Sidney Tarrow and Charles Tilly 1996b, 'To Map Contentious Politics', *Mobilisation*, 1, 1: 17–34.
McAdam, Douglas 1982, *Political Process and the Development of Black Insurgency, 1930–1970*, Chicago: University of Chicago Press.
McCarthy, John D. and Mayer N. Zald 1973, *The Trend of Social Movements in America: Professionalisation and Resource Mobilisation*, White Plains: General Learning Corporation.
—— 1977a, *The Dynamics of Social Movements*, New York: Withrop Publishers.
—— 1977b, 'Resource-Mobilization and Social Movements: A Partial Theory', *American Journal of Sociology*, 82: 1212–39.
McCarthy, Shawn 2009, 'Oil, Metals Pull Back as China Slows Buying', *The Globe and Mail*, 6 July.
McFarren, Wendy 1992, 'The Politics of Bolivia's Economic Crisis: Survival Strategies of Displaced Tin-Mining Households', in *Unequal Burden: Economic Crises, Persistent Poverty, and Women's Work*, edited by Lourdes Benería, and Shelly Feldman, Boulder: Westview Press.
McGuigan, Claire 2007, 'The Benefits of FDI: Is Foreign Investment in Bolivia's Oil and Gas Delivering?', La Paz: Christian Aid and CEDLA.
McNally, David 2006, *Another World Is Possible: Globalization and Anti-Capitalism*, Second Edition, Winnipeg: Arbeiter Ring Publishing.
—— 2009, 'From Financial Crisis to World-Slump: Accumulation, Financialisation, and the Global Slowdown', *Historical Materialism*, 17, 2: 35–83.
McNeish, John 2002, 'Globalisation and the Reinvention of Andean Tradition: The Politics of Community and Ethnicity in Highland Bolivia', *Journal of Peasant Studies*, 29, 3-4: 228–69.
Medeiros, Carmen 2001, 'Civilising the Popular? The Law of Popular Participation and the Design of a New Civil Society in 1990s Bolivia', *Critique of Anthropology*, 21, 4: 401–25.
Melucci, Alberto 1980, 'The New Social Movements: A Theoretical Approach', *Social Science Information*, 19, 2: 199–226.
—— 1984, 'An End to Social Movements?' *Social Science Information*, 23, 4–5: 819–35.
—— 1985, 'The Symbolic Challenge of Contemporary Movements', *Social Research*, 52, 4: 789–816.
—— 1989, *Nomads of the Present: Social Movements and Individual Needs in Contemporary Society*, Philadephia: Temple University Press.
Mendoza Mamani, Jorge 2005, Personal Interview, El Alto, 20 May.
Merida Gutiérrez, Henry 2005, Personal Interview, El Alto, 1 April.
Mesa Gisbert, Carlos D. 2005a, *Encuentro por la Unidad de Bolivia*, La Paz: Government of Bolivia.
—— 2005b, *Progammea Económico y Social: Plan Bolivia Productiva y Solidaria, un nuevo estado para todos*, La Paz: Government of Bolivia.
Miranda Pacheco, Carlos 1999, 'Del descubrimiento petrolífero a la explosión del gas', in *Bolivia en el siglo XX: La formación de la Bolivia contemporánea*, edited by Fernando Campero Prudencio, La Paz: Harvard Club de La Paz.
Mitchell, Christopher 1977, *The Legacy of Populism in Bolivia: From the MNR to Military Rule*, New York: Praeger.
Molina, Fernando 2005, 'Insurrección: una interpretación de lo que ocurre en las calles', *Pulso*, 10 June.
Montoya Villa, Beimar Josué and Rosa Rojas García 2004, *El despertar de un pueblo oprimido: estructuras de movilización y construcciones discursivas en la ciudad de El Alto, en el mes de Octubre de 2003*, La Paz: Musux Wayra.

Moody, Kim 1997, *Workers in a Lean World: Unions in the International Economy*, London: Verso.

Mouffe, Chantal 1979, 'Hegemony and Ideology in Gramsci', in *Gramsci and Marxist Theory*, edited by Chantal Mouffe, New York: Routledge.

—— 1984, 'Towards a Theoretical Interpretation of New Social movements', in *Rethinking Marx*, New York: International General/IMMRC.

—— 1988, 'Hegemony and New Political Subjects: Towards a New Concept of Democracy', in *Marxism and the Interpretation of Culture*, edited by C. Nelson, and L. Grossberg, Champaign: University of Illinois Press.

Nash, June 1989, 'Cultural Resistance and Class Consciousness in Bolivian Tin-Mining Communities', in *Power and Popular Protest: Latin American Social Movements*, edited by Susan Eckstein, Berkeley: University of California Press.

—— 1992, 'Interpreting Social Movements: Bolivian Resistance to Economic Conditions Imposed by the International Monetary Fund', *American Ethnologist*, 19, 2: 275–93.

—— 1993, *We Eat the Mines and the Mines Eat Us*, Second Edition, New York: Columbia University Press.

Nash, June and Helen Safa (eds.) 1986, *Women and Change in Latin America*, Santa Barbara: Bergin and Garvey Publishers, Inc.

Ocampo, José Antonio 2009, 'Latin America and the Global Financial Crisis', *Cambridge Journal of Economics*, 33, 4: 703–24.

Offe, Claus 1985, 'New Social Movements: Challenging the Boundaries of Institutional Politics', *Social Research*, 52, 4: 817–68.

Olivera, Oscar 2004a, 'For A Constituent Assembly: Creating Public Spaces', in *¡Cochabamba! Water-War in Bolivia*, edited by Oscar Olivera and Tom Lewis, Cambridge, MA.: South End Press.

—— 2004b, 'Petroleum and Natural Gas: Reconquering our Collective Patrimony', in *¡Cochabamba! Water-War in Bolivia*, edited by Oscar Olivera and Tom Lewis, Cambridge, MA.: South End Press.

—— 2004c, 'A Political Thesis', in *¡Cochabamba! Water-War in Bolivia*, edited by Oscar Olivera and Tom Lewis, Cambridge, MA.: South End Press.

—— 2004d, 'War', in *¡Cochabamba! Water-War in Bolivia*, edited by Oscar Olivera and Tom Lewis, Cambridge, MA.: South End Press.

Olivera, Oscar and Tom Lewis (eds.) 2004, *¡Cochabamba!: Water-War in Bolivia*, Cambridge, MA.: South End Press.

Opinión 2003a, 'Ante los conflictos el Gobierno asegura que hará cumplir la ley', *Opinión*, 15 September.

—— 2003b, 'Dos muertos y 20 heridos por enfrentamientos en Ventilla', *Opinión*, 10 October.

—— 2003c, 'Goni asegura que pequeña minoría pretende destruir la democracia', *Opinión*, 10 October.

—— 2003d, ' "Guerra del gas" provoca tensión social en el país', *Opinión*, 19 September.

—— 2003e, 'Opositores, COB y COR El Alto respaldan sucesión constitucional de Vicepresidente', *Opinión*, 17 October.

—— 2003f, 'Se abren tres piquetes de huelga de hambre', *Opinión*, 16 October.

Orellana Aillón, Lorgio 2004, 'El proceso insurreccional de abril: estructuras materiales y superestructuras organizativas de los campesinos regantes en el Valle Central Cochabambino', in *Ruralidades latinoamericanas: Identidades y luchas sociales*, edited by Norma Giarracca, and Bettina Ley, Buenos Aires: CLACSO, available online at: <http://bibliotecavirtual.clacso.org/ar/ar/libros/ruralidad/Orellana.pdf>.

—— 2006, 'Oligarquía capitalista, régimen de acumulación y crisis política en Bolivia', *Nómadas*, 25, October: 261–72.

Ormachea Saavedra, Enrique 2009, *Soberanía y seguridad alimentaria en Bolivia: Políticas y estado de situación*, La Paz: CEDLA.

Orozco Ramírez, Shirley 2005, 'Historia del Movimiento al Socialismo (MAS): Trayectoria política e ideológica', *Barataria*, 1, 2: 16–22.

Otero, Gerardo 2003, 'The "Indian Question" in Latin America: Class, State, and Ethnic Identity Construction', *Latin American Research Review*, 38, 1: 248–66.

—— 2004, 'Global Economy, Local Politics: Indigenous Struggles, Civil Society and Democracy', *Canadian Journal of Political Science*, 37, 2: 325–46.

Otero, Gerardo and Heidi A. Jugenitz 2003, 'Challenging National Borders from Within: The Political Class Formation of Indigenous Peasants in Latin America', *Canadian Review of Sociology and Anthropology*, 40, 5: 503–25.

Oxhorn, Philip 1995, *Organizing Civil Society: The Popular Sectors and the Struggle for Democracy in Chile*, University Park: The Pennsylvania State University Press.

Oxhorn, Philip and Graciela Ducatenzeiler 1998, 'Economic Reform and Democratisation in Latin America', in *What Kind of Democracy? What Kind of Market? Latin America in the Age of Neoliberalism*, edited by Philip Oxhorn and Graciela Ducatenzeiler, University Park: University of Pennsylvania Press.

Pabón Chávez, Julio 2005a, Personal Interview, El Alto, 30 March.

Panitch, Leo 2000, 'The New Imperial State', *New Left Review*, II, 2: 5–20.

Panitch, Leo and Sam Gindin 2003, 'Global Capitalism and American Empire', in *The Socialist Register 2004: The New Imperial Challenge*, edited by Leo Panitch and Colin Leys, New York: Monthly Review Press.

—— 2004, 'Finance and American Empire', in *The Socialist Register 2005: The Empire Reloaded*, edited by Leo Panitch and Colin Leys, New York: Monthly Review Press.

Patana, Edgar 2005, Personal Interviews, El Alto, 10 and 17 May.

Patzi, Felix 2005a, 'Rebelión indígena contra la colonialidad y la transnacionalización de la economía: Triunfos y vicisitudes del movimiento indígena desde 2000 a 2003', in *Ya es otro tiempo el presente: Cuatro momentos de insurgencia indígena*, edited by Forrest Hylton, Felix Patzi, Sergio Serulnikov, and Sinclair Thomson, La Paz: Muela del Diablo.

Patzi, Félix 2005b, Personal Interview, La Paz, May.

Peredo, Arturo 2003, 'La policía salvó a Bolivia del impuestazo', *El Juguete Rabioso*, 16 February.

Pérez Luna, Mamerto 2004, 'El desarrollo campesino indígena: ¿omisión u olvido?', in *Economía y sociedad boliviana después de Octubre de 2003: Análisis de un año de gobierno de Carlos Mesa*, edited by CEDLA, La Paz: CEDLA.

Petras James (with Todd Cavaluzzi, Morris Morley, and Steve Vieux) 1999, *The Left Strikes Back: Class Conflict in Latin America in the Age of Neoliberalism*, Boulder: Westview Press.

Petras, James 1997, 'Latin America: The Resurgence of the Left', *New Left Review*, I, 233: 17–47.

—— 2009, 'Latin America: Perspectives for Socialism in a Time of a World Capitalist Recession/Depression', available online at: <http://www.lahaine.org/petrasb2-img/petras_dec08.pdf>.

Petras, James and Henry Veltmeyer 2000, *The Dynamics of Social Change in Latin America*, New York: Palgrave Macmillan.

—— 2001, *Globalisation Unmasked: Imperialism in the 21st Century*, London: Zed.

Plant, Roger 2002, 'Latin America's Multiculturalism: Economic and Agrarian Dimensions', in *Multiculturalism in Latin America: Indigenous Rights, Diversity and Democracy*, edited by Rachel Sieder, New York: Palgrave Macmillan.

Platt, Tristan 1987, 'The Andean Experience of Bolivian Liberalism, 1825–1900: Roots of Rebellion in 19th-Century Chayanta (Potosí)', in *Resistance, Rebellion, and Consciousness in the Andean Peasant World, 18th to 20th Centuries*, edited by Steve J. Stern, Madison: Wisconsin University Press.

PNUD/UNDP 2005, *La economía más allá del gas: Informe temático sobre Desarrollo Humano*, Second Edition, La Paz: PNUD/UNDP.

Querejazu Calvo, Roberto 1975, *Masamaclay: Historia, política, diplomática y militar de la guerra del Chaco*, Third Edition, La Paz.

Quijano, Aníbal 2005, 'The Challenge of the "Indigenous Movement" in Latin America', *Socialism and Democracy*, 19, 3: 55–78.

Quisbert Quispe, Máximo 2003, *FEJUVE El Alto 1990–1998: Dilemas del clientelismo colectivo en un mercado político en expansión*, La Paz: TOHA/Ediciones Aruwiyiri.

Quispe, Benecio 2004, *Emergencia de la Burocracia Rural y Enajenación de la Soberanía Comunal (Municipio de Corque)*, Masters Thesis, Department of Sociology, La Paz: Universidad Mayor de San Andres.

—— 2005, Personal Interview, El Alto, 5 May.

Quispe, Felipe 2005a, Personal Interview, La Paz, 12 May.

—— 2005b, 'La lucha de los *ayllus* kataristas hoy', in *Movimiento indígena en América Latina: resistencia y proyecto alternativo*, edited by Fabiola Escárzaga, and Raquel Gutiérrez, Puebla: Universidad Autónoma de Puebla.

Ramírez, Franklin and Pablo Stefanoni 2005a, 'Anatomía de un levantamiento: potencialidades y límites del movimiento social alteño', *Pulso*, 10 June.

—— 2005b, 'La insurrección inconclusa: la proyección política de los movimientos sociales', *Pulso*, 17 June.

Ramos, Edgar 2005, Personal Interview, La Paz, 10 March.

Reinaga, Fausto 1970, *La revolución india*, La Paz: Ediciones del Partido Indio de Bolivia.

Rivera Cusicanqui, Silvia 1983, 'Luchas campesinas contemporáneas en Bolivia: El movimiento "katarista", 1970–1980', in *Bolivia, Hoy*, edited by René Zavaleta Mercado, Mexico: Siglo vientiuno editores.

—— 1991, 'Liberal Democracy and *Ayllu* Democracy in Bolivia: The Case of Northern Potosí', *Journal of Development Studies*, 25, 4: 97–121.

—— 2003 [1984], *Oprimidos pero no vencidos: luchas del campesinado aymara y qhechwa 1900–1980*, Second edition, La Paz: Aruwiyiri.

—— 2004, 'Reclaiming the Nation', *NACLA Report on the Americas*, 38, 3: 19–23.

Roberts, Kenneth M. 1997, 'Beyond Romanticism: Social movements and the Study of Political Change in Latin America', *Latin-American Research Review*, 32, 2: 137–51.

—— 1998, *Deepening Democracy? The Modern Left and Social Movements in Chile and Peru*, Stanford: Stanford University Press.

—— 2002, 'Social Inequalities Without Class Cleavages in Latin America's Neoliberal Era', *Studies in International Comparative Development*, 36, 4: 3–33.

Robinson, William I. 2004, 'Global Crisis and Latin America', *Bulletin of Latin-American Research*, 23, 2: 135–53.

—— 2007, 'Transformative Possibilities in Latin America', in *Socialist Register 2008: Global Flashpoints, Reactions to Imperialism and Neoliberalism*, edited by Leo Panitch and Colin Leys, New York: Monthly Review Press.

—— 2008, *Latin America and Global Capitalism: A Critical Globalisation Perspective*, Baltimore: The John Hopkins University Press.

Roddick, Jacqueline and Nico van Niekerk 1989, 'Bolivia', in *The State, Industrial Relations and the Labour Movement in Latin America: Volume 1*, edited by Jean Carriere, Nigel Haworth, and Jacqueline Roddick, Glasgow and La Paz: University of Glasgow Press and CEDLA.

Roediger, David R. 1999, *The Wages of Whiteness: Race and the Making of the American Working Class*, London: Verso.

Rohter, Larry 2003, 'Bolivian Leader Resigns and His Vice President Steps In', *New York Times*, 18 October.

Rojas, Bruno 2004, 'Los 'convenios de Mesa frente a las luchas y demandas sociales', in *Economía y sociedad boliviana después de octubre de 2003: Análisis de un año de gobierno de Carlos Mesa*, edited by CEDLA, La Paz: CEDLA.

Rojas, Carlos 2005, Personal Interview, El Alto, 20 May.

Roman, Richard and Edur Velasco Arregui 2007, 'Mexico's Oaxaca Commune', in *Socialist Register 2008: Global Flashpoints*, edited by Leo Panitch and Colin Leys, New York: Monthly Review Press.

Romero Ballivián, Salvador 2006, *El Tablero Reordenado: Análisis de la Elección Presidencial de 2005*, La Paz: Corte Nacional Electoral.

Rossell Arce, Pablo and Bruno Rojas Callejas 2000, *Ser productor en El Alto: Una aproximación a la dinámica productiva y el desarrollo local en El Alto*, La Paz: CEDLA.

Saad-Filho, Alfredo 2005, 'From Washington to Post-Washington Consensus: Neoliberal Agendas for Economic Development', in *Neoliberalism: A Critical Reader*, edited by Alfredo Saad-Filho and Deborah Johnston, London: Pluto.

Sachs, Jeffrey 1987, 'The Bolivian Hyperinflation and Stabilisation', *The American Economic Review*, 77, 2: 279–83.

Sader, Emir 2008, 'The Weakest Link? Neoliberalism in Latin America', *New Left Review*, II, 52: 5–31.

Salinas, Nestor 2005, Personal Interview, El Alto, 1 April.

Sanabria, Harry 1997, 'The Discourse and Practice of Repression and Resistance in the Chapare', in *Coca, Cocaine, and the Bolivian Reality*, edited by Madeline Barbara Léons, and Harry Sanabria, Albany: State University of New York Press.

—— 1999, 'Consolidating States, Restructuring Economies, and Confronting Workers and Peasants: The Antinomies of Bolivian Neoliberalism', *Comparative Studies in Society and History*, 41, 3: 535–62.

—— 2000, 'Resistance and the Arts of Domination: Miners and the Bolivian State', *Latin American Perspectives*, 27, 1: 56–81.

Sandoval Z., Godofredo and M. Fernanda Sostres 1989, *La ciudad prometida: pobladores y organizaciones sociales en El Alto*, La Paz: ILDIS-Systema.

Sawyer, Suzanna 2004, *Crude Chronicles: Indigenous Politics, Multinational Oil, and Neoliberalism in Ecuador*, Durham, NC.: Duke University Press.

Schneider, Cathy Lisa 1995, *Shantytown Protest in Pinochet's Chile*, Philadelphia: Temple University Press.

Schultz, Jim 2005, *Deadly Consequences: The International Monetary Fund and Bolivia's 'Black February'*, Cochabamba: The Democracy Center.

Scott, Rebecca 1972, 'Economic Aid and Imperialism in Bolivia', *Monthly Review* 24, 1: 48–60.

Sears, Alan 2005, 'The Infrastructure of Dissent: Creating and Sustaining Communities of Struggle', *New Socialist*, 52, July–August: 32–3.

—— 2007, 'The End of 20th Century Socialism?' *New Socialist*, 61, Summer: 5–10.

Selbin, Eric 2008, 'Stories of Revolution in the Periphery', in *Revolution in the Making of the Modern World*, edited by John Foran, David Lane, and Andreja Zivkovic, New York: Routledge.

Serulnikov, Sergio 2003, *Subverting Colonial Authority: Challenges to Spanish Rule in Eighteenth-Century Southern Andes*, Durham, NC.: Duke University Press.

Sieder, Rachel 2002, 'Recognising Indigenous Law and the Politics of State-formation in Mesoamerica', in *Multiculturalism in Latin America: Indigenous Rights, Diversity and Democracy*, edited by Rachel Sieder, New York: Palgrave Macmillan.

Silver, Beverley J. 2003, *Forces of Labor: Workers' Movements and Globalisation Since 1870*, Cambridge: Cambridge University Press.

Singer, Matthew M. and Kevin M. Morrison 2004, 'The 2002 Presidential and Parliamentary Elections in Bolivia', *Electoral Studies*, 23: 143–82.

Slater, David (ed.) 1985, *New Social Movements and the State in Latin America*, Amsterdam: CEDLA.

Smith, Gavin 1989, *Livelihood and Resistance: Peasants and the Politics of Land in Peru*, Berkeley: University of California Press.

Smith, Neil 2006, 'The Geography of Uneven Development', in *100 Years of Permanent Revolution: Results and Prospects*, edited by Bill Dunn and Hugo Radice, London: Pluto.

Snow, David A. and Robert D. Benford 1992, 'Master Frames and Cycles of Protest', in *Frontiers in Social Movement Theory*, edited by Aldon D. Morris and Carol M. Mueller, New Haven: Yale University Press.

Soederberg, Susanne 2004, *The Politics of the New International Financial Architecture: Reimposing Neoliberal Domination in the Global South*, London: Zed.

—— 2005, 'The Transnational Debt Architecture and Emerging Markets: The Politics of Paradoxes and Punishment', *Third World Quarterly*, 26, 6: 927–49.

—— 2006, *Global Governance in Question: Empire, Class and the New Common Sense in Managing North-South Relations*, London: Pluto.

Solares Barrientos, Jorge 2005, Personal Interview, La Paz, 5 April.
Solares, Jaime 2005a, Address to FEJUVE-El Alto Emergency Assembly, 11 May.
—— 2005b, Personal Interview, La Paz, 3 May.
Solón, Pablo 2003, 'Radiografía de un febrero', *Observatorio Social de América Latina*, 4, 10: 15–27.
—— 2005, Personal Interview, La Paz, 27 June.
Spronk, Susan 2007a, *The Politics of Third World Water Privatisation: Neoliberal Reform and Popular Resistance in Cochabamba and El Alto, Bolivia*, PhD Dissertation, Department of Political Science, Toronto: York University.
—— 2007b, 'Roots of Resistance to Urban Water Privatisation in Bolivia: The "New Working Class", the Crisis of Neoliberalism, and Public Services', *International Labor and Working-Class History*, 71, 1: 8–28.
Spronk, Susan and Jeffery R. Webber 2005, 'The Two Bolivias Square Off', *Canadian Dimension*, 39, 3: 17–19.
—— 2007, 'Struggles Against Accumulation by Dispossession in Bolivia: The Political economy of Natural Resource Contention', *Latin American Perspectives*, 34, 2: 31–47.
Stavenhagen, Rodolfo 2003, 'Indigenous Peoples and the State in Latin America: An Ongoing Debate', in *Multiculturalism in Latin America: Indigenous Rights, Diversity and Democracy*, edited by Rachel Sieder, New York: Palgrave Macmillan.
Stefanoni, Pablo 2003, 'MAS-IPSP: la emergencia del nacionalismo plebeyo', *Observatorio Social de América Latina*, 4, 12: 57–68.
—— 2005, '¿Quiénes son y qué quieren los radicales? Un mapa de los grupos que asedian a La Paz y se movilizan en el país', *Pulso*, 3 June 3.
Stefanoni, Pablo and Hervé Do Alto 2006, *Evo Morales de la coca al Palacio: Una oportunidad para la izquierda indígena*, La Paz: Malatesta.
Stephen, Lynn 1996, 'The Creation and Re-Creation of Ethnicity: Lessons from the Zapotec and Mixtec of Oaxaca', *Latin American Perspectives*, 23, 2: 17–37.
—— 2002, *Zapata Lives! Histories and Cultural Politics in Southern Mexico*, Berkeley: University of California Press.
—— 2005, *Zapotec Women: Gender, Class, and Ethnicity in Globalised Oaxaca*, Durham, NC.: Duke University Press.
Stern, Steve J. 1987, 'The Age of Andean Insurrection, 1742–1782: A Reappraisal', in *Resistance, Rebellion, and Consciousness in the Andean Peasant World: 18th to 20th Centuries*, Maddison: University of Wisconsin Press.
Striffler, Steve 2004, 'Class-Formation in Latin America: One Family's Enduring Journey between Country and City', *International Labor and Working-Class History*, 65, 2: 11–25.
Suárez, Hugo José 2003a, *Una semana fundamental: 10–13 octubre 2003*, La Paz: Muela del Diablo.
Suárez, Luciano 2005, Personal Interview, El Alto, 20 May.
Suggett, James 2009, 'Venezuela Says Clinton's Remarks Reflect "Profound Lack of Knowledge of Our Reality"', *Venezuelanalysis.com*, 9 July.
Sustar, Lee 2007, 'Where is Venezuela Going? Chávez and the Meaning of Twenty-First Century Socialism', *International Socialist Review*, 54: 14–29.
Tapia, Luis 2000, 'La crisis política de Abril', *Observatorio Social de América Latina*, 2, Septiembre: 3–6.
—— 2002, 'Movimientos sociales, movimiento societal y los no lugares de la política', in *Democratizaciones plebeyas*, edited by Raquel Gutiérrez, Álvaro García Linera, Raúl Prada and Luis Tapia, La Paz: Muela del Diablo.
—— 2004, 'Izquierda y movimiento social en Bolivia', in *Memorias de octubre*, edited by Álvaro García Linera, Raúl Prada and Luis Tapia, La Paz: Muela del diablo.
—— 2005, 'El presidente colonial', in *Horizontes y límites del estado y el poder*, edited by Álvaro Gacía Linera, Luis Tapia, Oscar Vega and Raúl Prada, La Paz: Muela del Diablo.
Tarrow, Sidney 1998, *Power in Movement: Social Movements and Contentious Politics*, Cambridge: Cambridge University Press.

Teichman, Judith 2001, *The Politics of Freeing Markets in Latin America: Chile, Argentina, and Mexico*, Chapel Hill: The University of North Carolinia Press.

The Economist 2003, 'What Will the IMF Say Now?' *The Economist*, 20 February.

—— 2008, 'An Axis in Need of Oiling', *The Economist*, 23 October.

Thompson, Edward P. 1963, *The Making of the English Working Class*, New York: Vintage Books.

Thomson, Sinclair 2002, *We Alone Will Rule: Native Andean Politics in the Age of Insurgency*, Madison: University of Wisconsin Press.

—— 2003, 'Revolutionary Memory in Bolivia: Anticolonial and National Projects from 1781 to 1952', in *Proclaiming Revolution: Bolivia in Comparative Perspective*, edited by Merilee S. Grindle, and Pilar Doming, London and Cambridge, MA.: Institute of Latin-American Studies, University of London David Rockefeller Center for Latin-American Studies, Harvard University.

Ticona A., Esteban, Gonzalo Rojas O. and Xavier Albó C. 1995, *Votos y wiphalas: campesinos y pueblos originarios en democracia*, La Paz: Fundación Milenio CIPCA.

Tilly, Charles 1978, *From Mobilisation to Revolution*, New York: Addison-Wesley.

—— 1981, *As Sociology Meets History*, New York: Academic Press, Inc.

—— 1985, 'Models and Realities of Popular Collective action', *Social Research*, 52, 4: 717–47.

Tilly, Charles and Louise Tilly 1981, *Class Conflict and Collective Action*, New York: Sage Publications.

Touraine, Alain 1981, *The Voice and the Eye: An Analysis of Social Movements*, Cambridge: Cambridge University Press.

—— 1985, 'An Introduction to the Study of Social Movements', *Social Research*, 52, 4: 749–88.

—— 1988, *Return of the Actor*, Minneapolis: University of Minnesota Press.

Trotsky, Leon 1977, *The Transitional Progamme for Socialist Revolution*, Third edition, New York: Pathfinder Press.

—— 2005 [1932], *The History of the Russian Revolution: Three Unabridged Volumes in One*, New York: Pathfinder Press.

Van Cott, Donna Lee (ed.) 1994, *Indigenous Peoples and Democracy in Latin America*, New York: St. Martin's Press.

—— 2000, *The Friendly Liquidation of the Past: The Politics of Diversity in Latin America*, Pittsburgh: University of Pittsburgh Press.

—— 2003a, 'Constitutional Reform in the Andes: Redefining Indigenous-State Relations', in *Multiculturalism in Latin America: Indigenous Rights, Diversity and Democracy*, edited by Rachel Sieder, New York: Palgrave Macmillan.

—— 2003b, 'From Exclusion to Inclusion: Bolivia's 2002 Elections', *Journal of Latin-American Studies*, 35: 751–75.

—— 2003c, 'Institutional Change and Ethnic Parties in South America', *Latin American Politics and Society*, 45, 2: 1–39.

—— 2005, *From Movements to Parties in Latin America: The Evolution of Ethnic Politics*, Cambridge: Cambridge University Press.

van der Linden, Marcel 2008, *Workers of the World: Essays Toward a Global Labour History*, Leiden: Brill.

Vanden, Harry V. 1986, *National Marxism in Latin America: José Carlos Mariátegui's Thought and Politics*, Boulder: Lynne Reinner Publishers.

Vargas, Humberto and Thomas Kruse 2000, 'Las victorias de Abril: una historia que aún no concluye', *Observatorio Social de América Latina*, 2, Septiembre: 7–14.

Veltmeyer, Henry 1997, 'New Social Movements in Latin America: The Dynamics of Class and Identity', *Journal of Peasant Studies*, 25, 1: 139–69.

Veltmeyer, Henry and Juan Tellez, 2001, 'The State and Participatory Development in Bolivia', in *Transcending Neoliberalism: Community-Based Development in Latin America*, edited by Henry Veltmeyer and Anthony O'Malley, New York: Kumarian Press.

Villarroel, Juan and Efraín Huanca 2004, 'Economía en crisis', in *Economía y sociedad boliviana después de octubre de 2003: Análisis de un año de gobierno de Carlos Mesa*, edited by CEDLA, La Paz: CEDLA.

Villegas Quiroga, Carlos 2004, *Privatización de la industria petrolera en Bolivia: Trayecto-ria y efectos tributarios*, Third edition, La Paz: FOBOMADE, CIDES-UMSA, Diacona, CEDLA.

Volk, Steven S. 1975a, 'Class, Union, Party: The Development of a Revolutionary Movement in Bolivia (1905–1952), Part II: From the Chaco War to 1952', *Science and Society*, 39, 2: 180–98.

—— 1975b, 'Class, Union, Party: The Development of a Revolutionary Union Move-ment in Bolivia (1905–1952), Part I: Historical Background', *Science and Society*, 39, 1: 26–43.

Vóz 2003, 'Una precisión de Evo Morales, "La marcha fue una consulta"', *Vóz*, 20 September.

Wade, Peter 1997, *Race and Ethnicity in Latin America*, London: Pluto.

Webber, Jeffery R. 2005, '"Agenda de Octubre" or "Agenda de Enero"? The Rebellion in Bolivia', *Against the Current*, 115: 13–16.

—— 2007, 'Bolivian Horizons: An Interview with Historian Sinclair Thomson', *Znet*, 8 November.

—— 2008a, 'Rebellion to Reform in Bolivia (Part I): Domestic Class-Structures, Latin-American Trenes, and Capitalist Imperialism', *Historical Materialism*, 16, 2: 23–58.

—— 2008b, 'Rebellion to Reform in Bolivia (Part II): Rebellion to Reform in Bolivia (Part II): Revolutionary Epoch, Combined Liberation, and Electoralism', *Historical Materialism*, 16, 3: 1–22.

—— 2008c, 'Rebellion to Reform in Bolivia (Part III): Neoliberal Continuities, the Autonomist Right, and the Political Economy of Indigenous Struggle', *Historical Materialism*, 16, 4: 67–109.

—— 2009a, 'Left-Indigenous Politics in Bolivia: The Constituent Assembly and Evo Morales', in *Hegemonic Transitions, the State and Crisis in Neoliberal Capitalism*, edited by Yildiz Atasoy, London: Routledge.

—— 2009b, 'From Naked Barbarism to Barbarism with Benefits: Neoliberal Capi-talism, Natural gas Policy, and the Government of Evo Morales in Bolivia', in *Post-Neoliberalism in the Americas*, edited by Arne Ruckert and Laura Macdonald, New York: Palgrave Macmillan.

—— 2010a, 'Venezuela under Chávez: The Prospects and Limitations of Twenty-First Century Socialism, 1998–2009', *Socialist Studies/Études Socialistes*.

—— 2010b, 'Carlos Mesa, Evo Morales, and a Divided Bolivia (2003–2005)', *Latin Amer-ican Perspectives*.

—— 2011, *Rebellion to Reform in Bolivia: Class-struggle, Indigenous Liberation and the Poli-tics of Evo Morales*, Chicago: Haymarket Books.

Weisbrot, Mark and Luis Sandoval 2007, *The Venezuelan Economy in the Chávez Years*. Washington, DC.: Center for Economic and Policy Research.

Weisbrot, Mark, Rebecca Ray and Luis Sandoval 2009. *The Chávez Administration at 10 Years: The Economy and Social Indicators*. Washington, DC.: Center for Economic and Policy Research.

Weisbrot, Mark, Rebecca Ray and Jake Johnston 2009, *Bolivia: The Economy Dur-ing the Morales Administration*, Washington, DC.: Center for Economic and Policy Research.

Weyland, Kurt 1998, 'Swalling the Bitter Pill: Sources of Popular Support for Neolib-eral Reform in Latin America', *Comparative Political Studies*, 31, 5: 539–68.

—— 2001, 'Will Chávez Lose His Luster?' *Foreign Affairs*, 80, 6: 73–87.

Whitehead, Laurence 1969, *The United States and Bolivia: A Case of Neo-Colonialism*, London: Haslemere Group.

—— 1986, 'Bolivia's Failed Democratisation, 1977–1980', in *Transitions from Authoritar-ian Rule: Latin America*, edited by Guillermo O'Donnel, Philippe C. Schmitter and Laurence Whitehead, Baltimore: The John Hopkins University Press.

—— 2003, 'The Bolivian National Revolution: A Twenty-First Century Perspective', in *Proclaiming Revolution: Bolivia in Comparative Perspective*, edited by Merilee S. Grin-dle, and Pilar Domingo, London and Cambridge, MA.: Institute of Latin-American

Studies, University of London and David Rockefeller Center for Latin-American Studies, Harvard University.

Wilkie, James W. 1969, *The Bolivian Revolution and U.S. Aid Since 1962*, Berkeley: University of California Press.

Williamson, John 1993, 'Democracy and the "Washington Consensus"', *World Development*, 21, 8: 1329–36.

Wilpert, Gregory 2007, *Changing Venezuela by Taking Power: The History and Policies of the Chávez Government*, London: Verso.

Wong, Joseph 2004, 'Democratisation and the Left: Comparing East Asia and Latin America', *Comparative Political Studies*, 37, 10: 1213–37.

Wood, Ellen Meiksins 1995, *Democracy Against Capitalism: Renewing Historical Materialism*, Cambridge: Cambridge University Press.

—— 2003, *Empire of Capital*, London: Verso.

World Bank 1999, *Entering the 21st Century: World Development Report*, Oxford: Oxford University Press.

—— 2005, *Bolivia Poverty Assessment: Establishing the Basis for Pro-Poor Growth*, New York: World Bank.

Yashar, Deborah J. 2005, *Contesting Citizenship in Latin America: The Rise of Indigenous Movements and the Postliberal Challenge*, Cambridge: Cambridge University Press.

Yujra Fernández, Alfredo 2005, Personal Interview, El Alto, 4 April.

Yujra Flores, Ricardo 2005, Personal Interview, El Alto, 2 April.

Zald, Mayer N. 1996, 'Culture, Ideology, and Strategic Framing', in *Comparative Perspectives on Social Movements: Political Opportunities, Mobilizing Structures, and Cultural Framings*, edited by Doug McAdam, John D. McCarthy, and Mayer N. Zald, Cambridge: Cambridge University Press.

Zald, Mayer N., and R. Ash 1966, 'Social-Movement Organisations: Growth, Decay and Change', *Social Forces*, 44: 327–40.

Zald, Mayer N., and John D. McCarthy (eds.) 1987, *Social Movements in an Organisational Society*, New York: Transaction Books.

Zavaleta Mercado, René 1972, 'Bolivia: Military Nationalism and the Popular Assembly', *New Left Review*, I, 73: 63–82.

—— 1983a, 'Forma clase y forma multitud en el proletariado minero en Bolivia', in *Bolivia, Hoy*, edited by René Zavaleta Mercado, Mexico: Siglo vientiuno editores.

—— 1983b, 'Las masas en noviembre', in *Bolivia, Hoy*, edited by René Zavaleta Mercado, Mexico: Siglo ventiuno editores.

—— 1998 [1963], *50 Años de historia*, La Paz: Los Amigos del Libro.

Zook, David Hartzler 1961, *The Conduct of the Chaco War*, New York: Bookman Associates.

Zubieta, Miguel 2005a, Executive Secretary of the FSTMB, speaking at a Public Forum. La Paz: UMSA.

—— 2005b, Personal Interview, La Paz, Executive Secretary, 23 June.

Zunes, Stephen 2001, 'The United States and Bolivia: The Taming of a Revolution, 1952–1957', *Latin American Perspectives*, 28, 4: 33–49.

Index

"Like what Karl Marx's *Eighteenth Brumaire* did for 1848, Webber astutely analyzes the alliances and ideologies of a powerful social movement that, while drawing its poetry from the past, is pointing the world to a different future. . . . In so doing, Webber provides the most innovative update of social movement theory yet available."
—Greg Grandin, New York University

"It is a rare book that helps to blaze new and promising directions for the radical socialist left. Yet, *Red October* does just that. . . . This is a magisterial work—theoretically sophisticated, ethnographically grounded, and historically nuanced. But more than anything else, it is a clarion call for radical scholars and activists to learn from a key flashpoint of anti-neoliberal insurgency."
—David McNally, York University

"*Red October* provides a compelling analysis of the infrastructures of solidarity, popular cultures of resistance, and oppositional forms of consciousness that nurtured one of Latin America's most militant social movements."
—Lesley Gill, Vanderbilt University

"*Red October* is without doubt the most solidly researched study and theoretically framed analysis of the popular movement in [Bolivia] that I have read."
—Henry Veltmeyer, Autonomous University of Zacatecas, Mexico

Bolivia witnessed a left-indigenous insurrectionary cycle between 2000 and 2005 that overthrew two presidents and laid the foundation for Evo Morales to become the country's first indigenous president. Building on the theoretical traditions of Marxism and indigenous liberation, this book provides an analytical framework for understanding the fine-grained sociological and political nuances of recent Bolivian class-struggle, state-repression, and indigenous resistance.

JEFFERY R. WEBBER is Lecturer in the School of Politics and International relations at Queen Mary, University of London. He is the author of *From Rebellion to Reform in Bolivia*.

Haymarket
Books
www.haymarketbooks.org

ISBN 978-1-60846-258-2 $28.00

52800>

9 781608 462582